WITHDRAWN

Middlesex County College
Library
Edison, NJ 08818

Just *Lassen* to Me!

A First-Generation Son's Story: Surviving a Survivor

Book Three: Survivor Learning

Harvy Simkovits

D1069782

WITHDRAWN

Just *Lassen* to Me!

A First-Generation Son's Story: Surviving a Survivor

Book Three: Survivor Learning

Edition 1.1

Copyright © 2019 Harvy Simkovits

Published by Wise Press

All rights reserved. No part of this book may be reproduced, stored, or transmitted by any means—whether auditory, graphic, mechanical, or electronic—without the written permission of the author, except in the case of brief excerpts used in critical articles and reviews. Unauthorized reproduction of any part of this work is illegal and is punishable by law.

This book is a work of non-fiction. The author and publisher make no explicit guarantees as to the accuracy of the information contained in this book. In some cases, the author has altered the names of people and places to protect their privacy.

ISBN-13: 978-0-9773957-3-6
ISBN-10: 0-9773957-3-1
Library of Congress Control Number: 2019900345

Because of the dynamic nature of the Internet, any web addresses or links contained in this book may have changed since publication and may no longer be valid. The views expressed in this work are solely those of the author and do not necessarily reflect the opinions of the publisher, and the publisher disclaims any responsibility for them.

Memoir Series by Harvy Simkovits

Just *Lassen* to Me!
Book One: Survivor Indoctrination
(An Amazon Bestseller)

Just *Lassen* to Me!
Book Two: Survivor Teachings

Just *Lassen* to Me!
Book Three: Survivor Learning

Contents

Part III: Ups and Downs of Moving On

Excerpt – Book Four: Survivor Surviving

Acknowledgements
About the Author

Welcome Back Again to
Just *Lassen* to Me!

Welcome back to the Johnny Simkovits and family saga. If you've made it this far, then we've gone through much together. "I can't believe Johnny did that!" and "What a charismatic character, cheat, bully, and even jerk he was!" have been things people tell me after reading Book One and Book Two of our Simkovits journey. They also have said, "It's amazing what your mother went through, not only in her life but also with her love." Some have asked, "How did you and your brother survive?" and "Do you and he get along today?" You may have wondered these things too. And you might look upon your own family with different eyes.

In this volume of the *Just Lassen to Me!* series, my kin will continue to shock and astound with revelations of unforeseen secrets, unexpected ploys, and gut-wrenching tragedies. I attempt to ameliorate my father's business shenanigans and money mischief. I try to ease my mother's distress vis-à-vis her incorrigible husband. But will it be enough to untie my dad's tangled web and build upstanding and respected men of his Simkovits sons? Will any of us be able to survive the snare of this forever footloose and tough-minded tenacious survivor? Will my mother be able to survive Johnny, and will Johnny be able to survive himself?

Hang onto your seat, and this book, for a continuing turbulent ride from this second son's survivor eyes into Johnny's world of fishy deals, family deception, and financial deceit. Watch as I, still young and naive, work behind the scenes to alter my father's hurtful and destructive ways and to impact and better the trajectory of our troubled family. Will it be possible to reshape the mold and soften the spells of Johnny?

Harvy Simkovits

Notes

This memoir series continues to employ Canadian spelling and writing conventions, and metric for most distance measurements.

At least 50% of the profits of this book will be donated to programs assisting victims of domestic abuse and violence.

Many individual and organizational names in this memoir series have been changed to protect identities.

Dedication

This book is dedicated to those who suffered the most under the hand and from the deeds of Johnny.

Book Three:

Survivor Learning

Part I:

Game Changers

Chasing a New Life

The late 1970s - the years before Dad left Mom for the third time.

Albert Vidor was a short, thin, cigarette-smoking Polish Canadian. He had a hooked nose, a crooked smile, and a squeaky voice. He spoke Russian fluently, having been born and raised in the eastern half of Poland that, at various times, had been a part of Russia.

One sunny summer day in 1978, Albert walked into the offices of Granite Real Estate in Champlain, NY. The firm was situated north of Lake Champlain, near the Vermont border. Behind the counter was Elaine Russ, a good-looking, dark-haired, 30-something woman.

Albert approached her and blurted out in his thick-accented voice, "I'm looking for the owner of this firm."

"That's my ex-husband," Elaine responded energetically. She eyed up and down this petite Pole, who was many centimeters shorter than she. But you can talk to me. What can I do for you, stranger?"

Albert stubbed out his cigarette in an ashtray on the counter. "My name is Vidor, Albert Vidor." His voice rose. "I'm looking to bring your firm business. I'm a real estate agent from Montreal, and I have rich clients who are looking for property around Lake Champlain. I can bring you lots of prospects if you are willing to work out an arrangement with me."

"Okay, let's talk," Elaine said. She stood and ushered Albert into her office. They reviewed real estate listings and made a commission deal for any business Albert would bring Elaine's way from across the border. For the rest of the day, they drove around the area to preview desirable properties.

A few Saturdays later, Albert returned to Champlain, NY, with John Simkovits. Elaine showed them several properties, one of which was a ten-acre peninsula jutting out into Lake Champlain on the New York State side of the lake.

As they walked around, Albert did the talking. "Johnny, you see this land here? If you buy this estate, you can keep the main house for yourself and subdivide the property into one-acre lots." He swept his hand around, like a male version of Vanna White on *Wheel of Fortune.* "What you get for selling the pieces will pay for the whole property. It's like you'll get the house and what's under it for free."

My father said, "Okay, Albert, good idea. Let me think about it."

Elaine said nothing.

The following Monday, my father was in his Montreal office. His secretary, Helen, was on the phone with a call that had just come in. "Is it Mr. Simkovits senior or junior that you wish to speak to?" she asked the caller.

She got the answer and then turned to my father, "Johnny, I have a call for you on line two from an Elaine Russ."

He said, "Okay, Helen, it's about a property I'm looking at in New York State. I'll take the call in my private office."

A moment later, he was alone and on the phone. "Hello, Elaine. It's nice to hear from you. To what do I owe the pleasure of this call?"

"Mr. Simkovits, I'm sorry to bother you," she said. "I need to tell you about the large lakefront property I showed you the other day."

Her voice hesitated. "I like to be straight with my clients. I'm sorry to tell you this, but what Mr. Vidor said about the property is not true."

She pressed forward. "I was feeling bad about what Albert had told you, so I wanted to tell you myself that the property cannot be subdivided and the pieces sold off. There is no way the zoning there can change. No one can build anything more on that peninsula."

My father was quiet for a moment. He then spoke calmly. "Thank you, Elaine, for telling me."

Elaine continued. "Mr. Simkovits, could you please not say anything to Mr. Vidor about this. I would feel bad if he knew I told you."

Dad took a long breath. "I understand, Elaine. And, please call me Johnny." He paused for a second or two. "By the way, in my appreciation for your honesty, please come and have supper with me one evening here in Montreal."

There was a pause at the other end of the phone. Then came, "Mr. Simkovits; Johnny; I make it a policy not to date my clients."

"Who says this is a date? And who says I'm your client?" He took a breath. "I just want to thank you for your honesty with me."

After another pause, "Okay, I could do that," she offered.

My father immediately added. "What about later this week? How's Thursday evening?"

A few moments later, Dad emerged from his back office. He shouted, "Helen, get me that schmuck Vidor on the line. I want to give him shit!"

Elaine told me that story years after my father's death. She added, "I had a policy about not dating married men. When I met your father for that supper, he told me he had separated from your mother."

She confessed. "I relocated to Montreal a half-year later; it was a big move for me. When I had gotten married to my first husband, I left Canada for Vermont and became an American citizen."

She looked away and then turned her eyes back to me. "In those days as a U.S. citizen, one could only hold a single passport. I renounced my Canadian citizenship when I moved south." She took a long breath. "When I came back to Canada after my divorce, I had to go through the Canadian Embassy in Boston to apply for Canadian landed immigrant status. It took nearly five months for the paperwork to come through."

She blinked a few times. "While I waited for the paperwork, I worked with my ex-husband in his real estate firm in upper New York State, right across the state line from where I lived in Vermont."

Elaine looked down. "To be honest, Harvy, it was mostly the pull from your father that brought me back to Canada. He and I had had many nice suppers with his Montreal friends: Vidor, Aras, and Celia. He wanted us to spend more time together."

Her voice tightened. "After your father and I had been going out for several months, a funny thing happened. One evening, while I was driving home to the West Island after we had a meal at the Troika, I noticed your father's Mercedes sports car ahead of me." She smiled. "It was hard to miss that spiffy red thing."

At 58 years old, my father drove a Mercedes 450 SLC. I knew Elaine was considerably younger than Dad, but I was surprised to learn that she had been under 35 when she had met him. She was barely ten years older than my brother.

There was a twinge of irritation in Elaine's voice as she recounted the story. "As your father drove west, I saw he didn't turn north to head to the Town of Mount Royal, where he said he lived." She pointed. "Instead, he continued west toward Dorval, where your mother lived. Since I lived in Pointe-Claire, the next town over, I followed him."

Elaine's eyes became narrow and intense. "I was shocked when I saw him exit the highway in Dorval."

When they first went looking for properties in New York State, Vidor must have told my father about Elaine being good looking and unattached. Dad probably took off his wedding ring when he and Elaine first met, and he removed it from his finger during their nights out.

Elaine took a breath, and her voice rose. "By the time I got home, I was livid. I called both Vidor and Aras, and I yelled at them for lying to me about your father being separated." She turned to me, seething, "They had this little boys' club about keeping such secrets from their wives and other women."

I stayed quiet as she spewed. "I called your father the next day and told him our relationship was off. I told him point-blank that I never wanted to see him again."

After a few long seconds, Elaine's tone quieted. She looked past me as if she were looking at an image projected on the wall. "I didn't see your father after that. Vidor and Aras were toast in my mind too."

She took another long breath. "However, I did like Aras's wife, Celia, and we maintained a friendship. She and I had dinner or supper together here and there in the city."

Elaine looked at me with a small smirk. "But you know how your father can be! When he wants something, it's hard to say no to him."

Her voice stayed calm. "About a year after I had blown off Johnny, Celia called me to a supper party at their apartment. Confidentially, she warned me about Johnny being there too. She even told me your father had arranged the whole thing, repeatedly asking her and Aras to have this small gathering for the four of us."

She looked away and then back at me again. "I don't know why, but I agreed to go."

Elaine took a sip from a glass of wine she had poured for herself. "Your father was very nice all evening, his usual charming self. We both had a fair amount to drink."

Her eyes blinked several times. "On the way out, as we headed to the elevators, he cornered me and said, 'Elaine, I want to be with you. Please let me come back.'"

She stared at the wall and said, "I asked him directly, 'What about your wife and kids?'

"He said, 'I'm going to leave Anne. I just need time to tell my sons.' He then crossed his heart and said, 'I promise.'"

She glared into the distance. "I said, 'Okay, Johnny, let me know when it's official, and then we can talk.'"

* * *

14

Mom brought me into the dining room of my childhood home, and we sat down. Her face was wet with tears. She blew her nose into a handkerchief. "After you and Steve called home on account of your argument in Vancouver, your father and I had a big fight."

Her breathing was labored and in short bursts. "Your daddy blamed your fighting on me." She could hardly look my way. "He screamed at me that I didn't raise the two of you properly."

Mom rolled up the sleeves of her blouse. I saw lightly-coloured black and blue marks on her arms and shoulders. "Look at this. He struck me so hard that I had to run out of the house to get away from him."

My heart started to thump. The bruises looked dark blue but seemed as if they had nearly healed. *Could my dad have done that?* He had never laid a hand on me, and only once had taken his belt to my brother when Steve had been a kid. I never saw or heard him hit Mom, though they had had their share of screaming matches.

Had she provoked his anger? I couldn't fathom what my mother was showing me. Part of me wanted to blame her.

A memory flooded my mind. When I had been home on a winter vacation during my last year in boarding school, Mom became distraught. She paced the floor with worry, her palm at her forehead. She told me, "Every night for the last couple of weeks, your dad has been coming home well after midnight, and he leaves in the morning before I get up. He hardly talks to me."

Before I headed to bed, her voice shook with despair. "Maybe if I could drink like your father, he'd take me out more, even love me more." Her eyes were wet. "I don't know what to do for him to want to be with me."

I could hardly look at her. I nodded, said nothing, and went to bed. I wished my brother were home—he was better at calming Mom when she was upset. But Steve was away for his first year at college. I went upstairs, hoping that Dad would be home soon.

A few hours later, Dad woke me from a deep sleep. "Come help me, son. Your mother is lying by the front door." His voice slurred, and I could smell the alcohol on his breath as he spoke. "It looks like she got herself drunk on Tia Maria and opened the door to cool off."

"What? What!" I rubbed my eyes. "But it's freezing outside!"

Dad pleaded. "I found her lying on the floor when I got home. The front door was wide open. I was able to push her inside and to close the door, but I can't get her into bed by myself. Please come and help me."

Lumbering, I followed my father downstairs. I grabbed firmly onto the staircase's railing to keep myself steady. When we got downstairs, the front entryway floor tiles were ice-cold to my bare feet. My insides felt the same.

Mom was lying on the floor, dressed only in her nightgown. She moaned, but I couldn't make out what she was saying. Dad said, "I'll grab her under the arms; you hold onto her legs. Let's carry her upstairs and put her into bed."

My mind craved sleep. I acted as if I were the Lost in Space robot following Dr. Smith's orders. I didn't want to feel anything, but just to get through this parental nightmare and go back to sleep.

Mom 5'4" frame weighed over 140 pounds. I was glad she didn't fight us. We carried her upstairs, put her on her bed, and covered her with a blanket.

Dad turned to me. "Go back to sleep, son. She'll sleep it off and be better tomorrow."

I nodded but said nothing, and hoped he would be right. While I turned toward my bedroom, Dad headed downstairs to the living room. He spent the night sleeping and snoring on the couch, the television blaring like it did every time he slept there.

When I rose the next morning, Dad was gone to work, and Mom was the one snoring in bed. When she got up hours later, she came downstairs with half-opened eyes and a hand to her forehead. She said nothing about the night before, and I pretended as if her drunkenness had never happened.

I told myself, *When I finish college, I'm leaving this frigging family forever.* I wanted to run far away from my cheating father and harsh-tongued mother.

Those thoughts of leaving my family helped me to survive them. But I hadn't realized back then that it was my father's continual abuse of my mother that had implanted those thoughts.

When I had come home from Harvard, I hoped things might get better between my parents. Now, as Mom showed me her bruises that she said came from Dad's fists, I wasn't sure if my coming home had been the right course. I sat speechless, my hand to my aching forehead, as Mom told me more about her altercation with Dad.

"After your father hit me, I ran outside and hurried down the block." Her palms wiped away her non-stop tears. "But he came after me in his car."

She glanced down toward the floor. "By the time your father found me, he had calmed down, but I was still upset." She pointed. "I tried to run down the street, to get further away from him." She moaned. "But, he chased after me."

She gasped for air. "Through the car window, your father told me he no longer loved me, and he no longer wanted to pretend he did. He said it didn't work anymore for us to be together, and he was leaving me for good."

Mom stopped to blow her runny nose and wipe her watery eyes. "Your father then turned his car around and drove back to the house without me."

I recalled that my brother had done a similar car maneuver with me in Victoria a week earlier, leaving me stranded on a sidewalk.

She continued to sob. "It took me a while to calm down and go back home. When I got there, your father was gone. He had packed some things and left."

I didn't know what to think, feel, or say. Had Mom's scorching tongue set Dad on fire? I wish Steve hadn't called home about our across-the-country quarrel. Was our sibling squabble the last straw that got my father to strike my mother and leave her for good? Or did Dad jump on an opportunity that my brother had presented?

What an idiot Steve was! What a schmuck Dad was too.

A week before Steve and I departed on our Western Canada excursion, Dad had approached Steve and me unexpectedly. It had been a sunny Sunday afternoon, and he asked us to take a walk with him around the neighbourhood.

On the way home, Dad suddenly stopped in his tracks and welled up in anguish, something I hadn't experienced before from him. His eyes watered as he bent over a little and brought his hand to his face. He blabbered about not having been a good father and husband.

Though a part of me did agree with him, I wasn't sure what he was trying to tell us. I said, "It's okay, Dad." Steve added, "You did your best." It suddenly felt as if Steve and I were the consoling adults to our child-like father. I didn't know what else to say or do.

Our father quickly calmed down. "It's okay, boys; please forget about it." We said nothing more and continued our walk. Now, five weeks later, I figured my father's distress had foreshadowed his pending departure from Mom.

To my mother's sobbing, all I could say was, "Please don't cry. I'm sorry this happened."

In my mind, I was scolding her. *Couldn't you read Dad's pending departure on the house walls? You are no angel in the way you aggravate him. I can't understand why you stayed with a man who has been unfaithful to you so many times.*

Her tears softened my hardened heart. I offered, "I'll talk to Steve and Dad and see what they say, okay?" *What the hell is going to happen to us now?* I wondered if I should have stayed at Harvard, or continued at P&G, rather than coming back to this mess of a family.

"Okay, son." She wiped her eyes again with the heel of her hands. "But with you, Stevie, and now your daddy gone from home, I'm going to be alone again." Her head dropped into her hands, and she began to cry once more.

On the drive back to my apartment, I still felt peeved at my brother for having lit the separation fire in our father. But I then realized that his Vancouver call home had only been the match that lit the fuse. The powder keg that exploded between my parents had been sitting dormant for years. If it hadn't been for our squabble in Victoria, it would have been something else to cause Dad to take an explosive leave of his wife for the third time.

Was Dad going to leave Mom for good?

I had come home from Harvard to help my family. I now felt I had failed.

* * *

18

Over the weekend, Steve and I talked briefly to Dad. The upshot was that our father had moved in with Elaine in her Pointe-Claire home. Dad then asked us to meet early Monday morning at JHS.

I had once met Elaine at the Troika. She sat between Dad and Aras at Dad's table. Her talkativeness and self-confidence reminded me of Lizabeth, the woman with whom Dad and I had supper two years earlier at Toronto's Blue Sky Hotel. As it had been with Lizabeth, it was unclear who Elaine was with and why. I knew Aras was married to Celia, so I surmised Elaine was with Dad, but I wasn't sure and didn't want to know.

During that Troika supper, I worked to stay pleasant and reserved. I didn't talk much with Elaine, nor did I speak in a glib tone as I had done with Lizabeth. Other friends of my father were there too. They acted as if everything were normal, so I didn't want to look foolish. I didn't ask or say anything to Dad, hoping this new woman might be a fleeting attraction.

In retrospect, I should have screamed at him about what he was doing, but I hadn't the courage. At least he didn't try to maneuver me into a precarious situation, as he had done at the Blue Sky.

I had worked to push the Elaine encounter out of my mind. The less I knew about what was going on, the less there would be to hide from my mother, and the less guilt I'd feel about being at the Troika with Dad and his friends. Whatever there was between Dad and her, I hoped the relationship would end as it had with his other women.

That Monday morning, Steve and I met Dad privately in his office. Our father spoke matter-of-factly. "I can't live with your mother anymore. I don't love her. We aren't right or even good for each other. Maybe we never were." He looked directly at us. "I shouldn't have come back to her after I left her the last time. She's too controlling."

Yah, but you did come back! And you're never to blame; it's always Mom's fault. She may be controlling, but you're domineering! Did you ever consider what's going to happen with her now? She's almost 60 years old!

Neither Steve nor I said such words to our father. Perhaps we figured there was no chance of changing his mind. Maybe we knew our parents' marriage had been over for some time. Then again, could we have been too timid to push against our patriarch?

My stomach ached with bottomless grief. I wanted to get in my car and drive away from my family the same way Steve had done to me, and the same way my father had done to my mother. I stood still in my disbelief and held back my angst. I wasn't self-aware enough to tell if I felt anger, grief, or heartache—perhaps it was rage, anguish, and despair.

Dad's voice quieted. He gazed at us with a soft look in his eyes. "When I left the house," he said, "I took a few things I needed. I still have stuff there that I'd like to get." He looked at Steve. "I don't think it's a good idea for me to see your mother right now. Could you get some of my things for me? I'll make a list."

I was grateful that Steve said yes. I wanted no part of being a valet service for my father. I didn't want to see Mom's long, sad face while packing a separation suitcase yet another time.

That evening, when Steve returned to our apartment, I said to him, "The last two times Dad left Mom, he moved into an apartment by himself. And he always came back after his relationship with the other woman turned sour." I sighed. "This time, he's moved into her home." I took a breath. "I guess it's final between him and Mom. He may never come back to her."

"We'll see," my brother said with little emotion. "But maybe that is so."

He and I didn't say anything more about it. I went into my room, closed my door, sat on the edge of my bed, and put my head into my hands. *How was I so lucky to get this badly broken family?*

My eyes watered. My parents' over thirty-year life together had ended with shouts and fists. I cringed. I suspected that both Steve and I had figured that Dad was going to leave Mom again one day. We both felt she had been clinging to a false hope of his remaining with her. Our reckoning had now become our reality.

My eyes continued to tear about our train wreck of a family. Even if we had told Dad to button his pants and stay home, would he have listened?

Seven months home from Harvard, I had no clue as to what I could have done differently to save us from ourselves. *We'll never be a family again.*

* * *

My father seemed to shift gears seamlessly when he started his new life with Elaine. He had had the advantage of having thought through his plan in advance.

Over the ensuing months, he spent his spare time renovating Elaine's house and landscaped the grounds. He hired contractors to attach a two-car garage to the main house. He hired others to install an in-ground pool and large stone barbeque in the backyard. He planted rose gardens and trimmed hedges. He almost single-handedly finished her basement as a replica of the red brick, burgundy wallpaper, and glass and mirror walls of the Troika's bar.

When the house renovations were complete, Dad invited Troika's minstrels, Sasha and Vladjec, to sing at his February birthday party and then at a summer barbeque. It was as if his life with Mom had become a washed-out memory, thirty-one years of marriage summarily cast aside.

During those months, I found it easier to be around Dad than Mom. He talked about what he and Elaine were doing and planning, while Mom talked about her lost past and stolen future.

Once when Steve and I huddled with our mother over a home-cooked supper in her kitchen, she blurted out, "I'm helpless and hopelessly here alone." She pleaded with my brother and me. "If you boys tell your father to leave that woman, he'll come back to me. He'll listen to the two of you."

From the way Dad had invested in Elaine's home, it felt as if he'd never go back to Mom. Steve and I worked to console her. "Mom, you need to make a new life for yourself. We know it's hard, but you have to try."

"I can't," she cried. "I gave everything to your father. How can I live without him?"

"Mom, you have to find a way. Please try."

She said nothing more to our appeals, and she may not have heard a word we had said.

The next time I was with her, she repeated the same refrain. I raised my voice. "Mom, I'm tired of your crying. You have to forget about Dad and focus on your life." I knew she didn't have much of a life before Dad left her, but I had to try to convince her to find a future.

She looked at me as if I were crazy. She raised her voice. "I can't. Your father was everything to me."

Perhaps if I had been a daughter, I might have better understood her anguish. I found it deeply painful to see her devastated. She added, "I do nothing but cry over the phone to my American and Czechoslovak relatives."

During the ensuing weeks and months, she hardly left the house. She only went out for regular weekly food shopping at the local mall. She spent hours watching TV soaps, perhaps to sympathize with others who had problems similar to or worse than hers.

Later, Mom found more about which to complain. "Your father doesn't give me enough money to live. I have to save on my stomach while he spends like crazy on that whore's house and at the Troika."

I never understood how Mom knew about Dad's spending on Elaine. Neither Steve nor I had said anything to her about Dad's hefty investments in Elaine's home. Someone in my father's world may have told her things, but she didn't divulge her source.

Mom's tongue could spit fire. At another supper, she looked at me and shook her fist. "Tell that bitch to get out of my husband's life! She stole my one-and-only love. She can go to hell!" Her eyes were on fire too. "What an old fool your father is. Can't he see that nobody will take care of him the way I do?" She took in a long breath, and it came out hot. "You'll see! Once he gets enough of her, he'll come back to me."

Being closer to Mom, Steve found reasons to avoid going to Dad's new home. I worked to give equal time to both my parents, though I probably gave my father more. It was more pleasant to be around him and his new "darling." Dad and Elaine's faces always wore smiles.

But when I spent time with them, I could never get my mother's voice out of my head. I could not fully enjoy myself knowing Mom was at home by herself while I was having Saturday suppers or Sunday brunches with my father and his mistress. I produced half-smiles and cut short my laughs.

Though it felt awkward to be around Elaine, she sidestepped the discomfort by talking about her and Dad's home remodeling ventures and adventures. She once chuckled as she looked out across the back patio. "Johnny loves to tell those landscapers and contractors what to do. You'd think he was directing the foremen in his factory."

Elaine seemed to understand Steve's and my predicament. Though she worked to be upbeat and pleasant with us, I more than once overheard her jest to Dad's friends, "To Johnny's boys, I'm just the wicked stepmother."

After the third or fourth time I heard her make that quip, I approached her. I looked at her and said calmly but firmly, "Elaine, you are not that. Please don't refer to yourself in that way."

She looked at me with surprised eyes but said nothing. She never uttered those "wicked stepmother" words again.

Some months later, when I was once more over at Mom's for supper, tears were pouring out of her eyes. She told me, "Elaine came over to my house the other day without warning. She wanted to talk to me, woman to woman." Mom was wheezing with despair. "She said that your father no longer loves me. She wanted me to let him go and to forget about him."

Mom screamed and cried simultaneously. "I can't believe that *piszkos csavargó* [dirty tramp] came here to my front door. I wouldn't let her step one foot into my house. I shouted at her through the glass of the front door, telling her to leave." She took another breath. "What does she want from me anyway? Does she think I'll let go of your father just like that? Why did she have to come here and make me feel worse?"

My mother's toxic venom confounded me. I had to endure a half-hour of her outrage because Elaine took it upon herself to confront what Dad himself had been avoiding. I repeated over and over again, "Mom, I don't know why she would come to see you." I suspected Elaine had hoped for an honest *tête-à-tête* and a truce between her and my mother. She certainly didn't know my mother.

Sometime later, Elaine told me, "I saw your mother recently. She said she wanted your father back, but I told her it was over between them, and she should try to move on." She took a long breath and looked away from me. "We said we'd leave each other alone. Your mother seemed fine about it."

Though I knew my mother wasn't fine, I told Elaine, "That wasn't the best thing, but it's now water under the bridge. There's nothing more to be said or done."

I said nothing to Dad about those conversations. I wanted to keep the peace among Elaine, Dad, and me. It seemed my parents' marriage was truly over, and my mother was only holding onto a shadow of what she thought she had. For the next few weeks, I shrugged my shoulders every time Mom recounted Elaine's unexpected visit until she eventually stopped talking about it.

A part of me respected Elaine for wanting to settle things between her and my mother. I wondered what Dad had said to her about his wife that had caused Elaine to knock on my mother's door.

* * *

Over thirty years later, after my father's passing, Elaine gave me another version of her and Mom's unplanned visit. She e-mailed me after I had told her what my mother had said about their encounter.

> Harvy, I never, ever went to your family home to confront your mother. I saw your mother only twice in the years I was with your father. The first time was when she came to my office at the real estate company where I was working. She asked for me and introduced herself with a fictitious name as if she were interested in leasing a store for a small business.
>
> I invited her into my office, and she spent five minutes in there looking me over while trying to talk about her 'business needs.' I knew who she was, having recognized her by photos I had seen, but I went along with her ruse. I knew immediately that Albert Vidor had his hand in this—giving your mother my office address and probably coaching her as to what to say.
>
> Our meeting was very cordial. Your mother left my office after having 'seen' me, which I surmised was what our meeting had been about!

That Vidor! Ever since Elaine revealed the ruse he had played on Dad about the property Elaine showed them in New York, it appeared he had become Elaine's enemy and my mother's confidant.

Elaine went on.

> The second time I saw your mom was probably four months later. My mum had answered the door while at my house in Pointe-Claire. She then came to tell me, 'You'd better go to the door; John's wife wants to talk to you.' Your mother had arrived by cab, and the driver waited in the driveway for her. I invited her inside.
>
> Our conversation in the entryway was short. Your mother told me, 'John is a horrible husband and a terrible lover, but I still want him back. I want you to tell him to come back to me!' I told her, 'I can't tell him what to do, but I will tell him about our conversation.' Again, it was very cordial, and she then left.

I was bewildered that my mother had replayed that woman-to-woman scene differently. These many years after my father's death, there was no reason for Elaine to lie about what happened. Perhaps Mom had embellished her story to get Steve and me on her side in her quest to get Dad back.

Elaine continued her recollections.

> I felt sorry for your mother. As time went by, I understood her situation more, but I never thought I was the reason for the breakdown of their marriage. I might have been your father's excuse at the time but never the cause of their breakup. Their marriage had been broken many years before and was irreparable!

She then added another twist I didn't know.

> I remember vividly the day your father left your mother for good. He sat in his car in my driveway, waiting for me to come home, about 6 p.m. He had several packed suitcases and was ready to move in. I was in shock!! Nothing like that was ever planned. We had been dating, but I had broken it off with your father when I realized he had lied about still living with your mother. After that supper party at Aras and Celia's, where we reconnected, he asked me for time to speak to the two of you and your mother. We continued dating, but there were neither plans nor a timeframe talked about.

> At the point your father was standing at my doorstep, I started to stammer. He immediately called his lawyer, Mack, from his car phone, then handed me the phone. Mack said, 'What are you doing, Elaine? This man gave up his family for you! You can't back out of this now!!' And so your father moved in...............

Mack had been a longstanding loudspeaker for my father. When our father wanted something, he rallied Mack to his cause and obtained his lawyer's support. I wondered why Mack went along with and contributed to my father's Machiavellian maneuvers.

Perhaps Mack had been the same way himself.

* * *

The weeks and months progressed slowly after my parents' third separation. On weekends, Mom occasionally took the provincial and city buses to visit her Hungarian Jewish friends in the city. Not feeling that she could work, and not having a car or able to drive, she had long, lonely days at home.

My mother happily did clothes sewing and mending for my brother and me, and cooked supper one night a week for each one of us. Later on, Steve got her to volunteer at the cafeteria of the Lakeshore General Hospital—the place where she had been hospitalized for her psych illness. Though she did volunteer for a day every week, I didn't know how she felt about working there. At least she was occupying herself other than staying alone at home.

Between her "Hi Loves" when Steve or I entered her home for supper, to her "Good night sweethearts" when we left, any cursory mention of Dad would trigger her. On one occasion, she voiced harshly, "I defended your Catholic father with my Jewish family in Košice. My brothers and sisters didn't want me to marry him and leave Czechoslovakia. He had had other women, but I gave myself to him. I married because I was in love with him."

Her face was tight; her hand was closed and shaking. "Your father promised me a life together in Israel; then he changed his mind and brought me to a cold Canada. After we had come to Montreal, I supported us as a seamstress while he needed to save every penny to start his business." She took a long breath. "For thirty years, I cooked and cleaned for him and you two boys. He promised to be faithful to me, and he repeated that promise every time he came back to me."

She raised her hand in a fist. "Then your father turns around one day and pretends I'm nobody!"

Mom's case was cogent, but I became coarsened to her constant complaining. Though I enjoyed her home cooking, I dragged myself to her home every week to digest another spoonful of her plight.

Mom sighed as her eyes wetted. She wiped her face with a handkerchief. "Even after what he did to me, I would take him back. I fell in love with him and only him." Her eyes pleaded, "He'll listen to you, son. Please, please tell him to come back home to me."

I felt torn but tried to distance myself from her grief. I said to myself that it was her pain and not mine. I continued to feel a tight knot in my gut

27

that wouldn't unwind, an ache in my heart that wouldn't subside, and a mark on my mind that couldn't be erased.

Being Dad's wife and our mother was the only world Mom had known. She had very few other options or opportunities. Maybe she was too proud to change her life once more due to a husband who had broken his vows many times. Perhaps she wanted to turn her dependency on Dad into spasms of guilt in her sons. Indeed, she was too scared to start anew without the man she had depended on for half her lifetime. Wronged women like her had been the subject of many Broadway dramas and tragic romance novels.

Though my mother's righteousness created a playable hand for her, she held no aces to win back our father. Both Steve and I just repeated the same words she refused to consider: "Please, Mom, forget about Dad and try to live your own life." Maybe she just couldn't.

After many months of sulking and sobbing, Mom tried to be more upbeat when my brother or I came for one of her home-cooked meals. Otherwise, we might find an excuse to cut our visits short or not to visit her at all. In between wanting to know about us, she let slip, "I don't keep the house as clean as I used to. I'm not as strong as I used to be. I may not be around too much longer."

Steve or I responded, "Don't be silly, Mom. You still have a lot of life in you," but she just stared at us.

Another time, when I brought over a girlfriend to meet her, Mom pointed out the window. Her eyes filled with tears. "Every day, I see an old couple from down the street walk hand in hand on the sidewalk. I thought my husband would settle down with me when he got old. Now he's completely taken that away from me."

I reminded her, "Mom, you have two sons, and possibly two daughters-in-law and grandchildren to come when we eventually settle down."

She responded, "But then you two would leave me for your wives and families."

* * *

My brother and I said little if anything to our dad about our mother's pleas and anguish. We let their third separation run its course.

The possibility of Dad returning to her stayed alive in Mom's mind for years. My father's favourite Hungarian expression unwittingly explained it. "*Nincs semmi a kezedben. Kapaszkodj jól.* [There is nothing in your hand. Hold onto it tightly.]"

Many months later, over one of her goulash suppers, my mother confided, "I always knew when your father was seeing another woman."

She took a long breath, and her eyes looked to one side. "It wasn't when your father came home late at night after I had gone to bed, or when he would disappear on the weekends with his business friends to play golf or whatever they were doing." Her eyes turned glassy. "It was when he got angry enough to hit me with his fist when he came home loaded. Only then did I know he had another woman."

Her eyes looked down at the kitchen table. "That's when I started calling your father's friends and asking them what was going on. One of them would eventually tell me the truth."

She looked at me. "When I then confronted your father about it, he'd stop seeing the woman and come back to me." She took another long breath and sighed. "But it was different with Elaine." She looked away, turned back to the stove, and she said nothing more.

Other than on that day, when Dad left Mom for good, and she showed me the bruises on her arms after Steve and I had returned home from our Vancouver incident, I never knew about my father's hitting of my mother.

Though my father had a violent temper, I didn't want to believe he could strike a woman and leave marks and bruises. I had deceived myself about him being better than that. Like with my mother, maybe my better beliefs about Dad were "Nothing in my hand that I was holding onto tightly."

Thirty-seven years later, on the anniversary of the day when Dad left Mom that third time, I came to wonder if it had been my brother's and my move out of our parents' house that, in part, precipitated Dad's departure from Mom. Maybe our father no longer wanted to come home to where he lived just with a spouse from whom he had grown apart.

I suddenly felt a depth of dread within the dryness in my throat. Perhaps Steve's and my Vancouver fight was the defining moment Dad had been waiting for. He had needed a something to grab onto to blame Mom for his departure.

* * * *

Help

My voice was troubled. "Mom no longer agrees to move out of the Dorval house." I was speaking to my father while Steve looked on.

It was the end of a workday on a windswept, late September evening in 1980, six weeks after Dad had left Mom. Dad and Steve were sitting at their desks in JHS's front office while I stood behind mine. My voice strained, "I don't know what we can do." My head pounded, and a weight pressed on my shoulders. I felt as if any possibility of peace in what remained of our broken family was dependent on me.

My brother and father had desensitized themselves to Mom's plight, as with her food-poisoning illness nine months earlier. It was up to my forcing the issue. I looked right at my father, though I avoided direct contact with his eyes. "Mom's still upset about your having left her, and she isn't willing to move out of the house."

With Mom's knowledge and verbal acceptance, Dad had put our childhood home on the market two months before he left her for Elaine. The plan had been for Mom and Dad to move into a condo closer to the city.

A month later, before Steve and I headed on our road trip west, my brother and I had been at Dad's office with his real estate agent. The agent had found a buyer and wanted both Dad and Mom to sign the Purchase and Sales Agreement.

Dad asked Steve and me, "Will your mother be willing to sign? Should I have the agent go ahead with the sale, or should we wait?"

Though I had a bad feeling in my stomach, Steve and I agreed that Dad's signature would be sufficient. We assumed Mom would go along. We all felt she would do better by living closer to her Hungarian Jewish friends in the city—immigrant families she had known for decades. Dad signed the document and told the agent, "Go ahead with the closing. We'll get Anne's signature later."

All of us were wrong. After Dad had left Mom, she refused to sign the agreement and wasn't willing to leave the house. Steve and I had tried to persuade her otherwise, saying, "Mom, you'll be much better off living in the city. You'll be closer to downtown rather than stuck here in the suburbs. You'll be closer to the people you know."

She came back strongly, "My life is here! I'm not leaving the house. Please don't make me." Maybe she just wanted to stick it to Dad.

Now, six weeks after Dad's departure from our childhood home, he was upset too. "If your mother isn't willing to leave the house, then the new buyers can sue us for damages. She needs to find herself another place to live within the next month. The money we get for the house will get her a nice condo closer to the city."

I felt entangled in a web, and I couldn't tear myself out. I desperately wanted to do what was right, but I had no idea of what was right for my parents. I couldn't understand why Mom was reluctant to do what Steve and I felt would be suitable for her. I shrugged. "Dad, I know. But I don't know what else Steve and I can do. She won't listen to us. We need help with this." I was at a loss.

Dad looked down at his desk and thought for a moment. He raised his head. "Okay, let me call Mack. Maybe he has an idea. He's dealt with separated couples before."

Steve and I stood in silence as our father grabbed the phone and called his long-time lawyer and Troika drinking buddy. Mack was on the line within a moment. Dad explained, "I signed a P&S with a buyer for the Dorval house." . . . "Anne is upset and not willing to leave the house." . . . "The boys don't know what to do to persuade her to move."

Our father listened for a few minutes and made a note. When he was off the phone, he gave me the paper. "Here, this guy is a psychologist Mack recommends. His name is Dr. Moe Gross, and his office is not far away. Call and make an appointment to see him. See what he recommends in this situation.

Dad had never considered that somebody in our family would see a psychotherapist. Mom had once told me, "I asked your father many times to go and see a marriage counselor with me. But he told me he didn't need it, and he also said, 'If you think you need somebody, go without me.'" Mom never went by herself for such help.

That evening, Steve and I talked to Mom about Dr. Gross. She said, "Okay, go see the guy if you think he could help us."

A couple of days later, Steve and I entered the therapist's home office. Though it was Dr. M. Gross on the nameplate on his desk, he asked us to call him Moe.

He was a balding man in his early fifties. His face was round, and his teeth crooked. His pudgy physique was seated in a big high-back chair, giving this short man a taller stature. He wore slippers instead of shoes as if he were right at home. Behind him, professional books filled a wall of bookshelves that went from floor to ceiling.

Steve and I sat at far ends of a long couch facing Moe. We explained our parents' recent separation and our current dilemma with their house. He kept his hand to his chin as we spoke. He asked questions to clarify what we had said. I then asked, "Moe, what do you think we should do?"

Moe thought a few seconds then offered, "First of all, you guys shouldn't be in the middle of this situation between your parents." He looked directly at one and then the other of us. His voice was serious but not stern. "You need to tell both of your parents that you can't be the ones to negotiate matters between them, even regarding your mother's house."

He raised a finger. "It's very unhealthy that the children, no matter how old and how caring, arrange such things for or between their parents. This problem and burden are theirs, not yours. You should be out of the middle of it as expediently as possible."

Moe was right. Steve and I had forgotten the similar advice we had previously gotten from Dad's lawyer, Mack. That recommendation to stay out of our parent's affairs had come from Mack nearly fifteen years earlier, when Dad and Mom had separated for the first time. I couldn't read my brother's blank face, but I suddenly felt relieved and stupid at the same time.

Moe shifted in his chair. His face was relaxed, and his voice stayed calm, but the latter remained serious. "Second, your mother shouldn't be forced out of her house where she has lived the last twenty-five years. She's right—her life is there. She should only move when she is ready and willing to do so."

He raised an open palm. "Your mother seems to be devastated by your father's leaving her. No one should force her to make another big change in her life until she is ready."

"So, what do we do about the P&S our dad signed?" Steve asked. My brother was leaning back casually on the couch as if he, too, were in his living room.

Moe looked at Steve and spoke matter-of-factly. "Your father signed it, which makes him responsible. He'll have to work out compensation for the buyer to break the agreement. It's unfortunate, but I don't see a better choice."

His eyes went back and forth between us. "If your father agrees to meet with me, then I can be the one to talk to him about this. It's not healthy for the two of you to be in a position that puts your loyalties into question, or puts you in a bind with your parents."

He took a long breath. "This situation is not of your creation, and it's not yours to resolve." His voice stayed collected, yet he was adamant. "Being their children, your job is to love and support both of them. If you are in the middle of their separation negotiations, one or both of them will feel manipulated by you for the sake of the other. It's just not workable."

As it had been with my Harvard psychologist nine months earlier—when I had suddenly stopped shivering after he had explained my condition—the lead weights attached to my mind, chest, and shoulders melted from my body and into the floor.

I looked at my brother. He seemed to be relieved, too, as he let out a breath. "Okay, Moe," we both said simultaneously.

Steve continued, "We can try to arrange a meeting for you with our father."

The psychologist leaned forward in his seat. "I need to see your mother too. My involvement won't help unless she agrees to it. They need to feel I can be objective in their situation. They can't feel that I'm working for the interests of just one of them, though most likely it will be your father paying for my services."

Moe retrieved a few business cards and handed them to us. "Tell your parents that they can call me if they want to talk before I meet with each of them." He wrote something on a piece of paper and handed it to Steve. "These are times I'm available next week. If they prefer, I can meet your father at his office and your mother at her home."

He looked directly at us. "It's okay for the two of you to arrange these meetings between each of them and me, or ask them to call me if they prefer." His eyes narrowed. "But after that, you need to be out of it. Do both of you understand?"

"Yes, Moe," both of us said. There was less tension in my voice. "One of us will get back to you soon," I added.

The psychologist had more to say. "And I'd like to meet individually with the two of you." His eyes seemed to look through us. "I work with many family business owners, including their spouses and children, to help them get through tough and tense family and business situations."

He pointed our way. "This situation with your parents must be hard for both of you. I can help you through it." He raised a hand. "There appears to have been ongoing trouble between your mother and father for a very long time. It must have had its effects on you, especially since you seem to be close to them."

He paused for a second, and his voice softened. "Your father can afford to do that for all of you. Deep down, I think he would want both of you to come out okay from this angst-filled situation between him and your mother." He raised a hand. "I would think he'd prefer to settle everything amicably and see the two of you undamaged by it."

"Okay," I said again.

"I hope you're right, Moe," my brother added.

Steve and I talked to our father that afternoon after the office staff had left for the day. Steve handed him Moe's card. "Dad, Dr. Gross says he needs to see you and Mom separately."

Dad's tone was short. "Why does he need me? It's your mother who won't cooperate."

"It's because this situation is between you and her," I said. "Dr. Gross wants Steve and me to stay out of it."

Steve put Moe's piece of paper on Dad's desk. "These are times he says he's available. He can come here if you want him to."

Dad looked down at the paper and then up at me. I sensed irritation in his voice. "Okay, tell him to come next Tuesday afternoon at two o'clock." His eyebrows were low over his eyes, and his face was tight. "How much does the guy charge?"

I dodged the second question for a moment. "I'll call Moe right now to let him know about the time." I walked to my desk and lifted the phone receiver. "He's $80 an hour," I said. "And he wants to see Steve and me too, to help us through this as well."

"Hesus, Maria!" Dad cursed, almost spitting. "A guy like that will eat us alive."

I gave no response while I dialed the phone. I didn't want to give my father a chance to change his mind.

That evening, Steve and I went to our mother's home. Though she was surprised that Dad decided to meet with Moe, she also agreed to see the psychologist on the day after, on Wednesday.

Later, at our apartment, I quipped to my brother. "I didn't know psychologists made house calls."

He looked at me with a slight smile. "I guess this one does."

Over the next week, Moe had private meetings with the four of us. In my first session, he explained. "People like your father like to feel in control. He wouldn't come to a psychologist's office but would meet on his turf." He smiled through his crooked teeth. "As for your mother, she'd feel more comfortable meeting at her home. She has no easy way of her getting here outside of spending hours on city buses."

Right after Moe had left Dad's office following their first meeting, our father called Steve and me into his private domain. He spoke confidently. "I agree with Moe that you guys shouldn't be in the middle of the situation between your mother and me. I've hired him to come up with a financial settlement between us."

His voice stayed crisp but calm. "I've called the real estate agent to tell him your mother will stay in the house. I told the agent to offer the buyer five thousand dollars to get out of the agreement I signed." His voice rose. "Otherwise, the buyer can kiss my ass and sue me."

I was stunned. Five thousand dollars was close to what my tuition had been in my last year at MIT.

Moe explained Dad's rationale during my session. "Your father is very money conscious. Five grand is small potatoes to him compared to what he is considering as a settlement with your mother. If she is more amenable to settle by remaining in her home, then it would have been worth paying the penalty to get out of the P&S agreement."

I was impressed with Moe's take on my father, as I had been with the psychologist's office wall that was full of books. I told him about my breakdown at business school before coming back to Montreal.

He leaned forward in his chair and offered quietly, "Harvy, you were under a lot of stress. You felt you were there for your father. Awful things were happening between your parents and with your mother."

He took a long breath. "I would have probably done all I could to keep you at Harvard, for it could have opened more opportunities for you in the future. But your departure from there is understandable. I respect you for

37

having come home to help your family; it's admirable." He looked at me with kind eyes. "I truly hope your efforts will be worth it for you."

No one had ever spoken to me that way. For only the second time in my life, someone wasn't telling me what I should do but was helping me to understand my circumstances. My heart had hope.

Moe added, "Harvy, it's hard to emerge as your true self in the shadow of your father. He occupies a lot of space in your life. It's time for you to create your purpose and build your self-confidence, both of which seem to be a challenge for you."

As he spoke, I looked only at Moe's chest and chin. I wasn't able to meet his eyes, but deep down, I knew he was right.

Moe shifted slightly in his seat. "If you want to make a positive impact in your father's business and your family, I can help you do that, and build your self-esteem in the process."

He paused and then continued. "Over the years, I've worked with family businesses and children of business owners." He kept his eyes on me. "And, if it doesn't work out for you to stay in your father's company, then I can help you figure out what you could do next."

I was amazed by the perspective this man had on my family and me. Though I felt a cloud was lifting from my mind, I still spoke shyly. "Moe, I think I like what you do. When I was at Harvard, one subject I enjoyed was organizational behavior. Though it was all new to me, I'd like to learn more about it."

Moe raised his hand once more. "Harvy, I can recommend courses for you on the human side of management. I can then help you apply those courses to your father's company."

He pointed my way. "You have the perfect environment in which to bring more sophisticated management approaches to your father's business. And I can help you sell your ideas to your father in ways he'll be less defensive about them."

My voice stayed sheepish. "Do you think my father will eventually allow Steve and me to run his company?"

Moe nodded slowly. "It's possible if you learn to do it right. You need to learn to 'drop handkerchiefs' for your father to pick up." Moe looked to one side then back at me. "If you don't mind his getting the credit for new initiatives, you can offer him hints in ways that he'd believe those new ideas are his." He smiled. "Then, when he wants his employees to act on those ideas, you can be the one to help his people implement them."

I was impressed. I was a parched throat taking in the quenching drink that I had been seeking all my life. I believed I could do what Moe was considering for me.

Moe must have seen my eyes widen, for he continued. "Another trick is to find areas, like a new product or service line, where you don't try to take control of the business away from your father. Instead of trying to wedge him out of his JHS throne, you could build a new venture under you." He pointed again in my direction. "If you are not in direct competition with your father for the leadership of the company, then you're not taking anything away from him."

Moe placed his right hand over his left, with the latter positioned horizontally. Then he raised the top hand to form a dome over his left hand. "The trick is to grow something new on what capabilities JHS already has. When you start forming your own business ventures, your father can act as your financier, and he'd be less likely to stick his nose into your business."

"That makes a lot of sense," I responded with energy. "I'd like your help to do this, and to figure out courses I could take to learn more about the human side of management."

"It'll be my pleasure, Harvy. You are a bright boy who has a promising future in front of you." He took a long breath. "By the way, you and I should meet for ninety minutes every week. We have a lot of ground to cover. I want to support you moving forward on both business and personal fronts." He smiled slightly. "It doesn't sound like you have any serious romantic interests; I can help you in that department too."

Moe's statements made my shoulders feel a little lighter and my spine a little straighter. I didn't know if he said all those things to make me feel good, yet I nodded my acceptance of his plan.

Moe was a much better choice than the consultant that my organizational behavior professor had recommended when I had departed Harvard. I had called and talked to that family business practitioner after reading his book. I didn't think my father would engage a high-priced U.S. consultant for my sake.

That American expert had a few too many "shoulds" and "musts." He professed that business founders must pass on their business during their lifetime, and should put their succession plans in writing. His assertive attitude might not fly with my father's approach to "Do things my way or hit the highway." Moe's "dropping handkerchiefs" method sounded like it better suited my family.

I had to be careful as to how I approached my father regarding my brother and me potentially taking over JHS. After I had felt more sure-footed with Dad—before he upped and left Mom—I gave him my Harvard professor's family business articles. Dad read them on a Sunday afternoon when we were at his country chalet. (It was never "our family's chalet" because Dad had bought it when he had been separated the second time from Mom.)

My father read those business articles while he sat across the living room from me. One of the pieces professed, "Family businesses take on the personality of their owner-founders; it can limit their company's growth and success." The other offered, "At a certain stage of development, family businesses should be turned over to professional managers."

I wondered how my father would react to those statements. Would he be upset about academics telling him to step aside and make room for a professional manager, something I was hoping to become? Could he entrust me (and Steve too) as his successors, and effectively plan for us to take over JHS? I sat still as Dad read, my insides stirring with anticipation.

When Dad finished, he stood, walked over to me, and pushed the papers back into my hand. "So, you think my business is my mistress? [One of the articles had alluded to that notion.] You think I should let other people run it for me?"

Yah, Dad, eventually. You aren't going to run it from your grave. But the harsh sound of his voice persuaded me to keep my mouth shut for now.

Moe helped me to understand what had transpired in that father-son interaction. "Your father's business has been his baby from its birth. It's very personal to him." He spoke matter-of-factly. "Your dad's *raison d'etre* is wrapped deeply around his company, and it's the source of his power." He smiled as if he had seen situations like this before. "Relinquishing his baby, or mistress, would make him feel like nobody; it might even kill him."

I now believed I had a local Montreal guide who listened well, who understood my family situation, and who would help me grow to be my father's eventual successor—if Dad would allow it.

Moe reiterated, "You are stronger by being aligned with your brother than trying to change things at JHS on your own. Your father would find it harder to say no if he saw the two of you united."

"I want Steve to be in this with me," I said. "I'm glad he has agreed to see you too."

Moe nodded his approval.

Later, at home, I said to my brother, "I like this Moe guy. I think he can help us."

"We'll see," Steve replied in his customary non-committal way. "Let's take it a step at a time."

Maybe Steve knew something I didn't. He had lived with Mom and worked for Dad longer than I had. For now, I was grateful that my mother's opposition about leaving her home had led us to Moe. I couldn't wait to grow bigger son-of-the-boss wings, and maybe *yaytsa* too, with this psychologist's help.

* * * *

3

Past Our Primes?

Nudge, nudge. "Harvy…Harvy…. Can you please get up?" Nudge again. "I can't sleep. Can you come downstairs with me and go for a walk? I need some fresh air."

The light was coming in through our bedroom windows that went wall-to-wall. It came in from the street lamps below and through the building windows across the street. My head pounded, and my burning, tired eyes could barely open. My ears and sinuses felt packed with cotton. "Gee, Dad. What time is it?"

"It's four in the morning, local time. Can you please, please come downstairs with me? I don't want to go by myself."

Can't he go without me? Why does he frigging need me? I need to sleep!

"Please, son," he repeated.

I lay there a few more seconds, put my hand over my eyes to shield them from the building lights outside, and said, "Okay, okay, Dad. I'll go with you. Give me a minute to get myself dressed."

It was late October 1980, several weeks after Moe Gross had come into our lives. I had recently turned 26. My father and I were staying in the Hotel Lotte, a large luxury hotel in the heart of Seoul's business and entertainment district. This business trip was my first to Asia, and it was our second night here.

Had Korea not declared martial law earlier in the year, Dad and I would have been here months earlier. He wanted to show me his Simkovits ropes in Asia while my brother watched the JHS fort in Montreal. Steve didn't come on this trip because Dad didn't invite him; my brother had never gone on an overseas business trip with our father.

When I had said goodbye to my brother before entering a cab with Dad to go to the airport, my brother only said, "Have a good trip, Harvy." Other than offering a half-smile, there was no telling sign about what he was thinking or feeling.

After Dad had awakened me on that early morning in Seoul, he and I dressed without a word and headed to the hotel lobby. I had to lean against the elevator's wall to keep myself from falling to the ground. I stared at the elevator floor while both of us remained silent. I thought about how little sleep we had gotten since we left home.

It had been twenty hours of travel from Montreal to Seoul via New York. We had had a four-hour, middle-of-the-night layover in Anchorage, Alaska. In Anchorage, Korean Air exited its hundreds of passengers from the airplane and had us wandering the airport. We walked around and sat drooped on hard benches in a virtually barren terminal. Not even a coffee shop was open.

"It can't take four hours to refuel," I said to my father.

"Maybe the pilots need some shut-eye," Dad responded. He tried to get comfortable in a seat at the gate.

"Wish we could get some shuteye too," I said. I slumped down as much as I could in my seat. "I'm sure the pilots have better seats than this."

Our plane took to the air as dawn was breaking over the snow-capped mountains that jutted out beyond the airport. Sleep was hard to get on the plane. When we got to our hotel in Seoul, we dropped straight into our beds.

The eleven-hour time change from Montreal made my mind beg for slumber, but my body wouldn't cooperate. I lay awake for hours, my head pounding and eyes burning. I wondered if I could handle such international travel.

I wanted to show my father—someone who had travelled across the Atlantic or Pacific almost every year—that I could keep pace with him. I had known him to be a resilient traveller who could function on little sleep. During our family trips to Europe, he could fall asleep at a moment's notice on a lounge chair, couch, or bed. If he had to, he could drive a rental car for many hours right after an overseas flight.

Now 60 years old, Dad seemed to have more difficulty with this trip. Though I too struggled with the jetlag, he was even more sleepless than I was. Now, on our second night here, rather than tossing and turning in bed, he wanted fresh air and some company. If it had been anybody else, I would have said, "Go on your damn walk without me."

When the elevator doors opened into the hotel's expansive lobby, we saw people milling and sitting about—perhaps other travellers suffering similar maladies due to the time change.

"Let's go outside," Dad said.

"But we can't go beyond the hotel property," I responded. "The military curfew is in effect until six o'clock."

Although the country's political situation was more stable than earlier in the year, there was still a midnight-to-4 A.M. military-imposed curfew preventing citizens and visitors from being on the streets at night.

"Would you rather go to the disco?" Dad asked, his face pleading for any alternative than going back to our room.

Because of the curfew, the discothèque on the hotel's top floor was open the whole night. Partygoers and jetlaggers could sit and drink through the wee hours until the sun rose and curfew lifted.

"No, thanks," I said.

Having dropped by the disco before we had gone to bed, I knew the place was body-vibrating loud. Headache-producing blinking and gyrating spotlights pointed and twirled in every direction. Though a stiff drink might help both of us relax and go to sleep, my stomach still ached from the big Korean meal we had had earlier that evening.

I looked at my father through my weary eyes. "Dad, the hotel disco is the last place my head and stomach want to be."

No restaurant or café was open in the lobby. My father repeated, "Let's go outside. We'll walk in the driveway."

The hotel had a large, partially covered, half-oval driveway. The ground beyond the building was wet from earlier rain, but the air hung still on this lukewarm fall night. The humid but crisp air refreshed my face as we stepped out of the building. I looked at the ground so I wouldn't trip over an irregular cobblestone and fall on my face.

Though some lights were on in the stores, restaurants, and offices across the street, they were lifeless inside. Except for the hotel's doorman— who reminded us not to go beyond the driveway—not another soul was in sight. In the distance, we could hear a police car siren wail.

Dad lit a cigarette and took a couple of drags. We strolled back and forth along the cobblestones. When we got to the sidewalk, I bent forward to glimpse around the side of our hotel building to see if anyone was risking the ire of the military police. No one was.

Not knowing what else to talk about, I looked toward the mundane. "Dad, did you see all the Parks, Kims, and Lees in the city phone book in our room?"

Dad was accommodating. "Yes, son. Half the people in this country have one of those last names. It's South Korea's way of simplifying its people's family names. It makes it easier for them to do business with the rest of the world."

I smiled through my tiredness. "I guess that's why everyone calls our Mr. Kim by his initials, CJ, instead of his given names, Ching Jun."

"Our" C.J. Kim was the President of Jin Dae, a Korean producer of electronic console stereo components, and an essential supplier to Dad's company. Over the last few years, Jin Dae had provided JHS with thousands of integrated radio chassis for various console models.

"That's right," Dad said. He took another puff of his cigarette and stared at the smoke as he blew it out of his mouth.

"Speaking about CJ, Dad; that was a crucial meeting we had with him yesterday."

I was glad my father was blowing his cigarette smoke away from me; otherwise, I'd have something else to unsettle my stomach. "Yes, son." His eyes blinked a few times from tiredness. "I hope CJ now understands the problem we are having with those goddamn plates mounted on their chassis' front molding."

The Jin Dae chassis included an AM/FM radio and both cassette and 8-track players, with all those components mounted in a single housing. A decorative black plastic molding enveloped the chassis housing on which the unit's control knobs and buttons were mounted. Seven brushed aluminum plates covered the black frame.

Those aluminum plates were designed and installed poorly, causing a severe aesthetic problem for several JHS console models. The Jin Dae chassis became despised by virtually every Sears store and warehouse across Canada. On more than half the chassis, the plates had warped or looked pitted, like they had been banged all over by a child wielding a kid's hammer.

I continued. "Dad, were you as nervous as I was when CJ's engineer, Mr. Lin, brought out that sealed box of chassis? He said it had come off Jin Dae's production line three months ago."

Dad pointed his cigarette at me. "Yes. CJ wanted to embarrass us. He had held back a box of finished chassis from their last shipment to JHS to prove to us the plate problem was not of Jin Dae's making." Dad took another drag. "I was sitting on pins and needles when Mr. Lin unpacked that container and showed us the chassis inside."

"Had those plates looked perfect, we would've had much explaining to do," I said.

My father turned slightly toward me and pointed his index finger my way. "If I had to, I would have air freighted CJ a few of the worst chassis we have at JHS, or I would have insisted he come to Montreal to see for himself how terrible the problem is."

Dad took a breath. "Anyway, we were lucky the package of chassis Mr. Lin opened showed some mild warping and pitting of the plates." Dad lifted his hand to make his point. "Sears's customers got so sensitive about the plates not looking right that Sears management stopped selling our units in their stores. Their floor salesmen didn't even want to show our products to prospective customers."

I had to work to keep one foot in front of the other as we walked along the hotel's driveway. I had to put one hand over my eyes and avoid bumping into my father as we sauntered along under the bright overhead lights. I rubbed soreness out of my eyes. "It's too bad. Had everything stayed the way those chassis looked yesterday, there might not have been such problems."

"But, you know what happened, Harvy!" Dad's voice elevated as it had been with CJ a half-day earlier. "Our goddamn cold Canadian weather made those thin plates warp and buckle even more, especially during shipments."

Dad made a fist. "The glue that held the plate onto the chassis housing was so strong that it didn't let the metal expand or contract as the outside temperature changed. It made the originally flat and smooth plate look pitted like shit after a while."

"Yes, I know, Dad." I kept my voice calm. I didn't want my father to get more excited. "CJ said yesterday that he'd fix the problem."

He pointed his cigarette toward me. "CJ has to if he wants more business from us, and to make more sales in Canada."

Dad was almost shouting as he took another drag. "Until he can get a thicker aluminum plate from his suppliers, or use more flexible glue, he'll have to put a second layer of plates onto each of the seven that comprise the face of the chassis." We had told CJ's engineer how to do it with special 3M double-faced tape. "Jin Dae has to follow our instructions," Dad exclaimed.

Dad, an experienced manufacturer, had been the one to suggest double-taping replacement aluminum plates on top of the existing pitted plates. That maneuver was much simpler than removing the defective plates, chiseling out the stiff glue, and then double-taping new plates onto the plastic housing.

He added, "It was good you and Steve went across Canada this past summer to fix the plate problem in every Sears store and warehouse. It did a lot to rebuild our credibility with the store salesmen and Sears head office."

I kept my head down so the hotel lights wouldn't be directly in my eyes. Steve and I had visited dozens of customer stores and warehouses west of Montreal. We repaired over 200 console units across the country, and we had shown the warehouse managers how to make repairs by themselves if any more deformed chassis plates turned up. Sears furniture salespeople and warehouse managers were pleased we had taken the time to make that significant gesture of goodwill.

"Those warped plates were like cancer," Dad cried. "You think you got it all, and then they appear again, even worse than before." Because of that, the electronics buyer at Sears' head office became so upset that he froze JHS console sales and warehouse shipments until JHS could repair everything.

I nearly tripped on a protruding cobblestone. I tried to find a silver lining. "It was a good thing you got a discount on future orders of Jin Dae's chassis."

"Yes, but the $3 U.S. per chassis concession we got on the 500 additional chassis I purchased yesterday is peanuts. It covers little of the damages we have incurred." Dad made a fist. "And because we have to pay Jin Dae by letter of credit, effectively paying them in advance for our orders, we can't withhold any payments from them if those new chassis have problems."

I tried to stay optimistic. "Didn't CJ promise to send us an electronics technician for a year at little or no cost to us?"

"He did, son, but who knows when that will be. He said he is training new techs to work for his North American customers. I don't think we'll see a guy from Jin Dae until well into next year." My father took the last drag from his cigarette. "But it's like closing the barn door after the horse *foot-scoffed*." Dad threw his cigarette butt onto the driveway and stubbed it out.

"What if we sue Jin Dae for damages?" I asked. "JHS has put a lot of extra labour into fixing their chassis, including Steve's and my trip out west."

Dad shook his head. "That would be hard to do, and too expensive. Jin Dae and their parent company have no offices in Canada, so there's nothing there to sue."

Dad blinked hard; perhaps his eyes were burning as much as mine. He continued. "I looked into it with Mack. He told me we'd have to get a judgement from the Quebec courts for damages, and then hire a lawyer in Korea or the U.S. to sue Jin Dae's parent company or its subsidiary. That's a costly proposition."

"It's too bad," I said. "Who figured it would be an aesthetic problem that would create such a fiasco?" I wondered if Jin Dae's chassis plate problem could permanently damage JHS's reputation and business.

Dad lit another cigarette. His voice rose again. "In my thirty years in manufacturing, I've never seen anything like it. Jin Dae chassis' aesthetic design is a bloody mess. They should have never created a unit with so many thin aluminum plates glued onto the chassis molding. Initially, it looked good, but it turned out to be a goddamn time bomb."

Dad motioned to a bench near the hotel's front door. We sat down. The quiet, lukewarm air seemed to help my eyes and stomach feel better. Dad continued to puff away, blowing the smoke away from me. I kept the conversation going to keep myself awake. "Could you believe the food CJ ordered last night for supper?"

Mr. Kim had taken us to a traditional Korean restaurant in our hotel. During supper, he must have ordered half the items on the menu. There was so much food in front of us that I nearly lost sight of the table. I could barely try half of it. I could hardly look at the Korean kimchee, let alone taste it. Other dishes, some delicious, required two glasses of water and a half bowl of rice to douse the spice burning in my mouth.

Dad offered a bit of a smile. "I'm glad you were there to eat it. I'm sick of this Korean seaweed food." He rubbed his protruding belly. "My stomach isn't used to it."

"What was Mr. Kim thinking?"

Dad smiled. "CJ was trying to be nice. He didn't expect us to eat everything. He knows Korean food is not to our Western tastes. He wanted to find a few things we'd like." Dad grinned. "He was trying to please us."

"I wish I would have known that beforehand." *Yah, Dad! Why didn't you tell me?*

My father responded, "CJ is looking for more business from us, so he's trying to compensate for our chassis problem through his entertainment budget. But I agree with you, son; he went overboard last night."

I put my hand on my churning stomach. I had forced myself to eat something slimy and squishy, having had no idea what it was. Dad must have seen my sickened face, perhaps green like the seaweed that had been in that kimchee. He raised his palm and gave a half-smile. "You'll know better next time, son. Just say which dish you like and eat as much as you can. Then push your plate away, raise your hands, and politely say you can't eat anything more."

I appreciated my father's belated tip, but I wasn't sure if my body was cut out for such overseas travel. I don't know how my father had done it over the years. Because he was having trouble sleeping on this trip, I wondered if his years of international travel were catching up with him.

Dad winked at me. "When we get to Japan in a couple of days, we'll see if we can find an Austrian or Hungarian restaurant in Tokyo. I could eat a good veal schnitzel or beef goulash, or even prime roast beef. You can't find our kind of food here in Seoul."

Dad finished his second cigarette and stomped it out on the ground. "Let's go back upstairs."

The driveway had looked immaculate before Dad arrived with his cigarettes. I imagined the doorman sweeping up the butts immediately after we went back inside. "Okay," I said. I hoped he and I could get to sleep. I could do without more wake-up calls in the middle of the night.

Dad made conversation while we rode the elevator. "We're going to see important people from Goldstar electronics this afternoon." His face looked serious. "In the U.S., Goldstar already sells a TV product line. I want to see if they would be interested in having JHS manufacture cabinets for them in Canada. Our company can also do electronic assembly work for them."

Dad's tone was glum. "We need to find another line of business for JHS. Console stereos are coming to the end of their life."

"Okay, Dad," I said with a yawn. "Must we have supper with them?"

"No, son." He smiled and then yawned. "We can skip that part." He turned toward me and put his hand on my shoulder. "Thanks for coming downstairs with me. Now let's see if we can get some sleep."

I half-smiled back. I hoped I could stay awake for those upcoming meetings.

* * *

Two mornings later, during breakfast at our hotel, Dad—now more wide awake—offered, "Harvy, let's go shopping. I want to buy a few things while we are here."

With time on our hands before our last supplier meeting that afternoon, Dad suddenly got a gift-buying urge. "What are you looking for?" I asked.

"Maybe some nice jewellery." He gestured for me to follow. "Come with me. I know where to go." He didn't say more.

We jumped into the back of a cab in front of the hotel. Dad immediately pulled a ragged piece of paper from his wallet and showed it to the driver. "Can you take us here?"

"Namdaemum Market? Yes!" The cabbie nodded and sped off a second before I got my second leg into the car and the car's door closed.

We made our way through the city, rushing through streets and dodging traffic. The cabby turned to my father. "You from the USA?"

"No, Canada," Dad said. "Montreal." His voice was upbeat.

The cabbie smiled. "Never been to Canada; too cold. Seoul warmer; more like New York City."

"I know what you mean," my father retorted. "I've lived in Canada for over thirty years, and I'm still not used to the winters."

The Korean man kept on talking. "Namdaemum Market is oldest and biggest market in South Korea, open day and night. Many stores and restaurants in city buy from there. What you looking for?"

Dad responded. "A good place to buy some nice jewellery."

The driver grinned wide. "For you or a lady?"

"Maybe both." Dad's voice stayed cool. "Do you know where we should go?"

The guy rummaged through a pocket and retrieved an oversized business card. When we stopped at a light, he wrote down a name. "Go see my friend at this store. His name Mr. Lee. He has nice things, and he gives you good price." He pointed to himself. "Tell him Mr. AJ Park, the taxi driver, sent you." The driver scrolled his name on the card.

Dad smiled back. "Okay, we'll look out for him."

As we neared the market, the cabbie turned his head once more. "You go see Sungnyemun Gate too?"

"What's that?" I asked.

"Great south gate to old city." The cabbie raised one arm over his head as if he were doing a one-armed pirouette. "Looks like giant pagoda."

I looked at my father. He looked back at me and said, "We'll see, son, after we do business at the market."

We were soon on the curb and started to wander through the market streets. The alleys were closed to vehicle traffic except for motorcycles and heavy-laden, hand-drawn carts of various sizes and shapes. Over the next half-hour, I followed Dad around like the RCA Nipper dog following his master's voice. My father scoped out a couple of jewellery stores. I eventually asked, "Don't you want to go to the place the cab driver told us about?"

"Soon, son. I want to see what's here first, see what things cost before we go negotiate with that Mr. Lee guy—if he has anything good to show us."

"Are you looking for anything in particular?"

"Cultured mabe and black pearls."

I had heard about cultured pearls before, but never the kinds Dad mentioned. "What makes those special?"

My father talked as we walked briskly, hunting for the next jewellery shop. "Mabe pearls are grown against the inside of the shell rather than in the meat of the oyster. They come out flat on one side and can look like a teardrop. They make for nice earrings."

He stopped in front of the next jewellery store. He pointed to a display window. "You see there. Black pearls are generally round and come from black oysters that only exist in a few places in the Pacific. You see them in necklaces and bracelets" He looked at me. "I heard we can get both mabe and black pearls a lot cheaper here in Korea than at home or in the U.S."

I suspected my father was getting these things for his new love, Elaine, but I didn't ask. After browsing more, Dad pulled out the card with Mr. Lee's name and store address. He showed it to a street vendor who pointed us in the right direction.

Mr. Lee's shop was an open storefront rather than a walk-in store. It was about four meters wide and two meters deep into a building that rose from the edge of the narrow sidewalk. The store's glass counters were just centimeters back from the sidewalk.

An older Asian man was standing behind a counter. On the wall behind him were glass shelves plus a doorway leading to a back room. Dad looked at the man and put out his hand with the card in it. "Are you Mr. Lee? I was sent here by Mr. AJ Park, the cab driver. My name is Johnny." He pointed to me. "This is my son, Harvy."

"Yes, I Mr. Lee. Good to meet you, Mr. Johnny and Mr. Harvy." He looked at me and then back to Dad. "How can I help you?"

"I'm looking for mabe pearl earrings and maybe a black pearl necklace or bracelet."

"For someone special?" Mr. Lee gave a bit of a grin.

"Yes," Dad said. He added nothing more, his face as blank as a dead president on an American bill.

"Where are you and your son from?" Mr. Lee asked. "Are you long in our city?"

"We're from Canada, and we're only here in Seoul for a couple of days on business."

"Will you be buying in Canadian or U.S. currency?"

"I have U.S. dollars and can pay you in cash if we can make a deal on some things."

I noted Dad was using the plural. I wondered how much he was planning to buy.

My father sat down on a stool in front of the counter. "Show me what you have; let's start with these nice earrings I see here in this counter."

I was hoping we were going to be there for half-an-hour, but Dad seemed to settle in for the long haul. He lit a cigarette and offered one to Mr. Lee. The short, thin man accepted the gesture. "I don't get to smoke Canadian cigarettes too often," he said.

My father lit the cigarette for him and said, "These are from Quebec. They're stronger than American brands."

Yah, they can grow hair on your tongue.

"American brands are like chewing gum," my father added with a smirk.

Mr. Lee took a drag and nodded his approval.

Very few other shoppers came by Mr. Lee's jewellery shop during this early part of the day. One by one, the Korean showed my father several pearl earrings, mostly priced in a $300 to $600 US dollar range. My father quickly brushed aside what he didn't like, but asked Mr. Lee to keep on the counter those items my dad wanted to consider. He showed close attention to a pair of tear-drop mabe pearl earrings in a gold setting, priced at $500USD.

After my father looked at the items under the glass counter, he asked, "Are these the best you have?" I was a little surprised by his question since I thought he was looking in a high-price range.

Mr. Lee took my father's comment in stride. He went to the shelves behind him to retrieve other items. The Korean brought forth a pair of black pearl earrings shaped in a teardrop, set in a gold and diamond setting. He said, "These are most special pearls. Come from Tahiti black oyster." The price tag showed a value two to three times higher than what my father had already seen.

Dad examined the earrings and puffed up his voice. "These are beautiful. What is your best price?"

"I cannot take less than $1300 for them," Mr. Lee said firmly but casually.

"Okay, let's put the earrings aside over here on the counter. I'd like to have them grow on me."

I had no girlfriend at this time. While Dad was looking at things for women, I perused the men's rings and tiepins displayed further down the counter case. On my ring finger, I sported a large MIT gold grad ring. Though I enjoyed the way my ring looked and felt on my finger, I wasn't into gift shopping as Dad was.

While Dad looked more closely at the earrings, I asked Mr. Lee if I could look at a small 24-kt tiepin I saw inside one display case. While Dad lit another cigarette, Mr. Lee brought out the tie pin, and I tried it on. Dad looked at me, pointed his cigarette at my tie, and offered, "That looks good on you son. Buy it for yourself." He turned to Mr. Lee, "You'll sell it to him for cash, with no sales tax, right?"

Mr. Lee nodded slowly. "Yes, for you, no tax."

"I'll think about it," I said. The piece's price was $55USD, but I wasn't sure if I wanted to spend even that little money on myself. That was chump change for Dad, but I rarely treated myself to flashy things I didn't need. I only wore my one-ounce, 14k gold, MIT ring because I felt I had earned it after spending five years there and obtaining two engineering degrees. Dad had bought it for me four years earlier for $85USD.

After nearly an hour at Mr. Lee's store, I was getting bored. I turned to my father, "I'm going to walk around a bit."

"Okay, but please be back in thirty minutes. I'll decide on these things by then, and then we have another business meeting to get to." I nodded but knew Dad was exaggerating. Our next supplier meeting was not until this afternoon.

My father turned to Mr. Lee. "Now, I want your very best price on these things here." He pointed to the white mabe pearl earrings and a black pearl bracelet. "And I want to think about these other black pearl earrings. Gosh, they are beautiful. Don't you think so, Harvy?"

"Yes, they are very nice." I wondered if my father was going to splurge today.

I turned and walked away. I wanted to find the Sungnyemun gates the taxi driver had mentioned. After being pointed in the right direction by another vendor, I found the large, 14th century stone structure. It had a two-tier, pagoda-shaped, tiled wood roof. I stared at the pagoda for a moment to try to hold onto the image in my memory. After I had walked through the massive gate and tunnel that separated two parts of the city, I promptly returned to the store.

My father smiled at my return and then turned to the store owner. "Okay, Mr. Lee, I'll accept your price on these things," he said, "as long as you throw in the tie pin for my son." He pointed to the piece I had tried on earlier.

Mr. Lee thought for a moment. "Okay, okay, Mr. Johnny. I do that for you." He looked into Dad's eyes. "And these earrings? Should I wrap them for you too?" He pointed to the $1300 black pearl teardrop earrings still set to one side of the counter.

Dad said, "They are gorgeous, Mr. Lee. I appreciate you dropping the price to $1200 for me." He took a long breath. "It's very tempting, but we have to run to a meeting right now. I want to sleep on it if you don't mind. I'll come back tomorrow and have another look before we go back to Canada."

"Okay, Mr. Johnny. I'll package these other things for you. I give you nice box for each."

My dad nodded. "Thank you, sir. It's been a pleasure." They shook hands and smiled.

When my father and I walked away from the store, I said, "Thanks for the tiepin, Dad." I was curious. "How did you do on your other purchases?"

He looked at me. "I got everything I was looking for, and at less than half what they would cost back home. Mr. Lee's jewellery was nicer than anything else we saw at those other stores in the market. That was a good connection the taxi driver gave us."

My father was grinning ear to ear. I suspected the unmentioned Elaine would be doing the same when she would receive those gifts.

I didn't ask how much my father had paid for his purchases. It was clear to me that Dad had no intention of going back for the more expensive black pearl teardrops. He had made the Korean think he had a bigger fish on the hook than he had had, thereby forgoing some profit on the lesser expensive items Dad purchased.

What I found most interesting was, unlike at his Montreal office, Johnny Simkovits got his price without raising his voice. My father had had an amicable negotiation with the store owner.

I was glad to do my part in my father's ploy. I received a little bonus for hanging around and being my father's son. I would proudly wear that modest, pure-gold tiepin during social gatherings for decades.

* * *

Dad and I continued bleary-eyed through two other legs of our trip—Japan and Taiwan. In Tokyo, we met with a manufacturing rep who supplied JHS with cassette decks. Then, in Taipei, Dad negotiated a deal with another rep who wanted to sell my father 1,000 inexpensive radio chassis that the manufacturer was discontinuing. Sight unseen, Dad offered the rep $8US apiece. The rep had asked for $12 per unit, half their original price of $24.

A day later, after consulting his superiors, the rep accepted Dad's offer. My father later told me, "We've used these cheap chassis in our Woolco products." He smiled. "They should be okay. We'll knock out a few inexpensive consoles and offer them to Woolco. They like cheap stuff. At a good price, those units will go fast."

I wondered if JHS needed those extra chassis. We already had 1,000 of them in stock at the company. It seemed as if my father had thrown out a price from his gut. I wondered if Dad was buying those units either to justify our being in Taiwan or to demonstrate his deal-making prowess to me.

As he had done in Japan, Dad asked our Taiwanese rep if he knew of a local television manufacturer seeking cabinet manufacturing in Canada, something JHS could provide. The rep said he would look into it and get back to us by telex.

Dad and I found an Austrian-Hungarian restaurant in Tokyo. But their schnitzel was so laced with rancid cooking oil that my stomach ached for a day. Dad, too, got sick to his stomach in the middle of the night, and he needed to go for another nighttime walk. As in Korea, we got very little sleep in Japan. I couldn't wait for the Asian food torture and sleep deprivation to end.

In Taipei, the weather was hot and sticky, like South Florida in the summer after torrential rain. Our dress shirts became soaked with sweat within minutes of being outside. On our last of two nights there, Dad took me to a massage parlour where we could relax by having haircuts and body massages in reclining barber's chairs. Young women performed the massages through our light shirts and slacks.

Through the shop's front windows, I saw advertising on billboards and flashing signs across the street. They were for more exotic parlours where one could get a fully nude massage. I couldn't decipher whether it was the recipient or giver who'd be completely naked. During our supper in Seoul with CJ Kim, the Jin Dae President had winked at me and said quietly, "When you come back by yourself to our country, I'll show you the *real* Korea."

I wondered whether CJ had meant places like the one I was now looking at in Taipei. Though I imagined my father taking his Montreal colleagues to such locales, buying more than massages, it seemed as if Dad were steering me away from such places. Maybe he was trying to protect his son from what he saw as "the real Southeast Asia."

When our business in Taipei was complete, both my father and I were draggy. We decided to cut our planned twelve-day trip short. We went to a Korean Air office to arrange to get back to Montreal three days early. Though I felt I missed seeing the exotic parts of Asia, I had had had enough travelling. After another 24 hours of flying back through Seoul, Anchorage, and New York City, I was relieved to get home.

My father thanked me for coming with him, and I thanked him for the opportunity and his gift. Yet it was hard for me to fathom my making such an arduous, eye-burning, stomach-aching, head-pounding overseas trip again.

Perhaps I, like my father, was getting past my prime for such things.

* * *

"This is sabotage!" Dad yelled. "Harvy, telex those Korean bastards that we're going to hold them fully responsible. Tell them what we have been going through and that we expect them to fucking pay for it."

It was early December, less than two months after our return from Asia. New Jin Dae chassis, now with double layers of faceplates, had recently arrived for JHS's busiest production month. The plates looked good, but the double-faced tape Jin Dae was employing to hold the second plate layer onto the first was not doing its job. Jin Dae had used a brand of tape that wasn't adhesive enough. In our cold Canadian weather, the top plate layer was separating from the bottom layer.

As per Dad's instructions, I immediately sent a telex to Mr. Kim and Mr. Lin. I worked to be a little more professional in my language.

> Dear Sirs:
> Because of our cold weather, your double-face tape is not sticky enough to adjoin new top plates to the bottom layer. We cannot understand why you didn't employ the 3M product we recommended to you when we saw you in October. We insist you do so in the future, or we cannot use your chassis in JHS production.
>
> We are trying to make your tape stick by heating the plates with a hot air gun, and then pushing the top layer down with the flat end of a piece of soft wood so as not to scratch the plates. We hold you responsible for the extra labour needed for our production. We want you or your tech here to show you the problem and what we are doing to fix it. When can we expect you?
>
> Our production is being compromised by your not applying our recommended fix for this plate problem. We cannot continue this way!!! Your negligence is sabotaging our relationship with our customers.
>
> Sincerely, John Simkovits, President, JHS

When we arrived the next morning, a telex was waiting from Jin Dae's chief engineer:

Dear Mr. Simkovits:
Our trained tech will be there in a month or two; we will let
you know. Mr. CJ Kim will come to see you in Montreal in
the spring. He will contact you directly.
Regards, JC Lin, Chief Engineer, Jin Dae

"Those son-of-a-bitch bastards!" Dad huffed. "They don't take
responsibility for anything."

My voice was edgy. "And those guys don't even know how to frigging
count! Remember the telex they sent us last month. It said we had requested
more replacement aluminum plates than the total amount of chassis we had
ordered from them."

I banged my fist into my palm. "It took me hours of work to review
our JHS and Jin Dae telexes for the last year to prove them wrong. What
bums!" I didn't say it, but thank goodness my brother had taught me to file
those telex correspondence.

I took a few seconds to compose myself. "I can't wait for Kim and his
Jin Dae tech to get here so we can show them what we are going through in
production. It's fucking ridiculous." It wasn't often that I swore, but I felt the
situation warranted it.

Dad nodded. "CJ still doesn't get the seriousness of the problem. He's
trying to keep his repair costs down, so he doesn't look bad to his superiors.
We may have to sue Jin Dae after all. They've cost us too much money, and
they haven't solved the goddamn problem."

Dad looked over at Helen. "Get Mack on the phone." He looked back
at me. "Son, I want both of us to meet with him soon." He pointed at me. "I
want you to explain the problems we are having in production because of Jin
Dae's neglect."

I thought for a second. "The story is long and complicated, Dad. If it
helps, I'll write it out for Mack to read, with dates and copies of our telexes."

"That's a good idea, son. Please get started on it today."

* * * *

4

Dropping Handkerchiefs

& Stretching Slinkies

Some months later, in early 1981, I sat in Moe's office for one of our weekly sessions. I had been his client for over four months, and I was frustrated.

"For a while, things were getting better at JHS," I said with annoyance. "But now, he resists nearly every new idea I have for making JHS operate better." I hit the arm of the couch with my hand. "He always has a reason why we shouldn't do anything new. He's saying my ideas are too expensive, or not worth the effort, that he's been doing it his way for years."

"What do you mean, Harvy? What are you trying to change?"

My voice strained. "Remember," I said as I pointed to Moe and myself, "we agreed for me to do that course last month in Ottawa regarding the people side of management?"

"Yes," Moe responded, nodding. He looked relaxed in his chair. His right foot out of its slipper and placed on his seat under his left thigh.

"A part of the course was on transactional analysis. You know how all of us have parent, adult, and child states within us, and how it's important to have adult conversations with people in the context of their work."

Moe smiled. "Unlike what your father does—yelling at people as if he were the parent and they the child."

"Yes, I guess." I hadn't thought about it that simply, but Moe was right.

I looked at him and stayed on my original track. "I'm now getting Eric Berne's book, the guy who developed that theory." Having been an electrical engineer, I hadn't needed to do much book reading in my years at MIT; but this psychological stuff interested me.

Moe raised a hand. "Yes, I know Eric Berne's work. I taught it myself when I was a professor of psychology at McGill."

"You were a professor? I didn't know that."

"I taught for a few years."

I nodded, and maybe my eyes widened. I was impressed by this man who was an air freshener for me, unlike my stuffy-air-creating father.

I continued. "And there were other sessions during my Ottawa seminar on how to manage conflicts between individuals. In one case, the instructor demonstrated how to be an objective third party between two people who needed to resolve their differences."

"Interesting," Moe said. "How did the instructor demonstrate that?"

I raised my hands as if they were two puppets talking to each other. I explained. "First, you have one person state their case as effectively as they can." I moved my right hand as if it were talking to my left hand. "Then, before the other person can talk, they have to repeat back what the first person had said." I moved my left hand as if it were talking back to my right hand. "The second person can present their position only after they accurately paraphrased what the first person had stated. Then the roles are reversed, with the second person stating their position and the first person paraphrasing what the second said, and so on."

"That's great," Moe said.

"It was neat," I offered with enthusiasm. "Through class role-plays, the instructor showed us how misunderstanding or preconceived notions could conflict. If the opposing parties can work to hear each other well, the conflict can disappear by clarifying where each person is coming from."

I was talking fast. "And if that's not enough, then the next step is to focus on what the two people agree on before focusing on what they don't agree on." I was almost out of breath. "That approach helps create something in common and generates movement toward a joint solution."

"Sounds like you liked the course, Harvy."

I hesitated and looked down. "Yes, I guess so." No one in my family had ever shown concern about what I liked and didn't like. It was hard for me to acknowledge my excitement about something.

"So, what's the issue with your father?" Moe asked.

I looked his way and picked up steam again, but not as fast this time. "One of the things the course covered was how to conduct effective performance conversations with employees. The trick is not to make the discussion about the employee's personality, or whether you like them or not, or about what they do outside of work." I pointed at Moe. "We learned that the manager starts by telling the employee what's working in their behavior at work and then telling them what they could improve upon."

"Okay," Moe said, using his hand to urge me to get to my point.

"After I got back from the course, I told my father we should do annual appraisals with our factory people and tie their salary increases to their work performance. I suggested that the foremen and I sit down with every employee to tell them how they're doing and how they could perform better." I pointed to myself. "We did it at Procter & Gamble when I worked there. If people don't know where they stand, then they don't know how and why they should improve."

"Okay. I'm with you, Harvy. So what's holding your father back from implementing your brilliant idea?" He grinned at me, showing his crooked teeth.

I raised my hand. "My dad right away said he didn't want to do it that way. He just wanted to do an across the board 3% cost-of-living increase for everyone. He said it would cost a lot more money if we gave bigger increases to people, and it would take the foremen too much time to talk to their people one-by-one." I looked down. "He said he wants to keep things simple."

My voice rose as I made a fist and looked at Moe again. "But what's 3% to anyone these days? That's no incentive!" I shook my head. "What my father wants to do is dumb. Some employees will come to him later and see if they could get more. If my father likes them, or he's in a good mood, he'll give them more money. If not, he could have the best worker standing in front of him, and he won't give them a penny more." I threw up my hand. "It's so goddamn stupid."

"Hmm." Moe thought for a couple of seconds. "What if we try a more subtle approach?"

I responded a little loudly. "Okay, like what?"

Moe's hands were folded on his paunchy belly, unfazed by my course remark. "Harvy, what if you tell your father that you want to try out something a little different for this year. You can say that if it doesn't work, then you'll go back to his way." Moe's eyes moved side to side. "What if you suggest that it won't cost any more money than what he was already going to spend on raises?"

"How is that possible?"

Moe put out his right hand as if he were conducting a choral group. "Make the average raise 3%, but vary it from let's say 1.5% to 4.5%. Offer your best or 'A' performers the highest percentage increase, offer the average or 'B' performers the 3% cost-of-living increase, and give the less than average or 'C' performers just half the cost-of-living. This way, you can reward the best with a 50% premium over the cost of living, and not penalize the lesser performers with no increase."

He pointed at me. "And if you have a problematic 'D' performer, then you can give them no increase and start building a rational case to let them go."

My eyes opened wide, and my chest rose a tad. I felt a little more hopeful. "Okay," I said, "that sounds like it could work." I grinned a little. "But with those 'D' performers, Dad usually kicks their ass out the door when they make a stupid mistake."

Moe smiled back. "Yes, he works on whim or impulse rather than on a rational basis." He looked right at me. "What you can offer is to document people's performance over time and to keep that information in the employees' files. This way, you are building a work history on every employee.

It will prevent your father from making salary and termination decisions based only on how he sizes up an individual."

He pointed his finger. "And it's important as to how you talk to your father about these ideas. As in your transactional analysis learning, if you come across as a 'Dad you *should* do this, or Dad we *shouldn't* do that' kind of parent stance, then your father will respond as a resistive parent. You cannot come at him head-on, but you can carefully drop handkerchiefs for him to pick up."

"Okay, you mentioned that 'dropping handkerchiefs' thing before. Tell me more about it."

Moe turned away then looked back at me. "You'll need to come across from the perspective: 'Dad, I'd like to talk to you about something important,' as if you were seeking his advice. He would then be more open to you and more amenable to making changes."

His face stayed somber as he spoke rapidly. "Your father likes to feel like a benevolent ruler to his factory court, so—from a transactional analysis standpoint—you need to approach him not as a bossy 'parent' or an upset 'child,' but from an 'adult-child' perspective."

Moe paused and then continued. "Your approach needs to be both rational and from a position of making him feel respected. He needs to feel as if he were the parent who makes the rules and offers advice to his son." He took another long breath. "In other words, Harvy, you're looking to get in his good graces. Again, you need to come from the position of 'Dad, I (or we) have an issue that affects the company. Can you help me solve it?'"

I nodded but was still confused. "So is that dropping handkerchiefs?"

Moe was now the one with a full head of steam. "We're almost there. What 'dropping handkerchiefs' means is that you could keep your eyes and ears open for opportunities to drop an idea or suggestion, and then let it go, not be attached to it. If your father doesn't grab hold of the idea right away, then he'll think about it consciously or subconsciously."

My mentor smiled. "Later on, he might come forth with the same or similar idea as if it were his own, as long as the idea makes sufficient business sense to him. If you don't mind his getting the credit for your ideas, then this approach can work."

I had to think about that one. How would I feel if I got no recognition for my suggestions? But if Moe's method got the job done, then maybe his approach was worth it. "I like your trick, Moe," I said as I smiled. "Did you know that at MIT, if one uses a trick more than once, it's called it a method?"

Moe's smile widened. "Here's the best part, Harvy. If your father thinks it's his idea, then he won't get in the way of your implementing it. Then you can move forward the way you see best," Moe pointed at me, "and get the credit you deserve by doing a worthy implementation."

"Okay, Moe. I see." I was impressed again. "I'll give it a try with this performance appraisal idea." I smiled. "I'll try to drop the thought at his feet so he can't but trip over it."

My mentor grinned again. "Let me know how it goes, Harvy. And if you need to talk in-between our sessions, because it's not going as you planned, feel free to call me." Moe's professorial hand rose again. "Situations like this are dynamic, and it's important to adjust to them as they change. I don't want you to lose opportunities because we hadn't had a chance to talk them over." He raised a hand. "And I don't charge for these short conversations, so take advantage."

I nodded. "Thanks, Moe." I was grateful he was taking a sincere interest in seeing me gain more influence over my father.

The psychologist had more to say. "And, before we end today, I have something for you. It's a brochure from NTL."

"That's the National Training Labs organization you talked to me about last time?"

"That's right. I'd like you to look through the catalogue and see if anything there interests you." He handed me a large booklet. "There may be courses in here that you'd want to try. NTL has many interesting programs in the area of applied behavioral sciences, which is their sophisticated way of saying 'human relations training and development.' They have summer programs in Bethel, Maine, only a few hours from Montreal by car."

"Okay, thanks, Moe. I'll look at it and let you know."

* * *

A couple of days later, on a Thursday evening, I stayed in the office doing paperwork after everyone had gone home. Dad also stayed late on Thursdays, before heading for his regular meet-up at the Troika. He was in a good mood this evening, as he often was before heading out to his favourite haunt.

He smiled at me. "Want to come out with us tonight, son? I'm leaving in a few minutes." His eyes were bright. "You can go home, put on a suit and tie, and then meet Elaine and me there." As usual, he didn't mention who else might be attending.

I enjoyed talking to my father privately about JHS business matters, but I was reticent to step out with him and his friends. The Troika was busy and loud on Thursday nights. Dad liked having his customary crowd at his table— Aras, Hans, and Mack. A girlfriend or mistress might be in attendance, but never a wife. Elaine fitted that bill for Dad.

The Troika scene didn't allow for much more than chatty table talk. In addition to donning the suit and tie to go there, I felt I had to put on a smile and display a forced laugh or two. It wasn't that I didn't enjoy the company of my father's friends. They talked about the latest government kafuffle, or about constructing or redecorating their country homes.

One cohort might complain about a departing woman employee, saying, "My best girl got pregnant again, leaving me high and dry for six months." He then grumbled about how he'd have to train a temp to fill in for that woman until she came back to work. It was funny how the other men around the table nodded their understanding and consoled their colleague as if a close family member had died.

Though I enjoyed the Troika's liveliness and the attention of being my father's son, that venue was no longer my kind of ambiance. After having a couple of drinks in unison with the Troika's escargot and rack of lamb, I'd get sleepy-eyed. After taking in secondhand smoke for more than an hour, I'd start to cough. After hearing the same stories and jokes, my ears would stop listening. After hearing a third person ask me, "So what else is new with you, my friend?" or "No special girl in your life right now, Harvy?" I'd want to scream and leave. I wasn't the talk-about-everything-and-nothing person or live-for-tonight entertainer my father was.

I did enjoy the music at the Troika. Sasha, on his guitar, and Vladjec, on his accordion, both with salesmen smiles on their faces, played anything I wanted to hear. The mellow *Midnight in Moscow*, the lively Russian *Kalinka* (where everyone sang along with the refrain), the exuberant *Hungarian Chardas*, and the staccato Slavic *Hot Canary* were my favourites. Those melodies put a wide grin on my face and filled my chest with bliss.

But I had to fight to keep thoughts of my mother from turning my outward smile into an inward frown. "No thanks, Dad," I said to my father's request to join him. "I'm a little tired tonight. What if I come to see you and Elaine this weekend?"

"Sure, son, whatever you prefer." Dad showed no disappointment, but I knew he'd be chagrined because I wouldn't be sitting, smiling, and singing by his side this evening. "We aren't doing anything this Sunday," he added. "Would you be interested in coming for brunch, perhaps around 11 o'clock?"

He grinned. "Would you prefer eggs benedict, or Belgian waffles, or blueberry pancakes this time? I'll ask Elaine to make what you like."

I smiled back. "You make it hard for me, Dad. I guess I'll go for the waffles this time. I like the way Elaine makes them with strawberries and whipped cream on the side."

Dad smiled back. "I always find something you like, huh, son?"

That Sunday, Elaine set out her fancy Limoges china, Waterford crystal glasses, and sterling silverware for our brunch. Dad wore a Polo shirt, slacks, and a cardigan. Elaine sported a colourful blouse and dark slacks. I wore pants and a sweater, but I felt as if I should have put on a three-piece suit for the fancy tableware in front of me. "You don't have to go through this trouble for me, Elaine," I offered.

"No trouble at all, Harvy," she responded. "You know me; I love to have you over and to give these dishes and silverware a workout once in a while." She chuckled.

I grinned. "I see you made my favorite—waffles!"

She glanced at my father and smiled wide. "Yes, a big bird told me you'd like to have that today."

Dad looked at her and nodded. A glint was in his eye and a fatherly smile on his face.

She turned back to me. "What's new with you, Harvy?" She winked. "Seeing anyone we should know about?" As usual, Dad let Elaine do the talking and have her ask the questions that I knew were on his mind. It bothered me less when Elaine asked.

I was seeing a woman near my age, a pretty school teacher I had met through the Canadian Youth Hostel. The CYH sponsored weekend bicycling and hiking trips in and around the Island of Montreal. My new friend and I had done biking and hiking together in the countryside, but it was a bit early to say she and I were steady. I offered, "I've met a couple of girls through the local youth hostel. I've been going on hostel trips with them, but nothing's serious yet."

"Take your time, son. No need to rush." Dad winked at Elaine. "Chase them for as long as you can . . . until they catch you." Dad talked calmly and caringly; he was very relaxed around Elaine.

Elaine laughed and threw up her hand. "Oh, Johnny! What are you teaching your son?"

I wondered what Elaine specifically saw in my father, but that question wouldn't get fully answered for some time. For now, they seemed to be enjoying each other's company.

Dad's face turned serious for a second. "He'll know when the right one comes along." His smile came back. "And when their hooks are in you, you'll never get them out." He winked at his partner. "Nor want to."

I tried to avoid thinking about my mother and the thirty-year marriage hooks my father had abruptly sheared off with industrial wire cutters.

Elaine looked at me. "Your father is such a charmer."

I looked down at my plate, for this conversation was too much man-woman talk for me. I changed the subject. "Elaine, can I ask you a question?"

"Sure, Harvy. What is it?"

"I've meant to ask you. In your real estate company, do better job performers get rewarded more?" I worked to keep my voice calm, though I was shivering a bit inside in bringing up a sensitive topic around my father.

"What do you mean, Harvy?" She looked at Dad and then back at me.

He showed no irritation as he might have shown my mother in a similar situation. He might have said briskly to Mom, "Don't talk about what you know nothing about!"

I focused on Elaine and kept my eyes away from my father. "I'm thinking about how we could better handle performance reviews at JHS. Do you think we should sit down and talk with people individually, and give better performers bigger increases?"

I stabbed a piece of maple-syrup-laden waffle with my fork. I wondered if I had said too much by dropping a glaring hint—perhaps a bright red handkerchief—in front of my father. "What do they do in your company, Elaine?" I forked the waffle in my mouth and chewed.

Elaine glanced again at Dad. He didn't return her look but continued to chew on his dry English muffin. She offered, "Our management does work that way with us. They sit down at least once a year with every employee and review how they are doing."

"Does sitting down with them one-on-one make a difference in how they perform their jobs?"

Elaine didn't hesitate. "Yes, I believe it does. People get to know where they stand in the eyes of management. They get to know what they are doing well and where they need to improve." Her eyes stayed on me. "It's common sense, I think."

"Thanks, Elaine," I said before my father could get into the conversation. "That makes sense to me." I kept my eyes on her. "By the way, these are great waffles. What do you put in them to make them so good?"

She went right along. "It's nice of you to notice. I put a little heavy cream into the milk. It makes the batter thicker and the waffles richer."

The following Tuesday afternoon, at our next JHS meeting, Dad turned to his foremen. Cigarette in mouth, he said, "I have a new idea for how we should give people raises this year." He placed the smoke into the ashtray. "Instead of an across the board increase, we will give them increases based on how good they are and how hard they are working for us."

I didn't know if Elaine had said more to my father about my inquiry after our brunch, but he acted just as Moe had predicted. Yet he hadn't given me any warning about raising the subject today.

He looked only at the foremen as he continued. "We'll work to keep the average increase to 3%, but vary it from 2-4%."

Dad's 2% to 4% range was narrower than the 1.5% to 4.5% salary increase range that I had proposed to him, but it was good enough. His voice turned hard. "And I want to know who the stragglers are. We should give them no raise if we keep them, or we should get rid of them if they don't improve." He flung his hand to one side as if he were throwing something away.

Everyone was quiet. Dad pointed at me as he continued to look at them. "Harvy will meet with you and talk to you more about it. He will make a system to decide who are our good people and who aren't. You'll have short meetings with each person to tell them what raise they got and why." He stayed on the road I had paved for him. "We want the good ones to get more money, and the worst ones to shape up or get out." He gestured toward the entrance door.

I looked at the foremen. Their faces were blank. "We'll work together on this," I said. "Your input will be important in deciding who should get bigger raises, who should get smaller ones, and who shouldn't get any at all."

Baptist offered, "That's new."

Georges tapped his knee with his pointed finger. "It's good if we tell people how they are doing and on what they need to improve."

I leaned slightly forward in my chair and winked. "Other than yelling at employees on the production line?"

Everyone smiled, but no one laughed. Our foremen understood the big boss's familiar way.

Dad ignored what I had said. "Yes, and the lousy ones better improve, or they're out," he chimed. "We'll give this a try for now and see how it goes. If it doesn't work the way we want, we'll go back to what we used to do."

I worked to keep my face from breaking a smile.

* * *

My mother seemed to be doing better with Moe's help. Over a home-cooked supper, she told me, "Moe encourages me not to sit at home all day and cry over your father. He tells me to go see my friends."

I smiled with relief. "That's great, Mom. What do you do with your friends?"

"The weekends can be lonely, so I go see them on Sundays, and we play gin rummy."

Thank goodness for that game! Even my brother enjoyed it when he was in the mood.

Moe had told Steve and me to encourage our mother to go out and do things. He had said, "If it's only my telling her to get out of the house, she may not. But if we all tell her, she more likely will. And the more she does to rebuild her life, the less pressure there will be for you and Steve to take care of her."

I attempted to stretch the slinky a little further with my mother. "What about going on a vacation this winter?"

Mom raised her voice a tad. "None of my friends have money to go anywhere. I barely have any money myself; your father doesn't give me enough to live on." She had once mentioned that she had only $5000 accumulated in her name after years of saving pennies where she could.

I countered. "But can't you go to Florida in January when it's cheaper? I know you don't like the cold winters."

She spoke sternly. "It's too much trouble for now. I don't know who I'd go with."

I pulled at whatever levers I could. "What about your friend, Irene?" Irene was a Jewish Hungarian family friend, both a survivor of the Holocaust and a former seamstress as Mom had been.

My mother's voice became terse. "Irene doesn't like to spend money. She'll only come if I invite her and pay for her, and I can't do that now."

"Okay, Mom, but I hate to see you stuck here in the cold. I'll even give or lend you the money if you want."

She looked at me as if I were crazy. "No, I don't want your money. I'll go away when I get the separation allowance I need from your father."

With Moe, Steve, and I pulling together, Mom eventually invited her friend to go with her to Florida for a week, with Mom paying for their flights and hotel. After they had returned, I was over at her home again. "How was your trip?" I asked.

"It was very nice and warm. Irene and I had a good time." She was smiling.

"I see you have a nice tan." Her skin was a bronzy brown.

"We were on the beach every day. It was so good to get away from the cold."

"So will you do this again soon, maybe with Irene once more?"

"No, I don't think so. That woman doesn't like to spend a penny on anything. When we went out to a restaurant, I was the one who always paid." She looked intently at me. "I can't invite her again because she'll expect me to pay."

"Maybe you can find someone else to go with?"

She came back abruptly, her eyes again looking as if I were crazy. "Who do I know who can afford to go away?"

Similar to my stubborn father and abstinent brother, it was easier to point my mother to a warm Florida pool than have her take a plunge.

* * *

It was overcast on this late-Sunday afternoon in March of 1981. A car drove slowly down the empty street where the JHS plant stood in an industrial section of St. Laurent, a suburb of Montreal. In a moment, the car returned from the opposite direction, this time turning into the JHS parking lot. The vehicle stopped by the loading dock doors. They were on the side of the building that was obscured partially from the street.

A man exited the car and walked to the front office door and stood under the overhead light. He looked around to see if anyone was watching. No one was. He unlocked the front door, took a breath, opened the door, walked in, and quickly locked the door behind him. He entered the security code to disable the alarm system.

It was dark in the front office, with the only light diffusing in from the street through the thin curtains covering the office windows. The man didn't turn on any overhead lights or desk lamps. He walked swiftly yet softly through the deserted office. He kept on his thin leather gloves as he switched on the copy machine. The old thing squeaked to life.

He headed for the private offices, his footsteps the only sounds that echoed down the hallway. He entered the boss's office, turned on a desk lamp, and turned toward a credenza cabinet sitting along one wall. He slid open the cabinet door and rummaged through neatly stacked documents. He pulled out a folder and walked back toward the copy machine.

While duplicating several pages, the copier ground and squeaked as it expelled yellowish photocopy paper. The man fumbled with the copies as he stapled and folded them. He then put them into his jacket pocket.

When the deed was complete, he turned off the machine, put the document back precisely where he had found it, and closed the credenza door. Before he exited, he glanced around the office to make sure he hadn't moved anything else. He saw that the stapler was back where it originally sat.

He reset the security system, waited for the confirming beep from the alarm company, and walked back through the front entrance. He locked the door and returned swiftly to his car. Outside, he glanced around again to confirm that no one had seen him. He entered his car and drove away quickly, back in the direction from where he had come.

* * *

"What are we going to do now, Moe?" My arms were on my knees as I sat bent over, looking down at Moe's slippered feet. "My father got pissed off when he heard my mother went to see a divorce lawyer."

It was April of '81, over six months after Moe Gross had entered our lives. Dad had made Mom a divorce settlement proposal through Moe, but it had been more of a take-it-or-leave-it offer. Moe wanted to help my mother make the right decision about Dad's proposal by getting her a legal opinion.

Late one afternoon, my father heard about my mother's move from his lawyer, Mack, who had been contacted by Mom's lawyer. Dad bolted out of his private office, both his Simkovits gun barrels blazing. "That divorce firm she went to is the biggest shyster practice in the city," he yelled. He looked at Steve and me. "They will suck us dry with their fees."

Dad didn't know for sure if Moe had been the one to take Mom to see that lawyer. He still blared, "Moe was supposed to keep this between your mother and me, and not get the goddamn lawyers involved." He huffed as he threw up his hands. "Moe didn't do his job as he promised. I don't want to see that guy anymore."

Steve and I sat still and said nothing.

A week later, Dad again walked out of his back office after another phone call with Mack. He threw his reading glasses onto his front office desk; the spectacles bounced on the desk mat. He screamed, "Your mother's new fucking lawyer got confidential financial information about JHS directly from the company's statements." He looked around the room and spoke with certainty. "Somebody from here gave them that information."

My father's face was red. His hand was in a fist as his eyes darted intensely at Helen, Steve, Rob, and me. "I'm going to fucking crucify the bastard when I find out who it was."

Dad's bookkeeper stood and defended himself. "Johnny, there's no reason for anybody here to do such a thing."

Helen followed, "I never go into the company's private papers." She pointed in the direction of Dad's back office. "I don't even know where you keep those things, other than somewhere back there."

Dad glared at Steve and me. "Do you guys know anything about this?"

I shivered in my seat. I stayed as still as I could while I shook my head slowly. My brother said, "No, Dad. Who would want to do that?"

Dad lowered his tone a touch but still barked loud. "I don't know, son, but those lawyers now know about JHS's income and assets. That's private company information that no one knows except for us here and our accountants."

Son-of-a-bitch, I said to myself, but I otherwise kept my mouth shut and eyes looking down.

Now, days later, in Moe's office, I sat on his couch, my elbows on my knees, my hands held together tightly, and my head down. "My father yelled today about the lawyers you took my mother to see. Did you give them a copy of the financial statement I photocopied for you?"

I was the one who had snuck into my father's private office weeks earlier to copy the company statements for Moe. He had asked me for that information, without my mother or father knowing of his request.

My body shuddered through my torso when I showed Moe those documents. My voice quivered as I told him what Dad, Steve, and I each owned in company assets and shares. Moe then responded, "To be fair to your mother, her attorney should know what assets your father holds in his company."

Though I typically stayed faithful to my father on financial matters, I agreed with Moe that Mom should get a fair shake. Dad had never been generous to her. He gave her only monthly allowances for groceries and household needs. For years, she had to produce receipts when she bought new things for the house, like a new vacuum cleaner. Mom's bruises from her and Dad's final fight had haunted me. I decided to help Moe by clandestinely getting the JHS information he wanted to show her lawyer.

Though I felt ashamed for being disloyal to my father, I knew there was no one else who could do this for my mother's sake. Steve preferred everything being in the open. Had he known about Moe's request, he would have told Dad about it or refused to go along.

I had said nothing to Moe, my mother, or my brother, about my father's offshore money. If that information got into the hands of Mom's lawyer, it would implicate me directly as the source.

I didn't want her lawyer to blackmail my father, or for Dad to have trouble with the Canadian tax authorities. Even more, I didn't want anybody to accuse me of knowing anything about his hidden stash. Giving Moe a copy of JHS's statements was the most I would do. I hoped my action would help my mother.

Moe stared at me as I repeated my question. "Did you give those statements to my mother's lawyer?"

Moe replied calmly. "I didn't give or show your mother's attorney the actual statements. I only shared, in round numbers, the value of JHS and how much your father owns." He looked straight at me. "Neither your mother nor her lawyer knows where I had gotten those numbers."

I leaned further over my legs, hardly able to look at Moe. "My dad's pissed about it."

Moe's voice stayed collected. "Harvy, your father is beating the bushes, hoping to find out where your mother's attorney got the information. These lawyers have their ways to obtain such information from their sources. They really don't need you or me."

I raised my head a bit. "I hope you're right, Moe. I'll be in deep shit if my father finds out I copied those statements for you." I had no idea what Dad would do, but he'd undoubtedly yell, scream, and threaten. "By the way, Moe, my father told me he doesn't want to see you anymore."

Moe looked at me with a blank face. "I'll give him a call and talk to him."

"I wish you luck, Moe."

Years later, I wondered about Moe's ethics in the way he played the lawyer situation between Mom and Dad. Because I desperately wanted to trust this man's help for my family's sake, I had given him the benefit of my knowledge and doubts. Perhaps he had stretched the slinky a bit too far with me.

I was glad my father never checked with JHS's security company to find out that someone had entered the offices on a previous Sunday afternoon. He then could have linked that to the few of us who had access.

Though my father never found out how Mom's lawyer obtained financial information about JHS, he refused to see Moe again. It made no difference to Dad that Moe had dropped useful handkerchiefs regarding JHS.

Moe had offered a clever idea about obtaining a vendor booth at a fully subscribed Canadian Consumer Electronics Show. He had said to Dad, "There is always a spare booth or two that they hold back for those who know how to get those spots. You may need to pay off a manager to get into their good graces to obtain a booth for JHS."

Dad liked the idea. He knew how to pass money under the table to motivate gatekeepers.

Moe had also dropped the idea of JHS marketing its sub-contracting manufacturing capabilities to other companies. Dad picked up Moe's handkerchief and soon obtained business from his friend, Ralph Lieb of Gusdorf, a manufacturer of knockdown (ready to assemble) wood cabinets.

In the end, my father saw those ideas as his own, giving no credit to Moe's indirect suggestions. I pleaded with my father, "Continuing to work with Moe can help JHS and our family."

He responded, "Why should I do anything with him? The guy's done nothing for me."

That was perhaps a downside to Moe's approach. There was little credit given to the one who had dropped the handkerchiefs.

"Steve and I are still going to see him," I said assuredly to my father.

Dad waved his hand. "Do what you want, but I don't want him to come here anymore."

* * *

Some weeks before Dad ousted Moe, my brother had gotten riled about a purchasing issue that he and Dad debated in the office. It was the usual father-son skirmish about a supplier. This time my brother threw a mug at the floor, shattering the cup, and then he stormed out of the building.

Helen had once chased after Steve after a previous argument between these two headstrong men. This time Dad threw up an arm and waved it toward the door. "To hell with him. Let him go."

No one followed Steve out the door this time. As she went to grab a broom to sweep up the mess, Helen turned to Dad. "You're going to drive that boy away if you don't stop criticizing him."

Dad looked at her and shook his fist. "What's the fucking difference? He fights me on every little shitty thing, no matter what I say or how I say it."

Steve was back in about a half-hour, after having walked around the block. By then, Moe had arrived for one of his regular JHS appointments. He and Steve spent the next half-hour talking privately in one corner of the office. I don't know what Moe said to Steve, but my brother was calm and collected afterward. It was as if his and Dad's altercation had never happened.

I thought Steve and Moe had been making progress in their work together, as I had with our psychologist. After my father had ousted Moe, I was surprised when my brother told me at home, "Harvy, I'm not going to see Moe anymore."

"Why, Steve? I thought things were going well between the two of you."

He looked at me with little expression on his face. "I have my Catholic church and my world travelling to help me feel better about myself. I don't need Moe."

All I could say was, "Moe's helping me, so I'm continuing."

Steve turned away and said nothing more. When my brother set his mind, no one could change it, especially neither Dad nor I.

* * *

After Dad ousted Moe, even Mom didn't want to see him anymore. Over one supper, she told me, "Moe helped me a lot. He got me out of the house and to go on a vacation. But I don't want to continue with him."

Between bites of her stuffed cabbage, I asked, "Why not?"

"My divorce lawyer costs me lots of money. Your father now refuses to pay for Moe's sessions with me. I can't afford him on my own."

I understood what my mother was saying. I, too, felt dependent upon Dad and JHS. I was glad I had invested most of my JHS bonus money into Canadian life insurance investments—a legitimate tax-free stash of my own. If I ever needed money, I could borrow from their cash value. Though Dad was more generous with his sons than with his wife, I still feared he might one day pull the money plug on me.

Mom never mentioned that Moe had given her lawyer JHS's private financial information, and I never told her my clandestine part in the matter. I had done what I could to help her. It was now in her lawyer's hands to get her a fair settlement from Dad.

As the summer of '81 turned into fall, I was the only one in my family who continued to work with Moe. From that point forward, my father grumbled every month about the bills he had received from Dr. Gross. One day, Dad approached me with Moe's invoice in his hand. "What are you doing with that guy? Do you need to see him so much?"

I looked into my father's peeved face. "Yes, Dad. He's still helping me." I didn't tack on: *in dealing better with you and our fucked-up family*.

From then on, whenever I suggested a change for our plant, our father raised his eyebrows. He probably wondered if my ideas were coming from Moe. Some had, and some hadn't, but Dad had no way of telling. He never asked about my sources, and I never said anything to divulge them.

One time, Steve and I asked the fire department to inspect our factory's water, pneumatic air, and safety equipment. We didn't tell Dad about it until the town's fire truck was at the JHS factory door. "The town just wants to do a spot plant inspection," we told him. "They do this regularly for the factories around here." We weren't lying, but neither of us mentioned that we had initiated the call to the fire department.

Steve and I walked two firefighters in and around the building. One asked us to test an old copper, soda-acid fire extinguisher by turning it over in the grass behind the plant. When we did, liquid sputtered out of its hose for a second or two. The extinguisher was dead and perhaps had been that way for years. Steve ordered new halogen units, many times the cost of those acid extinguishers.

When Dad heard about the "impromptu" inspection results, he looked at Steve and me with his face red. He pointed his reading glasses at us. "You two guys are causing me trouble!"

Dad couldn't ignore the fire department orders to replace our fire extinguishers, among a list of other non-negotiable recommendations. After we had explained the plant needed these items for safety reasons, Dad waved his hand dismissively. "Do what you want, but you're costing the company money."

Even though our father was condescending, Steve and I got our way. I was pleased that my brother and I were still making improvements. We were careful never to ridicule our father, either in his presence or behind his back.

When Steve went off on another extended trek to East Africa, I suggested to Dad, "To save factory heating cost, what if we put in ceiling fans and install insulated panels over our factory windows?"

Dad got up in arms. "Why are you bothering with such things that have a negligible benefit?" He was almost shouting.

After I had done heat savings calculations, I tried again. I showed my father that it would take four to six years to repay the investment, a decent return based on the return-on-investment standards I had learned at P&G.

His face was stern. "Your savings are only in theory!"

Though I was irritated, I didn't get fazed. "We'll do the work ourselves in the factory, employing our people to build the insulated panels and install the fans. It'll pay for itself in the long run."

Dad looked at me over the top of his eyeglasses, as if he thought I had nothing better to do in his company. "In the long run, none of us will be here, and maybe not this factory either."

A week or two later, I came back at him one more time during one of our production meetings. He finally consented. He glibly said to the foremen. "Harvy wants to give our people something to do while business is down. He is wasting your time and our money, but we'll do it while we are waiting for customer orders."

In addition to Moe guiding me to install a better performance appraisal system in the company, I held other plant coordination meetings with the foremen, including Steve, when he was around. I didn't let my father know about those meetings. Exploiting Moe's ideas, I worked to have line workers inspect and test for quality problems all along the manufacturing process, rather than my Uncle Edo just doing his completed-units testing at the end of the line.

Sometimes I was unruffled by my father's ongoing resistance, but other times it annoyed me. Didn't he see I was trying to do productive things that would benefit the whole company and keep our factory people working?

I began to sense that my father was jealous of Moe. Moe turned out to be much more than the marriage psychologist and divorce mediator Dad thought he had hired.

When I realized my father might be feeling competition from my psychologist, I told Moe to stop sending his bills to JHS. To make his time more affordable, I cut my sessions to an hour instead of ninety minutes per week, and I paid him out of my pocket.

When Dad stopped getting monthly bills from Moe, he became more relaxed about my JHS initiatives, and he no longer mentioned Moe's name.

* * * *

Writing on the JHS Walls

It was the winter of 1982, more than two years after I had returned full-time to JHS, eighteen months after Dad had left Mom, sixteen months after our family had begun working with Moe, and nine months after the rest of my family had stopped working with him. The writing began to emerge on the JHS factory walls.

It started with Dad curtailing our weekly foreman production meetings. I don't know what triggered his move, but one day in the office he said to my brother and me, "We aren't so busy in the factory. We don't need weekly foremen meetings anymore."

Though Dad had made his formal declaration, I still carried on my clandestine foremen gatherings in the plant. I later worked out our collaborative decisions with Dad, with Steve offering useful opinions when I could get them.

At the end of one production meeting, I told the foremen, "What if each of us makes a similar suggestion to my father over the next week on this issue." I smiled. "If it's only my telling him he's drinking too much Kool-Aid, he probably won't decide. But if all of us, in our way, tell him he's overdoing it, he might make the decision we need." Moe had fed me those lines.

The foremen looked at me and smiled. Moe's little tricks didn't always work, but we were trying.

Unexpected things then happened to put a pen in my hand to rewrite my family business future. The chassis plate problems with our Sears models went from bad to worse. From late 1981, and into 1982, JHS sued Jin Dae for lost business. The court case took a year of legal maneuvering. I provided documented and oral testimony. Dad paid $5000 to a forensic accountant from Roger Delliard's firm to assess JHS's losses with Sears. We moved the case from Mack's office to an international law firm in Montreal.

JHS eventually won the case on a technicality: neither Mr. CJ Kim from Jin Dae nor his superiors from the parent company appeared in the Quebec court in response to our court-ordered summons. The Quebec superior court ruled in JHS's favour on an over one-million-dollar judgement against Jin Dae and their parent.

The international law firm had told us to worry about money collection only after the court ruling would be in hand. Up to that point, JHS had spent $12,000 with that firm to win the suit, more than doubling what JHS had spent with Mack's firm and our accountants.

Our law firm then said what we already knew, that Jin Dae and its parent company had no assets in Canada to seize. Dad didn't want to go through the expense of suing the Korean supplier in either the United States or Korea. He yelled at our lawyer, "I'm not pissing away another $25,000US with a bloody New York or Korean attorney with no guarantee of having any money recovered."

Though JHS had won a sizable judgement, Dad let the suit go, and JHS didn't collect anything from anywhere. I did wonder, after the time and trouble we went through to win the lawsuit, why my father had no stomach to pursue the case further. Maybe he just wanted a reason to yell at the lawyers.

More problems surfaced. Our Woolco sales rep in Toronto, Jeff Peters, called my father one day. He was in desperate need of money. I overheard their call that Dad had put on the speakerphone in his private office. Jeff said, "Johnny, you know my wife. She doesn't work, and she spends like crazy. I need cash soon, or I'll be underwater." I thought it might have been Jeff who had money issues, though I wasn't sure what that was.

Jeff had a close colleague who was high up at Woolco. That friend asked my father to help Jeff by advancing him $25,000 from JHS. Dad was going to pay that amount to Jeff anyway, as commissions for $500,000 of consoles that JHS was to produce and ship to Woolco in the coming months.

Instead of Dad directly loaning Jeff the money from JHS, Dad took Jeff to his Montreal bank and requested a $25,000 line of credit for the guy, to be guaranteed by JHS. Jeff's commission payment would then be paid directly to the bank to repay Jeff's loan.

All seemed well until the bank called Dad three days after it had consummated the loan. I was there when the call came in, and Dad again put the conversation on his speakerphone.

The bank manager asked, "Mr. Simkovits, when should we stop honouring Mr. Peter's cheques?"

"What do you mean?" my father asked. "How much money has he taken against his bank line?"

"It's now over $27,000."

"But we agreed that the limit was $25,000." Dad's voice elevated. "You should not be cashing cheques above that amount."

"Mr. Simkovits," the banker responded. "You brought the gentleman to us. We thought he was your friend, so we have given him a bit of leeway. We wanted to check with you before we stop cashing his cheques."

"Cut him off right away!" My father shouted. "JHS took responsibility for only $25,000, what we owe the guy in commission payments. I'm sorry, but I cannot take responsibility for the amounts over and above that. That was our arrangement."

"Okay, Mr. Simkovits," the manager responded, "we'll do what we need to do at our end."

Then the unthinkable happened with our Woolco line. The 1000 inexpensive radio chassis Dad bought from our Taiwan rep (when Dad and I had been in Taipei together) turned out to be defective. They were riddled with intermittent electronic problems due to poor circuit board soldering.

When Jin Dae's tech finally arrived from Seoul in the spring of 1981, we immediately put the fellow to work on the Taiwan chassis problem. He worked tirelessly, testing, and repairing every unit. He had to fix some units again after they had gone into a console. Even so, those chassis continued to have erratic electrical problems.

JHS's second-largest customer sent Dad a lawyer's letter. It stated that Woolco was cancelling several orders due to electronic deficiencies with those Taiwan chassis. Jeff's commission would disappear as a result, and JHS held the bag on the majority of Jeff's bank loan.

Some months later, Dad told me, "Jeff got in trouble with the Royal Canadian Mounted Police. They charged him with the unlicensed and unlawful duplication and distribution of sex videos."

I wondered why the guy had two VCRs sitting on top of the big television in his den. He had said that one was his, and the other one was a machine he "borrowed from a neighbor." That story seemed too odd to be true.

Once the walls came down around Jeff, JHS lost its connection to an important customer. Woolco soon dropped their whole console stereo line, and JHS never did business with them again. Dad threatened to sue Woolco for cancelled orders. But when Woolco sent an electronics inspector to JHS, the guy found too many erratic defects in a large sample of our finished products. Thus JHS had no legal legs to stand on.

Even our independent Sears sales rep, Joe Steiner, had seen the writing on the JHS walls. Sears had declined a reorder from JHS because Dad had set the price high on a good-selling console model (one that didn't have the Jin Dae chassis).

Joe then tried to get Dad to manufacture console units under the JHS brand name—the first time Dad had ever done that. Dad set those prices high too, and he made only short production runs of five models. When Joe couldn't find customers to buy the JHS brand, he abandoned us for a full-time sales job with a furniture company. Dad roared, "That Joe *foot-scoffed* on us!" He pointed to himself. "Now, I'm the schmuck that has to peddle those goddamn JHS units to every little shitty retail store across the country."

Though Joe told Dad that he could still sell units for JHS at the same time he had a full-time job with a furniture company, Dad barked, "That shyster won't be able to ride two horses with his one puny ass."

The final straw hit my son-of-the-boss back when we shipped a higher-quality model to Woolco. In the front office, Dad, Baptist, and I were discussing how many of the wall-unit-sized stereos could fit into a truck. Baptist said, "We can only fit 48 of them vertically in the van."

Dad quickly responded, "I don't want to feed the trucking company. We can put two or three more on top by laying them on their backs."

All of my outside seminars and work with Moe had told me we should trust our employees. Baptist had more experience than I had on what pressure a heavy cabinet loaded with electronics could take. I came to the foreman's defense. "Dad, let's play it safe and go with just the 48 units."

Dad said, "No, I want you to put in a few more on top."

Baptist's voice showed annoyance. "Johnny, I won't take responsibility for the additional units."

Dad's face turned on fire. His eyes were piercing. He glanced past me, looked straight at Baptist, and shouted, "Do as I say. I'm the boss here." He pointed to his chest and yelled, "I'll take the *FUCKING* responsibility."

After a few shipments had gone out to Woolco warehouses, it turned out Dad was right; nothing got damaged with the extra units put on top. But, for me, the personal damage had been done. Dad didn't want anybody, including his son, his heir, and his future, to suggest what he should or shouldn't do in his company. In his leaking, perhaps even sinking JHS ship, he wanted to be the sole captain at its helm, right to the very bottom of his dying industry. That moment illustrated where I stood with my father.

Maybe Dad felt a threat by my growing influence. Perhaps he sensed that Moe was having too much say in JHS through me. Dad's increasing age and declining business might have made him hold tightly onto being the master of his company's declining destiny.

Or was he terrified that his business was coming apart at the factory seams? Was he trying desperately to keep the factory walls together through his sheer will? There were a few times I had caught him at his desk, glassy-eyed, a pensive look on his face, no telling what was on his mind.

I'm sure a part of our father wanted his two sons to learn from him and take over his business, but he never saw us ready to take hold of the reins.

Steve and I may not have had what it took to operate his business competently. Even if we had known what we were doing, would Dad have allowed us to take control? Though there seemed to be less and less in our father's hands for his holding onto—and, as in his favourite Hungarian expression—he held onto it as tightly as ever.

Later that same week, I went to see Moe. I cried, "I want to apply to that American University/NTL Master's program in Washington, D.C."

After Moe had introduced me to NTL, I took a few week-long, human relations training seminars with that behavioral science organization. I also attended a Gestalt psychology program in Montreal. I was drawn to such training, as a starving young bee was attracted to spring clover. Though I felt I had a lot to learn about human beings, especially myself, I had enjoyed the courses and the instructors I had met. I saw a new career for myself. With Moe's continuing help, I felt I would succeed.

Tears were in my eyes as I sat glum-faced on Moe's couch. "I've had enough with my father and the problems in his company. I want to love him and not fight with him anymore."

I took a long breath and raised my hand. "It's been nearly two-and-a-half years since I came back to Montreal. I now realize my father would never relinquish anything to anyone, including me. There is no future for me at JHS, and the company has no bright prospects either."

I rubbed my eyes with my palms. "And my brother's no ally. He's off again on one of his overseas trekking trips, and he won't be back for months."

Steve was in Israel for five months. Though I was now driving his Mercedes sedan, it was little consolation for not having him stand with me in pushing up against Dad.

Moe said, "Harvy, your brother is finding his way to keep his sanity concerning your father. He's taking those long excursions for his self-preservation."

I raised my voice. "But it's not helping me or us! With Steve gone to Timbuktu, I'm here alone against my father." I turned my head to wipe a tear from my eye without Moe seeing it. "I've had it with both of them. I want to leave JHS to go back to school."

Moe nodded his understanding.

I told my father about my plans. To my surprise, he was dismayed. He asked me to have dinner with him, and he wanted me to invite Moe. My father hadn't talked to the psychologist in fifteen months.

A few days later, the three of us met. Dad's voice was conciliatory. "Harvy, I want you to stay at JHS. Go do your courses if you want to, spend whatever time you want with Moe, but you could stay here at the same time." His facial expression was soft, and his voice stayed calm.

I recognized my father's appeasing MO, but this was the first time he ever used his shtick on me. He continued. "JHS will pay your course tuition. You can even keep on doing your production meetings with the foremen."

Several months earlier, Dad had found out about my clandestine foremen meetings by unexpectedly walking in on one. He had looked surprised but said nothing. My father just turned around and walked back to the office. Now was the first time he mentioned it. He put his hand near mine. "Do me a favour son and stay with JHS." He sounded sincere, but I wondered if he was.

From the day I walked back into JHS from Harvard, Dad had promised me responsibility. He had said, "I'm going to teach you everything I know about business and manufacturing." I now knew it was too hard for him to do that. It was too much of, "Do as I tell you and not as I would do" from him. It wasn't that he didn't want his sons to follow in his business footsteps; he just couldn't let go. He needed to be the kingpin, the head honcho, the top dog, the court ruler, the big boss. Everybody else knew it, and now I did too. My tiger father could never change his ingrained stripes.

At a previous counseling session, I had told Moe, "It's too bad that my father can't even be like Don Corleone in the *Godfather* movie." I described one scene where the dons were meeting in Corleone's office. The Godfather's son, Michael, led the conversation on behalf of the family. Then one of the other dons turned to Don Corleone, "Is what Michael's saying what you also want, Godfather?"

Don Corleone responded calmly, "Michael is now making the business decisions for the family. What Michael wants, I want."

After the other dons had left, the Godfather turned to Michael and asked calmly, "Is your proposal what you want, Michael?" Michael said yes, and Don Corleone nodded, "Okay, it's done."

I felt dejected that Dad couldn't even once defer to me.

Moe had looked at me. "Your father has shown, again and again, that he can't hand over the company's reigns. You have what you have with him, and you need to make your choices based on that. If you stay at JHS, at least you'll have your eyes open as to what you are up against."

I lowered my head. "Maybe I was fooling myself, Moe. My father hasn't made it easy for me." I looked at my mentor. "I even tried to make things work with Steve."

Moe nodded. "Your success seems to be mixed there too, Harvy. Your brother continues his defiant behavior with your father, continues to seek his escapes from JHS, and he isn't there for you."

I smiled a bit. "I'd hate to think of plotting against my brother. Michael Corleone eventually had Fredo killed, you know."

Moe smiled too. "Yes, Harvy, and I don't see you being that type."

But, in one way, I was doing just that. I knew, but said nothing to Steve, about our father's offshore money. Not even Moe knew what I knew about Dad's Cayman stash. Perhaps I was fooling myself, but I felt those hidden assets were a different matter from what Steve and I could build at JHS.

As I sat with Dad and Moe over dinner, my father talked as kindly and caringly as I had ever known. I felt he was baiting me. It was similar to what he had once done to Baptist when he wanted the guy back as JHS's electronics foreman. I now knew my father's penchant for not keeping promises, and his temper tantrums, and his inability to defer to anyone, including his sons. Like a scorpion, he couldn't change his stinging nature, even for one who would carry on his legacy.

"I'm sorry, Dad, but I've decided," I said. "I'll help you as much as I can until I start my new master's program next month in Washington, D.C. It's a non-residential program, so I'll be living in Montreal while I commute down to D.C. once a month for three to six days at a time. I can help you here and there if you need me."

My father turned to my mentor. "What do you think, Moe?"

Moe answered sincerely. "Johnny, it's Harvy's decision. He's a grown man now and needs to put his career interests first."

My father lowered his eyes, indicating he wasn't pleased. He added nothing more, and we ended the conversation there.

My dad may have felt that Moe had a big hold on me, but that wasn't true. Moe hadn't worked to influence me one way or another in my next career move. He had only exposed me to a new possible direction.

I wasn't running away from Dad or toward Moe. I was heading toward a future of my making. I was to enter a new college program birthed only three years earlier. I'd be at the forefront of the applied behavioural science field, obtaining a Masters in Human Resource Development and Organizational Development at American University in Washington, D.C.

For the first time in my 27-year-young life, I was writing my Simkovits chapter. I had been a top student at MIT but had little passion for my father's electrical engineering direction. I had detested Harvard Business School and the reason why I had been there—to please my father and have the education he had never obtained. Now I was moving forward with my career, life, and future. It was to be of my making and not my father's.

I departed JHS in June of 1982, thirty months after I started. Dad agreed that JHS would pay for my studies at AU. Perhaps he saw the excitement in my eyes for the new frontier I was approaching. Maybe he was also apologizing for having put me through the trauma of Harvard, the angst of his and Mom's separation, and his boisterous bossiness at JHS. Whatever it was, I gave him a big hug and thanked him several times for his help and support.

He responded, "You're very welcome, son."

* * * *

6

Oh, Brother!

During the '70s and into the '80s, my brother devoted much attention to our local Catholic parish. Wearing a white shirt and grey suit, he disappeared every Sunday to go to services and then church committee meetings. He once said that he considered becoming a Roman Catholic priest. He later confessed, "I want to have a family one day, something the Catholic clergy prohibits."

Some months before I departed JHS to start my new master's program in D.C., Steve had left Montreal for a year to travel to East Africa and the Middle East. He had begun his trip in Kenya, where he participated for a month in an outdoor leadership-training program. He then hopped onto an overcrowded train—local travelers sitting on the roof—that crawled through the Sudan desert on its way to Egypt. Steve was making his way to Israel.

Part of me envied my brother. His itch for adventure was an excellent excuse to get far away from our father's shouting at work and our mother's crying at home. Perhaps he wanted to get away from me too.

My schooling had been my way of distancing myself from my family. But my parents didn't have to worry about my making my way through a forest, jungle, or desert in foreign lands. Mom did warn me once, "Don't break your head in school for the studying you are doing." But Mom and Dad always knew where I was. I wasn't going to get kidnapped by a poacher, become lost in the wilderness, or risk entanglement in a religious conflict or civil war.

After Steve had made it safely to Israel, he tried to join a rural kibbutz. At first, the kibbutz gatekeepers didn't believe he was Jewish. It took the help of an Israeli friend of Mom's to get him accepted into that fold. She vouched for my brother as the son of a female Hungarian Jew.

Steve stayed and worked at the kibbutz for five months. My father later joked, "Steve is lucky the Jewish heritage passes down through the mother. If the people there had asked him to pull down his pants, he certainly wouldn't have been accepted as a Jew."

I smiled slightly but said nothing.

I rarely, if ever, received a card or letter from Steve during his world travels. Once in a while, he called each of our parents, or he wrote a letter or postcard to them, which they later showed me. His notes from Israel talked about his working the earth by planting, weeding, and harvesting vegetables. He participated in Shabbat services every week, studied the Torah, adhered to fasting days, and danced in circles at weddings and celebrations that seemed to happen every week.

One day, Mom and Dad received a curious message from Steve. He wrote, "I'm going to make a big change in my life."

Both of my parents had considered that Steve might turn to Judaism. Though Dad was a staunch Catholic, he had no disdain for Jews. He had many Jewish friends and had married Mom. We knew that rabbis could have a wife and as many children as they desired. Israel plus kibbutz plus Torah-reading seemed to sum up to a Jewish conversion for my brother.

Steve wrote again. "I'm going to take a week or two off my sojourn in Israel to come back to Montreal and take part in a religious conversion." To our surprise, he added, "I'll be baptized as a member of the Church of Jesus Christ of Latter-day Saints."

When I next visited Dad at his office and Mom that same night at home, both of them yelped, "Steve wants to become a Mormon!" Both of them showed worried eyes and had an edge in their voices. "What will your mother say?!" Dad exclaimed. "What will your father think?!" Mom cried. I, too, was baffled that Steve would make a more extreme and unexpected choice. His previous cards and letters had never mentioned Mormonism.

I already knew my brother's righteous ways. Before he had left for Africa, he discovered and threw away a few girlie magazines I had tucked away on a high shelf in our apartment's hall closet. When I found them missing, I fumed into his room, "Steve, did you throw out my magazines?"

He spoke matter-of-factly. "Yes, I did, down the garbage chute."

"Why didn't you tell me the magazine bothered you? And why didn't you ask me to take them away before you threw them away?"

His look was stern and voice curt. "That garbage does not belong in our home."

Steve's moral ethic was positioned way above any courtesy to me. I told him, "I'm upset that you didn't even say anything before acting unilaterally with something that was mine."

He replied, "Okay," and turned away. Heck, if he was going to ask for my permission on anything

After reading Steve's letters to me, each of my parents urged, "Harvy, Stevie won't listen to me. Can you talk to him before he gets baptized into that screwy religion? You're his brother. See what you can do to change his mind."

None of us knew much about the Mormon faith, except that followers once had many wives and hordes of children. We knew Mormons followed strict rules against smoking, drinking, and caffeine—every vice Dad enjoyed.

Though I wondered why my brother would ever listen to me, I told Mom and Dad I'd try talking to him. Perhaps I, too, felt it my duty to confront my brother about his decision before it was too late.

When Steve arrived in Montreal, I picked him up at the airport and brought him back to our apartment. After small talk about his travels, I dove into his Mormon quest. "What's your conversion about, Steve?"

He shared what inspired his enlightenment. "I had a Mormon roommate on the kibbutz," he offered calmly. "He knew I was looking for a religion to follow, so he encouraged me to seek the truth for myself about Mormonism."

Steve's hand floated in the air like a priest giving a lesson. "After finding out more about it, I went to pray by the Sea of Galilee to seek a sign." He gestured downward. "I lay on the grass to take a nap." Steve's hand reached upward. "As I fell asleep, I received a revelation from an angel saying, 'The Book of Mormon *is* the Word of God'."

My dear brother has fallen off a religious edge! On the other hand, didn't I have a revelation during my hospital stay while I was at Harvard? Then again, look at how that turned out.

Steve's voice stayed priestly soft. "The Latter-day Saints follow the Book of Mormon in addition to the New and Old Bible Testaments. The Book of Mormon is about Jesus coming to North America after His Resurrection." He took a long breath. "Jesus revealed himself to the native people here before He ascended into heaven."

My brother's tone seemed deadly serious. There was a smile on his face as if he had discovered a long-lost friend. He continued. "From that revelation, written tablets were made and buried in Upper New York State. Guided by God, Joseph Smith discovered those tablets in 1820."

My eyes were rolling, but I tried to hang in there with my brother's new beliefs. Steve elevated and lowered his hand methodically as he spoke. "Joseph Smith claimed the native people of North America to be one of the Lost Tribes of Israel. Guided by God, Smith translated those tablets, and they became the Book of Mormon."

"Yah?" I found myself deeply dubious about my brother's new dogma. His move from Catholicism to Mormonism—with a matzo ball and latkes (or perhaps a falafel and hummus) side trip through a Jewish kibbutz—had come with no warning.

Though Steve had been a rebel in our family, I felt he now jumped into the deep end of a spiritual pool. I suspected he chose Mormonism because it was foreign to our family. He could hang his new religion over Dad's head, declaring by his action that he was now a better man of faith than our father.

"Steve," I countered. "You are asking Mom, Dad, and me to buy into your quick decision without ever having given us an inkling of your wishes, or a chance to comment on it, or to influence you otherwise. Don't you think you're moving too fast?"

Steve's eyes narrowed, and his face became tense. "Harvy, I've made up my mind. I'm contacting our local Mormon church tomorrow. There's one here in the West Island of Montreal. I'll convert as soon as possible."

I recalled our altercation in Vancouver. My brother had given me no chance to talk things out with him. He just called Dad to say he was leaving me and flying back home. This time, he gave our family no chance to talk things through before he had unilaterally decided to commune with a higher religion. When Steve set his mind, there was no changing it. Like our father in business and at home, my brother's family MO was to decide and then announce.

"Okay, Steve," I said. "None of us are pleased about what you're doing, but it's your life. I'm not going to stand in your way." *Not that I could.*

I returned empty-handed to both my parents. "Steve's mind seems fixed," I said to each of them. "There's nothing I can do."

Mom sighed, but Dad called Moe Gross. "Steve wants to turn Mormon. Can you change his mind?" I was amazed that Dad, desperate for help, went to someone he didn't trust. Maybe he figured Steve might listen to Moe.

Over the phone, Moe responded, "I can talk to him, John, but I can't promise anything,"

To my surprise, Steve agreed to meet with Moe. Afterward, Moe came to see Dad and me at JHS. He looked directly at my father and raised an open hand. "I talked to him about his decision. But like in your company, it's difficult to have an employee come back when they have both feet out your factory door and into another employer's company."

Dad nodded his understanding. "That's too bad. Is there anything more we can do?"

"I don't think so. Your son's mind seems to be unmovable."

Over the next weeks, I learned more from Steve about his new church. He told me, "Mormons see themselves as devout Christians who deeply believe in the teachings of Jesus Christ. Our founder, Joseph Smith, restored the original church and Christianity taught by Jesus. Mormons will stay devout to Jesus—and keep our faith in God and His Church—during the time leading to Jesus' second coming. We are thus, literally, 'The Latter-day Saints.'" He used his fingers to make quotation marks in the air when he said those words.

I amused myself by thinking Steve couldn't have found a better way to one-up our father than to one-up his Roman Catholicism. All Mormons were considered saints. Steve could claim unequivocally that he and his Mormon colleagues had a better faith. And by adhering devoutly to the Christian commandments, he'd be a shining and constant reminder to our father—a man who lived the ten commandments as if they were loose suggestions—of his first son's superiority.

Because no one in our family was Mormon, neither Dad nor Mom nor I were permitted to watch as Steve became baptized into his new faith. I wouldn't have gone even if I had been allowed. Though I accepted Steve's new religion to be what my brother wanted and needed, it didn't mean I had to agree and participate.

From what I had learned from my brother, Mormon orthodoxy defined ridged family and religious roles for men and women. The two sexes sat separately for much of the church services, with the men going to different religious-education sessions than their spouses. Those practices seemed archaic to me, not in my cup of religion. I had shared these concerns with my brother in the days before he got himself fully submerged under baptismal waters. He had accepted those notions as a given.

Steve returned to Israel to finish the kibbutz stint. After he had come home for good, he found the only single female of his age in his local Mormon church—a convert like him.

He and his fiancée married within a year. A child was soon on the way. About that, Steve once joked. "Harvy, do you know the Mormon form of birth control?"

"Okay, Steve. What is it?"

His chuckle was slightly-forced. "Abstinence or none at all."

I grinned a bit but said nothing. Steve was working to be opposite to our father. Little did he realize how much he was just like our dad, except their life manifestations differed. Steve became married to his church as much as Dad was married to his business. Neither of them listened to outside opinions other than to justify their own.

Over the ensuing years, Steve became elevated to lay minister in his church. The church then "called" him to manage the regional Mormon family history centre. His voice gelled into a soft monotone, like a pastor speaking to his devoted flock. My brother never raised his voice in public. He engaged his slightly-forced smile or soft chuckle when he thought something was funny.

Elaine once shared with me, "Your father came home from the office one day and told me that your brother came to see him. Steve had said that he had gotten a promotion within the church. Johnny then told me, 'Today, Steve said the church promoted him to a Mormon elder. Tomorrow, he'll tell me he's God.'"

I did hear from Steve's wife that he could get angry and break things at home. I never pried or said anything about it, for I knew his frustrations were remnants of being raised by our volatile parents. Steve once volunteered, "If my wife and I ever become cross with each other or the kids, we stop what we are doing, get on our knees, and pray."

Dad complained to Elaine and me about my brother's new religion, but he rarely said anything directly to Steve. On the other hand, Elaine could put her two bucks worth on the table when riled. She once recounted, "When Steve comes over to our home, he can go on and on about his new religion. You'd think that guy's a saint."

She took a big breath. "Of course, your Dad says nothing to him, but I once got fed up. I pointed my finger at him and said, 'Steve, I was born and raised Catholic like your father. And, like your father, I may not be the best of Catholics.'" She tapped her finger hard on the table. "'And maybe I have a thing or two I don't like about Catholicism and the nuns and priests that I had had in school.'" Her face was stern like a school nun taking a ruler to an unruly child. "'But Catholicism is my religion. So please don't come into our house and lecture us about Mormon this and Mormon that. I would certainly not do that to you.'"

She crossed her arms as she continued to look at me. "After my statements, your brother stopped trying to convert your father and me."

I nodded. "I know what you mean, Elaine. He tried doing the same to me until I raised my hand and emphatically told him to stop. He even did it to our mother until she said the same."

It could have been worse! Steve could have become a Moonie or Hare Krishna. Though my brother's spiritual route was certainly not mine, he seemed to be content with his choice. He found the creed he needed and went for the whole testament. Though I rarely thought well of my brother, I hoped his Bishop and his God would bless him for his steadfast devotion.

I had thought I could get closer to Steve by working with him at JHS. I had thought I could repair our sibling relationship by our moving in together.

We once had a MASH party *chez nous* with our combined companions to commemorate the conclusion of that television series. Everyone who came, including Steve and I, dressed as our favourite character from that show. We huddled together in front of the television, everyone there being "our friends." My strategy with Steve seemed to have worked awhile.

In the end, it didn't work out the way I had hoped. Steve abandoned our family for his new religion, as Dad had abandoned our mother for his new mistress. In late '82, the same month that my brother became engaged to his girlfriend, I started looking for another place to live closer to the city.

The following spring, before Steve married and moved into a new home near their church in Montreal's West Island, I relocated to an apartment closer to the city and closer to Moe Gross. Steve and I were now on very different paths that only touched in connection with our parents. I wondered if he and I would ever again do anything "just the two of us."

* * * *

Family Business Ties that Bind

Our father signed company cheques to my brother and me as we looked on. "Thanks, Dad," we both offered after he had finished. We stood a meter away from his desk, like two trained dogs waiting patiently for a steak bone from their master. I presented an appreciative smile while Steve showed little expression. It was as if he had expected what he received.

It was June 1982 and the end of another tax season at JHS. Dad's company had to file corporate tax returns by the end of the month. Over the previous weeks, Roger Delliard's accounting firm had descended onto the premises to audit accounting ledgers, spot-check inventory counts, and complete JHS's returns.

From the time I had returned to JHS in 1980, Dad continued to pay my brother and me a year-end company bonus. Sitting at his front office desk, Dad reiterated once more, "JHS has used up its Canadian small-business tax credits. Instead of the company now paying 50% corporate tax on its profits, I'm declaring a bonus to you guys. Your personal tax rates are much lower than JHS's corporate rate or my individual tax rate, so you will obtain more cash from these bonuses than if the company held onto the earnings."

Earlier in our conversation, Roger had supported Dad's giving his kids those bonuses. "Johnny, both Stephen and Harvy hold shares in JHS, and they both have worked here not only as employees but also as directors." He spoke confidently. "There's nothing wrong with them taking this kind of money from the company. It's a legitimate way to split the company's income across its owners."

"Yes," our father concurred. "Why feed the government when you don't have to." Not even my brother, known for his staunch honesty, could argue that point.

Now that our father had signed the company's tax returns, Dad handed us our bonus cheques. It was more than a year's salary for most JHS employees. Dad put the cheques in our hands, his voice calm but authoritative. "Boys, now don't piss it away."

I was no longer a full-time JHS employee. While pursuing my part-time graduate degree at American University, I had no other income. Outside of my studies, I got involved in the local Junior Chamber of Commerce. Moe suggested I offer myself to their volunteer board as a place to develop my organizational skills. I did and became elected to a VP position, but no remuneration was involved. JHS bonuses would keep me going until I graduated from my master's program.

Though I wondered why I deserved this extra money for being a Simkovits son, I was thankful both to my father for the perk and to Revenue Canada for offering the tax incentive. Every cheque I got from JHS not only helped to build my independence but also allowed me to show my father I was responsible with his money.

I wondered if this family business benefit was Dad's capitalistic way of keeping money out of government hands while showing generosity to his sons. Or was he breeding a financial dependency in his offspring? Perhaps it was both.

I did feel like a privileged progeny, though I hoped I wasn't conceited or arrogant about it. I didn't live large as my father did with his friends. I didn't want to become exceedingly reliant on his money graces. My father expected only a cordial thank you in return for his company's cheque. He never asked for anything more.

Roger had encouraged Dad to have JHS pay my American University tuition and travel expenses to Washington, D.C. "Companies can pay the education expenses of their directors," he said.

JHS took my education expenses as a deductible business expense, so it cost the company half of the gross amount. My JHS bonuses then adequately covered my modest Montreal apartment and living expenses.

Before he converted to Mormon, Steve had spent his bonus money on his horse and on the multi-month trips he took around the planet. I squirreled away what extra cash I could into safe investments, like bank CDs and whole life insurance policies. I wanted Dad to see me as not "pissing away his money." That's what my brother did!

Dad certainly was more generous to Steve and me than to our mother. Mom continued to live on a monthly stipend that barely covered her house and personal expenses. Moe had told Steve and me that our parents' money issues should stay between them, that we shouldn't get involved. I felt a small, shriveled space next to my heart regarding my brother and me winning out and our mother not.

Though I was moving forward in a new profession, I still felt addicted to my father's money gifts. Though I was working to curtail my reliance, I continued to take his money when offered. I shivered at the thought of ever being cut off.

Occasionally, I found myself staring into space, questioning myself about the grip my father seemed to have on me. I shook off my stare by telling myself Dad was big-hearted to his sons. I would continue to show respect and gratefulness in my dealings with him.

When I walked out of the JHS office that day, I couldn't wait for the day that I could break free from our dad's money grip. I longed for success in my new course of study. At the same time, I felt the pull of wanting to be my father's primary beneficiary, especially regarding his offshore money.

My worst fear was to disappoint my father once more by having no job prospects after his company paid a sizable investment in my newfound direction. With five years behind me at MIT, half-a-year at Harvard, and soon, two years at American University, Dad had spent heavily on my future.

I sat in my dumpy Datsun before driving off. I thought more about my complicated connection to my father. I wanted to prove to him I could be both a good saver and make an independent living. I lived in a modest one-bedroom apartment in an inexpensive yuppie area on the edge of the city. I hoped to find a worthy profession and position by way of my new college program. AU/NTL wasn't my father's preferred HBS, but my course of study was organizationally-related, and it excited me. I felt I had found a good compromise for my career.

Before I started the car's engine, I looked down into my lap. Though I was still on the quest for the Simkovits pot of gold buried in an offshore haven, wasn't I now following my own path to get there?

I banged my palm on the steering wheel. Unlike my father, I didn't have a high-maintenance life or greedy comrades like Mack. I only went out to classy restaurants when my father invited me, or when I took my mother out for a fancy dinner or supper for her birthday or on Mother's Day.

I had long ago relinquished my Playboy Club Keycard, and I curtailed my use of the American Express company credit card Dad had given me—except to pay for my university expenses. I didn't need to impress anyone with what I drove, where I lived, or how I entertained. I desperately wanted to be unlike my father, but was I succeeding?

I started my five-year-old Datsun, two years older than any Oldsmobile Dad had ever owned. I wondered why I was so careful with money. As a kid, whenever I wanted something, my father would ask, "Do you need that, son?"

My answer was usually a somber one as I averted my eyes. "No, Dad, not really, I guess." I never felt indulged by my parents. Into my adulthood, I never wanted or expected extravagant presents. Maybe I never felt worthy of indulgence.

My frugality could have been connected to my parents being savers. They had lived through The Depression and World War II. Maybe I was like my mother, who, as a seamstress and homemaker, saved every piece of thread and cut of cloth, and she made sure that leftover food was put away for another day. She counted her dollars and change before and after every trip to the grocery store.

At JHS, Dad didn't open his wallet unless he could see a return on any investment. It was incredible how he splurged at places like the Russian Troika. My father bought season tickets to Montreal Alouettes football and Canadiens hockey games to entertain his customers and business colleagues, and sometimes to treat his sons. He gave thousands of dollars each year to the Slovak Catholic Church, his Slovak social club, and to help needy Czechoslovak immigrants start anew in Canada. He indulged where he wanted to be the big man in his community circle and business campus, and a sugar daddy to his friends and mistress.

I no longer wanted such things. Dad's ways had caused torment at home for my mother. Their incessant fighting about both money and my father's indiscretions created angst in me.

I touched my hand to my wallet, where I had tucked away my bonus cheque. I wanted my father to notice my prudence with his money, so that he'd trust me with his fortunes, both onshore and off. And, in case he'd abandon me as he had done to my mom, I was going to save as much as I could from what he had given me. I didn't want to become almost penniless like my mother.

From what I could tell, my only vice was my eating. I worked hard on staying fit through skiing in the winter and cycling and hiking in the summer. But I could never get rid of the love handles that had developed from my mother's homeland cooking and our shared indulgence for sweets. Food was my escape. I craved rich Eastern European food, anything chocolate, almost anything ice cream, especially when I was feeling blue.

There were times when I gained ten to fifteen pounds in a matter of months, then fought to lose the excess flab over the next year. Perhaps I was obsessed, a slave to my culture's rich Hungarian goulash, potato gnocchi, sweet cucumber salad, and chocolate crepes for dessert. My stomach felt sick when I sensed Mom forcing meals on me. I then felt guilty when I tried to curtail the role that gave her the most pleasure—feeding her kids.

Perhaps I was as obsessed with my mother's cooking as I was with my father's money. Every week when I visited her, she continued to push her Hungarian fare as Dad continued to push his bonus money on me and his

"One day, my son, what's mine will be yours." His fatherly promise dripped in my mind like a trickling water faucet that wears away a sink's enamel.

I put my car in gear and headed for home. What kept me moving forward was the thought that, once my AU master's degree was complete, I'd find a job in another city and never again be in either of my parent's clutches. My personal growth and self-sufficiency—and not an obscure religion—would be my salvation. That focus would break me free of the ties that bound me to my father and for me to survive my seemingly senseless family.

* * *

In April of 1983, near the end of my first year of grad school in D.C., I was once more in my father's front office with Dad, Roger, and Roger's junior associate, Norman. We were going over my tax returns due at the end of the month. Steve, having already signed his tax documents, had left for the day.

My father looked at me as if he were conducting business as usual. "Harvy, we are going to deduct your last year's American University tuition from your income taxes. We'll do this every year you're in graduate school, so you'll pay less tax on your yearly bonus."

I was surprised. "But, Dad!" I retorted. "Aren't you already paying for my tuition through JHS, taking it as a corporate tax deduction? Should I then not deduct the same expense personally?"

Roger's assistant, Norman, offered, "Harvy, college tuition is a legitimate deductible personal expense in Canada."

Dad added, "We did it when you were at MIT and Harvard. Don't you remember?"

I quickly glanced at Norman and Roger and then looked back at my father. "Yes, but back then, we only got a single tax benefit from my tuition—the deduction on my personal taxes. Now that JHS is paying my tuition, wouldn't this be double-dipping—using the same tax deduction for both the company and me?"

Roger spoke. "It's better you have the money in your pocket than it sitting in the government's coffers."

I shook my head. I knew that my brother, a man who thumbed his nose at every tax deduction trick, would have raised his chin, stiffened his lip, and dug in his heels. He would have insisted his tax returns not receive the second tuition deduction. Though I was used to my father looking for every tax loophole, it had never involved my having to sign on any dotted line.

Norman, a handful of years my elder, looked at me. "Harvy, can you show me how this coffee pot over here works. I could use a cup."

I stood and led Norman into the small kitchen area adjacent to Dad's front office. My father raised his hand. "Make some for all of us, Harvy. Roger, do you want some too?"

The senior accountant raised an open palm, "No thanks; that stuff this late in the day keeps me up at night."

Norman and I walked the few paces to the coffee machine located in a small alcove off the main office. When we got there, he spoke to me quietly, like a caring big brother. "Harvy, there's no Revenue Canada tax rule against making both the personal and corporate tuition deductions."

He smiled. "Frankly, I did it when I went to accounting school. The company I worked for paid my tuition, and I also deducted it from my income taxes." He raised a hand. "The government never cross-checks these things—they have better things to do." His voice was assuring, "A lot of working students do this. You don't have to worry about it."

Jesus! That's just about what my father tells me about his offshore stash. Legitimate tax deduction or not, might these accountants to money moguls like my father be taking drags from the same tax-avoiding cigar?

My gut didn't feel right about it, but my tax returns lay prepared on the desk I had used during my years working for my father. Roger, Norman, and Dad looked at me as if they all expected me to go along without raising a fuss. Their double tuition deduction meant more after-tax cash for me. I lowered my head and focused on the brewing coffee and said, "Okay, Norman, if you say so."

I served a cup of coffee to Dad and then went back to my old desk. I parked myself in my seat, picked up my pen, and put my signature on my returns. There was no point fighting a losing battle while Dad wielded his accountant guns. I figured the extra tax-savings was par for the course for well-off people who can afford high-end accountants.

After receiving additional tuition deductions for the calendar years I attended American University, I figured Canada's government ended up paying better than two-thirds of my AU master's degree program costs.

Thank you, Revenue Canada!

* * * *

Not My Cup of Business Tea

No Asian television manufacturers came through for Dad and JHS after our overseas trip in the fall of '80. After I had departed JHS for my master's program, Dad made one more attempt in late-1982 to find new business for his company. He used his connections in the Quebec government to get funding for a business development trip to Paris.

My father was to meet with executives at TVF, a French television manufacturer. As with Korea's Goldstar, he wanted to interest TVF to employ JHS to manufacture their televisions for the Canadian market.

Accompanying Dad to Paris were Roger Delliard's associate, Norman, and Brad Moore. Brad, a manufacturing engineer, was a close friend of Dad's. He had recently retired from the Canadian division of a multinational technology corporation.

Soon after that Paris trip, I visited my father in his office at the end of a workday. Norman, who was taking over more of Roger's work with JHS, arrived soon after me. My father was less busy after five o'clock, and JHS was on Norman's route home from downtown Montreal. Norman knew that, at this happy-hour time of day, Dad might splash a little Grand Marnier or VO cognac into a cup of tea.

Norman was a heavyset family man with a clear and calm tenor voice—perfect for an accountant who might need to calm down an irate business owner. Today, Norman wore a big smile and carried two briefcases, one in each hand. After saying hello and shaking hands, Dad smirked at Norman and said, "Always two briefcases, huh Norman?"

Norman was prepared. "I need two to keep me balanced."

I smiled. "Norman, I don't think that accountants should get into stand-up comedy."

Norman chuckled back. "In my profession, you have to find any way to spruce it up, for the accounting tedium can kill you."

Dad laughed and came back with one of his own. "And do you know how accountants are like women?"

"I think I've heard this one before," Norman remarked.

Dad didn't offer Norman the opportunity to say more. "It's because company owners like me can't live with you or without you." He chuckled.

"I can't outdo you, Johnny," Norman said. He deferred to where his business bread was buttered.

On this day, business came before tea sprucing up. Dad handed Norman a document. "Here, I received this love letter from the provincial government. Before they fully repay JHS, they want more goddamned information about our trip to France." Dad's face was tense. "Didn't we send them everything?"

My father didn't wait for an answer. His fist banged the table. "I'm sick of this government baloney. Let the bastards sue me if they want any of their seed money back."

The provincial government was going to pay for half of Dad's business trip to France. I knew my father customarily padded his expenses, probably to cover nights at the Moulin Rouge or another risqué Paris venue. I wasn't surprised the government wanted additional reporting from him.

Norman perused the papers for a moment, and then he spoke calmly. "This isn't a big issue, Johnny. They want to know how you calculated the fees of the advisors involved in this project—both for your engineer friend and for me."

Norman looked at my father as he spoke. "All you need are detailed breakdowns both from my firm and from Brad. I'll have my office put something out to you for my time." He smiled. "You'll have to get the same from him."

"Okay," my father said, calming down. "I'll get something from him."

Being a longtime friend and colleague of Dad's, the retired Brad may have given his time to the project for free in exchange for the trip to Paris. Dad might have to produce a phantom invoice for Brad's effort. In business and government funding, anything goes with Johnny Simkovits.

While Dad handled the cognac, he asked me to pour coffee for him and make tea for Norman. I declined a spiked drink, saying, "I've got studying to do tonight."

Norman looked at me. "How's that new university program going for you, Harvy?"

I figured my father had told Norman about my leaving JHS to go back to college. As usual, someone else was asking questions on behalf of my dad.

I perked up. "So far so good, Norman. I've already done several courses: organizational theory, counseling psychology, and personal career development." I counted them out on my fingers. "I'm enjoying them." I was saying that more for my father's ears than for Norman's.

"Sounds interesting," Norman said. "All that can be useful in business."

I nodded but added nothing more. Though I was 28 years old and drawn to my new field, I felt young among my American University classmates. Most of them were human resource and consulting experts, ranging in age from 35 to 55 years old. I felt like an amateur in a field of organizational professionals. Moe had encouraged me, saying, "The skills you are learning are for life. They are important to any and every organization."

In a self-assessment for my career development course, I had learned that I was a people-oriented analytical-thinker. I was unlike my father, an outgoing entertainer and hard-driving doer. I cared about finding ways to motivate and include people, as I had tried to do at JHS. On the other hand, my father cared about people at work only when they helped to achieve his ends. He could cast them aside when they no longer suited his purpose.

It interested me to learn how my father and I were different, though it scared me to think that tough-minded, self-absorbed entrepreneurs like him ran much of the world. I wondered if I could ever help his kind to see the benefit of a more humane and collaborative way.

What I didn't say to Norman was that my graduate coursework was very foreign to me. At MIT and Harvard, I never had to read so many textbooks or to write so many papers. My engineering problem-set mind now had to wrap itself around an applied-behavior-science curriculum. The homework assignments were challenging, especially since I wasn't an efficient reader—my nemesis also at Harvard with its case method.

Thank goodness I had Moe helping me not to get overwhelmed. He had told me, "Instead of closely reading everything, and underlining and highlighting lots of text, look for the few main ideas in every article and book chapter. Write those down in your notes, even within the article or book chapter."

I tried to follow his advice, but it still felt as if I were learning Swahili. "Will I make it through this program?" I had asked my psychologist now turned mentor.

"Yes, of course," he told me. "Keep on working at it. Things will get easier over time." That was the same line I had heard from my Harvard professors after a couple of months there, and I hadn't felt anything getting less complicated.

I hoped Moe would be right. I was glad I wasn't working full-time during my part-time studies, as many of my AU classmates were. I was relieved I didn't have a wife and family to compete for my attention. It was hard for me to grasp how many of my classmates carried on a job, marriage, and family, and then spend the time needed for this rigorous coursework. (Some of my colleagues would leave jobs or divorce wives by the time they got their new degree.) I was very fortunate in my life circumstances, and I knew it. I didn't want to squander this opportunity.

Dad nodded and offered a small grin to the accountant's comment about the practicality of my degree program. He spoke right behind Norman. "I think Harvy will be a professional student for most of his life." Though

Dad said that with tongue in cheek, I was glad he had a sense of who I was. I did enjoy being in school.

Norman turned to my father. "Did you hear anything from TVF? Are they interested in having you manufacture products for them here in Canada?"

Dad looked down at his desk. "I've had no indication. Those big companies are slow as molasses to make their decisions." He took a breath. "We need to find a new line, or JHS will be sunk very soon. There is little market for consoles anymore, especially after the trouble we had with both Sears and Woolco."

JHS's chassis problems with Jin Dae seemed to have punctuated the end of the console stereo industry in Canada. Consoles had been a dying breed for years, except maybe in a console connoisseur's basement.

Dad continued. "As you already know, Norman, JHS has been making more money on its cash investments than in its production. We are still peddling units here and there to small electronic retailers and distributors I found in Canada and New York State, but we can't keep going this way."

Dad had been spouting similar words for years, yet he hadn't uncovered any new ventures for JHS. Regarding TVF, televisions would be more complex to manufacture, requiring a high-level quality control and electronic testing, perhaps more than JHS and my father were capable of handling. Maybe his French connection saw no future for television sets in wood cabinets.

Those TVG executives possibly needed a Canadian partner with younger blood like mine rather than aging men like my father and his retired chief engineer friend. But I had discovered through my years at JHS that my younger blood wasn't cut out for either travelling or working with my father.

Norman turned to me. "So what about you, Harvy? Any great business ideas for your father's company?"

I had heard the same question before. And I had learned the hard way that JHS was my father's company and not my brother's or mine, though Norman knew that Steve and I held most of the company's ownership. Dad had structured his business shareholdings years ago to give Steve and me the most financial benefit from his company. Steve and I held the growing common shares in the corporation while our dad held control through his fixed-priced preferred shares.

While I pondered Norman's question, he dug further. "Didn't you want to start a solar business? What happened there?"

"It was a good idea in theory," I responded. "But it didn't have long legs from an engineering standpoint."

Edo's Cousin Alex, who lived in Ottawa, had designed a solar-assisted heat pump system that saved energy costs in a home. He had built a prototype at his house and tested it for a couple of years. He showed me his design and documented fuel savings.

The device looked promising. It was an 11'-high wooden housing containing a 10'x10' tilted glass pane on one side, which allowed the sun to heat a compartment that held a heat pump condenser. The unit used baffles to adjust outside airflow, keeping the heat pump compartment warmer in cold weather and cooler on hot days. That "heat pump under glass" could warm and cool a home more economically during any season of the year.

Initially, I became excited by the idea of building my own business under the auspices of JHS—as Moe had once suggested. JHS could build the wooden and glass housing and assemble the air-movement baffles and the unit's controls. I'd then have to market the units at home shows and to develop installation and maintenance crews.

Dad had told me, "If you get into this solar project, then I want the first production model built at Elaine's and my home." With that statement, I knew Dad was into my project with both his feet and JHS's money. We engaged JHS's designer, François, to start work on production blueprints.

When my engineering head later kicked in, I realized that we would have to significantly enlarge Alex's device to make a decent dent in reducing a house's energy bills. There was an intuitive simplicity to his design, and it would generate some home-heat savings. But it would be almost as if one had added a large picture window onto a house's south wall and then labeled the house "solar heated." One would need much more than a 10'x10' glass to make a significant dent in a house's heating bills. Such a large unit in a wood cabinet would be prohibitively expensive to build.

I decided to back out of the project. My father said he understood my decision and the deficiency of Alex's design. I still felt as if I had failed my father, JHS, and myself.

In my father's office, Norman's face was long. "That's too bad, Harvy. I was hoping you might help JHS find something new to get into."

My eyes looked down. Norman was right. My disappointment in the solar project had made me shy away from trying anything else. I guess I wasn't the "if you don't succeed the first time then try again" type of businessman that my dad had been in his early years. Or maybe I now knew better as to what it was like to work with my father. I didn't want to take a chance of building anything under his auspices and then have him second-guess or blame me if I lost money. I had gotten weary of wrestling for every little thing I tried to do at JHS.

When Norman finished his tea, he headed home. Before Dad locked the office for the night, he looked at me and said, "That Norman is a great guy. He and Roger have been the best accountants I've ever had. They've helped our company and me a lot."

Dad didn't elaborate. I knew that Roger had been a big help back in '75 when Revenue Canada had sued Dad for corporate tax evasion. Roger had been an expert witness for my father, instrumental in preventing my dad from being convicted of criminal charges for tax fraud.

But maybe not all of Roger and Norman's help had been on the up and up. I knew that Roger had advised my father not to worry when I had come home from Harvard with a bank receipt that showed I had transferred $100,000USD from my Boston bank account to Dad's Cayman Islands account. (The interest from that money, which Dad had given me, had been used to pay my Harvard college expenses.) After I had left Harvard, Dad directed me to make the money transfer to Cayman.

My dad continued, and a glint was in his eye. "Norman recently got into trouble, you know."

My ears perked up. "How so, Dad?"

Dad had a childish smirk on his face. "While we were in Paris, the guy had a little too much fun." His grin widened. "I took him out to the Moulin Rouge. There, things started to get a bit risqué."

My father lowered his voice as if he didn't want anyone to hear us, but there was no one else present. He winked at me. "We had a few drinks, and Norman found himself a girl." He chuckled. "Or maybe the girl found him." He put his tongue into his cheek, and he batted his hand in the air. "I told him to be careful with her, but he didn't listen."

Dad looked toward the entrance door and then back at me. "Soon after we came back to Montreal, I got a call from Norman. He said he had caught something there. He wanted to know if I could connect him to my doctor." He raised one hand. "Norman was afraid his family doctor, who also sees his wife, might say something to her." Dad grinned again. "So I sent Norman to my guy, and he got fixed up."

"Wow, Dad!" I said. I had never taken the straight-laced Norman to be that type of fellow. He came across as a puritanical family man with a good marriage. But under the influence of my carousing father, even the most upright citizen could be turned into a libertine.

My father looked at me in earnest, and he wagged his finger. "Don't say anything to anybody about this, for Norman's sake."

I nodded but wondered, *Why the heck does he tell me such things?*

* * *

Thirty years later, I met with Norman for lunch at a Montreal smoked meat deli. The now elderly fellow was still spry. He reminisced. "I still remember the great trip I had to Paris with your Dad. I was amazed at how your father got the Quebec government to pay for it."

He smiled. "Here was your father, an Eastern European immigrant, getting Quebec funding to do business in France. I hand it to him; he had pull somewhere in the government and the gumption to ask for a handout."

I added what I knew. "There was a Slovak Canadian fellow who was with the Quebec Finance Ministry. The guy came to the Slovak Business Association balls, and my father knew him well. Maybe my dad had leveraged that relationship to get the government seed money."

"I see," Norman said.

He scratched his head. "On the other hand, it seemed to me that your father and his engineer friend, Brad, were only going through the motions over there in France. It didn't look like they wanted to do business with that TVF Company. They never got into any hard negotiation, only surface exploration. I felt I was there for the ride and not much more."

"Yes, Norman," I offered. "That seemed to be the last straw for my father and JHS. Soon afterward, he liquidated JHS and retired from manufacturing." I took a breath and added, "After I had left for graduate school in D.C., my father didn't feel Steve could run the company by himself."

Norman took a bite of his smoked-meat sandwich. "Yes, Johnny stopped working with my firm after he retired; he didn't need us anymore. But we stayed good friends, and he invited my wife and me to his retirement party." His eyes were on me. "It's too bad that JHS had to shut down. Your Dad had been over thirty years in business, hadn't he?"

"Yes, he had had success. He saw both the beginning and the end of the console stereo industry in Canada. Though he made good money and got out, it's hard to see a good run end." I took a bite of my sandwich." It would have been hard for Steve and me to continue it. Dad wasn't an easy guy to work with."

"Yes, I know, Harvy." Norman's face went from serious to a smile, and he wagged his finger at me. "But he did know how to have a good time."

I didn't mention what my father had told me about the naughty "good time" Norman, Brad, and Dad had had in Paris. Each one of us carries secrets: some innocent, some inconsequential, some life-altering, and some life-defining. Who was I to judge? Dad's kind of sweet entertainment was not for my cup of business tea.

* * * *

9

Money Ups and Money Downs

Dad sat at his Troika table in front of his colleagues and friends. He bragged, "I made $8000 U.S. in one night at the blackjack table in Cayman."

Elaine chimed in, "Johnny could also lose thousands any given night." She smiled. "Yet he always came out of the casino with his shirt on and me by his side."

Everyone at the table chuckled, including Dad.

Decades later, after Elaine had told me that anecdote, she added, "One night in Las Vegas, your father got so drunk he lost over $20,000 at the blackjack table." Her voice soured. "I was so upset at him; he could have donated that kind of money to a better cause." She raised a closed hand. "And I was upset at the casino for allowing him to play in his condition." She turned her head away and then back to me. "But you know how your father could be. He doesn't listen to anyone when he's drinking."

I nodded as she continued. "After that big loss, Johnny was quiet the whole next day. I don't know if he felt guilty or nursed a hangover." She took a breath. "I said nothing to him. It wasn't my money he had thrown away."

I was glad she had waited thirty years to tell me that story. Whether Dad could afford the money or not, I could wring his neck today for such foolhardiness. But back then, it had been very different.

* * *

Several months into my AU master's program, Dad asked me to go to Freeport, Bahamas. It was a vacation trip to help him recuperate from a bout of angina. At 62 years old, he had taken ill suddenly and became hospitalized for a week. After he got out of the hospital, his doctor recommended he take another week off from work.

Elaine had taken too much vacation time from her real estate job, and Steve had returned to Israel after having been baptized Mormon. I was between courses in my graduate program. My father said, "Harvy, come south with me for a week. We'll have a good time."

I was apprehensive about going away with Dad once more. The last time was for our Asia business trip three years earlier. The travel had been grueling, and we both had little sleep. A year later, Mom asked me to travel with her to Bermuda to help her recuperate from a gynecological procedure. (She had roped me in by saying she had no one else with whom to go.) Dad was now cashing in his travel chits with me; I couldn't bow out.

Dad wanted to go to Freeport instead of his favoured Cayman Islands. He found an inexpensive, last-minute, late-spring package. We'd take a direct flight to Grand Bahamas Island, a less taxing trip for him. I would have preferred checking out Cayman, a place Dad had spoken about for years. I deferred to my father's wishes, for he had been the one in the hospital, and he was paying for our trip.

On our first full day on Grand Bahama Island, Dad unwound his typical way—lying and sleeping in a lounge chair by the pool. We lay there for the morning and half the afternoon.

Because it was late in the season, the place lacked vacationers. Though the island weather was warm and breezy, and the beach sported hot, silky sand, I found little else to do besides taking a walk around the property or going to swim in the pool—I wasn't an ocean swimmer. For most of that day, I sat next to Dad. I read a magazine or one of my course books while he trumpeted out elephant snores as he snoozed.

I left my father's side once or twice for a half-hour. When I returned, he woke and clairvoyantly said, "Where have you been, Harvy?" I responded, "I went to get some exercise," or "I took a look around the place." Though he looked away and then returned to sleep, I felt bound to his side. I said nothing about it; I was there to help him recover.

Late that afternoon, he and I got dressed and visited the island's International Bazaar. Dad bought costume jewellery for Elaine and various trinkets for his few remaining JHS staff. When I showed interest in a carved Bahamian knickknack, he pulled out his wallet and put money into the vendor's hands. I raised my hand in protest, "Please, Dad, you don't have to."

He replied, "Let me do it, son. It's my pleasure."

Though his move made me feel like a child, I didn't want a struggle. I lowered my eyes and offered a muted, "Thank you."

That evening, we went out for my father's favorite vacation meal. While he ate filet mignon, I had Caribbean lobster tails. Chewing on his steak, he said with a smile, "While we are here in Freeport, let's go deep-sea fishing one day."

"Sure, Dad," I responded as I downed my lobster. "Whatever you'd like."

But ocean fishing wasn't my sport. When my brother and I were kids, Dad once took us deep sea fishing while we vacationed in Florida. Both Steve and I got seasick, having to lie down in the boat's main cabin for most of the trip. Not having much else to do in Freeport, going fishing sounded better than listening to Dad snore half the day by the pool.

When we finished our supper, my father added, "Harvy, let's go have fun at the casino."

My childhood feelings surfaced again. Part of me was okay with shadowing my dad around Grand Bahama Island, but another part didn't want to be here. "Okay," I said again. We grabbed a cab and headed to Freeport's Princess Casino.

Freeport's only casino was a one-story complex that was bigger than a Canadian football field, maybe even two fields. Before going to the gambling tables, we went to see the casino's burlesque show.

The seventy-five-minute spectacle included singers, dancers, jugglers, and a magician. Handsome male vocalists wore black and white tuxedos, while pretty women singers sported long, sparkling gowns that showed bare necks and shoulders. Male performers were accompanied by provocatively dressed women assistants—in black pants with a long slit down the side.

In between the main acts, an entourage of well bosomed, round butted, high-heeled women strode gracefully to flashing lights and drum beats. They high-stepped in sync to lively dance music. They wore long nylons and glittering tight one-pieces from breast to crotch. Most wore glittering pasties over their nipples. A few, sporting high shimmering tiaras balanced on their heads, were topless. I enjoyed watching the sexy ladies.

Dad and I smiled and laughed through the performance. I saw him glance at me a few times, perhaps to see if I enjoyed the show as much as he. I did! It kept my mind off how the rest of the evening might go.

I knew my father's casino routine. After the entertainment, he was going to sit for hours at the blackjack table until he could barely keep himself upright. Having had his earlier half-day nap, we could be in this building until the wee hours.

Being with Dad was going to be a tedious chore, but I was there to look after him. I hoped that I might win enough money at the tables to make worthwhile my having to be by his side.

Our visit to the Princess brought back memories from a decade earlier. In the early '70s, for two Christmas vacations over three years, Dad had brought our whole family to Freeport beaches and the Princess Casino. Steve and I had been in our late teens, below the Bahamian legal gambling age of 21, though above Quebec's drinking age of 18.

On our first excursion to the Princess, our father made Steve and me dress in dark suits and white shirts. We wore black neckties that Dad tied into Windsor knots for us. The fact that Steve and I were underage hadn't deterred him. He told us, "Walk tall and straight. Act as if you belong there."

Dad shepherded us into the casino. Mom, decked out in a long dress, wore her best gold bracelet and earrings. After exiting a cab, we followed a crowd of people climbing the casino's front steps. Mom walked in front of Steve and me while Dad was right behind us.

I glanced to one side to see one of the doormen eyeing me. I kept my face subdued and strode with a straight gait, promenading into the casino as if my dad owned the place. Here, on my first visit to the Princess, our father could claim ignorance of the legal gambling and drinking age if anyone asked to see our passports.

Inside the casino, lights flashed and bells rang eighteen hours or more per day as a crowd of people played the slots. But Dad didn't go for such mindless games. "Slot machines require no skill," he said. Instead, he did his gaming at the blackjack table.

Before sitting at any gaming table, Dad took us to the casino's burlesque show. I suspected Dad wanted to make sure Mom obtained enough of the nightly entertainment before the men took a spin at the tables.

After we sat down, Dad grabbed a waiter and ordered screwdrivers for my brother and me, a Dubonnet for Mom, and a scotch on the rocks for himself. When the drinks came, he leaned toward my brother and me and said softly, "Sip it slowly, boys, and not through the straw. Otherwise, the alcohol will go straight to your head."

I looked around the place and saw no one there close to my age. During the hour performance, I kept the lower part of me obscured by our small table. I had to turn my eyes away from the scantly-dressed dancing ladies so as not to get overexcited. I worked to keep a straight face. Dad glanced my way and smiled.

My father had previously taken our family to such a venue in Montreal. We had seen a similar show—including dancing can-can girls—at Le Caf' Conc' supper theatre at our city's L'Hôtel Château Champlain. It was for a New Year's Eve celebration after I turned 16 and Steve 17. The host didn't question my brother's and my age, especially after Dad discretely put a $20 bill into his hand. After we had taken our seats, Dad winked, "I know the maître'd; I bring many customers here."

Watching with googly eyes here at the Princess, I worked to stay subdued during and after each act, softly clapping as if I were a royal prince. Cigarette in mouth, Dad offered hearty applause after each performance. Mom and Steve clapped too, but not as exuberantly as Dad.

After the show, we strolled to the blackjack tables. Dad gave my brother and me $50USD each. He offered Mom the same. While she went off to play the slot machines, we three men sat side-by-side at a $5 table, with Dad in the middle.

When I had been 14, Steve and I had played roulette (with a $10USD stake from Dad) at the El San Juan in Puerto Rico, during a night excursion from our Caribbean cruise ship. Now was the first time we played casino blackjack together, and with a more substantial stake.

I sat upright on my stool and kept myself calm as the dealer dealt the cards. I wanted my father to be proud of my behaving like a man and not an exuberant teen.

Dad showed my brother and me when to draw a card, when to pass, and when we could take a chance to double down on our bets. He ordered drinks for us—they were free to players. He permitted Steve and me to have one more screwdriver, saying quietly, "As I told you before, sip it slowly and not through the straw."

A funny thing happened as the minutes turned into a half-hour and more. Steve and I started to win. After the first hour, I figured I had well over a hundred dollars in chips in front of me while Steve had an even bigger pile. Neither one of us showed any excitement or counted our money. I guess we both felt doing so would be bad luck or too adolescent.

After being ahead awhile, Dad started to double and triple his bets. From that point on, his chip pile dwindled. A couple of times, he pulled out another $50 from his wallet, and he lost that too. Saying nothing as he chain-smoked cigarettes, Dad started to take chips from Steve.

Steve, too, said nothing about Dad's "borrowing." I could see my brother's face looked a bit peeved every time our father took a small handful of Steve's chips to re-stake himself.

I gradually pushed my chips to the other side of me so Dad couldn't mooch from this son. Having had several drinks by now, my father tried to sneak his hand over to my stash. I leaned my body forward against the table so he couldn't take anything without having to pry me aside. Getting nowhere with me, he kept on taking from his first son.

Over an hour later, Mom returned. "Johnny, let's go home. It's late. I lost the fifty dollars and another ten from my own money. I'm ready to go to bed."

My father's eyes glazed over from his drinking. He looked as if he would fall over if anyone would shove him. Ordinarily, he resisted Mom's requests when he was having fun, but this time he was amenable. "Let's play one last hand," he said. There were only a handful of $5 chips remaining in front of both Dad and Steve. They pushed their chips forward into their betting boxes.

By now, I had become disgusted by Dad's stealing and losing my brother's winnings, his stinking of alcohol and cigarettes, and his trying to pinch my chips. *Screw it!* I pushed everything I had into my betting box. I didn't know how much money was in my pile, and I didn't want to know. I didn't look at my father or brother to see their reaction. *Win or lose; I don't care.*

The dealer dealt the cards. My groin tingled. I had an 18 showing on the table—pretty good cards, but it could easily be a losing hand. The dealer showed a nine on top. A face card or ace would give him 19 or 20, and I would be toast.

Both Steve and Dad's card hands were in the mid-teens. In turn, they each asked for another card. They both pulled face cards and went over 21, instant death. Steve's accumulated stash was now gone. Hundreds of dollars of winnings had vanished entirely, mostly via Dad's hand.

When the dealer came to me, I fanned my hand over my cards to decline another. I wanted to force the dealer to beat me. The croupier had dealt face cards to Dad and Steve, so maybe the next ones would be small. The dealer turned over his hidden card; it was a 5, which made his hand 14. He had to pull at least one more card. There was a chance he could still tie or beat me, but there was a bigger chance he would go bust. He pulled a 2. The dealer now had 16 to my 18, and he had to draw again.

My God, he could go over 21.

He pulled another card. It was 9, and he was toast.

My father grabbed my shoulder, jumped up, and screamed. "Hurrah! Harvy, you won!"

I didn't jump up. I smiled and stared at the pile of chips as the dealer paid me out, swapping green $25 chips for my red $5 ones.

I started to count my pile. Above the $50 I started with, there was over $240 more. It was about enough to cover what Dad had spotted himself and the rest of us during the evening.

Dad was grinning ear to ear. "Good boy, Harvy! Now give me your chips. I'll cash them in, and then we can go."

Being underage in the casino, I agreed to have him do the money changing for me. Before I handed my father the pile, I snuck a white $1 chip into my pocket as a souvenir of my first big gambling night.

Cradling my money chips against his body, Dad walked to the cashier window. I was exuberant for my good luck, and I couldn't wait to tuck a couple of $100 bills and more into my wallet.

What!! When Dad turned around from the cashier's window, he was stuffing the bills into his wallet. Before he put it into his pocket, he took a $20 bill and put it into my hand. "Here, take this for your good work tonight."

I was astonished. I had won that money, and Dad now took most of it. My smile left me, and my head lowered. Should I say he was being mean? *But it's his money; he never said I could keep my winnings.* I don't think he would have expected me to repay him his $50 if I lost the original stake.

A lump formed in my throat. I felt a little used and cheated, but I buried my thoughts and feelings. I decided not to make a scene. If I did, Dad might not bring me to a casino again. My father was happy about my good luck. Perhaps that and $20 was enough of a reward.

A couple of years later, after I turned 20, Dad took our family back to Freeport again for the Christmas holidays. I was still underage but close enough to have no qualms about walking into the Princess. This time I spotted myself $50 each night we went to the tables. After two or three evenings, again at the $5 blackjack tables, I came out ahead by nearly $200. I don't remember how Dad or Steve did; I didn't care. By the end of that vacation, I felt redressed to have earned back most of my previous forfeiture to my father. And, for luck, I had brought the $1 Princess Casino chip with me, keeping it tucked in my suit pocket.

As I exited the casino on that last night of our second Bahamian vacation, I flipped that $1 chip into the air and caught it in my hand. I was learning not to depend on my father.

Those underage gambling outings were now years behind me. This time, after the Princess Casino's show, Dad and I strolled to the blackjack tables. We ambled around so my father could stake out a spot for us. As I followed him around, I wondered if I was a German shepherd protector or puppy dog trainee. *You're here for him, Harvy; let him do what he wants.*

My father soon parked at a $5 table where he could sit on the end—the last to get cards from the dealer before the dealer got his. I sat in the seat next to him. He started his play slowly, with only $100 on the table. As I pulled out my wallet, Dad said, "Put your money away, son." He smiled as he put another bill on the table. "Here's a hundred for you. Play with it."

"Okay, Dad." It appeared the days of his absconding with my underage winnings were behind us.

Dad started with the minimum bet per round. He ordered vodka on the rocks for himself while I settled for a dark rum and Coke—both were complimentary. By the time we had finished our drinks, my father had lost his first stake while I was down a little from where I had started. He said, "Let's move to another table. This one isn't lucky."

I nodded and stood.

Nearby was another table with two open seats. Starting with a second $100, Dad repeated his pattern. After winning several double bets, double downs, and double plays—along with a bunch of loud "hurrahs" after a double drink—my father had a healthy stack in front of him. It was more than he had lost at the previous table.

Like Dad, I started with conservative play. I placed minimum bets to start, doubling down on my cards only if I had a 10 or 11 showing. If I lost a few hands in a row, then I doubled my bet to hope for a win to recover my losses. Though my strategy was sound, my luck was not as good as my father's this night. Less than an hour later, I had only a few chips left. *Shit!* It dawned on me that I had left my lucky $1 Princess Casino chip at home.

Dad had gotten a couple of complimentary Cuban cigars from a passing cigarette hostess, having given her a big smile and a few $1 chips for her trouble. He was happily puffing away. At every big win, he threw a few dollar chips toward the black-suited dealer, and he took a big drag on his smoky cigar. "For you," Dad said to the man, "for bringing me good luck."

The dealer took the chips, smiled a thank you, and loudly proclaimed, "For the boys." He tapped the chips vigorously on the table for everyone to hear—especially the pit boss—and sent them down a tip slot.

Unlike Dad, I nursed my second drink. Over the years, I found I didn't have the alcohol stamina my father had. Both my head got fuzzy and my eyes tired by the time I finished a second. I now felt light-headed, not only from my drink but also from Dad chugging away on his stogie. Feeling bored and not very lucky, I said, "Dad, I need a break. I'm going to walk around."

"Okay, son, but don't go too far. This table is lucky for me, and I'm staying." He turned his head a bit more my way. "Come and see me if you need money."

I raised my palm. "No problem, Dad." I didn't want more of his; I had my own. "Good luck over here," I said and walked away.

I roamed around to the other gaming tables. I continued to hear big "hurrahs" coming from Dad in the distance as he won big hands. He was so loud, and his deeply accented voice so distinctive, I sensed other players in the vicinity turn their heads to see what was causing the happy yelling.

I went over to the craps table. I put my remaining chips down and pulled another $50 from my wallet.

Dad didn't like craps. I had learned the game the last time I was here at the Princess. I had casually watched other people play. I occasionally asked questions of the croupiers or the players next to me. Everyone was friendly and willing to help out a green player as long as I wasn't in the way.

The thing I enjoyed most about this dice game was it went much faster than blackjack. You could place many bets at one time. For good and bad, one could win and lose more quickly. Knowing my father didn't like this game, I could play it without his looking over my shoulder.

After thirty minutes of ups and downs, I "crapped out" and was out of chips. "Damn," I said to myself, "I really should have brought that lucky $1 chip with me."

As I started to walk away from the table, I heard a big shout from behind me. "Harvy, Harvy, where are you? Come here!"

It was Dad. He repeated his yell.

I walked promptly over to my father's table, holding myself back from running. I saw that Dad had the whole table to himself. I wondered if his boisterous shouting or stogy chugging had chased away everyone else.

A waitress served Dad another drink. A fresh cigar was smoldering in an ashtray. He stood on wobbly feet and looked at me with glassy eyes. "Harvy, where have you been? I've been calling for you."

My father stank of liquor and smoke. I responded, "I've been over at the dice tables, Dad. What's going on?" I tried to keep my voice steady and calm.

He didn't answer my question. He looked at the chips on the table and then at me. He sounded giddy. "Here, son; take these chips and put them into your jacket pockets." I looked down at the table and became astonished. In front of him were big piles of black $100 chips.

My father handed me fists full of chips. "Hold onto these; don't let me play with them. I'll use what I have left here." Remaining on the table were handfuls of red $5 and green $25 chips.

I didn't count the black chips that Dad had handed to me, but there must have been three or four dozen of them. It was enough money to pay for a third of my two-year master's degree tuition, or over a year of my Montreal apartment rent. Dad's voice was loud but slurred. "Now leave me alone and go sit somewhere. But don't go far; I might need you again."

Reluctantly, I did what my father said. I walked two tables behind him and sat at an empty table. My jacket pockets were bulging. I felt like a pack mule for my father's winnings, and at his beck and call.

Dad continued to play, cheer, drink, and suck at his cigar. I hoped he's wasn't going to burst a blood vessel, though a part of me wouldn't be surprised, yet another part of me felt guilty for thinking that way. *Am I going to survive this night with this guy?*

The fumes thickened around Dad, hovering like smoke from a Boy Scout cookout. I pushed my chair away from the spotlights, hoping to disappear into the darkness between tables. I averted my eyes from players and waitresses as they walked past me. I knew that the man over there was my father, but I didn't recognize the guy. I wanted to pretend I didn't know him.

Is this the way he relaxes and has fun? Though I knew my father could get loud with his friends after a few drinks, I had never seen him this rowdy before.

I closed my eyes to try to calm my nerves and to block out the lights, bells, and people around me. A long twenty minutes later, Dad yelled again. "Harvy, Harvy, come here!" I opened my eyes. From his seat, Dad was looking left and right. I stood and sauntered toward him. "Yes, Dad," I said quietly. I hoped my father's tone would match mine.

It didn't. "Quick! I need some chips," he shouted. "I have to double down on these bets. Give me a few from your pocket."

I looked at him. "But you told me not to give you anything back."

"It's only for these bets." Dad had green and red chips scattered among three betting boxes. He had 20, 10, and 11 showing in his three hands. The dealer showed a small card. "I have to double down on the 10 and 11," he shouted. "I have great cards here, and I have no more cash on me."

I handed him a small fistful of black chips.

He turned back to the table and said, "Now go away and let me play. But don't go far, I might need you." Dad then looked at the dealer and acted as if I were no longer there.

I walked back to where I had been sitting. When I got to my chair, I heard a loud "Hurrah!" behind me as my father won the hands he had been playing. I wished he had lost so we could go back to our hotel. I sat down again, feeling bound to this outrageous fellow I called Dad.

I looked at my watch. We were well into the next day. I closed my eyes again and tried to breathe through the choking smoke and my choke collar.

Fifteen minutes later, my father shouted, "Harvy, Harvy, where are you?"

I went to him again. "What now, Dad?" My voice was irritated.

He motioned toward himself. "I need a few more chips. *Please,* son, give me some."

By now, I was more than annoyed. I pulled out every chip from my pocket and put them on the table in front of my father. Calmly as I could, I said, "Here, Dad, you can have everything back. I'm tired. I'm taking a cab back to the hotel."

He had a surprised look on his face. He tried to stand but was tipsy; he fell back into his seat. His eyes were glassier than before. He stank of his vices. His voice hardly lowered. "What are you doing? Please stay with me." His face, eyebrows raised, was that of a confused child.

I saw the dealer eyeing me, but his face remained blank. He looked at my father. "Sir, would you prefer to pass this hand?"

I looked at the guy. "Can you or someone here make sure my father gets a taxi back to our hotel when he's finished?"

The dealer nodded. He relayed my message to the pit boss as he pointed at my father. The boss nodded too.

I looked at my father, my voice raised and slightly stern. "Sorry, Dad. It's way past midnight. I'm tired, and I've had enough. Play as long as you want, but I'm going back to the hotel."

I turned and walked away from him. He shouted, "Harvy!" several times, but I didn't turn around or look back. I walked across the casino, straight out of the building, down the front steps, and stepped into a cab.

I was both pissed and distraught during the ten-minute ride back to the hotel. *What an idiot my father could be!* But I had never walked out on him before. *Should I go back?* I hoped he would make it back to our hotel safely. *Will he be angry at me?* Might he have another bout of angina or a heart attack? *Will he still love me?*

I gave extra money to the driver as I exited his taxi. "Could you look out for my father back at the casino and bring him back here safely?" I described my father and his attire, and I gave his name. The bulky black Bahamian said he would try to keep an eye out when he got back to the casino.

I sat in the hotel lobby for fifteen minutes, wondering if I should grab another cab and return to the casino. If I did go back, would Dad and I pass each other in separate cars?

I stood and headed for our room. *Screw it! I'm not chasing after the bum!* He hadn't been my kind of father this night, just a stinking drunk playing with his filthy money.

Before I left the lobby, I asked the front desk person if he could watch for a short, heavyset guy wearing white pants and a red jacket. "He's drunk a bit too much," I offered. "If he's in any distress, you can call me in our room, and I'll come and get him."

Little expression showed on the dark man's face. "No problem, Mr. Simkovits. I'll make sure your father gets to your room."

I went to our room, got undressed, and went to bed, but I couldn't quiet my mind. I looked at my watch. It was over 45 minutes since I had left my father's side. I worried he might not make it back in one piece. Might he have another attack? Might he get robbed as a defenseless drunk? I thought about getting dressed and going to find him. But he might worry when he didn't see me in our room if he got here before I returned.

I lay awake. My eyes scanned the darkness for a sign.

More than an hour after I had left him at the casino, I heard the room door unlock. I feigned sleep and kept my back to the door. I could tell it was Dad by the way he lumbered around. He stayed quiet, turned on only the bathroom light, brushed his teeth, and lay down on his bed. I could only relax after I had heard his breathing deeply as he lay on top of the covers.

I woke early the next morning to my father's violent snores, like cracking thunderbolts. My eyes burned from tiredness; my lungs ached from smoke; my chest was heavy from having left Dad. *Shit! Am I still here?*

I couldn't get back to sleep. I got up, sat on the edge of my bed, and rubbed my eyes. I looked around the room. Through the thin light, I noticed a large stack of $100 bills on the dresser. *Dad's winnings?* At least there was something positive about our first night at the casino. I didn't dare touch his take.

I got up, put on my shorts quietly, and opened the sliding glass doors that led to the patio of our ground-floor room. I stepped outside and sat in a chair. Dad continued to snore like a hyena.

Leaving the sliding door slightly open, I sat and waited on the patio. It was a warm but cloudy day. I tried to read a magazine. I squeezed my eyes shut to try to get the tiredness out of them.

I couldn't get my mind off the previous night's events. My throat was parched, and I had a hard time swallowing. *What mood will my father be in when he wakes up?* Will he be irate? Would he cut our vacation short and have us take the next plane home? Will he disown me for having left him?

I focused on the ocean in the distance. The way my father had acted in the casino—more like a big kid than a grown man—had infuriated me. He had treated me as his goddamned servant, but I feared his ire even more than I respected my own. I dared not move from where I sat. I didn't want to abandon my father again.

After what seemed like forever, I heard my father's snoring suddenly stop. The bed creaked. "Harvy, are you here, son?"

A dry lump buried itself in my throat. My voice was meek. "I'm out here, Dad." The words cracked as they came out of my mouth.

Dad put on shorts and stepped out onto the patio. He rubbed the sleep from his eyes with his palms.

I could hardly look at him. My eyes stayed glued to the ground a few meters in front of me. Out of the corner of my eye, I could see his hair was sticking up and to one side. He pushed it down on his head and into place. He sat next to me and spoke softly, "Are you okay, son?" He was sober.

My body felt frozen. My jaw muscles were tight and sore as if they had clenched and gnawed on a casino chip all night. I couldn't say a thing. I nodded my head slightly, but I wasn't okay. I felt horrible.

I felt ashamed for abandoning my father when he counted on me. I was enraged by his treating me like a frigging employee. I was angry at myself for coming on this stupid vacation. I wanted to run into the ocean and be eaten by sharks. I sought an island hole to bury myself in limestone. I wished to hang myself like a coconut on a palm tree.

"I came home with over $2000 last night," he offered. Maybe he thought I would feel better knowing his success, or perhaps he was trying to rub it in. I felt his stare. "I don't understand why you left me," he said.

I looked away and stuttered. "Sorry, Dad, but I had had enough for one night." I couldn't say more. My throat was closing, and I could barely breathe. My eyes turned wet.

"What's bothering you, son?" His voice was gentle.

It was one of the few times I could remember my father seriously and sincerely asking me about how I felt. Could I tell him I hated his incessant drinking and smoking, and his lurid shouting? Could I say I resented being his casino pack dog, hauling his winnings and answering his call? Could I go further and tell him I loathed his hitting my mother and leaving her high and dry, screaming at his company staff, and prancing around with other women at his precious Troika. Could I tell him I despised his hiding money in Cayman and thumbing his nose at the Canadian taxman, and, especially, for what he wanted me to become—just like him, with an "I wish I had the opportunities you have, son," tacked on. I couldn't find words or the courage to speak.

I sat stiff as my father's question echoed in my head. I wanted to run away as far as I could, but I didn't dare bolt from my father's side once more. I looked toward the Caribbean horizon and held in my tears as best as I could. I shook my head and said nothing.

My father sat in place for what seemed like an eternity, also saying nothing.

My paralysis held me fast. On the one hand, I loathed becoming like an RCA Nipper dog, my father's prized mascot at his master's heel. On the other hand, I sat petrified in losing my privileged position as my father's favoured son and the worthy heir to his fortunes. Though he told my brother and me that he loved us and would never abandon us, he had said the very same to our mother. She no longer had any place in his life, tossed aside as if she had been an at-will employee.

My voice got small as my throat constricted. I felt pulled by two polarized poles—finding a future far away from my family while keeping a close connection with my father and his fortunes. Though Dad's perpetual deception of the government weighed on my conscience, I still wanted to be first in line to his hidden legacy. I felt unclean for craving my father's stash, but I consoled myself by thinking I'd do something beneficial with that money other than hoard it in an offshore haven.

I needed to survive long enough to be bestowed those sums. I didn't want to become crushed by either giving in to Dad's desires for me or by my longing to be different from him. I wondered how much of my sanity and soul I was ready to sell.

Dad looked again at me. "Did it bother you how I acted last night?"

All I could do was nod my head and stare into the distance.

Dad didn't pry further into my discomfort. He put his hand on my arm, and I dared not recoil from his touch. "Okay, son; let's go for breakfast. It's late; I bet you're hungry."

I nodded again. I wiped a tear from my cheek and uttered a muted "Okay."

"Let's get dressed and go," he added matter-of-factly. "We can talk over breakfast about what we want to do today."

Dad had sensed my deep discomfort about his ways of having fun, but I was grateful he didn't pry into my distress. For the remainder of our week together, Dad cut back on his rowdy drinking. We spent his casino winnings on steak and seafood suppers, a second shopping trip to the International Bazaar, another Princess Casino show, a couple of evenings of more muted gambling, and one deep-sea fishing excursion.

For the fishing trip, Dad hired a guy right off the dock to boat us a few kilometers offshore to the island's reef. Out there, the guide's small boat heaved and pitched in the Caribbean waves. The pungent smell of the live bait made both of us sick to our stomachs. We chucked our breakfasts into the ocean—to feed the fish instead of catching them. We cut the outing short and didn't attempt another.

Later in the week, while Dad and I lounged by the ocean, a couple of girls my age appeared at the other end of the sand. Dad looked down the shoreline. "Hey, Harvy; let's throw a football."

Having nothing better to do, I said, "Okay, Dad."

I kept my back to the young women as Dad and I tossed the ball back and forth. After a few tosses, he heaved the ball further down the shore, toward the girls now splashing in the water. Dad chuckled as he lofted the ball as far as he could down the sand and into the sea. I retrieved it, walked back a few paces toward my father, and threw it back to him. He then smiled and heaved it past me once more.

I knew what my father was trying to do, but I didn't latch onto his bait. I avoided looking at the women or talking with them. What was I going to say? "I'm here in Freeport to grown-up sit my father," or "Hey, come and see my dad smoke, drink, and gamble," or "Guess what we did on a fishing boat the other day."

After a few more of my father's football lunges, I grabbed the ball, strode back to my chair, placed the ball on the sand, and buried my head in a book. Dad said nothing as he came back to sit next to me. I prayed that he didn't think I was gay.

When Dad and I returned to the Princess Casino blackjack tables, he kept his drinking in check, and his "hurrahs" more muted, though he continued to smoke as if his cigarettes were candy. After sitting awhile at one table, he spoke in a soft tone, "So what bothered you the other night when we were here?"

I knew I had to offer something. I glanced at my father, took a breath, and said, "I guess you weren't acting like the father I was hoping for."

Dad looked down at his chips, nodded his head a bit, and said, "Okay, son."

Neither he nor I said another word about it.

Dad didn't take in another chip haul that week. We exhausted his first night's winnings. I wondered if I now cramped his style, not letting him be the man (or big kid) he enjoyed being.

Somehow, Dad was good at putting uncomfortable pasts behind him. He never mentioned our upsetting casino night again, even after we had returned to Montreal.

As time passed, I wondered what kind of drug my father was pushing that kept me bound to his side. Whatever it was, it felt as if I couldn't cut myself off.

Months earlier, during a session with Moe, my therapist had told me, "Be patient, Harvy. Time is on your side regarding your father's business."

Though Moe and I had been speaking about my having a growing impact on my father's company, his statement could have applied to all my father's fortunes.

I was relieved to get home after seven long days and nights of being by my father's side. I worked to bury what had happened between him and me.

When Moe later asked me how our holiday trip went, I said, "Fine," and left it there.

Some days later, I came across my $1 Princess Casino good luck chip. I pulled it out of a sock drawer and stared at it for a few seconds. I walked out of my apartment, went down the hallway, opened the garbage chute, and tossed the coin into the darkness.

It turned out our Bahamian holiday would be Dad's and my last vacation with just-the-two-of-us. He never asked me again—and neither did I ever ask him—to go on another father-son trip.

* * * *

Cash-Ins and Cash Outs

Starting in the early 1980s, Dad flew with Elaine to Cayman for a two-week holiday. For those stints, Steve or I held the JHS fort, though Dad called in every second day to see what was going on in the office and factory.

Every time Dad returned home from his trips south, he sported a dark tan and bragged about his casino winnings—he never mentioned any losses.

One time, when I was again with him in his private office, he looked at me like a car salesman who had had a great year. "Cayman is booming, son! There is a lot of real estate development going on there." He grinned. "A lot of American businessmen are taking advantage of the tax-free gains."

Though no one was within earshot, he lowered his voice. "I bought a property with the money I have over there." He pointed southward.

I pointed south too and asked coolly, "How much does Elaine know about that money?"

His intense eyes looked at me as if I were a naive kid. "She knows nothing, son."

His face relaxed as he pawed his hand at me. "You don't need to worry about Elaine." He nodded in the direction of his island paradise. "She thinks my money over there comes from here; and that I keep a bank account there only for convenience. She doesn't know anything more. Only you and I and my accountant know about what I have hidden there."

Dad looked down at his desk and then up at me. "You know, Harvy, you and Stevie come first for me. My money is mine, and Elaine has assets of her own. If something happens to me, then between Stevie and you, you know where my assets are." He pointed to the floor. "Both of you know about the money we have here in JHS." He pointed my way. "And you know about the funds I have down there."

I nodded. Since the time I had rejoined JHS, Dad had permitted Steve and me to participate in the accountant's end-of-year-review of the company's financial statements. Both of us also knew the manager at JHS's bank. Dad, Steve, and I sat on a legitimate multi-million dollar business, separate from his illicit holdings in Cayman.

Though I didn't know how much Dad had stashed "over there," I knew where Dad hid his precious Cayman business cards—in the top drawer of his back-office desk. They were critical Cayman contacts I'd need for the day my father would no longer be with us. As far as I knew, my brother knew nothing about those connections.

"What about Elaine's house, Dad? I know you spent a lot of money there." Dad had done additions and many upgrades to Elaine's Pointe-Claire property.

Dad responded without hesitation. "She and I have an agreement. She will pay me back my investment when she sells the house." His tone was calm and quiet. "I've kept track. I've put $50,000 into her home, and I trust her for that amount. Her property will appreciate a lot more because of what I've done there. "

He raised his hand, palm toward me. "The only cash I give Elaine is a monthly salary for household expenses. She's not the kind of person to take advantage."

I was surprised yet encouraged by my father's openness with me. I hoped he was right about Elaine not wanting much more from him than what he had said.

Whether or not I was making a fully conscious choice, I worked to stay invested in my relationship with Dad. Two or three times each month, I joined him and Elaine for restaurant suppers or dinners at their home. (I also went to see my mother every week to keep the parental scales balanced.) Because my father continued to be kind to me, by his company paying for my graduate studies, I wanted to be kind to him.

I said little to dissuade my father regarding his Cayman stash. I had heard his offshore money defense many times: "In '48, the Czechoslovak Soviets took everything I had. Our Quebec separatist government could do the same here. I don't want to put myself in such a position ever again."

There was no use arguing with my father about his hiding and hoarding of money. I offered my silence and tacit acceptance, for I desired his love and the possibility of being first in line to his offshore legacy. That father-son agreement was never signed and sealed, but it was a belief I held onto.

I could only hope I was playing my cards right for now. But there was never an absolute certainty with Dad.

My offshore gamble weighed on me, generating stomach aches and sleepless nights, but my perpetual silence to his outrageousness was the only gaming option I saw. Part of me felt as if Dad owed me that money for what I had to endure with him. I felt repulsed by what I was doing, but I never told my father to take his offshore cash and go to heaven or hell with it.

I had no idea what my future with Dad's money might look like, especially how I might clean up its illicitness after he was gone. Or would I, by then, be in so deep that I might have to perpetuate his government deception?

Though I was agnostic, I asked the God I knew for his ultimate forgiveness for the sins I might be amassing. I hoped I could make it up to Him a little later in my life.

* * *

During my father's Cayman years, I met several of his island friends when they visited him and Elaine in Montreal. They came to Canada only in the summer, for those sun-, surf-, and sand-worshipers wouldn't set foot in our cold country at any other time.

I met these Cayman guys at Dad and Elaine's home during a weekend barbeque, at the Troika during some of my father's Thursday night gatherings, or at Dad's office where they came to talk business.

One Cayman Yankee, Larry Younger, was a skin-and-bones thin, deeply suntanned, Hawaiian-shirted guy with a made-in-Las-Vegas smile. He must have worn over a troy pound of gold jewellery around his neck and on his wrist and fingers, topped off by an expensive Rolex watch.

Dad told me privately, "I met Larry through my Cayman lawyer, the one who had set up CANEX for me. Larry's a real estate agent." He smiled. "He finds me nice condos to rent on the beach every time Elaine and I go down there."

Larry came only once to visit my father in Montreal. While I was hanging around Dad's office late one afternoon, Larry sauntered up to me and said, "Let me tell you, Harvy! There are money-making opportunities around every corner in Cayman. Son, you need to come down there and see for yourself." He was grinning from sideburn to sideburn. "There's a boom going on, and you don't want to miss it."

Larry put his hand on my shoulder. "Cayman's a great place to live too. It's an absolute paradise, not overbuilt like a lot of other islands in the Caribbean." He winked. "Sonny boy; there's a lot of fish to catch in the sea where we are, including many pretty ones on our silky, sandy beaches."

From my angle, Larry was a sand blowing, used beach salesman who liked to chase other peoples' wallets. I wondered why my father, who limited and tastefully wore his gold props, couldn't look past Larry's jewellery-laden physique and overly bronzed body and see his sun-weathered shallowness.

Though Larry was energetic, and his pole-thin physique and toothy grin perhaps attractive to some, I only smiled and nodded at his pompous advances. I didn't engage him in a conversation about his fish-laden (maybe fishy too) Cayman paradise.

I never saw Larry again in Montreal, which was a great relief.

During one Cayman vacation, while tanning with Elaine on the beach, my father unexpectedly overheard a man speaking Slovak to his family. Dad approached the guy and introduced himself. Though it turned out that the man, Juan, had been born and raised in Mexico, Juan's father, a Jew, had emigrated from Czechoslovakia to Mexico before WWII.

Juan and my dad became instant friends. In the following year, Dad and Elaine traveled to Mexico City for the bar mitzvah of Juan's eldest son. The next summer, Juan and his family came to Montreal for a month-long summer holiday.

When Juan and his family came to Montreal, my father introduced me to a beefy friend and his bulky spouse and kids. Dad later told me privately, "Juan always buys a row of three seats on an airplane so that he and his wife can sit side by side."

In Montreal, the two couples exchanged lavish gifts. Juan gave silk ties, alpaca shawls, and Mexican tequila to Dad and Elaine. Dad offered Quebec maple syrup, Oka cheese (made by Quebec Roman Catholic monks), and Slivovica plumb brandy to their Mexican friends. Dad and Elaine toured Juan's family around the city to see the sights and to taste the food of every ethnicity. On weekends, they took excursions to Quebec and New York State's countryside. From what I could tell, they laughed, drank, and had a fun time together.

Like my father, Elaine was an excellent host. She said she had run a country inn in Vermont before getting into the commercial real estate business. An avid reader of home design, food, and glamour magazines, Elaine had a knack for choosing suitable gifts, decorating a room tastefully, and cooking delicious meals. She served her dishes with little accents—not only putting a variety of fruit into her breakfast pancakes and muffins but also adding extra berries on the side for a bit of flair.

I imagined Dad and Elaine's days and nights filled to the brim by hosting Juan and his crew. Though the two of them gave Juan and his family big airport hugs and kisses when they departed back to Mexico, they seemed exhausted and relieved when those appetites were on the plane home.

141

A week later, over supper at an Italian restaurant near Elaine's home, my father told Elaine and me about a money conversation he had had with Juan. This conversation was the first time that Dad included me in such financial discussions. I felt honoured to be a part of it.

Dad offered, "Juan wants money from me. What do you think I should do?" He looked down at the drink in his hand. It was not clear as to whom Dad was addressing his question, Elaine or me. He added, "The guy's family needs money to help out their business in Mexico."

"What does he specifically want?" I asked while I glanced at Elaine.

Unlike my mother, Dad's mistress had a sound mind for business. She also had a good way with people. In her youth, as the only daughter of an entrepreneurial father, Elaine had been a tomboy. In her early adulthood, she became a professional drag race car driver. She could handle herself well in any male milieu. Her wide smile, hearty laugh, and dark eyes could set any person at ease.

She also knew how to smooth out my father's rough edges, get sensitive conversations going, or patch a problem if he blew a fuse. She even knew that my father might promise more than he could or would deliver.

Elaine spoke right after me, her voice terse. "What have you promised him, Johnny?"

Dad fidgeted in his seat. He didn't look directly at Elaine or me. "He's asking for between a quarter and half million U.S." He looked at us. "Should I do it?"

I had no idea how much total cash my father had stashed offshore, and I didn't think Elaine knew about Dad's hidden money in Cayman. I offered shyly, "That's a lot of money, Dad. What's it for, and what kind of return will he be giving you?"

Dad obliged. "Juan tells me that he and his brothers want to expand their manufacturing operation in Mexico City. He is offering 15% interest each year for three or four years, after which he will return the capital."

Whether Elaine knew it or not, I expected Juan's 15% payments would be in cash, which my father could pocket offshore. I said nothing more for now and looked at Elaine.

"Johnny," Elaine said, her finger pointing at him. "That's just what *he* told *you* about his business." She pointed to herself. "I heard other things from his wife." She raised her finger further. "I suspect the family's operation down there is in trouble, and they are looking for an investor to bail them out."

Elaine's tone became resolute. "We hardly know these people. Yes, they were good to us in Mexico, but we know nothing about their business and family. And I'm not sure how good his relationships are with his brothers."

"They have a sibling partnership," Dad responded. "From what he told me, their business has been a going concern for decades."

"What have you told him so far?" I said, repeating Elaine's question that my father seemed to be skirting.

Dad raised his voice. "I told him nothing. I said I'd think about it."

I had an inkling my big shot father may have said more. I had heard him tell business colleagues and personal friends, "If you need any help, come and see me." He was never specific about what kind of support he could provide—moral or financial—which left the door open for interpretation.

"What kind of recourse would you have if Juan reneged on paying you back?" I asked.

"That's a good question, son," he said.

I wondered why my father would be careless with his cash with an unknown quantity like Juan. If the man's business was, in any way, bloated like him and his family, then Dad's money could be at risk. I had known my father to ask for hard collateral from any Montreal colleague who asked him for a loan. Juan's friendship might have been the Mexican's way to get my father to drop his money defenses.

Elaine saw an opening. "Johnny, you won't be able to do anything if the guy doesn't give you your money back. Will you go down to Mexico and sue him?"

Her voice was calm but serious. "And you don't know if Juan or his kin are into any of those Mexican cartels." She raised a hand. "Don't you remember when we met his kid brothers in Mexico? They looked like muscle men for the mafia."

Her voice turned stern, like a Mother Superior speaking to an unruly child. "It's too dangerous to get yourself involved in a business where you have no control and in a country that you know little about."

I was impressed with the way she protected my father from himself. "I think Elaine's right, Dad," I said. It concerned me that my father might be careless with our financial future. "And, if they're good friends, won't they understand if you say no to their request?" I added.

Dad took another sip of his vodka. "Okay, okay; I'll call him. I'll say I have my money tied up elsewhere."

I sighed relief and knew not to say another word. Elaine, too, added nothing more. I was glad she and I had joined forces to keep Dad away from questionable characters and a lousy money deal.

A couple of days later, Dad broke the news to Juan as planned. I then heard from Dad that Juan stopped calling him, and his wife no longer returned Elaine's calls or letters. The two couples never saw or talked to each other again.

Throughout his Cayman years, Dad made several fair-weather island friendships. They seemed to end as quickly as they had begun.

* * *

On another end-of-day in the office, over a cup of coffee, Dad told me, "Elaine's a smart lady. She's helped me a lot with my investments down there."

"Yes, Dad, I know," I offered, referring to Elaine's smarts.

I continued to wonder how much Elaine knew about my father skirting Canadian income taxes on his Cayman dealings, but I never asked her about it. If she didn't know, then I didn't want to be the one to divulge to her what I did know. If she did know, I didn't want her to know that I also knew. That Johnny Simkovits double-bind had me keep my mouth shut.

Elaine's value became Cayman sky clear after my father had put $300,000USD into a Texas land development project with a guy named Stew McDuff—a property developer. Dad said that Stew was the offspring of a wealthy Cayman American family who owned much property there. He lent Stew the $300,000 for two years at 15% interest, payable in cash.

From what I understood, there was no cloak-and-dagger transfer of a suitcase of money in such deals. In Cayman, a bank draft was enough. Maybe Dad saw this McDuff deal as a way to become connected to a bigwig family on the island.

When the two-year money term was coming close to its end, Dad, Elaine, and I were again having supper at the Italian restaurant near her West Island home. Chewing on his osso buco, my father declared, "Stew wants another year with my money for his Texas project." There was a slight hesitation in his voice. "He says it's not yet ripe for me to get my money out at the end of our original two-year term."

The three of us talked back and forth for thirty minutes about whether my father could trust Stew on getting his money back after the loan extension. Dad was worried Stew was going to stretch the repayment out further or renege on it. While Dad's voice rose in frustration to Elaine's questions about the deal, her tone remained steady and calm.

Because we talked over thirty minutes about the situation's ins and outs, I sensed that Stew could be another shady Cayman character. Perhaps Dad had detected something fishy about that man or his project. I eventually looked at my father and asked, "How did you decide to get involved in this arrangement?"

He obliged. "Stew came highly recommended by Larry Younger, the real estate fellow who came here a couple of summers ago."

Oh, that fast-talking, gold-hauling guy?

Now I became worried. I wondered if my father was losing his senses by getting in deep with superficial Cayman socialites. I was at a loss as to what Dad should do to get his money out safely.

Elaine's face looked pensive. After a moment, she picked up her wine glass and spoke calmly. "Johnny, what if you tell Stew you'd be interested in doing other projects with him once you get your money out of his current development."

Dad and I looked at her. Her eyes shifted left and right as she spoke. "If he thinks you're a bigger fish to fry, he wouldn't dare renege on your current loan agreement. He wouldn't risk losing your good graces if he could get you deeper into another deal the next time."

I was impressed by Elaine's strategy. Dad immediately nodded and said, "Okay."

The very next day, my father called Stew and carried out the charade. The next I heard, Dad got his money back from Stew by the original deadline, including the two years of loan interest.

A month later, as predicted by Elaine, Stew came calling with another investment opportunity concerning a Tennessee coal mine. Dad initially showed interest, asking for more documentation on the project. He later backed out, saying that his money was committed elsewhere. Stew continued to call, but Dad said he rebuffed Stew's requests for more funding. My Dad and his shrewd mate had outsmarted a Cayman fox.

As with Dad's Mexican friend, Juan, I never heard my father mention Stew's name again.

* * *

Over the years, Dad said he came out ahead in his Cayman property and money-lending deals. Unlike with Dad's gambling losses, Elaine never mentioned anything to the contrary, so I trusted my father's reporting.

One night, after coming home from one supper discussion, I couldn't get to sleep. I worried if my father might find himself one day in a financial gutter if he continued his fly-by-money Cayman Island friendships. Was he being an intelligent investor or an addicted gambler looking for the next big score?

Though I was intrigued by Dad's Cayman cash-ins and cash-outs, I wondered if I could follow in his offshore finagling footsteps. The only star my father seemed to pursue was one that had a dollar sign written on it. He seemed to have no other purpose than to pack his pockets with offshore money chips. In my mind, I asked again why he wanted to stash money over there. In my head, he responded, *To build a cushion that the government can't grab from me.*

As I drifted off to sleep, I felt there was little I could do to change my father's ways. I couldn't be disloyal and sell him out to Revenue Canada. If I confronted him about his deceptions and distanced myself from his manipulations, as my brother had done, then I'd risk losing my connection to him and his growing fortune. His offshore money-making and tax skirting captivated me, but I was also worried about it. Dad had no qualms about what he was doing. *Could I ever pull off what he does? Could I live by his sly and scheming ways? Did I even want to?*

The next morning, I woke up thinking about Steve. I loathed the thought of being like my overly virtuous brother. He relinquished even legitimate tax deductions on his income taxes if he didn't like the way they smelled. The previous April, during tax season, Dad had said to Steve, "Why are you feeding the government? Just go ahead and take that personal deduction off your income!"

I didn't remember what the specific deduction was, but my brother responded, "I don't feel right about it."

Dad came back, "Everybody takes these deductions. Even the accountant would tell you to do it. So why can't you?"

In my mind, I agreed with my father, but Steve saw it differently. His voice became terse, and his face turned tight as he looked at Dad. "I don't like doing what you do!"

Dad threw up his hand and turned away. "Then do what you want, but you are a goddamn fool." I understood our dad's ire. By not taking legitimate tax deductions, Steve handed right back to the government a portion of the tax savings that Dad's company was gaining by giving Steve an annual income and bonus.

As I jumped into the shower, I wondered which Simkovits was the most damned. Was it my father who skirted tax law at every chance, or my overly righteous brother who dishonoured his forbearer at every opportunity? Perhaps it was me for having turned against my brother (and mother) to stay loyal to Dad. I felt I would fall into an eternal abyss if I leaned too far toward either my father's unfazed illicit money ways or my brother's staunch ethical purist course. I wondered what I feared most: to be cast aside by my father or cast out of my conscience.

Over cold breakfast cereal, I pulled out an AU/NTL course textbook, but my mind couldn't focus. Being an insider in my father's offshore affairs was too enticing. Leaning in my brother's direction gave me little confidence in my financial future. I had worked too long to gain my father's trust and to keep his secrets.

I banged my fist on the table. I hoped I wouldn't have to contort myself on the tightrope I was walking. I didn't want to lose my balance and fall to my ruin.

I took a long breath. I consoled myself by considering I would one day stop playing Dad's tax-cheating money game, reconcile his dubious dealings as best I could, and do better than earn tax-free income from his hidden hoard.

I shook my head and tried to concentrate on my textbook, but I couldn't. I hoped I wouldn't get drawn too deeply into Dad's skirting ways. I wanted to keep my hands relatively clean, not have to become more like my father to outlast him. How far would I have to go to show my loyalty and worthiness to him without losing myself?

I thought of Moe. He had talked about our working to bolster my self-esteem. Perhaps I lacked the self-confidence to make something of myself without my father. I felt I had to do what was necessary to steer my father's fortunes eventually into legal waters. I also hoped that my new career course, and Moe's mentorship, would help me find some greater good to work toward and to achieve some personal solace.

I clasped my hands together tightly as I looked down into my book, trying to block out my preoccupation. I prayed I could manage the costs of what I was doing.

* * *

Soon after Dad got his money out of the McDuff development deal, his Cayman mood shifted. Over fettuccini alfredo at our regular gathering place for supper, he sounded off to Elaine and me.

"Excuse my French," he said, "but Cayman is too fucking expensive. Everything there is double the price." His face tightened as he raised his voice. "And it's hard to get there from Montreal—we have to fly through Miami, or Texas, or Timbuktu. I'm getting sick of going there."

Though I agreed with my father's enlightened view, I didn't say a word. I didn't want his feeling overly influenced by me concerning an offshore move. I didn't want to sound like a scared animal running away from a fox's paradise. "Whatever you think best, Dad," I offered.

Elaine spoke right behind me. "I'm with you, Johnny." I was surprised by her quick agreement. She grabbed her glass of wine, took a sip, and added nothing more.

Perhaps Elaine had dropped handkerchiefs with Dad about getting out of Cayman and finding safer moneymaking and friend-creating hunting grounds. I wondered if the McDuff clan there had put out a "do not deal with Johnny Simkovits" mark on my father after he backed out of Stew's coal mine deal.

Maybe Dad felt he had had a good run in Cayman. Perhaps it was time to take his chips off the island's gaming table and walk away with his winnings. No matter, I was glad both Dad and Elaine were becoming tired of the likes of people like Larry, Juan, and Stew.

Decades later, after Dad's death, Elaine told me more about their decision to leave Cayman. She offered, "In Cayman, your father bought an oceanfront lot and hired an architect—someone he found through Larry—to create plans to build a house."

Her voice elevated. "I couldn't believe it! What was Johnny thinking?" She pointed. "It was going to cost that man a fortune to build there since everything had to be imported (concrete blocks, lumber, furniture, etc.)." She huffed. "And what did we need a house for on an island that's only fourteen miles in circumference?"

Her eyes glared into that sandy past. "Your father knew how opposed I was to the idea of building in Cayman." She took a breath. "A month later Johnny got a call from Larry saying he had found a customer to buy the lot. Johnny then called me, and I right away said, 'Sell it!'"

She took a second to compose herself. "Six months later, the bottom fell out of the Cayman real estate market. Your father would have lost $200,000 U.S.!"

As far as I knew, Elaine never knew how much the Cayman Islands had been a money-hiding, tax-avoiding haven for Dad, or maybe she did know but wasn't saying.

Though I wondered, I never asked her about what she had and hadn't gathered about my father's Cayman money mischief. I was glad that Dad's days there were over, and he had gotten out ahead in that island's money betting and cash hiding game.

* * * *

Part II:

Looming Horizons and Havens

11

Retirement Planning

One Sunday afternoon back in the spring of 1973, when I was eighteen and Steve nineteen years old, Dad took the three of us for supper to Carlos, his favourite Italian restaurant in the city. It was the middle of our parents' second separation. Steve and I were home from college for spring break.

When Dad finished his fettuccini alfredo, he pushed his plate away and lit a cigarette. My brother and I sat still as he said, "I spent many summers as a kid working on my grandfather's farm." There was a proud look on his face. "It was in a little hill village outside of Košice." He looked at us. "I was just a kid back then."

Steve and I nodded. We were careful not to interrupt our father in the middle of recounting a story. He continued. "When I worked for my grandpa Gabor, he was already a long time retiree from farming." Dad smiled. "Grandpa spent his last three decades on earth tending to his chickens, goats, and cows." He crossed his index fingers. "He crossed pear, apricot, and cherry trees to make new kinds of fruit." Our father's grin widened.

Dad took a swig of his scotch. "I worked for Gabor for many summers. Every morning, he was up before sunrise." He pointed at himself. "Grandpa had me rise with him to milk the cows and feed the chickens." He gestured toward the distance. "Until the sun came up, we had only a gas lantern for light." He pointed his fuming cigarette at Steve and me. "Every

154

day, I had to get up and do what he asked of me. If I would dare say no, he'd right away send me back home to my father."

Dad took a puff and chuckled. "Every night, before he went to bed, my grandpa took a shot of Slivovica." He smiled wide. "That strong plum brandy kept him alive well into his nineties." He winked. "He buried three wives, you know."

There was certainty in Dad's voice, as if Slivovica were not only a life-extending elixir but also a remedy for surviving any marriage.

Dad looked down at the table as he put his hands in his lap. The cigarette continued to burn between his fingers. "When I was 28 years old, a few years after the war, Gabor passed away in his sleep. His housekeeper found him the next morning." Dad took a deep breath. "He had died peacefully in his bed. He was 94 years old."

My father looked at Steve and me; a soft expression was in his eyes. "That's the way I'd want to go when it's my time."

At this early stage of my life, my father being merely 53 years old, it was hard for me to fathom that he would ever die.

* * *

A decade later, after Dad had turned 63 in early 1983, he told us more about his retirement plans.

At 28 years old, I was in the midst of my graduate studies at American University. After he had returned from Israel, Steve was again working for Dad. Every month or so, the three of us met at JHS. It was our way to stay in touch with essential matters regarding Dad and the company.

After Dad had once more proclaimed "Business stinks!" he looked at Steve and me. He spoke calmly. "Elaine and I have decided to sell her West Island house."

I was a little surprised. Dad had moved in with Elaine two-and-a-half years earlier. He had spent a wad of money to renovate her home, building a garage, installing a swimming pool, and replicating the Troika in her basement. After that much investment, I couldn't understand why they were leaving their upgraded abode.

Steve and I said nothing as Dad continued. He smiled. "Elaine and I will be moving into two places. One is an apartment in the Snowdon area of Montreal, just south from here. From there, I could easily drive to JHS or go downtown with Elaine to meet our friends."

"Okay," I said, waiting for the other shoe.

Dad's grin grew. "The other place is a house in Peru, NY, on the shore of Lake Champlain. It's eight kilometers south of Plattsburgh, about an hour's drive from our new apartment." Dad gestured toward the distance. "Elaine and I will spend long weekends and holidays there when we aren't travelling."

"Why there?" my brother asked.

Dad's eyes widened as he looked at Steve. "I want to retire there eventually. I want to enjoy the rest of my life, living in the countryside as my grandfather did for thirty years."

"How did you find the place?" I asked.

"Elaine has a good nose," he offered. "She found the property, and I bought it." He looked back and forth between Steve and me. "I hope you guys will come down there often to visit us."

Dad never consulted his kids before he made any big moves. We both said, "Sure, Dad," but our enthusiasm didn't quite match his.

* * *

Some months later, I had my first chance to see Dad's new lakeside home. Until then, it had been under renovation, with Dad and Elaine spending extended weekends managing the reconstruction. They didn't want any friends or family distracting them until they were ready to display their new digs.

On a Saturday in late spring, I drove to Peru, NY, for the first time. I told Dad I couldn't stay overnight because of schoolwork I had to complete. It seemed better not to stay over, considering the bind I felt regarding my mother.

Nearly three years into their separation, Dad and Mom still hadn't settled their divorce. I wanted to avoid her incessant interrogations whenever she got a whiff of my visits with my father and Elaine. Though I never lied to Mom, I worked to keep my visits chez Dad short and unknown to her. I couldn't tell who I was protecting more, her or me.

I drove down I-87 south of the Canadian border on that warm but sunny late-spring day. I turned off the interstate south of Plattsburg and headed for the ragged edge of Lake Champlain. When I reached the shore road, I turned south and followed the lakeshore. Very soon, to my left, was the Peru marina and boat launch my father had mentioned. Across the road, to my right, was the Old Gun & Rod Shop that he had also cited.

I recalled my father telling me he hated guns and that he had never owned one. I was glad of it, yet I wondered why he, a veteran of the Second World War, never possessed one.

That lakeshore gun shop made me wonder what kind of shooting matches might take place between Dad and Elaine over the coming years, as had happened between my parents ever since I could remember. So far, there hadn't been any shots fired or misfired between him and his mistress. I questioned whether my father could live with any woman without eventually sparking verbal rounds, maybe even physical ones, though I hoped he could restrain himself.

Past the gun shop, I saw a double driveway on my left. It came up quickly. In my nervous anticipation, I whizzed by it and had to turn around down the road.

Two pairs of brick pillars, each about 6' high, stood across the entrance and exit driveways to Dad's property. A thick chain hung across the left pair of posts, blocking the exit. A similar chain lay on the ground between the right driveway columns. *I guess that's where I'm supposed to turn in.*

I drove down a new asphalt path that was perhaps a meter wider than my car. The driveway went straight for about the length of a soccer field. On my right was a large horse paddock and what looked like a small barn. Beyond the paddock's back fence was a wall of thick spruce trees.

To my left, perhaps ten paces past the parallel exit driveway, were three-meter-high arborvitae tightly packed together. They obscured the view to the neighboring house and the public boat launch I had passed alongside the lakeshore road.

I passed another row of arborvitae placed perpendicular to the driveway. Those bushes partially obscured what lay behind it. The driveway opened to a large asphalt parking lot surrounded by massive maple and oak trees. Parked there was Dad's fiery red Mercedes sports coupe. Past the car was what I had been waiting to see: Dad's big stone house. *Wow! Dad got fancy in his older age.*

My father had already told me what he knew of the house. "It was built fifty years ago by a New York City financier," he had said with a grin. "That man died ten years after finishing the place, and the house then got sold to the founder of the Meyer Pharmacy chain. Meyer lived there for several decades with his family." Dad liked the house having a rich pedigree.

His smile widened. "About a year after old man Meyer died, we learned that the property was for sale. None of his kids could afford the place—they had inheritance taxes to pay on their father's estate."

He raised a hand. "Elaine had known about the house when she worked in the area as a real estate agent. When she saw it was available from Meyer's estate at a good price, she told me to grab it." Dad clenched his fist and grinned again as if he had reeled in a big tuna.

I admired my father for finding good deals. Upon first sight, the house took my breath away.

I climbed out of my car and took a closer look. I noticed the intricate granite stonework of the house's exterior walls. No stone was the same size or shape, the pieces having been cut in different rectangular sizes and fitted together like a jigsaw puzzle. The outside face of each stone was chiseled to give it a three-dimensional look.

Each of the house's windows contained twenty small panes of glass held together with lead trim. Windows were ganged together in groups of four, allowing lots of light to enter and providing good views of the outdoor. I looked upward to see a steep roofline that held the second story, with gangs of windows inlaid into the roof. *This is quite the retirement home!* The house was vastly different from the split-level house on a postage-stamp lot in which I had grown up. *Would I get used to Dad's new life here?*

Dad had witnessed my arrival. He came outside through a side door and trotted toward me with his hand held up in greeting. "Hi, sweetheart; glad you could make it!" He offered a wide grin, grabbed my upper arms, and kissed me on both cheeks. "How was the drive down? Any problems at the border? Were my directions okay?"

"Yes, Dad; I got here in less than sixty minutes from Champlain Bridge, just as you had told me." I pointed toward the road. "But I missed your entrance past the gun shop. It came up fast on me."

My father poked me in the shoulder. "I should put a big neon sign in the middle of the road for guys like you." He offered another wide grin.

He motioned for me to follow. "Here, I'll show you around before we go inside. Elaine is busy in the kitchen; she's making phone calls and preparing lunch. I don't want to disturb her."

Maybe he wants to show off the place a little.

He gestured toward the barn and paddock behind us. "Look there!"

I saw a two-meter [six-foot] satellite dish mounted on a concrete and metal pedestal. "We installed that dish this week," Dad said. "We can get hundreds of channels from two different satellites." He pointed to the sky to show me where the satellites were situated, and then he looked back at me. "When we go inside, I'll show you the new electronics setup I installed in the den."

Dad's face was jovial. Even after thirty years in the consumer electronics business, he never tired of gadgets. I was pleased that he was happy with his new house toys. When he was happy, everyone else felt good too. He was certainly at the epicenter of this family constellation, though my mother now was way out of his orbit.

"Harvy, let me show you the stable."

"Is that what that little barn is?"

He walked toward the paddock. "It's a small stable yet big enough for two horses. Your brother could bring his horse down from Montreal and ride here. If his horse has a girlfriend, she can come too." He chuckled. "For now, I keep our riding mower in there." He pointed around the property. "I hired a kid who comes every two weeks to cut the grass."

"That's nice," I said. I was glad it wasn't I who had to show up regularly to cut Dad's grass.

I was also skeptical that my brother would cart his horse from the "horsey town" of Hudson, Quebec, to Peru, NY, to ride here. Over the years, Steve's steed had been his escape from Dad's continual shouting at work and Mom's inconsolable crying at home. Steve's bringing his horse here, like my staying overnight or cutting this property's grass, would be tantamount to us fully accepting our father's new life with Elaine. I anticipated that Dad's horse stable would remain a riding-mower shed for the duration.

I was curious and wanted to stay on the topic of my father's new digs. "Dad, how much property do you have here?"

"Six acres," he responded.

He pointed again. "It goes from the road," he gestured toward the main road, and then he turned and pointed past the house, "to about fifteen meters behind the house. And you can see how wide it is, from the arborvitaes that follow the driveway to the trees on the other side of the corral."

"That's pretty big." I eyed the distances and did some quick arithmetic in my head. I figured Dad's six-acre number was two to three times what it was in actuality. I knew his penchant for exaggerating. Not having my brother's tendency to contradict, I nodded and said nothing.

Dad continued. "We're going to change a lot more outside here when we finish our work inside the house. I'm going to plant poplar trees along the driveway and next to the main road." He motioned toward the entrance where

I had entered the property. "In the median between the entry and exit driveways, we'll plant nice maple trees with gardens in between."

He smiled. "That'll be Elaine's project for next year." He was as excited as a horse with a bucket of fresh apples. "She will plant nice flowers and put down some good shit…, oops, I mean fertilizer." He grinned and winked as he covered his mouth with his hand, like a little kid that accidentally swore in front of a parent.

Dad looked far away, well beyond the main road, and said, "In the distance are the Adirondack mountains. In the winter, you could come here to ski."

Dad was well into his sales pitch. He knew I liked to alpine ski, a sport I acquired in high school and had done every winter since. "Lake Placid is only fifty minutes away," he added. "You could even bring your girlfriend." He jabbed his finger again into my upper arm.

I wasn't seeing anyone special at this time, though I did have women friends. I might feel edgy in bringing any of them to my father's new extravagant home.

My mother still wore her wedding band, but my father didn't. The thought of my parents' unsettled divorce would ruin my appetite no matter how much of a good time I might have chez Dad. I had to give myself time to get used to this fancy place. I looked at my father and borrowed a standard line from my brother. "We'll see, Dad."

Over the coming years, I would impress a couple of girlfriends with Dad's lakeside digs. They felt special here as they lay in the thick lawn grass, lounged by the lake, ate lunch on the patio, or had Sunday brunch in the dining room with Dad offering mimosas. I felt a bit lascivious in leveraging the largess of Dad's new layout to delight and excite my women friends. I was still young, so what the heck!

Dad must have seen a pensive look on my face. "Come on, son; I'll show you the lake." His face was bright. "I have another surprise for you."

We came around to the main entrance of the house that faced the lake. Dad and I stood on a fieldstone landing and looked out over Lake Champlain. I realized that Dad's new home and the surrounding land sat on a plateau. A three- to five-meter cliff dropped to the shore. Gigantic oak and willow trees stretched out over the water, sheltering the house from not only the sun but also the eyes of passing boaters. Though Dad enjoyed being a gregarious party host, he liked his privacy too.

He and I stood on a landing that was at the top of a concrete staircase and iron railing that stepped down to the water. The lake was dark blue; the sun shimmered off the waves. Evergreens and brown hardwoods lined the shoreline into the distance. The trees hadn't come out this early time of year.

There were a few white sailboats on the water, taking advantage of the sunny day and spring wind. I stood next to my father as we looked out together. "This is beautiful, Dad. You can see many kilometers away."

Dad pulled out a cigarette and lit it, using his cupped hand to protect the fast flickering flame expelled from his Dunhill. Maybe the smoke was another reason why he wanted to show me around outside. He smiled as he motioned across the lake. "Directly north is Plattsburg's public beach. It's only 20 minutes away by boat. The water is shallow there, so it's warmer for swimming. We'll go there sometime this summer."

I nodded my understanding as an offshore breeze sent a chill through my body. I could see that my father wanted me to venture into his new world: the large property, stone house, satellite TV, riding corral, lake view, warm beach, younger partner, new life. He never understood that those things weren't as important to me. What I had wished for was to have Dad around more, for his showing interest in my life, and his not shouting or screaming at people, including Mom. My wishes rarely came true.

As an adult, I wanted my father's acceptance and support of my new professional direction. I was moving forward in my career, but Dad's legacy still looked like a carrot at the end of a stick that my father dangled out across this finger lake. I told myself not to rely on Dad's money, but to make my way in my life. I needed to become self-made like him.

I didn't want to stay dependent on my father as my brother continued to be, Steve now having worked at JHS for nearly a decade. My new graduate training would be my ticket to self-sufficiency and freedom from parents. I wanted to make my father proud. I wanted to show him that I was worthy of his promise.

My eyes moved to a large, forested landmass situated about a half-mile offshore, occupying about half of the lake's view. It was a rocky, craggy mass covered in thick forest. "What's that island over there, Dad?"

He offered, "That's Valcour Island. It's about three kilometers long and less than a kilometer wide. It has a few small beaches and many hiking trails." He pointed to a structure on the island. "Other than that red lighthouse facing us, nothing can be built there."

I looked back at the house. "This is a very exclusive place," I offered.

"Now you know why I bought it, son."

I hoped this lakeside plateau would give my father the retirement he sought, similar to the hilltop his grandfather had lived on for thirty years.

Dad looked down at the shoreline as he leaned against the iron railing. "I'm going to put a fifty-foot [fifteen-meter] dock into the lake and buy a motorboat this summer." He turned to me, again smiling ear to ear. "You can come here anytime to water ski. That's my surprise for you."

"That's neat, Dad."

I enjoyed water skiing as much as downhill skiing. Though my father sounded excited about the prospect, I wasn't sure what kind of boat driver he would be. I looked at him with a skeptical eye. "I didn't know you could drive a motorboat, Dad."

"Isn't it like driving a car?" I couldn't tell if he was serious or sarcastic.

"Not quite, Dad. There are no brakes. And I think you need a separate boat licence."

He puffed away. "Elaine was a racing car driver. She knows how to drive a boat if I can't."

Elaine had mentioned that she had been an amateur racer in her late teens, driving Corvettes in quarter-mile drag races in places like Napierville and Mascouche drag ways in Quebec. I wondered what kind of boat driver she might be. Dad winked. "And we have good friends in the area who have waterski boats. They can help us out if we need it."

"Okay, Dad, we'll see." There was my brother's line again. I was glad that we were a few months away from that kind of summer adventure.

I looked out over the lake and then back at the house. I again felt unfamiliar with this lavish lifestyle that Dad was building with Elaine.

His new house was a far contrast to the simpler, suburban life we had had in Dorval. He had spent much money renovating our childhood home when we first moved in, but his work there had been modest compared to the house and life he was building here in Peru. A family weekend event at our home would have been Dad barbequing steaks on a small charcoal grill or Mom serving supper in front of a TV that had only a handful of channels— not a whole satellite dish system as he had here.

When Dad had lived at home with Mom, the biggest thing we did as a family on summer weekends was to drive into the Laurentian Mountains to spend a day lounging by and swimming in a small hotel pool. Dad now had a whole lake for that. I hoped I wouldn't drown from the largesse.

Maybe I was feeling jealous on behalf of my mother. I understood my father was now much older, had more money, and didn't have the impediment of raising two young boys. I still felt a loss for our family.

After Dad had finished our house upgrades in Dorval, he balked at doing more. It later took my mother years of begging and complaining to get a new beige living room carpet when the old brown one wore out. It took more begging for her to get updated furniture when the old couch and chair cushions showed wear and tear.

I wondered if the same would happen between him and Elaine here in Peru. She seemed to be in his grand graces now, maybe even the right woman for him, but only time would tell with Dad. When he'd stop spending, that would be the time to watch for trouble.

I wondered if my father's new home enticements were his way to compensate my brother and me for having left our mother. Or was this his way to lure us into his new life with Elaine? Reading his underlying motives was never easy.

Dad did buy a boat that summer, named Cloud 9. It was an older, 28-foot, cabin cruiser, bought second hand for $25,000. Cloud 9 was big enough to sleep four. Occasionally, it housed a guest or two when Dad's lake house was full.

My father didn't drive that whale of a boat. When I, for the first time, went across the lake with Dad and Elaine, she drove the boat. Her lead-weight hand pushed down hard on the throttle. With her gunning that boat, we made it to Plattsburgh Beach in minutes. I held onto my cap and towel for dear life.

Not able to smoke his cigar during the ride, Dad commented harshly. "Elaine, stop being such a cowboy driver!"

His tone didn't faze her. She kept the throttle out full and acted as if she hadn't heard what her partner had said. The wind blew through her hair, and the smile on her face told me she was enjoying the speed. I noticed that the boat made such a huge wake that water skiing would be dangerous. I'd consider it only if I wanted to take my life into Elaine's hands. It was way too early for that.

I went water skiing only once from Dad's new dock. One of his Plattsburgh friends came over with his proper speedboat. It was fun being lifted out of the water and pulled by a boater who knew what he was doing. After that occasion, the water skiing pressure was off. Neither Dad nor I suggested it again.

Some years after Cloud 9's purchase, Elaine said, "We'll need to sell the boat because it's too big for just me to take out. I need a crew to run it, and your father doesn't want to go out anymore. We'll need to trade it in for an 18-footer that one person can handle."

Oh, oh. I didn't dare ask if my dad was getting seasick from Elaine's speedboat driving.

Within a year, a smaller boat replaced Cloud 9. Elaine still did the driving, and I found excuses for not going out with her and Dad.

Dad turned back toward the parking area. "Before we go inside, son, let me show you a couple more things.

Though I was getting weary of the tour, I nodded and followed.

My father pointed to the part of the house that was next to the driveway. "That was the old garage," he said. "Because the exterior of that space matched the rest of the house, we gutted it and turned it into a family room. You'll see it when we go inside."

"I hand it to you, Dad. You like to keep your head and hands working together." I wanted to be happy for my father's latest and greatest. I also wondered if he yelled at his contractors here the way he did at his JHS employees. "It looks like you've thought of everything."

"That's not all, son." He was exuberant as he continued to point around the property. He told me about constructing a new grassy area in front of the house that "will become a place to play soccer," and new walkways of coloured stones that "will look like a mosaic." He wanted me to get the whole picture, whether I wanted it or not.

My dad was into making big impressions, though my head by now felt as if it had been stamped full like a used passport. He pointed again. "And there, I'll build a stone and granite barbeque pit that will cook enough Delmonico steaks for forty people at one time."

Dad, Elaine, and I are standing on the new stone mosaic walkway that Dad had built. Behind us are Lake Champlain's Valcour Bay and Valcour Island. The dog is Muffie, a Tibetan Terroir, and successor to Orphee, Elaine's former dog. The late-1980s.

Dad was beaming. He pointed to his prospective soccer field. "We'll have outdoor garden parties here, like our Canadian Slovak Professional and

Business Association's summer barbeque. We'll raise a tent for a hundred people, and bring down the musicians from the Troika or Hungarian Club so we can have good gypsy music." He winked at me. "Of course, you and Stevie are invited."

I wasn't the gregarious party person my father was. I preferred smaller gatherings of good friends over big bashes of colleagues and acquaintances. "How will I ever be able to stay away?" I said with a forced smile.

My wife and daughter, standing at the stone barbeque my father had built 27 years earlier. Wood or charcoal fueled it. Dad could cook 40 steaks at once on the grill, and the counter space could hold the wooden plates he used to serve all that beef. c. 2008.

* * *

167

Over the ensuing years, Dad and Elaine would come to host many Slovak Business Association summer barbeques in Peru—complete with a big tent and Troika singers, Sasha and Vladjec.

Once, over eighty ethnic Montrealers descended on the place for Johnny and Elaine's hospitality. They ate their fill of Polish sausage and calf's liver appetizers from a Hungarian *boucherie* in Montreal. Following the appetizers were thick, juicy steaks that came from a local Plattsburgh butcher.

Every man had a drink with the host. The women hovered around Elaine and talked about endless things. Dad kibitzed in Slovak, Hungarian, Polish, Ukrainian, and Russian, though English was his language with me and my brother. There wasn't an Eastern European dialect in which Dad didn't have something funny to say. The Hungarian toast "to your health" transformed into "to your ass;" Russian eggs turned to Ukrainian balls; Polish sausage to "you know what."

A big bar was arranged outside with an array of libations, including Slivovica and other homeland brands. Dad knew what everyone liked to drink; no one ever complained about anything lacking in the liquor department. My father shone in being the center of attention. He wanted everybody to have a good time.

All through the afternoon, Sasha and Vladjec played as they meandered around the tables. They serenaded guests with a broad array of Eastern European melodies. They played popular English pieces too, like "Memories" and "The Way We Were" for the women and the theme song, "Speak Softly Love," from *The Godfather* movie for the men.

The latter song fit Dad's personality of being a godfather to his Montreal Slovak community. Dad did business with or helped find work for many of his cohorts. One long-time Slavic friend approached me and offered, "Harvy, your father is a giant among us."

I felt awkward overhearing the happy hubbub. Though everyone at the party seemed to bask in my father's party glow, I didn't feel as connected to them. I politely smiled and laughed, but didn't feel the countryman kinship they seemed to carry.

Steve was present, but he drank only his customary 7-UP. He hung out with JHS suppliers he knew while I hung around with people I had met at the

Troika or Slovak Ball. I didn't enjoy hanging out with my brother. When we were together at Dad's parties, I felt as if he were trying to monopolize conversations, holding the attention to himself and away from me. Perhaps he felt the same about me.

Sasha on guitar, Vladjec on accordion, and Dad (third from left) are whooping it up with a couple of friends at a Peru, NY garden party. c. 1990

One of Dad's friends approached me and said, "You're the son who looks more like your father." Another offered, "You're the one who went to MIT—the perpetual student who has a big smile like your dad's." Another woman asked, "Aren't you the older brother?" I shook my head, and she said, "I thought you were older than Steve." Though a part of me was flattered by being in the first-child position in her mind, I felt peeved that she couldn't keep my brother and me straight.

After the party, I was amazed that no one got in an alcohol-caused car accident on the way back to Montreal. I figured that most of those Eastern Europeans knew how to hold their liquor. To be safe, Elaine brewed pots of strong coffee well before closing time. Most of Dad's male friends smoked sweet cigars or foul cigarettes. The cops or Canadian border officers would smell only smoke if they detained an intoxicated driver.

169

Dad's East German friend, Hans, became rickety after drinking a little too much. He stammered and swayed as he walked around the tables, having a drink with this man and that woman. Thank goodness that his drier wife drove them home.

Dad later told me, "Sometimes, Hans and Kathy stay overnight with us to let him sleep it off." He offered a half-smile. "One year, he had a big fight with her about his drinking. Without warning, Hans upped and left her here. He took the car and drove back to Montreal alone, and she had to find her way home with a friend." Dad grinned. "Being as high as he was, I don't know how he made it through the border station, but he did."

The morning after the party, I was having breakfast with Dad and Elaine. I stayed overnight while Steve had left to go back to Montreal well before the event ended. I looked at my father and said boldly, "It was a great party, Dad. It must have cost you a fortune."

My father smiled as he sipped on a mimosa. "It's not too bad, son. Our Slovak Business Association gives me a budget for the tent and tables. They offer me so much per person for food and wine. I do spend more, for the extras, like the musicians and hard liquor."

"Not any more than he'd spend on a big night out at the Troika," Elaine ribbed with a grin.

Dad continued as if he hadn't heard her remark. "On the other hand, the alcohol and steaks are a lot cheaper down here in Plattsburgh than in Montreal, so it's a big advantage for everyone to come here instead of having the party there. And the association doesn't have to rent a hall." He smiled. "Everybody chips in to help with the food cooking and table serving, so it works out well in the end."

Elaine smiled and offered, "Your father does nothing but enjoy the festivities. Good old Joe, the CSPBA President, does the barbequing on your father's big grill."

She took a sip of her drink. "The wives bring most of the salads and fixings. I hire a couple of extra people to help out for the day with the setup, serving, and cleaning, but that's about it." She winked. "Heck, if I want to clean up after so many Slovaks."

Count on Dad and Elaine for finding a way to pay for their extravaganza effectively, and to sit back and enjoy it.

"Did you have a good time, son?" Dad asked as he refilled my mimosa.

"Certainly, Dad." I lifted my glass to him and Elaine. "Both of you know how to throw a great party."

* * *

I was near the end of my endurance for Dad's new house tour. "Can we go inside, Dad?" I asked. "It's getting chilly."

"Sure, son, but allow me to show you one last thing."

My eyes looked down. "Okay, Dad, one last thing."

Dad motioned to the right side of the house. "Over there, we'll build a new two-car garage next year, with a covered walkway to our new mudroom next to the kitchen." Dad's voice was like that of a journeyman giving a pointer to his apprentice. "It's going to take time to get that project going. I want to match the new structure to the existing house."

He finished his cigarette and stubbed it out on the ground. "It's going to cost an arm and a leg for the granite walls and special roof tiles, but I don't mind because it's a good investment in the house." Dad generally balked at spending more than he needed to on anything, but this time his face was bright. "I got a good deal on the house, and it'll be worth much, much more when the renovations are complete."

Dad had said magic words that got my attention. "How so, Dad? What's your arrangement here?" I found my father's money deals instructive.

His face got serious, and he spoke softly. "For now, I'm renting the house from the Meyer family. I'm doing it through their corporation in the Cayman Islands. They have given me the first option to buy the place, if and when I want to. Until then, I pay them a monthly rent."

My voice turned serious. "What about the work you're doing? Won't they own your improvements?" I wondered what kind of deal my father had gotten himself.

"It's not a problem, son. They allow me to deduct any permanent house improvements I make against the rent I pay. As long as I put money into the house, in addition to paying the regular upkeep, I can live here rent-free." Dad smiled. "They're happy that a buyer like me came along who would take such good care of the place."

I remained skeptical. "Well, what about the sale price, Dad? Couldn't they screw you later, after you make these improvements, by playing with the price when you are ready to buy?"

His face stayed relaxed. "Don't worry, son; we have that figured out. The owners and I negotiated a formula for calculating the sale price in connection to the money I put in for permanent improvements. I have to keep good records and my contractors' receipts. Meyer's corporation in Cayman has to agree to the improvements I want to do."

He took another breath. "It's totally up to me if I want to buy the place or not. I have control. If I later don't want to stay, then they get my improvements, but I wouldn't have had to pay any rent to live here."

This arrangement seemed odd to me, but Dad appeared pleased with it. Over the years, he had bought and sold industrial, residential, and land properties in Montreal and Cayman. Real estate seemed to be Dad's other mistress. Considering how much time he spent on it, it might have been his more preferred interest.

Hoping that Dad knew what he was doing, I let go of my concerns. I figured that if Elaine had smelled something fishy about this real estate deal, she would have steered Dad in a better direction.

"Let's go inside, son. Are you hungry? Elaine is preparing a nice lunch for us."

"Yes, I could eat," and perhaps curtail this tour for now.

* * *

Dad led us to an oversized front door. I followed him inside. Thick, smooth granite stones framed a black door and its sidelight window. The entryway opened into a wide, dark-brown tiled hallway. A wide beige carpeted staircase and walnut wood banister lead to the second floor.

Me and my girlfriend, who later became my wife, visiting Dad, Elaine, and Muffie.
Summer, 1991.

Elaine was nowhere in sight. Dad looked at me. "Would you like me to show you around inside before or after lunch?"

I felt torn. "Maybe the nickel tour for now and the quarter tour later."

Dad pointed up the staircase. "I won't take you up there now, but we have three bedrooms upstairs. Besides the master bedroom over the den, we have two guest rooms on the opposite side of the house." He smiled. "You can stay in one of those when you come overnight."

I nodded but said nothing.

Dad turned left. "Let me show you the living and dining rooms."

We entered a beige shag-carpeted, sunken living room. I was taken aback by its cathedral ceiling and the nearly floor-to-ceiling windows on the side of the room facing the lake.

And that wasn't all. Opposite the windows was a massive fireplace made of stone that matched the outside of the house. It was as tall as I was and equally wide. As I looked around the room, I offered, "This is amazing!"

Dad had a smirk on his face as if he had expected my reaction. "Now you see another reason why I got this place. The inside of the house is gorgeous."

Getting fatigued from touring, I looked beyond the living room. "So, is that the dining room there?"

"Yes," my father said. We walked across the living room and up a couple of steps into a dark wood-paneled dining area. A solid walnut table, large enough to seat ten, filled the room. More lead-lined windows were on the north wall, providing yet another view of the lake.

On the opposite wall was a matching walnut buffet cabinet and hutch that reached close to the ceiling. It was full of wooden door compartments below, drawers in the middle, and glass door compartments in the hutch. I could see that matching glasses, plates, and serving dishes filled the cabinet and were placed neatly inside.

Dad gestured toward the big wood cabinet, continuing his presentation with the enthusiasm of a listing agent. "Elaine is very organized, meticulous, and has a good eye. She wants everything to look nice. Because I asked her for no reimbursement for the improvements I made at her Pointe-Claire home, she bought the furniture, linens, bedspreads, cushions, dishes, and other stuff we needed for this place. She even got this beautiful big buffet and hutch. Aren't they nice?"

"It seems she is doing a great job, Dad. By the way, where is she?"

Dad pointed to a large swinging door to the right of the big buffet. "She's in the room next door, in the kitchen with Orphee." Orphee was Elaine's black and white Hungarian Puli.

"Before we go in there, I want to show you one last thing. Dad motioned to the end of the dining room that faced the back of the house. "See that wall?"

I nodded through my tour fatigue.

"Next year, we're going to open that wall, put in French doors, and build a cozy solarium that will match the rest of the house."

I tried to stay enthralled. "One second, I think you've thought of everything, and then the next second, you show me something else that's impressive. What else do you have up your refurbishing sleeve, Dad?"

My father's eyes were proud and bright. "I want this place to be my retirement home until the day I'm gone. My grandfather lived until he was 94. Like him, I want to be around at least another 30 years, and to enjoy my retirement." He lowered his voice. "And, when the time comes, I want to go as fast as he did." He pointed his finger upward and then to his head. "Just like a brick falling from a building and onto my head, and *Boom!* I'm gone."

"You liked your grandfather, didn't you, Dad."

"Yes, I could talk to him. He was more of a father to me than my own father was. He let me come to his farm every summer for a month or more to work with him. He gave me lots of advice about life. I very much respected him."

Dad didn't elaborate, but I wondered if that advice was about cigarettes, alcohol, wheeling-dealing, and women. I wondered what the next decades would bring, and if my father could live those years with only Elaine.

My mother's thirty years with him had brought many ups and downs. Dad and Elaine held more in common than my parents. They smoked like chimneys, held their liquor like drinking pros, enjoyed renovation projects, went jet setting to the Caribbean and Europe, and partied regularly with their friends. Might that translate into the long life he desired?

My father pushed through the swinging door that led to the kitchen. I followed right behind. On the kitchen floor was Orphee lying on his belly. That big, 45-lb., fluffy thing stood and started to bark. He then happily jumped onto my father's thigh.

Dad's tone was soothing. "Yes, Orphee, you missed me." My father took a small ball that was on the floor, and he quickly thrust it down a hallway toward the den. "There, Orphee. Get it! Get it!"

Orphee went barreling for the ball and came rushing back seconds later with it in its mouth. "Good boy; that's a good boy," Dad said. "Now, give it to me." He took the ball and petted the dog vigorously.

"You and that dog!" came from a booming voice in the kitchen. "I swear, I think you're more in love with him than me." It was Elaine, and she was smiling.

"Howdy stranger," she said. She approached me, put her hands on my shoulders, and gave me a set of kisses, one for each cheek, customary for Canadians. "Glad you could make it. Has your father given you the big tour of the place?"

"Hi, Elaine." I smiled. "Yes, I'm quite impressed and overwhelmed. Both of you have done a lot of work here, and everything looks great."

Elaine bent down and showed an open hand to the dog; then, she pointed to the floor. "Orphee, sit!" she said.

Orphee complied without hesitation or complaint. He looked at her with his longing eyes and a panting tongue.

Elaine turned to me. "It hasn't been easy, especially with your father, who likes things done yesterday. If these walls could talk, the stories they could tell." She laughed.

"It's a good thing we both like to be organized and get things done," Dad retorted.

"Otherwise, we would have killed each other by now." Elaine's face had a big smirk. "For sure, I've stopped being a lumber hauler for your father." She batted her hand in the air. "The wood I had to bring down here from Montreal in his company station wagon, you'd think I was an importer." She smirked again. "That father of yours can be a slave driver."

"Come on, darling; it wasn't that bad." Dad's face showed a boyish grin.

Elaine's continued to look half-serious and half-comical. "Two or three times a week, he had me make deliveries of 2x4s, plywood, molding, and who knows what else from his factory to the house here for the den renovation." She batted her hand again. "I felt like one of his hourly employees. I pity the people that have to work for him day-in and day-out."

"Now, you are making me upset, Elaine." Dad looked at me and pleaded his case. "All that material is cheaper in Montreal than here in New Your State. I bought it through JHS and from our long-time suppliers."

His eyes became intense. "I only asked Elaine to drive that shit down here because she has an American passport. The border guards wouldn't let me or any of our employees bring materials from Canada without having to pay import duties." He raised his hand. "All she had to do was drive. We had people at both ends loading and unloading the station wagon for her."

She pointed to her shoulder. "Yah, but the last trip was the straw that broke this camel's back." She looked at me. "I had things I needed to do in Montreal, and your father wanted me to drop everything to cart his lumber." She turned to him with caring eyes and touched him on the cheek. "Darling, you can be very demanding. It's a good thing you're such a nice slave driver."

"Yah," Dad responded, his face turning a bit red. "I had to plead with her to do it. Otherwise, the men here couldn't finish their work." I couldn't tell if he was understanding or annoyed. "Afterward, I bought her two dozen roses. You can see them sitting there." He pointed to a glass vase on the kitchen counter in which were long-stem red and pink roses.

Elaine smiled. "Your father can be very nice when he gets down on his hands and knees."

The conversation was getting a little too prickly. I changed the subject. "Show me what you've done here in the kitchen. And maybe you can show me that den you were talking about, Dad." I figured I'd rather get more tour than be in the middle of something between Dad and Elaine.

Dad offered, "I have to say, Elaine had good ideas and saw many possibilities." He pointed to an area in front of us. "Before we go to the den, do you see this space here?" Dad motioned to an open area adjacent to the kitchen. We knocked down half of the old nanny quarters and put in a breakfast nook and a mudroom for the back entrance."

"Nanny quarters?" I asked.

Elaine came in. "Yes, we left the nanny's bedroom and bath but demolished its adjoining living space. My mum can stay in that room when she's here with us." She gestured with open hands as if she were Vanna White showing a solved mystery puzzle on *Wheel of Fortune*.

"Sounds and looks good to me," I said.

Dad offered, "It's a good thing Elaine's mother, Jean, is short and thin. The little bedroom here is just her size."

Elaine looked intently at him. "Now, be careful about what you say about my mother, Johnny." Her eyes were intense, yet her face was half serious and half smirking. "She's petite!"

"And she has a lot of pep for her age. She's still running on all cylinders," Dad said. He looked at her. "I can certainly see where you get your energy, sweetheart."

Elaine's mother was about Dad's age. It was amazing how the much taller and more robustly figured Elaine had grown out of that tiny, thin, delicate mother of hers. But that little lady could carry a conversation a mile a minute if you gave her a chance.

"Your father is such a charmer, Harvy," Elaine added. "He certainly has been very good to my mother, including her in our social life, and having her come and stay here with us."

I couldn't help thinking that my mother wasn't as lucky, having gone to parties with Dad only a couple of times each year. Every month or two, on a Saturday night, they had had friends over to play cards. I don't remember the two of them ever going out on their own.

I shook away my thoughts. "Let's see your new satellite setup, Dad."

He turned to Elaine. "How much more time do you need before we sit down for brunch?"

"I've been busy on the phone this morning with lighting and furniture stores. I've now got three different quiches in the oven and a big bowl of cut fruit in the fridge."

"Are you expecting an army?" I asked.

Her eyes opened wide. "I wasn't sure what you'd like, so I made three different types of quiche. I can freeze what's left. Anyway, your Dad helped earlier by squeezing fresh orange juice." She pointed to the dining room. "The table is set."

I could see her checking things off in her mind. "What if you guys go see the satellite installation in the den, then wash up, and be back here in 10 minutes or so?" She looked at me, "I hope you came hungry, Harvy."

"Yes, I know you already, Elaine. I'm ready to eat a whole quiche myself."

"The apple does not fall too far from the tree," she said. "I'm glad you have a good appetite like your father."

And it's a good thing I exercise to stay reasonably trim.

Dad cut in. "Okay, son; that's enough kibitzing. Let me show you the den."

"Johnny, when you're there, tell Harvy what happened the last time your Montreal factory crew came here. I'm sure he'll get a kick out of that story."

She turned to the dog. "Orphee, you stay here." Elaine's hand was up again, indicating to the pet that he shouldn't move.

Orphee lay on his belly with his ball between his front paws. He looked longingly at Elaine, panting away in short bursts. He didn't budge from the cool floor. "Good boy; stay with mummy," Elaine repeated.

I figured Elaine couldn't train my father as easily as her Puli. I hoped that her good humour and assertive manner would maintain my father's interest and keep him in line.

I followed Dad toward the den. Before we left the kitchen area, a compartment on the inside wall drew my attention. "What's this, Dad?"

"Son, that's a dumb waiter." He must have seen a surprised look on my face, for he explained. "Old-man Meyer lived here as an invalid until his death, so he put in that thing."

Dad pointed down and then up. "It goes from the basement to the second floor above us. I'd show you how it works, but it needs electrical improvements to bring it to code. I could do the wiring myself, but I need a licensed electrician to finish the job properly for town inspection."

He smiled. "It's going to transport wine up to the kitchen from the new wine cellar I'm building in the basement." He quieted as he pointed upward. "When I'm old and sick in bed, Elaine will use it to bring me meals upstairs."

"I heard that," Elaine said sternly. "Heck, if I'm going to serve you hand and foot, mister."

A smirk formed on my father's face as he turned toward her. "No, darling, you misunderstood me. I said that *your mother* could serve me in bed if I'm ever sick."

"Leave her out of this too! You'll either stay healthy or get your own damn food and medicine." She said that with a chuckle.

Dad ignored Elaine's comment. He looked at me and continued. "I built the cedar-lined cellar in the basement by myself, with Edo's help."

Though Elaine offered no further comments, I imagined her thinking, *Johnny needs somebody around to tell them what to do. Better it be his brother than me or my mother.* I was grateful that it was Edo helping Dad rather than me. My uncle had a lot of patience for working with his brother, though he could crave a couple of beers afterward.

"Okay, now come and see what I've done in the den." Dad headed for the hallway.

Exiting the kitchen, we stepped down into a brightly lit, wood-paneled, chocolate brown, shag-carpeted room. "This is it, son. What do you think?"

"Wow!" I said.

Contractors had installed a pair of sliding patio doors where double garage doors had been. Wooden benches with cushion covers hugged the walls below the windows on opposite side-walls. A huge, burgundy, V-shaped couch and lazy boy chair filled the center of the room. Dad pointed to the wall behind us. "Look at this, son."

My eyes opened wide. A large built-in walnut cabinet with glass door compartments filled the front wall. In the middle of the structure was a large TV with a set of external speakers scattered around the other shelves. The TV was on, but the volume was low. "Gee, Dad, this is a great room. I bet you are going to spend most of your time here."

"You're right. I love this place. Our people from JHS's factory-built it exactly to my specifications."

Dad raised a hand. "An electronics guy I hired has done a great job helping me install the satellite operation and to connect it to the TV and the other baloney we put in here."

He pointed to a floor-to-ceiling bank of shelves near the back of the room. The shelves were full of components: VCR, a hefty amplifier, cassette deck, radio tuner, turntable, and other electronic boxes that controlled the satellite dish. His voice elevated. "We put all that crap on these back shelves so we wouldn't have to clutter the cabinet around the TV. I installed the wiring in the walls and made the connections myself. I'll show you."

Dad grabbed a couple of remote controls. He fiddled with their switches and adjusted several knobs on the components on the shelf. While he checked out his new toys, I tried out the lazy boy chair in front of the TV. It was leather.

I found the lever for the chair's footrest. I watched the 40" screen as Dad checked a bunch of stations coming from one satellite. "You see, son. I'm going to get sports from all over the world." He pushed a button to swing his dish to another satellite, and then he checked out more stations.

My eyes started to close. Though I had been a good student at MIT, I had found no electromagnetic attraction to techy things. I was glad to be in my new AU/NTL program that taught me progressive ways to deal with people within organizations. For Dad, employees existed to do his bidding. For me, I saw them as people working together to serve customers well and not just to make maximum profit.

I had given away nearly six years of my life pursuing my father's prized college plans for me, and nearly three more in working for him at JHS. Those long years had revealed to me the directions I didn't want to pursue, though I wished my revelation hadn't taken so long. I was now heading in a better career direction. I hoped Dad thought so too.

Elaine walked into the room. "Are you guys ready? My quiches are on the table."

"Yes, sweetheart; we're fooling around to see if everything is working with the satellite system. Everything looks good."

"Then wash up, you two, and come for brunch."

A few moments later, we were sipping from Elaine's tall, tapered champagne glasses filled with mimosas. She pointed with her sterling silver pie cutter. "This quiche is ham and cheese, the way you like it, Johnny." She turned to me. "I know you prefer vegetables, Harvy, so this one is asparagus and broccoli. And, the last is tomatoes and onions."

"The rabbit food is for you guys," Dad said. "And tomatoes and onions don't like me anymore. I'll stick with the ham and cheese."

Elaine served. Dad lifted his glass. "Chin, chin. Here's to having you here in Peru with us for the first time, son."

"Cheers to the two of you as well," I remarked enthusiastically. "You're getting this place whipped into shape." My voice quieted. "By the way, what's the story that Elaine mentioned regarding the den? We never got to that."

Elaine looked at Dad for a long second. "You tell it, Johnny."

He looked back at her. "Okay, but only if you promise not to interrupt."

She smiled. "Okay, okay, Johnny, but can't a modern girl get a word in edgewise?"

"Only if you don't take over, sweetheart."

They looked at each other for a second or two. I glanced down at the table, not wanting to be in the middle of Dad and Elaine hashing things out with their eyes.

My father turned to me. "We had my best guys from the factory: Edo, Georges, Guido, and Guido's best employee, Pedro, come down here for a couple of weeks. They helped us renovate the den." He took a long breath. "Because we were not busy at JHS, I had them come here while still paying them their regular salaries." He smiled slightly. "It was like a working vacation."

Elaine couldn't help herself. "And who do you think was doing the cooking for those four hungry guys, plus your Dad to boot?"

"So who's talking?" Dad chirped with a hint of annoyance in his voice.

Okay, Johnny, go on." She looked at me. "You see what I have to put up with, Harvy." She laughed, and Dad did too. I smiled but stayed out of their space.

My father continued. "We're not permitted to import workers from Canada to do jobs here in the U.S. They'd need a work visa, and hell if I'm going to bother with that baloney for only two weeks of work. So I told those guys to tell the U.S. customs agents that they were coming down to go fishing on Lake Champlain and that they were going to stay here with us."

Dad forked quiche into his mouth and kept on talking. "The first week, everything worked fine. We made a lot of progress in renovating the den. But we couldn't finish everything, so I had them come back a couple of weeks later for a few more days." His eyebrows rose. "Well, the U.S. border guards got suspicious."

Elaine roared, "Can you imagine, Harvy! Here's a Slovak (your uncle Edo), a Frenchman (Georges)," she counted them out on her fingers, "an Italian (Guido), and a Spaniard (Pedro) saying they were going fishing on Lake Champlain. They're good workers, but those guys can hardly string two English sentences together. That moment with the U.S. border official must have been priceless."

Dad was chuckling too. "The customs guy asked them to open the back of their station wagon. They didn't find any fishing rods but only tools, along with the rest of their luggage. The guards then told them to come inside the station, where they interrogated them in separate rooms. They didn't have their stories straight, so U.S. immigration turned them around and sent them back to Canada."

I started to laugh too. I put my napkin over my face to keep from spitting out my food. Though I liked those fellows, I couldn't stop thinking about how that border scene must have looked. Dad's men must have been factory worker deer frozen in border guard headlights.

Dad continued. "Here we are, sitting and waiting for them. Georges calls us from a payphone on the Canadian side, wondering what they should do." His voice rose. "Boy, was I pissed off." He waved his hand in the air. "What a bunch of fucking clowns; *excusez mon français.*"

Elaine couldn't stop laughing as she put a palm to her chest. "I bet they stood there at the border station and flipped a coin as to who should call your father with the bad news. You know how upset Johnny can get."

"My father gets upset? I didn't know," I said with a chortle. Luckily I had no more food in my mouth.

Dad's tone was loud and severe. "I blasted them for their stupidity."

I caught my breath. "So how did you get those guys here?"

Dad's face was stern as he wagged his fork. "I told them to try it again the next day, but from a different border crossing." He took another bite of his quiche. "Another border station is situated just a few kilometers off the highway, on a less busy road. I told them to leave most of their tools at home—I have plenty here."

His eyes were penetrating. "I told them to throw fishing rods into their trunk, put on the right kind of clothes for fishing, start early in the morning like they were going out on the lake, and to get their story straight with the border guards." His voice was thunderous.

The tension in my father's face subsided. "They finally got here the next day, and we had breakfast waiting for them. Those bums will give me a heart attack one day."

The front side of Dad's Peru house, in 2008, looking the way it did in the 1990s, except for the overgrown and unkempt vegetation. Almost as much house jutted out the other side of the central section (pointing left, toward the lake) as did on this side. The boy is my son, Johnny's grandson.

"That's a precious story, Dad. I hope the rest of the week went better than the way it had started."

Elaine jumped back in. "Your father had them working here like busy little Quebec beavers. They got everything done in one less workday than we planned. They headed back home with no problems at the Canadian border and a good story to tell."

"*Une*-believable," Dad said with a Slavic drawl. "If those guys ever got lost in the woods, they wouldn't be able to rub two sticks together."

"You know how to pick them, sweetheart," Elaine said.

I said nothing more. My heart went out for Dad's JHS gang, for I knew those workers were among JHS's finest, and they had to put up with a lot from their boss. I also hoped Elaine's sugar and spice would continue to mix well with Dad's salt and vinegar.

Elaine changed the subject. "So tell me, Harvy, how's your Washington, D.C. program going? Will we see you graduate soon? Is it working out for you?" She didn't say, *better than business school.*

I was used to my father's ways. I knew Elaine's questions were Dad's. I looked straight at her. "I'm very much enjoying my courses. I'm halfway through the program now and will finish in about another year. I hope both of you will come to my graduation."

Because Dad and JHS were supporting me through the D.C. program, I felt it only fair that he and Elaine come to see me walk for my degree. Knowing they were coming, Mom would probably stay at home for the event. She hadn't seen Dad in three years, and she would probably sob and shrill in the same breath if she encountered him and Elaine together.

"We'll be happy to come," Elaine said. "Let us know the date well in advance. Your father keeps us very busy with his travel plans."

"It will be nice to be there to see you get your diploma," Dad said. He offered nothing more.

I hoped that I hadn't disappointed him too much by not going back to Harvard or another business school. I wasn't sure where I would be after my D.C. program was complete. I secretly hoped it wouldn't be Montreal.

* * *

Some months after my first visit to Dad's Lake Champlain home, I stopped by my father's office near the end of a workday. He was alone. After our greetings and kisses, he unexpectedly said, "Harvy, I want to tell you something important."

Those were captivating words to my ears. Such terms were frequently followed by a financial secret my father wanted to reveal. "Okay, Dad," I said.

He hardly took a breath. "I want you to know that I own the Peru house through CANEX, my corporation in Cayman."

I was surprised and a little shocked but didn't let on. Dad had said he was renting his Lake Champlain home through the previous owner's company in Cayman. Nearly a decade earlier—after his Revenue Canada court case was settled—he had told me that he was going to close CANEX. "I thought you shut-down CANEX a long time ago, Dad," I said, my voice expressing concern.

Dad spoke matter-of-factly. "I decided to keep it as a shell company to hold the Peru house. It allows me to transfer more funds offshore through the rent I pay for the house."

"So why are you telling me this now?"

He didn't hesitate. "Because I want you to know that I'm going to move my offshore money from Cayman to Luxembourg."

"Luxembourg, Dad?" *Not another offshore money haven!* I barely knew where that small state was in Europe. "Why there?"

"I think I told you part of the reason. I'm tired of going to Cayman to get access to my money." He reiterated, "I made good investments there and then decided to sell everything I had. Cayman is too far away, and it's too expensive."

"What's so great about this Luxembourg bank? Isn't it also far away?"

Dad had an answer. "The Lux bank offers better investments than keeping my money in a bank account or CDs earning next-to-nothing interest." He gestured away from himself. "I can also get access to my money from anywhere in the world where the bank has branches, even here in Montreal. I won't have to travel far to get to my cash."

Wow! A money-hiding offshore bank on our Canadian soil! Who and where the heck are they, and how did my father find them? And how do such banks pull off tax-skirting right in our country's backyard? My mind was exploding with questions about my father's admissions that came out of his mouth as if they were old news. Count on Dad for finding a new and improved money hiding trick!

I wondered if it was a good time to ask questions. I knew if I asked too much, Dad might think I didn't have the *yaytas* for his brazen offshore banking behavior. I then might not hear more from him. So I came forth with one crucial question. "So, what's going to happen to CANEX?"

"I'm not sure. Maybe I'll buy the Peru house personally and then close CANEX; I'll see."

More Johnny Simkovits' money moves! Why should I be amazed?

My father spoke quietly. "I'd like you to come sometime to my Lux bank. I want you to meet the people there in case something happens to me."

Dad was now 64 years old. His manufacturing business had been slowing for years. I wondered if and when he was going to retire. I knew retirement was a touchy subject with him. Whenever Elaine asked him about it, he'd say, "So you now want to put me out to pasture?"

I kept my mouth shut to see if Dad had more to say. He obliged. "It would be good for you to get to know the Lux bank manager. The bank is in the Alexis Nihon Plaza in Westmount."

I now had an answer to one of my other questions. The comforting news was that my father still wanted my involvement in his hidden money— or was he telling me such things to keep me dangling on a hook? Luckily, Alexis Nihon Plaza was only a fifteen-minute drive from JHS, not the many hours across land and sea that Cayman was.

I gathered my courage. "Is that safe, Dad, to bring your money here to Canada?"

My father looked at me as if I were naive. "My money isn't going to be here, son. It's going to be sitting at the bank's head office in Luxembourg." He pointed outside the building. "They have a small branch office in Montreal that will manage my investments and allow me access to my funds." He was confident, as if his money hiding were no big deal, no problem, and no sweat.

My stomach started to churn, but I didn't want to project surprise, eagerness, or judgment. "Okay, Dad, whatever you think is best." I figured my father would do what he wanted, whether or not I was for or against it.

Be it with women or his money, when Dad got tired of a romance or a haven, then he looked toward the next horizon. There was no need to ask more now; I could wait until he'd take me to his new bank. I'd then learn how he pulled off finding a Luxembourg institution in Montreal and how he was hiding his untaxed money right under the nose of Canadian authorities. I looked at him. "Let me know when you want me to go with you."

"Okay, son; I will." He didn't indicate when.

Part of me felt seventeen again, the time Dad had taken me to the *Banque de Genève* to open his first offshore account. Back then, the youth in me felt privileged to know my father's secrets and to be close to him. I would have done almost anything to be his good boy, his chosen son, his confidant, the legate of his offshore legacy.

But there was another tide rising in me. The money that my father had tucked away safely offshore was now coming onto our Canadian shores. I had no idea as to what tax dangers and police perils might come from that move. I considered whether this money maneuver, like the new Peru home, was a part of Dad's crafty retirement planning.

What more would he have in store, and what further involvement might I have?

* * *

I wondered if my father's Peru environs had been famous for anything in American history. One time when I went to New York State, I stopped off at the Plattsburgh public library. I discovered that the sizable forested island that lay across the bay from my father's house was famed for a battle between British and Colonial naval forces at the onset of the American Revolution.

In the fall of 1776, on the other side of that long, narrow island, General Benedict Arnold and his fleet of 800 ragged rebels fought a major battle against a British armada. Arnold's small fleet took on many superior British numbers. The British ships had sailed south from Lower Canada to seize control of Lake Champlain before the onset of winter. Though Arnold's troops damaged a portion of the British fleet in the battle, Arnold's forces lost many more ships and men.

In the aftermath, while the British were tending to their losses on the lake side of the island, Arnold regrouped in Valcour Bay (the bay my father's lakeshore home overlooked). That night, under cover of darkness, Arnold snuck what remained of his fleet right past the British armada, sailing south toward the rebel stronghold of Fort Ticonderoga. When morning broke, the British saw Arnold's retreat and gave chase.

The faster British warships on his heels, Arnold realized the futility of his escape. He grounded, abandoned, and burned what was left of his vessels to avoid the enemy's capture of his men and ships.

By foot, Arnold led over two hundred men to the safety of Fort Ticonderoga before the pursuing British and Indian ground forces could overtake them. Having slowed British advances on Lake Champlain, the Colonists soon lauded Arnold for his courage and determination in holding back the enemy.

Reading the history of Arnold at Valcour Bay, I thought about my father, who was a larger-than-life figure for me. Like the rebel general slipping past the British, Dad was a rebel who worked to dodge our Canadian government.

My father had his reasons for not trusting the government. The Hungarian fascists forced him to fight in a horrific war, and the Czechoslovakia Communists later seized his budding electronics business in his hometown of Košice. Indeed, his desire for freedom from any man or land fed his craving for clandestine cash. That desire had also undercut his commitment to any country.

When I arrived at my father's home that afternoon, I stood on the concrete landing that overlooked Valcour Bay. I imagined my father still standing on the bridge of his business after thirty years in his adopted land. He was seen by most as an upright Canadian citizen and a lauded immigrant, not one who might be captured and shackled for tax-skirting shenanigans.

I wondered how long my father could sail out of the reach of Revenue Canada's gunships. Might he have to incur large losses to survive his money-finagling and cash-hiding ways? He had once dodged a Revenue Canada cannon a decade earlier. He was fortunate to have evaded criminal charges for writing off obsolete inventory and for sneaking his concealed CANEX corporation right past Revenue Canada's nose.

I glanced down at the water's edge in front of Dad's Peru home. I wondered whether I would become like my father—a rebel to the tax laws of my land. Would I be a loyal co-conspirator, keeping my father's secrets? Or might I become a turncoat, delivering him (and perhaps myself) to Canadian tax authorities?

I looked out again past Valcour Island to the other side of the lake. At 29 years old, I still wondered how much I would have to become like my father to be able to survive him. Would I develop into an honorable man or a self-serving one, and in whose eyes?

What about in my own?

* * * *

12

Old Dog Training

Elaine was good at keeping things light. One evening, over coffee and dessert in her and Dad's new den, she glanced over at Orphee as he lay on his cushy dog bed in the corner of the room. "I like my dogs well-trained," she said. "Orphee was sent to obedience school when he was a pup."

In addition to the usual litany of heel, lie down, roll over, sit, and paw commands, Orphee had an uncommon ability.

Elaine looked at her canine. "Come here, Orphee." She pointed to where she wanted him to stand, which was right next to her. The dog came, wagged its tail, and stood where she had indicated. "Now sit!" she instructed.

Orphee sat. His longing eyes stayed fixed on her, and his tail wagged back and forth across the carpet.

Elaine picked a grape from a fruit bowl and kept it in her hand. "Now watch this," she said to me. With her other hand, Elaine gently grabbed Orphee's lower jaw and held it horizontally. "Orphee, be still," she calmly commanded. She placed the grape on top of the Puli's nose and softly but firmly repeated, "Stay, Orphee, stay!"

Orphee obeyed. He balanced the grape on his shaggy nose without whimpering, barking, or dropping the fruit. He sat in place; his eyes looked crossed as they tried to stay focused on what sat on his nose.

After a couple of seconds, Elaine said, "Okay, Orphee, you can get it."

In what seemed like a millisecond, the dog flung the fruit into the air then grabbed it in its mouth. The grape was gone. Orphee looked again at his mistress, wanting another.

"Good boy, Orphee." Elaine patted her dog on the head. She threw him another grape, which he caught in his mouth before it would hit the carpet.

Dad laughed, "He does it for me too." He picked up a grape, motioned to Orphee to come by his side, and repeated what Elaine had done. When Orphee completed the drill, Dad offered vigorous pets. "Good, dog, Orphee! Good dog!"

Orphee was up on his hind feet, front paws on Dad's knees. He offered a big bark and panted with excitement.

Elaine turned to me. "He'll do it for you too, Harvy." She smiled. "Here, take this grape." She put one in my hand.

I repeated Elaine's playful act, asking Orphee to sit, then to stay still as I gently held his jaw and put the grape on his nose. After a few seconds of watching him balance it, I said, "Okay, Orphee, you can get it."

The grape disappeared in half a second without falling to the floor. "Good dog, Orphee," I offered, patting him briskly. Smiles were on all our faces. I looked at Elaine. "I guess he doesn't like to eat his grapes off the floor."

Playing with Orphee cut the tension concerning Dad being separated from Mom and living with his mistress. I wondered whether Elaine had also completed partner obedience school so that she could keep my father in line. Would her ways work on him as they did on her dog? Then again, how much might my father allow any woman to train him?

* * *

I never asked Elaine what attracted her to my father. I didn't want to be nosey about their bond. I tried to accept their relationship the best way I could. I still wondered why she wished to live with a hard man like him.

One evening at their Peru home, a couple of years after they had finished the house renovations, Elaine, her mother, my father, and I were sitting together in their den. Elaine told a story. "Like Johnny, my dad was an entrepreneur, a street-smart person." She glanced over at her partner and smiled. "He was a big, burly guy, like Johnny."

She looked at me. "My dad was in the used car business, owning many dealerships in and around Hamilton, Ontario." She glanced at her mother and continued. "It was amazing to see my father next to my petite mother." She smiled again as her voice elevated. "Mom could disappear in his arms. He could almost crush her with his hugs."

Jean, Elaine's Mom, stayed silent but smiled in agreement.

Elaine's tone turned a tad terse. "My dad laid down the law with my older brother and me." Her tongue went into her cheek as if she and her brother never quite followed her dad's orders.

She looked my way again. "Your father knows this story." She took a deep breath. "One late afternoon, in the winter, when I was 27, my father got a call from his brother, my Uncle Joey. Joey was in the fuel oil distribution business, and he had a fuel delivery he needed to do." Her hands and arms spread wide. "He drove these big fuel tankers through Southern Ontario."

I listened closely. Even Jean, normally chatty, didn't interrupt as Elaine continued. "Because my uncle didn't have another driver available, Dad volunteered to ride with him to a small town past Toronto. Dad and Joey felt they could spend some brother time together in the cab."

She took a deep breath. "The weather was awful that day and into that night. The wind was blowing snow over Highway 401 between Toronto and Windsor. We didn't think anything of it because Dad's brother had been driving those routes for years."

Her voice hesitated, but she powered through it—the racing car driver she was—as she looked over at her mother. "Hours later, Mom got the call from the Ontario provincial police. The oil truck had run off the road at a sharp curve in the 401. The truck had turned over on its side, leaked oil, and blown up." She threw a hand into the air while her eyes looked down. "The fire was so intense that the provincial police had to close the highway in both directions."

I sat frozen in my seat as Elaine took another long breath and continued. "By the time the fire was put out the next morning, there was little left of my dad and his brother."

She looked at her mother. "After the police had called my mum, she called me in Vermont—where I was living at the time—and shared the terrible news. By the time I got to her home, their bodies had been placed in plastic body bags and transferred to the morgue." Elaine lifted her arms as if she were carrying one of those bags. "When we went to identify the bodies, Dad and my uncle were so badly burned that what remained of each of them was no bigger than a Husky dog."

There were neither tears in Elaine's eyes nor a waver in her voice. It was as if every retelling of this story had made her stronger. She looked again at her mother. "It was just Mom, my brother, and me from then on."

Jean piped in, her speech as matter-of-fact as Elaine's. "It was a big loss for us." She looked at her daughter. "I loved your daddy; he married me right after I finished high school."

Jean took a drag from her cigarette. She could go smoke-for-smoke with both her daughter and my father. She offered. "I was an adopted child, you know. I never knew my birth parents. I lived with my adopted parents in Southern Ontario until I was 13." She pointed her cigarette into the air. "After my adopted mother had died, another relative took me in."

That's interesting! Dad, too, had been placed with relatives after his mother died when he was only three years old.

Jean's voice stayed unemotional. She spoke as if she were giving us "just the facts" as Sergeant Joe Friday might do on the TV detective show *Dragnet.* She offered, "My new guardians had another daughter close to my age, but I found her unbearable."

She looked toward Elaine. "Luckily, your father found me when I was 17." She smiled slightly. "He was 26 at the time and right out of the army. We met at a street dance in Branford, Ontario." Her eyes blinked a few times.

"We soon ran away together to his family in the Eastern Townships of Quebec."

Jean spoke so impassively that I wondered if her upbringing had happened in a previous life. She pointed her cigarette toward her daughter. "Your daddy and I got married a year later. It was soon after I found out I was pregnant with your brother."

She took another drag and blew the smoke into the air. "We later moved back to Southern Ontario, where you were born."

She gazed at Elaine. "Your father took me away from an intolerable situation. He loved me, worked hard to support us, and gave me two kids and a good life. I never needed anything, and I never wanted to remarry after he died in that truck fire thirty years after we met."

I now better understood more of what attracted Elaine to my dad. He reminded her of her father. But unlike her mother, Elaine didn't want to be dependent on a man. Time would tell how forces would play out between these two strong-willed and self-assured Canadian Huskies.

* * *

Some years later, the relationship between my father and Orphee offered another clue regarding what Elaine saw in her partner.

During the last couple of years of Orphee's life, my father regularly took the dog to his office. Dad played fetch with him in the corridor, took him for a walk every few hours, and had him give paw handshakes to everyone who came through JHS's front door. It was as if Dad were a boy again, playing with a faithful companion.

Dad liked to tease Orphee by pretending to throw a ball down the hallway. Orphee chased after the phantom ball, not finding it, of course. He then ran back to Dad and cocked his head as if he were puzzled. My father then showed Orphee the ball, and the dog barked excitedly. Orphee lowered himself onto his front paws as if he were ready to give chase, and the dog barked again to encourage his master to toss the ball.

Dad chuckled. "Orphee, you are so much fun!" He threw the ball for his canine mate, and Orphee fetched it faithfully.

When Orphee got hungry or tired, he retired into Dad's private office, where my father kept the dog's food bowl. Orphee lay down under Dad's big desk for a little shut-eye. He was a very good dog.

While at their Peru home, Dad fed scraps off his plate to their pet. Elaine chided him. "Johnny, please don't feed Orphee from the table. He'll get used to it, and then he won't eat what I put out for him."

Dad said, "Okay, sweetheart," but then he did the same at the next meal.

Elaine scolded him again, half-seriously. "You and that dog, Johnny! You'll undo the work I put into training him."

"I'm sorry, sweetheart; I won't do it again."

But my father couldn't stop himself. He offered, "The way Orphee looks at me with his big, sad eyes, I can't help myself."

"You two are incorrigible," Elaine said to both Dad and the dog. She looked and pointed at her pet. "Okay, Orphee, it's time for you to lie down in the kitchen." She led the dog there and pointed to his bed. "Now, stay here."

The dog obeyed. Dad then lowered his head and shoulders as if he were a kid told he couldn't go out and play with his best friend.

At seventeen years old, in the summer of 1987, Orphee passed away. Elaine had him cremated. Soon afterward, she worked with Dad to bury Orphee's ashes on the front lawn of their Peru home. Elaine took a video of the ceremony.

My father dug a 12" square, 6"-deep hole. He gently placed Orphee's ashes into the hole and then covered them with dirt.

It was humorous to watch my dad and Elaine push, pull, drag, turn, and place a nearly 100-pound, 8" thick square piece of granite—remaining from the construction of their new garage—on top of Orphee's grave. Elaine said, "I want the grave covered with that stone so that other dogs in the neighborhood won't smell Orphee's ashes and dig him up."

Dad placed a decorative flower pot on top of the granite block. There he planted daisies. He'd plant new flowers there every spring.

The most revealing part of Elaine's video was the moment when Dad placed Orphee's ashes into the grave. My father instantly burst into tears and started to sob like a child. He covered his face with a hand and whimpered, "Orphee was such a good friend. . . . I miss him so much." He continued to wipe tears from his face as he scooped loose dirt and placed it over the ashes.

Years later, Elaine told me, "In all our years together, I never saw Johnny cry like that over the loss of anyone or anything."

Orphee had found Dad's heart. They had seduced each other well.

I hoped Elaine could keep my aging father's heart open and accessible for all of us to enjoy. Dad was a lot more fun to be around that way.

* * * *

New Horizons for Me

It was time to leave Montreal for good.

It was August of '84, two months shy of my turning thirty. A few months remained until I would complete my AU/NTL master's program. My practicum (a significant client application paper) and a final comprehensive exam were my last obligations. I'd receive my degree in Washington, D.C., the following May.

On the home front, my parents were four years into their separation skirmish, seemingly fought by sloth lawyers in a slow-motion movie. If I was to build my independence and maintain my sanity, I needed to get out of the city of my upbringing. I made plans to leave my brother, my mother, my father, and what friends I still had in Montreal.

Most of my English-speaking compatriots had moved out of Quebec during the mass Anglophone exodus of the late 1970s. The rise of the Quebec separatist movement, and the ascendance of the Party Québécois into power in 1976, had sent waves of English Quebecers west to Toronto and beyond.

It was my turn to join the movement by getting as far away as I possibly could, but I wasn't getting away just from the separatists. I was heading to Vancouver, BC, the balmiest climate in Canada. Since I had no steady girlfriend, my departure would be that much easier.

Earlier in the summer, I had spent a month in Vancouver. I looked for a place to live and carried out intense job hunting. I had several prospects. Among the possibilities was a construction engineering firm that was looking for a more human touch in its engineering projects. Another was B.C. Telephone that had a training and development group they were growing. My contacts in Vancouver had told me to get in touch with them when my feet were planted firmly on the west coast. That was my plan.

During my time out west, I had made a few friends through a New Age psychology retreat centre on Gabriola Island off of Vancouver Island. I had taken a weekend program, *The Development of the Mind, Body, and Spirit*. I liked that holistic stuff—especially hanging out after sessions in the hot tub under the stars.

Upon returning to Montreal, I terminated my apartment lease and got myself ready to tell both Mom and Dad that I was leaving town for good. I no longer cared about what they thought.

In his JHS office, Dad sat behind his desk that was as old as I was. He stared at me, looking incredulous as I stated my news. His tone turned concerned. "How will your mother feel about your moving away?"

I looked directly at him, no wavering in my voice. "I'm telling Mom tonight. I'm leaving September 1."

For two-and-a-half years, I had tried my hand in his business and worked alongside my father, but we knew how that had turned out. There was little he'd let go of, and he fired my mentor Moe at a time when I thought we had been making progress. Unlike my father leaving my mother without warning, I was leaving my family with advance notice.

That evening, I sat at Mom's kitchen table eating her scrumptious Hungarian stuffed cabbage. After I had told her my news, her jaw opened wide. She wiped a tear from her eye. "What will your father say?"

Though my parents had not seen each other since the day they had separated, they evoked each other's name when it was convenient. Their desire to keep this grown bird near their nests didn't cause my veering off my flight path. I was going to miss my mom's cooking and clothes repairing, but not her sighing and pining. "Dad already knows," I told her.

From the time I had come home from Harvard, I had done what I could to help my mother get through an undefined psychiatric illness. I had tried to soften the blow of Dad leaving her. I had given confidential information to Moe to help Mom's lawyer gain leverage with Dad. To my dismay, the lawyers made little progress, and my mother was stuck. She refused any therapeutic help. She still held onto her magic wish of Dad coming home to her, as he had done the previous two times he had left her.

As for my brother, Steve and I had joined forces awhile to make useful changes in JHS. But Steve had cast me out of his car in Victoria, BC, leaving me stranded on a sidewalk. He later travelled to Israel, abandoning me to fight my solitary battles with Dad. He unexpectedly turned Mormon in what seemed an attempt to make himself better than the rest of us. It reminded me of the times that Steve and I had biked around our hometown when we were kids. He had raced off ahead of me so he could see his friends without me. He now left our family in the dust for his new religion.

I felt alone and at a loss. My plans for JHS succession and helping my family had unraveled. Then again, had I been realistic with my aspirations to alter the trajectory of my dysfunctional family? I felt like a far-off moon with little gravitational pull on this family constellation. Was I now desperately jettisoning myself from their orbit? Perhaps, but I didn't feel they had given me a good reason to spin around them.

Within months of having wedding rings on their fingers, Steve and his wife became pregnant with their first child. Steve put his focus on his family and church and had less time for our parents. He came late to every meal with Mom and meeting with Dad, saying, "I had something important at home [or church] to attend to first."

At one meet-up at Dad's office, Steve told Dad and me, "Mormons are in church almost the whole day on Sunday. We have morning services and afternoon religious-education classes. Mormons reserve Monday nights for family, where we pray together and talk about the scriptures."

My brother spoke as if he were a missionary speaking to a prospective flock member. He added, "We wear sacred underwear that protects us from the evils of the world."

I couldn't believe that anyone could think prayer and underwear could tamp down every human vice and desire. Dad and I nodded but said nothing about Steve hanging his religion over our head.

After I had left high school, I stopped practicing any form of religion. I shunned not only bleeding Jesus images but also Christian crosses wielded like swords.

Steve added, "For the rest of my life here on earth, I'm working to seek my place in the afterlife and the Second Coming." Steve walked tall as if he had been assured a place with Jesus while the rest of us risked an eternal inferno.

I suspected my brother received many pats on the back from his church elders for embracing his new religion—undoubtedly more gratifying than Dad's continual message of "Steve, you could do better!"

On a couple of occasions, I had met and talked to Steve's new colleagues. They were full of smiles and offered a "God be with you" friendliness that felt sickly sweet. When they spoke about their religion's founding, they held onto their Joseph Smith story as if any wavering would cause them banishment from an afterlife.

Then again, maybe I was jealous that they had something to hold onto that made them feel special and blessed. I was holding tightly only onto the possibility of a career and the promise of my father's offshore money that would build my financial independence.

Unlike my brother, I held off on wanting a wife and family until I felt more grounded in my new profession. I wasn't sure I wanted kids, afraid that I might screw them up because of my childhood of nighttime parental fights. As time passed, I distanced myself from my brother's new life, being with him only when our lives intersected around Mom or Dad.

Perhaps it's easier to hand over one's life to something grandiose when one finds it hard to believe entirely in oneself. To his credit, my brother found a way to liberate himself from our parents through his religious devotion. On the other hand, I remained under my father's influence, both with his promise of a treasure buried under offshore sand and in wanting to be his preferred son. Perhaps I loathed my brother for the new light he followed while I remained mired in my father's shadow.

As I was closing in on my second master's degree, I was determined to get as far away as I could from my crazy family.

Because Mom's lawyer claimed my parents to be common-law spouses under Quebec marital law, he got the provincial court to freeze Dad's assets. Dad took trips to Czechoslovakia to obtain documents to claim that his and Mom's 1949 civil marriage was "separate property." Knowing my father, he may have even bought off a Košice town administrator to get the official documents he wanted.

Mack's firm argued in Montreal court that Czechoslovakia's marital laws trumped Quebec common-law, thus denying Mom's financial claim on half of her husband's assets. Their case meandered through the court like thick maple syrup, the kind that makes hard candy that could break a tooth.

There was nothing sweet about my parents' pending divorce. I was tired of hearing about the continued court stalling and legal stalemating. My mother whined, "My lawyer is a big bum who can't get anything settled."

I figured Dad was in no rush to move things along with her. I surmised that being at a standstill with Mom allowed him to delay marriage to Elaine. Dad never liked his knots tied tightly.

Mom continued to condemn Dad and "that other woman," yet she hoped for a miracle that he'd wake one morning and come back to her. Like in the Hungarian expression, she held firmly onto nothing in her hands.

My father continued to pretend that their separation was no big deal. He blamed Mom for not accepting his "reasonable" divorce offer of $500,000 in cash and the house in which she lived. "I won't give her a penny more!" he bellowed to Steve and me.

I suspected that our father's house in Peru, NY, was worth more than his settlement offer to Mom. But what did I know? Dad kept that house asset hidden in his CANEX offshore corporation. That financial move, plus the fact that Steve and I owned most of JHS via our common corporate shares, made it look as if our father owned little. I felt he was a bum with Mom, but I was afraid to divulge to her what I knew about Dad's offshore shenanigans. It was easier to pretend naivety whenever she asked questions about Dad's wealth.

In turn, Mom cried to Steve and me, "It's not enough that I was home for thirty years washing his socks and ironing his shirts while he was out making business and who knows what else with whom." Her voice howled. "Your father owes me half of everything he owns."

My parents' dripping separation faucet felt like water torture. After four years, I had had enough. "I've decided," I said with no hesitation to both of them. "I'm moving to Vancouver. I'll come back to visit you over the holidays. I'm only a plane ride away." I mimicked my Dad's *It's no big deal*, with a little of Steve's *We'll do it this way from now on.*

I didn't even fear my father cutting me off financially, or his requiring me to pay for what remained of my master's program. I was getting the hell out of our family's soap opera and heading west. I needed a clear sky, fresh air, and a new start. I felt there was nothing that could stop my leaving a place where I saw little hope for my family and a limited future for myself.

* * *

Some weeks before my Montreal departure, I went to see Moe, to tell him my decision to leave the city. He knew I had visited Vancouver a month earlier to seek employment and make connections.

Moe had helped me through the AU/NTL program. There had been times when I felt overwhelmed with piles of social science reading and long papers to write. When I had been an engineering student, I stuck with technical courses that had problem sets and final exams rather than writing assignments and comprehensive papers. Though my engineering thesis advisor had urged me to take a technical writing course, which I did, beneficial effects from that investment had long worn off.

Moe had offered ideas on how to annotate and summarize my book readings so I wouldn't get overwhelmed. He offered suggestions on how to focus and write my term papers. He didn't give up on me the way I sometimes did on myself.

Once I told him, "All these readings and class papers are too alien to me." I looked down at his feet. "I got a frigging D in a paper that was half the grade of one of my courses."

"I'm sorry to hear that, Harvy. How did you do in the rest of that course?"

"I got an A-minus for the first half, which is fine. But the second half was taught by a different teacher. He made his evaluations only on the final assignment. He didn't include in-class participation." I put my head in my hands. "He said my paper made no sense."

Moe thought for a couple of seconds and said, "So then you averaged a C+ for the whole course, Harvy." He gestured his open hand at me. "That's okay! You passed." Moe's voice was buoyant. "So, what's the problem?"

My head down, my voice became deflated. "I never got a frigging C in a college course before."

"Don't be so hard on yourself, Harvy. Your C is a passing grade. You're in graduate school, so who the heck will care about it afterward?" He was looking right at me. "You don't plan to do a Ph.D., do you? You are working on getting your credentials and then finding a job in your new field. From what I recall, the rest of your grades have been As and Bs, so why should one C be a big letdown?" There was no question in his question.

Though it grated on me to obtain a poor grade in anything, I took in my mentor's point and lifted my head. "Okay, Moe. I guess you're right."

Moe wasn't able to help with one big cloud that had loomed on my horizon. At the end of '83, when I was still two subjects and the practicum short of completing my AU degree, I became worried about my job prospects.

Before I considered leaving Montreal for Vancouver, I started sifting through newspapers and putting out feelers for jobs. No prospects surfaced. Because I didn't have a U.S. work visa, I couldn't explore the American frontier without a sponsoring company.

The U.S. was still recovering from the savings and loan crisis and the resulting recession of '81-'82. Why would an American company go out of its way to sponsor a Canadian fresh out of a grad school?

I hadn't maintained my French language skills during my many years of university education in the U.S. I now looked toward English Canada, especially Toronto. But Canadian unemployment rates were even higher than in the U.S. Having only once found a job outside of JHS (at Procter & Gamble eight years earlier), it felt awkward to seek my first job in a new field. Because my graduate program was new to AU, their career centre couldn't help me much. I felt like a freshwater fish flailing in a salty ocean.

I began to think that my second graduate degree had been a waste of time. If I couldn't come out of the university box and find employment in the field of my choosing—an area different than my father's wishes for me—then I felt he'd look down upon me. I feared his seeing me as unworthy, and my future would then be lost. Dad was beginning to ask what I was going to do once my AU studies ended. I didn't have an answer.

Moe had told me not to be concerned about finding a job until I had my degree in hand. But I couldn't stop worrying.

And there was something else. In the previous three years, after Moe had come into my life, I had a couple of intimate relationships with women. One even lasted nearly a year.

Sharon was a sweet and caring school teacher who had a warm smile and a love for kids and the outdoors. We had met through the Canadian

Youth Hostel Association and went on many bicycle trips together. Our connection was also bolstered for a time by our having survived an almost fatal car crash.

One late fall evening, as the outside temperature was hovering around freezing, Sharon and I drove to the city to see a movie. A car with a teen driver and two elderly passengers had skidded on the icy road and hit the wall of an underpass. Their vehicle had come to a stop some distance directly ahead of me, in my lane. If I didn't keep my wits about me, someone might die!

To prevent my auto from crashing into the stopped and disabled car, and after pumping my brakes to no avail on that icy pavement, I veered into another lane. I collided with another vehicle that was traveling alongside mine. Both of our autos swerved and turned 180-degrees to face the traffic that was coming down the highway. Luckily, the oncoming cars stopped in the nick of time, not hitting any of us. Though my auto received major bangs and dents, I had avoided hitting—and perhaps killing the passengers—of the car that had stopped at the bottom of the underpass.

After determining that no one was hurt, and after the cops had arrived to assess the situation and help the affected people, Sharon and I drove home slowly in the continuing freezing rain. She praised my quick thinking in preventing anyone from being killed, including us. Though the incident shook her and me, when we got back to her condo, we proceeded to have the best lovemaking I had had up to that point in my life.

Because both Sharon and I enjoyed the outdoors (hiking, bicycling, skating, and cross-country skiing), I hoped our relationship would go far. Alas, we didn't last, for I was still young in the intimacy department. I was not astute in knowing when she needed a hug, wanted her hand held, or desired just to cuddle on the couch. Indeed, I hadn't had good role models for emotional intimacy.

Regarding women, my life continued to remain dry for many months. Then, in December of 1983, in D.C., I met a svelte, short-haired, sandy brunette named Allie at a holiday party during one of my AU/NTL sessions.

Allie's eyes expressed warmth and caring. She had a broad smile and sported a trim body that she carried gracefully. I felt drawn to her. We had an animated conversation about the graduate programs we both attended. She was pursuing a social science degree at another college in the area. She and I smiled and laughed freely with each other, which I took as a good sign.

To my chagrin, I fumbled around to ask her out, and she—perhaps thinking I wasn't interested—left the party before I could collect my courage. I didn't catch her last name and had no way of contacting her. I walked out of that party deflated. *All my human relations schooling and I couldn't even ask her, someone who seemed interested in me, for a date.*

That incident, combined with the ending of my relationship with Sharon and my angst about finding a job in my new field, triggered deep despair. When I returned to Montreal, I was distraught. I stopped seeing or calling Moe. I didn't answer or return his phone calls or the calls of any friends. The days of my next D.C. course session came and went, with me not participating. I got calls from the program director, but I neither picked up the phone nor called her back.

Instead of talking to anyone, I cocooned in my small apartment for weeks, doing little more than sleep twelve hours a day. I stared at the ceiling for hours, both during the day and in the middle of the night, not caring what would happen to my seemingly pathetic life. I ate ice cream, cake, cookies, and chocolates until I was sick, and until my clothes grew tight.

I mindlessly surfed the TV channels, going to sleep with *The Johnny Carson Show*, hoping he could say something funny to ease my sense of failure. I laughed at Johnny's punchlines and hoped for a sign to find an exit ramp from my descending spiral. But when I opened my eyes the following mornings, I was back into my funk.

Somehow I was able to get myself up and out of my cave every week. I showered, shaved, cut my fingernails, and put on a good face. I visited my mother at her home and my father at his office—to show them I was still alive.

When they asked how I was doing or how my graduate courses were going, I avoided their eyes. I offered, "Everything's fine." I never stayed long with them, and I rushed back to my apartment cave, turned hole, turned ditch, turned bottomless pit. I no longer wanted to live. I saw no life ahead of me besides being a failure, incapable partner to any woman, and disgraced son.

Dad and Steve said nothing about my downheartedness, as if they were oblivious to my condition. It was like the time they hadn't noticed Mom suffering through her psychiatric problem. Either they were blindly unaware, or I hid my misery well.

My brother was off doing his religious thing; there was no way I'd talk to him. I never got comfort or relief from his words. And hell if I was going to let him offer me any of his standard religious lines, like "Jesus is with you," and "Let's pray to ease your pain."

My mother sensed my mood. She asked, "What happened to you, Harvy? You're not your usual happy self." I stayed tight-lipped and said nothing to reveal my distress. I kissed her goodbye after eating her supper and said, "I'll see you next time." I headed back to my cave and bed, not sure if there would be a next time.

No friend, nor family, nor Moe came to my apartment to see if I was alive. I imagined the police or EMTs breaking down my front door and carrying me away in a padded wagon, but no one came. Though I would have hated such an ordeal, I wondered what such inaction meant about how much my family and friends cared about me. *Do they even see and know me?* I felt even lonelier.

I felt ashamed, as I had during my Harvard breakdown four years earlier. But this collapse was different; it went on for days, then weeks, even months. I couldn't snap out of it as quickly as I had done before. I had no idea how to get myself back to normal—if there ever was such a thing for me?

One morning, I stood in a shivering cold shower to try to wake myself from my self-torment. *What the hell is wrong with me?!* I put my dropped head into my wet hands and screamed at my lost life and wretched family. I hit the wall with my fist to try to bang sense into my world. Nothing came. I turned off the shower and dragged myself back into my bed, having only my TV for company. At least I didn't have to explain myself to Johnny Carson.

I wanted no one, especially my father, to know my plight, my giving up, my feelings of dread and unworthiness. I was failing at making him proud, and of making it on my own the way he had done. I yearned for his respect, acknowledgement, even anointment. I wanted to prove my worthiness, but I was feeding my worst fears of becoming nobody. I couldn't stop myself. More than having lost my belief and trust in my therapist, I had misplaced the same in myself.

I had thoughts about drowning in my bathtub or jumping off my apartment's balcony eight stories above the city street. Though my head filled with an eerie daze as I looked down from my balcony at the cold, snowy streets of Montreal, I couldn't let myself fall over. Something held me back. Little did I realize that I was fighting my father within me, the father I wanted to please so much. Rather than get angry at what he had done to our family, I loathed myself.

Moe was persistent. He kept calling every week or two and left voice messages. I didn't answer his calls. I felt I had failed him, and maybe vice versa. I had tried to find my future with his guidance but felt our efforts had been futile. I wanted to die and let everyone mourn, even suffer, the loss of me.

After several months of funk, I woke one morning realizing that I couldn't erase my family or do away with myself. I don't know what had shifted, but I felt a little different that day. I called Moe. I went to see him and to tell him what happened with my job-hunting, and about my disappointment regarding the nice woman I had met. My chest was heavy, my throat dry, my eyes wet with tears. I held myself as best I could from crying. I was both angry and sad about my worthless life.

Moe asked, "Was anyone at that party connected to the woman you met?"

"No, nobody!" I asserted.

"Who introduced you to her?"

My mind spun as I stared at my psychologist. My body felt as if a Taser had stricken it. "Son-of-a-bitch!" I declared. "One of the people who had hosted the party had introduced us." I had forgotten that fact. "She may have known her."

I was incredulous. Had I been that frigging stupid, or completely blinded by my months of moping? Had I come to see Moe at the beginning of my downslide, I might have had a second chance with Allie. I felt my heart sink once more for the opportunity that was now long gone.

Moe probably saw my distress. "Harvy, you are only 29 years old. There's much more time left in you than in old fogies like your parents and me. When you are my age, the rest of us will be long gone. You'll be married to a wonderful woman and have great kids together because you knew what it was like growing up with a father who wasn't around much."

Moe grinned through his crooked teeth. "Have patience; don't give up; you're an intelligent and sensitive guy with whom any decent woman would want to be. Just get out there and try again until you find one who deserves you."

He raised a hand. "Many women can make you happy; you only need to push yourself out the door and into their view. Don't let the punches and letdowns take the wind out of you."

Having had a father, mother, and brother who blocked fresh air from getting into my lungs, I sometimes found it hard to keep my breathing going.

Over the next weeks and months, Moe helped me reconnect with my friends and complete my studies. He reminded me that there was much breath left in me. I owed the man my life.

When I got back on my feet that spring of '84, I told my father that it was going to take me an extra six months to finish my program's practicum. I'd officially graduate the following year. I paid for the one course I needed to retake so he wouldn't find out about my skipping that session. Dad seemed okay about my delayed graduation.

During one of our subsequent sessions, Moe offered words I hadn't expected. "Harvy, I'm sorry if I may have pushed you too hard in your graduate program. Maybe it was more difficult than both you and I had expected. That might have caused you to give up and stop seeing me."

I admired Moe's integrity. On the other hand, I wondered if he might have better protected me from myself. Not wanting him to feel bad about what I had done to myself, I said, "That's okay, Moe. I'm back now, and that's what counts."

He nodded his understanding.

I don't know if Moe had ever thought about sending me for psychiatric evaluation due to my depressive episodes, but I was glad he never suggested it.

As a Simkovits son, I feared my stigmatization as a "lesser than" rather than "a better man." I hoped that I was over what I had gone through and that my funk wouldn't return. If it did, I was going to find a guy like Moe no matter where I ended up.

In my years of having Moe as my mentor, I continued to withhold what I knew about my father's offshore affairs. I protected my father, perhaps thinking I was also protecting my future. Also, I didn't want Moe to think less of me for hiding Dad's concealed money and for my aspiration for that clandestine legacy. I couldn't break my promise to my father, not even with my closest confidant. I felt Dad's stash was my aspiration and burden alone. I wasn't willing to relinquish that narrative quite yet.

* * *

Six months after getting my life back, and weeks before packing up and shipping out of Montreal to Vancouver, I was sitting on Moe's couch for perhaps the final time. I started saying my goodbyes to the man who had been, for four years, my therapist, my mentor, even my friend.

It hadn't been Moe's idea for me to move west, and he hadn't tried to sway me one way or another. I had prepared myself to express my thanks for his ongoing help through my ups and downs.

Before I could open my mouth, my mentor leaned forward, "Harvy, before you say anything, I have something to tell you."

My eyebrows rose. "What's that?"

"I'm starting a new company. I'm forming a partnership with a computer consultant here in Montreal to start a new firm in computer-assisted management training."

"Hmm, how does that work?" Though I had been a student of electrical engineering and computer science, my recent HRD training told me that computers couldn't effectively train people skills to managers.

Moe raised his hand. "I can't tell you a whole lot about the technical side of this; that's the domain of my new partner, Irvin. What I do know is that the price of computers is rapidly coming down. There are now software companies that want to develop management training delivered on PCs."

"*Okayyy*," I said, with a hint of skepticism in my voice. I wondered where he was going with this. I was here to say my goodbyes.

Moe didn't slow. "A software company, Edware, is coming out with a suite of management training products that they want to distribute around the world."

I shook my head. "Computers can't train people as effectively as professional trainers." I disowned my engineering background; I was an HRD guy now.

Moe leaned forward. "That's what I first thought too, Harvy. Then Irvin showed me the Edware software. It's quite advanced with lots of interactive material. The computer takes an individual through a series of exercises to have them think and learn about the way they lead, motivate, and develop people. There are modules on communication, influence, decision-making, and other management skills. There are simulations, assessments, exercises, and applications. They look like good educational tools, and they will continue to get better."

"But that kind of learning requires human interaction and feedback. Computers can't…"

"You're on the right track there, Harvy." He raised an open palm to stop me. "That's why we don't want only to sell this product to organizational training departments. We want to create training centres where participants will interact not only with the computer but also with a trainer. Many participants would share the trainer's time."

Moe pointed to himself. "Irvin and I want to pioneer the best ways to perform this computer-assisted management training. We want to show that it's an economical alternative to traditional classroom training."

Using his right hand, Moe drew a circle in the air. He kept his left hand in the center of the ring. "The computers will be there to be an efficient extension of the trainer, in the middle of this circle. The trainer will serve many learners who are working on the machines." His right hand moved along the circle's circumference.

I was unsure. I grabbed at a technical straw. "Why a PC platform and not Mac?"

Moe smiled. "You'll have to ask Irvin that kind of question; he's the computer guy. What I know is that the training software is being built for PCs first. We have several machines on order, and Irvin has set up a demo in our office."

I was impressed. Not only was Moe knowledgeable outside his field of expertise, but he and Irvin were wasting no time to get their new company running. Though I knew Moe liked to grab onto opportunities in front of him, I was taken off-guard by his salesman manner with me. My father, brother, and mother had stopped giving my counselor the benefit of the doubt, but I still did. "So what do you want from me, Moe? I was about to say that I'm moving to Vancouver on the first of next month."

His voice calmed. "Okay, Harvy, no problem. I know your mind is fixed on leaving Montreal. But before you go, please do me a favour. Come down to our new offices next week and try out the Edware material."

His hand was still in the air, as a professor making a point to a student. "Allow me the benefit of your new HRD education to help us figure out good ways to train trainers on this material. Over the next few weeks, help us perfect our education model so that we can duplicate it across our planned training centres." He pointed at me. "You can do a literature search for us to validate the efficacy of computer-assisted training." Then he offered magic words to my ears. "I'll pay for your time."

I was blown over. My psychologist and mentor wanted to hire me? I wondered what I should do. The only advisor I could consult with was the one in front of me, and I knew where he stood.

Moe must have seen my eyes and ears perk up. He raised a hand. "Harvy, more and more software companies out there will be making computer-assisted training products. Edware has put five million dollars into their venture, and other developers are coming along quickly." He took a deep breath and added, "Irwin and I have each put $25,000 into WISE to get the firm going."

I had never seen Moe this excited. It was as if he were attached to batteries under his therapist's chair. He kept going. "We'll eventually open centres across the whole country, maybe even in your Vancouver."

He gestured toward me, his hand open. "Irvin has good connections with corporate clients here in Montreal and Toronto, and he knows computer technology." He pointed to himself. "I have know-how in psychology and education, and I have many small-business clients who need to develop their managers." He raised his other hand. "Together, we can be at the forefront of the best ways to disseminate this new management training in Canada."

I thought for a few seconds and then raised an open palm. "Okay, okay, Moe, I'll have a look. I have time before I leave Montreal." Though I had AU/NTL coursework to complete, I had nothing to lose by looking at Moe's software programs. "So, when do you want me to come over?"

It occurred to me that my father had been at the start of a new Canadian industry back in the early 1950s, the record player manufacturing industry. So why couldn't I be at the beginning of the computer-assisted training industry thirty years later?

* * *

The following week, I went to meet Irvin and to test drive the Edware product.

Irvin, ten years Moe's junior, was soft-spoken and came across as a prudent spender. He had purchased four PC Junior packages, with memory and floppy disk enhancements and dot-matrix printers, for a $1000USD per workstation, a good deal in those days. Irwin had connected the equipment himself. He showed me how to run the computer operating system and install the software.

Over the next two weeks, Moe worked to change my career flight plan. I became the first employee of WISE Management Development Centres, his and Irvin's new company. We determined a fair salary for when my graduate studies would be complete, and an hourly rate until then.

Moe added a maraschino cherry onto his whipped up plan for me. He knew I had to complete a practicum for my master's degree. My mentor suggested I do my project at WISE. He said, "We need to define our product and service offering clearly and to decide what markets to pursue first. We'll have one or two sales and marketing people coming on board over the next couple of months. When they're here, you can facilitate a day-long retreat to help us strategize our first year's game plan."

I was still a newbie in my HRD/OD field and felt Moe had a good idea and much to offer me. A Montreal job in hand could be worth more than my two or three prospects in Vancouver. "Okay, Moe. It sounds like this could be good for both of us." I suspected we understood that my pending master's degree could add to WISE's credibility in the corporate training marketplace.

Moe's voice turned serious. "There's one other thing, Harvy. Our relationship will have to change."

"What do you mean?"

"If you are going to work for Irvin and me, I can no longer be your personal counsellor. I can still help to mentor you in the context of our work here at WISE, but you'll have to find yourself another professional for personal matters. It would be too awkward otherwise."

I nodded. "Okay, I get that, Moe." I felt a pang in losing Moe that way, but what he said made sense. I also didn't see any issue in having my psychologist become my boss. If Moe was okay with it, then so was I.

Over the next few weeks, I found myself a new apartment in Montreal. I located a therapist, a leader from a Gestalt psychology training program I had been a part of in the city. I figured that if my WISE gig didn't pan out, I could still head for Vancouver, with or without a connection to Moe and WISE.

In the meantime, I was helping to start and build a new business that focused on growing managers. I'd extend my engineering background by learning about PCs. Perhaps my half-year at the Harvard Business School would come in handy too.

Both Mom and Dad were elated when I told them I was staying in Montreal. They seemed a little anxious that I'd be working for Moe, but I didn't care. I had given them a big gift by remaining in their city for now.

My brother didn't say anything one way or another about my new path, but what Steve thought didn't matter to me. I didn't owe him an explanation of my life decisions and visa versa. *Mon frère* had his new religion, and I had my new career; he had his church, and I had Moe. Time would tell as to which one of us got the better deal.

* * * *

Next Horizon for Dad

A warm, radiant sun filled the western sky on this cool late-summer evening in 1984. Dad wore a blue suit without a tie, while Elaine sported a silky beige top and tight navy blue skirt that went a little below her knees. I wore dark slacks and a button-down shirt.

We were sitting in Luigio's, an Italian restaurant within walking distance from my father and Elaine's new *pied a terre* in Montreal's Snowdon area. The small, quaint establishment had red on white tablecloths and burgundy curtains draping the windows. The place had the ambiance of the Troika but without the wandering minstrels. The fare was excellent but less expensive— the way Dad liked family meals out. Elaine enjoyed Luigio's wine selection and was friendly with the owner and staff.

For our main courses, Elaine and I had veal Oscar while Dad ordered osso buco with a side of fettuccini. As we ate, Elaine lifted her wine glass. "Here's to you, Harvy, for finding yourself a job and soon finishing your master's degree. You must feel good about both." She smiled and glanced at my father. "And your father is certainly happy that you'll be staying in Montreal for now." She turned back to me. "Good luck with your new position at WISE."

I was a couple of months into my work with Moe. Moe and Irvin had hired a salesperson my age with a training background, while I was to become a training specialist. My job was to evaluate and create flowcharts and manuals for the software products that came from Edware and other computer-assisted training vendors. We had trial customers from Moe's client base who were willing to test our management training products. Things were progressing well. "Thanks, Elaine," I said and lifted my glass to hers.

Dad lifted his scotch and pointed his finger. "Be sure those WISE guys don't screw you. Make sure you are getting the salary you are worth."

I don't think Dad appreciated my working for the man he had kicked out of his office a few years earlier. It was ironic that my father was concerned about my salary when he was skimpy in that department with his JHS staff.

"Don't worry, Dad. They're giving me a decent salary. It'll be $3000 per month when I'll be full-time after my degree program is over. The rent for my new apartment is only $350 a month, so I'll be way ahead." I was as cheerful as Moe always was and my father could be.

I eyed my father and continued. "And there may be an opportunity to buy into the firm. Moe and Irwin want to create WISE Training Centres across the country. They are putting together a prospectus to go out to business people they know." I kept my voice professional, as if I were talking to a fellow businessman. "They plan to sell a 20% stake in the firm. It'll be in chunks of 2% for $50,000 each to 10 investors. I'm thinking about getting in on it myself."

My father responded as if his entrepreneurial pants were on fire. "Don't pay too much to buy in." His voice was loud. "For the start-up work you are doing, those guys should give you a discounted price, even shares for free." He raced along with his train of thought. "Rather than giving them $50,000 cash for a stake, tell them you'll work for them free for a year."

"That's a good idea, Johnny," Elaine said. Her voice stayed cool and calm, perhaps giving Dad a message to keep his the same.

My father hadn't finished, though his tone was less agitated. "And be careful about getting into a partnership deal. Partnerships rarely work for minority shareholders, even with a signed agreement. Those guys can take your money and do what they want afterward. You'll have no recourse."

"I'm sure Harvy will think this through carefully, Johnny," Elaine added. "There's lots of time. No need to give him a lecture on it now."

I, too, wanted my father to calm down. Maybe he didn't like that Moe had a growing influence on my future. "I'll be sure to get your help in making that arrangement," I said. But I didn't want my father to look over my shoulder and tell me what to do.

Dad settled down. "Okay, then." He took a swig of his drink and placed the glass onto our cluttered table.

I followed him by throwing a bone onto the tablecloth. "Maybe you'd want to get in on this deal too. It will be a big moneymaker when we have centres established across the whole country."

His eyes opened wide. I bet he had already been thinking that way. "Okay, Harvy. If Moe can get nine other 2% investors, then tell him I'll take the last 2%." He wagged his finger as his face turned serious. "But only if they treat you fairly."

I smiled inside for how well my father could leverage his assets for my benefit. It mattered not that he hadn't seen Moe in years. Money deals were money deals. He probably figured I'd be there to watch over any investment he'd make. He was like Elaine's Orphee going after a steak bone.

Elaine took a sip of her wine and changed the subject. "Your father has news for you and your brother." She looked at him as he forked pasta into his mouth. It was rare for Dad to talk about hard subjects without being poked. Elaine knew how to do it without involving a cattle prod. My ears perked as my father cleared his throat. "I'm planning to liquidate and close JHS."

What?! It was now my turn for my voice to elevate in my head and my eyes to open wide. I sat stunned. Dad had directed his manufacturing ship and crew for thirty years. His statement had come out of his mouth as if his decision had been no big deal.

He spoke without looking at me; his eyes focused on the table. "I'm 64 years old, not a spring chicken anymore. I know you aren't interested in working for the company, and I don't think Steve could keep it going by himself."

My father took a long breath. "I've had enough these last few years of trying to keep the business afloat. And I had that case of angina a couple of years ago." He took another swig of his drink and touched his chest. "At my age, I don't need any more headaches or a heart attack."

Though Dad was nearing the customary retirement age, he remained spry. He was still able to match any man on the dance floor and at the bar. "Wow, Dad," I said. "Closing JHS is a big decision. What are you going to do after that?"

My father had been the top dog, head honcho, king of his JHS hill since before I was born. Over that time, he had conducted over fifteen hundred weekly production meetings, and he rebuked his foremen innumerable times when things didn't go the way he wanted. He had gone through over seventy-five hundred days of salespeople coming to his front door, suppliers calling on the phone, and piles of purchase orders, contracts, and cheques to sign. He had visited his Montreal and Toronto customers countless times for design and engineering meetings, to negotiate prices and delivery, to schedule production and shipment, and to ask or beg for orders. For well over a thousand nights, he had entertained valued customers and essential suppliers at his favourite Montreal haunts—along with their swanky food, stiff drinks, stirring songs, and spicy women—well into the wee hours.

There had been almost as many nights when he came home exhausted, his head hitting the pillow for a few short hours before going back to his four successive factories, from Common St. to Nazareth St. to Saint Patrick St. to Delmeade Road—his babies from their birth.

How did he so suddenly, so matter-of-factly, so unemotionally, relinquish all that? What will it now be like for him to abruptly curtail his life as a salesman, a manufacturing man, and a businessman?

Dad spoke as if nothing dramatic had happened. "First, I need to liquidate the inventory, which will take three to six months to complete. And I need to find a tenant for our factory—I still want to hold onto the building as an income-producing property." I was amazed that he had his business closing already planned.

He added, "I'll make a new section of offices for myself in the corner of the building. Then I'll rent the production facility, the main office, and the woodworking machines to another cabinet manufacturer, like to a company that can make TVs or knock-down furniture." He looked at me. "I already have feelers out to people I know."

Though I knew it was time for Dad to consider the next phase of his life, I had no idea he could pull the retirement trigger so quickly. Perhaps Elaine had told Dad that he didn't need the business pressures and headaches anymore. I wondered what my father would do when he no longer had both a factory kingdom to go to every day and an office throne on which to sit.

Elaine chimed in. "Your father needs to relax more, and he doesn't need the money."

Dad came back. "After my next birthday, I'll be collecting from the deferred annuities that Maury Reemer established for me years ago, when I sold most of my industrial and apartment buildings. I'll receive nearly $200,000 each year from those investments and my government pension." He batted his hand. "There is little point for me to make more money after that. The government would take away in taxes more than half of any other income I'd make."

I didn't say it in front of Elaine, but there would be a big chunk of tax-free income coming to my father from his offshore assets. It was possibly more money than he could spend, but time would tell.

Elaine raised her hand. "We'll have more opportunity to do things at the Peru house. You know how your father loves projects. And the Slovak Business Association has been after your father for years to become their president. Now he'll have time for that."

"Yah, I need that position like I need a hole in my head," Dad snapped back. "It's a lot of goddamn work for no pay." He looked at me for sympathy, but I said nothing. Dad would need to keep his mind occupied.

Elaine fired back. "Well, you aren't going to sit around and do nothing, Johnny. They need your good business thinking in the association." She turned to me. "That association doesn't even have a formal charter or tax-exempt status so that members can legally deduct their donations. They're so fly-by-night that they're lost in the dark."

Yah, and I'm looking at one of those fly-by-night guys. There was something about Slavic businessmen like my father. They preferred sidestepping the legalities and administrative details rather than pay the lawyers and accountants to create a fully legit association. I kept my not-so-kind thoughts to myself.

Dad looked at Elaine, and his voice softened. "I'll get involved in business investments and projects here and there. And we'll spend more time travelling, huh darling?" He took a breath. "We'll spend the summers at our place on Lake Champlain. And I want us to go to Czechoslovakia every fall, in addition to the winter trips we take south to the Caribbean." He lifted a hand. "Maybe we'll go to South America too, like to Brazil and Argentina."

Elaine winked. "You know I still have my job, Johnny. I'm not ready to retire quite yet." She was over two decades younger than Dad. "But my property-management company won't miss me as much during the colder months. We could continue to go south in the winter and Europe in the fall." I noticed she said Europe and not just Czechoslovakia.

I was glad it was Elaine rather than me going behind the Iron Curtain with my father in mid-November when he could take advantage of cheaper transatlantic fares. The thought of travelling through a cold, clammy, communist Czechoslovakia near the onset of winter made me shiver. Though Czechoslovakia wasn't colder than Canada, I preferred going to warmer places during times close to igloo season. I glanced over at my father. "Does Steve know about your plans?"

His eyes were on me as he held firmly onto his vodka glass. "I want you to come to the office this week; I'll tell him then." His eyebrows fell. "Since he got into his new religion and then got hitched, he's been so busy with other things that he hardly works for me anymore. His family and church come first for him, never JHS, which supports him."

Dad's voice rose. "The Mormon scripture says, 'You should honor your father,' but Steve never does."

Steve had been our father's main topic of complaint ever since I had worked for JHS. But Dad never put his foot down with his first son, other than yell at him about purchasing issues. I consoled myself that I never gave Dad reason to complain about my character.

Decades from now, Elaine would confirm my perception by telling me, "Sometimes your father complained about both his kids not appreciating enough the education and opportunities he gave them. But he never had any specific criticism of you, Harvy, as he did with your brother."

It was true that Dad and I had played each other as favourites, but our closeness had stained my relationships with Steve.

Though I had pressed Dad more than once to fire my brother for his insubordination, my father's closing of JHS might be the next best thing; it would take away Steve's safety net, and he'd have to find a real job. "Okay, Dad, whatever you want," I said. "When do you need me at the office?"

From what I knew, my brother hadn't squirreled away money into secure investments as I had done. Perhaps he thought our father would support him forever. I wondered how Steve would handle our father's news.

Decades later, after my father's passing, Elaine mentioned more about Dad's decision to dissolve his manufacturing business. "Your father desperately wanted you and Steve to continue JHS, but both of you had made it clear you weren't interested. On many occasions, I encouraged him to sell the company instead of waiting for the day you'd have to liquidate the assets for potentially ten cents on the dollar. I told Johnny, 'If you love your boys, then you need to dispose of your company and invest the money, rather than your sons having to sell everything under duress when you're gone.'"

She took a long breath as her eyes looked into the past. "It was a difficult decision for Johnny. But based on my urging over many months (if I may take the credit), he agreed that it was the best way to go."

I appreciated Elaine's good head and her persistence with my father. It made my and Steve's lives a little easier.

Some years later, Dad's long-time and now retired secretary, Helen, offered more about my father's decision to close JHS. Over dinner at her and Georges' home, she said. "Your father was sad and upset about your leaving JHS when you did, Harvy. He had been counting on you to take over the business with your brother. He also felt that Stevie could not run it on his own."

"Yes, I know," I responded with a sigh. "But my father didn't make it easy for any of us," I added, staring at her. I considered Helen and her husband included in my statement.

"I know," she responded, her face solemn. "Johnny realized that there was nothing he could do about your decision, so he accepted it."

My departure from Dad's company might have been a trigger for my father to consider closing JHS's manufacturing business. Dad's ultimate dream for his company's future was over, and that was truly unfortunate for him and our family.

I could understand my father's profound sadness about ending his thirty-year run; it must have hurt deeply. I didn't know if he realized that his hands, along with his sons' hands, had hammered a stake into the future of our family business.

* * *

Later that week, the three Simkovits men met at JHS's factory office after everyone else had left for the day. We had met this way every two to three weeks when I had worked at the company. We now did it only once a month or quarter, when Dad wanted to discuss important things, as he did today.

I sat at Helen's desk. Since I didn't work at JHS anymore, I didn't want to sit at my old desk opposite Dad. I played along as our father talked, pretending to hear Dad's plans for the first time. There was no sense in Steve's knowing I had been privy to our father's decision before he was in the know. I wondered how Steve would react to being cut off from his JHS livelihood.

"Boys," Dad said, looking our way. "I'm closing our production operation before the end of this year." He looked at my brother. "Stevie, I'll help you find another purchasing job if that's something you still want to do."

I kept my jaw from dropping on Helen's desk. In front of my eyes, Dad had softened the termination blow for his first son. Was he now going to become a job-hunting agent for Steve?

I didn't believe our father was giving his first son any life-learning lessons. Why couldn't Steve find his way from here, like I was doing? It grated on me that Dad could complain big time about Steve's lack of consideration toward him, but he still put himself out for his first offspring. Instead of screaming at them for their craziness, I bit my lip until it almost bled.

My brother nodded but showed little reaction to our father's announcement. "Okay, Dad," he said blandly. Perhaps he figured that this day had been coming, or he didn't want to show vulnerability in front of me.

Our father continued. "I want to sell off the garbage we have in inventory, and then find a tenant." He talked calmly. "Everyone here knows that the company hasn't been doing well these last few years. Business has been slow, and we haven't been able to get projects going with any offshore TV suppliers. If it weren't for the income from JHS's cash investments covering the losses we are having in production, we'd go bust."

Dad looked down. "And I'm not a young guy anymore. It's time for me to relax." He said nothing about his lack of confidence in Steve keeping the business going on his own, or about his frustrations in working with his first son. He also said nothing about his disappointment in my having left the company. Perhaps it was too late for such declarations.

Steve mimicked my standard line. "Okay, Dad, whatever you want." I couldn't tell if he spoke that way because I was in the room. He had been taking much time off from JHS for family and church obligations; maybe it didn't matter to him that Dad was closing the company. "When will you tell the office staff and factory people?" he asked.

Dad looked at him. "I'm planning to tell the foremen at the next production meeting. They will tell their people afterward, and I'll tell the office staff. We'll start letting people go soon, but we'll need a few employees for a while to help me liquidate our stock and organize the place for new tenants."

He pointed to the factory and continued to speak matter-of-factly. "I'm planning to rent the place, with the machinery included. We'll need to reconfigure the offices so I can have a space for myself. I'm hoping to close the company by the end of this year."

Steve continued with his questions. "Are you considering a pension or severance for your best employees, like your foremen, especially the ones who have been with you for a long time?"

Count on my brother to be the first one to call for Dad's support of JHS employees. In this case, Steve had a point.

Dad responded. "They'll get unemployment benefits if they can't find another job right away. Our foreman, Georges, has been with JHS the longest. We gave him and Helen a big money gift a few years ago when he made it to 25 years with us. We paid for a living room full of furniture for their home."

Dad took a moment to light a cigarette. "I don't think we need to give him or anyone else anything more. They are still young enough to work." He took several puffs. "I'll give them good references, and they have their RSP [Retirement Savings Plan] pensions they've contributed to over the years, as well as their Quebec and Canadian pension plans that the company paid into on their behalf." He pointed his cigarette at Steve. "And they have their basic health insurance from the government. I don't think they need anything more."

I felt a pang of nepotistic guilt. Dad's company was paying for my master's degree program, which amounted to six to twelve months of salary for most JHS's employees. "You should give something to your best people, Dad," I offered. "They stuck it out with you all these years." It was rare for my brother and me to agree.

Dad looked my way. "I'll think about it." But it seemed as if he had decided.

I cared the most about Helen and Georges. They had been with Dad from the early days of Montreal Phono. I had known both of them since I was a kid. They always had smiles for me and something nice to say. If our dad wouldn't help them now, then Steve and I could make it up to them down the line.

* * * *

New Havens and Deeper We Go

Steve and I sat motionless in our chairs, perhaps still taking in our father's proclamations of closing JHS. In the lull, Dad changed the subject to what I had never been told or hadn't foreseen. "Boys, I'm planning to buy a condo in The Bahamas, maybe in Freeport on Grand Bahamas Island."

"How come, Dad?" Steve blurted out, his face showing puzzlement.

"What's that about?" I said, right behind my brother.

Dad repeated what he had once told me. "I'm getting tired of going to Grand Cayman. It's too far away and too expensive to stay there." He didn't say anything about the money he had stashed in that island haven.

He then offered words that made me shudder. "I want to establish Canadian non-residency status. I will obtain Bahamian residency so that I will no longer reside in Canada for tax purposes."

"Why, Dad?" I asked, beating my brother to the question. *And why didn't you say anything about this when we had supper together earlier this week?* Maybe he thought I wouldn't ask many questions in front of Steve about his Bahamian chess move. Or perhaps he didn't want to say much about it in front of Elaine.

Dad looked at us. "I have to start taking my pension and annuities next year. The Bahamian government doesn't tax personal income. If I'm a non-

229

resident of Canada, the federal government here will withhold only 15% of my pension payments for federal taxes. Otherwise, I'd have to pay an over 50% tax to them and Quebec if I lived here. As a legal Bahamian resident, the difference would come tax-free to me.

"Is this legal?" Steve asked.

"For sure," Dad said. "There's nothing to worry about. Lots of people do this to save on income tax."

"But as a non-resident, Dad," I added, "don't you have to live outside of Canada most of the time?" *What's my father thinking?!*

"That's why I have the Peru house, so I don't have to come back to Canada. I could stay there as much as I want to. You guys, as well as my and Elaine's friends, can come to visit us in Peru anytime."

Dad had had this non-residency thing planned all along. I was stunned, not knowing what to think or feel. What would Steve's and my life be like with our father living far away?

He continued calmly. "At the beginning of my Canadian non-residency, I'll only have to be out of the country for the better part of a year. After that, I can come back to visit anytime." He gestured at Steve and me. "And, you guys are invited to come down to Freeport and stay with us there too." He smiled as if he had developed a foolproof plan. "I'll buy a small condo there for Elaine and me."

Dad spoke confidently. "Either of you can even use the condo when Elaine and I aren't there. Elaine's mother will come to spend time with us too."

Yeah, right! I don't even like Freeport! The last time I had been there with Dad, he played blackjack at the Princess Casino while I was bored as shit in his shadow. Doesn't he remember that I had become so pissed by his yelping, and by being his money chip pack mule, that I abandoned him at the card table? *If he leaves for Freeport, he'll be beaching by day and gaming by night without me.*

On the other hand, it might be healthy for Dad to get away and relax more. It would mean Steve and I would be more in charge of JHS's interests in Montreal, not only the old factory building but also the other properties that the company owned.

It would be easier if Dad stayed in Canada. I wouldn't have to deal directly with *mon confrere,* and I could keep more of my attention on my new job with Moe and WISE. I imagined our father calling Steve and me every day from his Freeport condo balcony to tell us to do this or that for him. I could see Steve procrastinating on his JHS assignments, putting his church responsibilities first, and I'd have to pick up the slack. Because of my work at WISE, I didn't want to take care of my father's properties and manage my brother as well.

I grabbed for another chisel with which to chip away on Dad's non-residency pyramid. "What does Elaine think about this? Doesn't she still want to work?" I wanted to remind him about what she had said over supper two nights earlier. I didn't think she'd want to live the life of a beach vagabond, reading crime novels (or being a part of one).

My father looked at me. "She's okay with these plans, son. It'll take three years to obtain my Bahamian residency. By then, she'll have had enough of working for her employer. She'll be ready to take more time off and spend it with me." Dad smiled and invoked one of his expressions, "What's good for the gander is good for the goose."

I had no idea whether Dad was telling it how it was or how he wanted it to be. He seemed confident that nothing would get in the way of the tax-savings maneuver he was planning. Possibly, I'd have to find a way to raise this issue with Elaine without upsetting my father.

I tried another angle. "Why go to Freeport, Dad, and not a more interesting place like Nassau? There are more casinos there, and it's a real town. There's more to do."

Dad was unmoved. "During the winter, there are a lot of cheap charter flights to Freeport from Montreal. And, Freeport is only a short puddle jump from Fort Lauderdale or Palm Beach. It's much easier to get to, and a much less expensive place to buy a condo."

I could imagine Elaine wilting from the Freeport boredom. Other than deep-sea fishing, playing golf, gambling at the casino—all of which Elaine didn't do—what remained was lying by a beach or pool with a book, or shopping at Freeport's one and only International Bazaar. For me, it was a rich man's paradise that was good only for turning white skin into brown toast.

"Why does it take three years for you to get a Bahamian residency?" Steve asked. I stared at him, surprised by his question. Where were my brother's contradictory ways when we needed them? Maybe Steve was pleased to see Dad banish himself to an offshore spit of coral and sand.

Dad looked at my brother. "I need to have a footprint in The Bahamas for two years before I can apply for permanent residency. My lawyer there says that I could have it within a year after that. Until then, Elaine and I will stay there two to three weeks every month or two during the winter season. It'll be enough to claim residency."

Those Bahamians make this easy! They must be building a tax-haven cottage industry of North Americans seeking to skirt income taxes.

My head began to pound, and my stomach started to churn. I wasn't entirely sure if I would be better or worse off by Dad becoming a Canadian non-resident. I didn't want to deal with my brother, even though he and I would have more control of the JHS steering wheel if Dad were deep-sea fishing and blackjack playing in the Caribbean.

I needed more time to think this through and to talk to Dad privately. Though it seemed as if his decision to leave Canada was a done deal, there was still time. Maybe Dad would change his mind after he and Elaine spent two years living out of Canadian suitcases on Bahamian limestone.

Steve looked at his watch and excused himself for a church commitment. I hung around awhile longer.

Not wanting to seem overly eager, I typically waited for my father to broach the subject of his offshore money. But there was a missing piece to Dad's non-residency, money-hiding, and tax-evading puzzle that nagged at me. I couldn't say anything with my brother in earshot but now seemed a good time. "Dad, can I ask about your plans?"

"Sure, son, anything." Dad was amenable when he was approached right.

"What are you planning to do about CANEX?" I kept my voice quiet, and I didn't employ the words "offshore shell corporation." I continued.

"You told me you are moving everything from Cayman to a different bank in Lux. Doesn't CANEX still own your Peru, NY house? What will happen when you plant yourself in Freeport and no longer travel to Cayman?"

Dad responded calmly. He repeated what he had once told me. "I'll close CANEX soon, and then I'll move the rest of what I have in Cayman over to Lux before I move to The Bahamas." He spoke confidently. "I'm going to have JHS buy the Peru property from CANEX before I let go of my Canadian residency. Through that purchase, I can move some of the company's cash over there too."

I was astonished by how my father had found a new money-haven cat to skin. If it weren't for my stomach churning from the stench, I might have been enthralled and impressed.

Dad stood and motioned toward the front entrance, indicating he wanted us to depart for the evening. He offered, "Once we close our manufacturing operation, JHS will exist as a holding company for the property assets we still own here," he pointed to the ground, "including this industrial building." He took a breath. "Once I have my residency established in The Bahamas, then I can legitimize my offshore assets. I'll pay minimal Canadian taxes on any of my income from here, and no tax on my money held over there." He pointed south.

He donned his jacket and talked matter-of-factly. "I'll have only withholding taxes to pay on my Canadian RSP, my company and government pensions, and the life annuities I own. I'll save well over a hundred thousand dollars in taxes each year from my annual income, and even more when I redeem my JHS shares."

Dad was on a roll, but something still bothered me. "Dad, by JHS owning the Peru house, aren't business owners forbidden to live in a property that their holding company owns? Isn't there a tax problem when a company holds property that a shareholder lives in?" Over the years, I had learned a tax accounting thing or two from Dad's auditor, Roger Delliard.

"I've got that figured out, son." He spoke with a touch of sarcasm in his voice, as if I were a naive kid. I hated it when he did that, but I said nothing as I gnawed at my lip. He continued. "Elaine and I aren't married.

She'll sign a lease with JHS in her name for the Peru house. This way, there's no direct connection between me and that property."

He took the last puff of his cigarette and confidently blew the smoke upward, away from me. "Elaine's an American citizen and can easily reside in the States. Eventually, she will let go of her Canadian residency and pay taxes only in the U.S., which will be cheaper for her than paying in both countries as she does now." He smiled. "Relinquishing her Canadian residency will save money for her too."

I wondered how much Elaine knew of Dad's plans for her. Would this modern goose go along with her scheming gander partner? "Are you sure that this will work, Dad?" My voice was skeptical. I was amazed at how my brazen father could continue to deny the taxes due to his adopted country of thirty-five years.

"Sure, there's no problem," he said. "As far as the U.S. IRS is concerned, the Peru house is owned by a Canadian holding company. As far as Revenue Canada is concerned, it's rented by an American with no connection to me. Nobody besides us will know otherwise."

"Okay, Dad," I said as I looked at his feet. A troubling feeling gnawed at my gut. I wondered if Dad truly knew what he was doing.

I desperately looked for another place to poke holes in his plan. "Does Elaine know about your maneuvering concerning the house and CANEX?"

My father became a tad edgy. "She knows enough, as much as she needs to know." His tone softened. "She's okay with my getting my non-residency in The Bahamas."

I wondered again how much my father had told her. I thought about asking her, but how could I put my nose between them? Could I broach the subject without upsetting either him or her?

Dad looked at me in a kind, fatherly way. "The rest of it, Harvy, you already know. There's nothing to worry about, son; I've worked out everything. In case something happens to me, you know where to go and find the people who know where my money is 'over there.'" He was referring to the Cayman and Lux bank business cards he kept hidden in the drawer of his back office desk.

My father repeated a promise he had made over a year earlier. "And I'll take you to meet the Lux bank manager here in Montreal, the guy I told you about."

I had mixed feelings about meeting that bank manager. On the one hand, I'd be pleased to know more about my father's offshore stash. On the other hand, I'd meet a banker whose job was to help affluent Canadians skirt their fair share of taxes. I wondered how I would act with such a fellow. Would I be cordial, or would I slap him in the face, literally or with my words?

"How much does Steve know about this?" I was worried about having a slip-up or awkward moment with my brother about Dad's offshore dealings.

"Just what I told both of you today. Steve knows nothing more about CANEX or Lux." Dad reiterated, "Only you know about those things."

Could I be sure that my father was straight with me? Then again, why would he lie? He'd tell me the truth about his money, wouldn't he?

My head felt airsick not only from Dad's cigarette smoke but also from everything he had divulged. His offshore assets were moving to Luxembourg with a still-mysterious Lux bank branch situated in Montreal. *Was he going to keep his promise and take me there one day?*

The Peru, NY house would be sold to JHS by CANEX, after which Dad would close CANEX in Cayman. *Was he going to close that shell corporation this time?*

Dad would apply for Canadian non-residency status in Freeport Bahamas. *Would Elaine unwittingly go along for the tax-avoiding ride?*

Elaine would rent their Peru home from JHS, utilizing her name and U.S. citizenship as a front for my father. *Would she let Dad ride on her American coattails? And, would she be yet another person from whom I'd have to keep my father's hidden money secrets?*

My brother didn't know about Dad's offshore affairs. *Would Dad's growing web of deceit put even of more of a wedge between Steve and me?*

There was another reason why my father's financial finagling bothered me. He and my mother hadn't finalized their divorce. Her attorney and Dad's lawyer were still battling it out in Quebec court. Mack was doing everything he could do to delay any settlement. I again figured Dad wanted to put off any marriage overtures by Elaine.

I didn't want to get into my mother's situation right now. I stuck to the advice I obtained long ago from both Moe and Mack—to stay out of my parents' separation.

But there was a growing heaviness in my heart that my mother was going to get stiffed. Every week she clipped coupons from the newspaper, bought the cheapest food for herself, and hardly went out or on vacation. She worked to save every penny she could from the meagre separation allowance she received from Dad.

I wondered if, one day, I would have a tense faceoff with my father regarding my mother.

* * *

Before closing his manufacturing company's doors for good, Dad helped Steve find another purchasing job. That position was with a small-business owner Dad knew in Montreal. My father had indicated to the owner that he would invest in his company. Hiring Steve as the purchasing agent became a part of the grander deal.

A few years later, the owner of that business let Steve go because our father had not invested in his company. Dad then got my brother into a second company via a similar agreement. Time would tell how long that arrangement would last.

I had turned thirty just before Dad closed JHS at the end of 1984. I found it curious that he had never kept any samples or even photographs of the hundreds of record player and console stereo models he had built over the decades. Those products could stock a record player museum or fill a console collector's photo album.

Maybe my father wasn't proud of his products, or perhaps he preferred selling his extra units for cash. Or had he figured that those electronic devices wouldn't last the test of time? My take was that manufacturing had only been my father's way of making money. The growing numbers in his bank statements were more meaningful than his preserving any vestige of what had contributed to his affluence.

Dad found a trio of young Korean Canadian entrepreneurs to lease his factory building. They produced TV cabinets for Sanyo, a Korean TV manufacturer. Their business was similar to what Dad had attempted to do years earlier with Goldstar—importing TV chassis from that Korean supplier and assembling them into cabinets in JHS's factory.

The people who ran that TV assembly business had the overseas connections that my father didn't. No matter, Dad no longer needed the manufacturing headaches, and he would collect $15,000 per month on his facility.

After JHS closed as a going concern, only one employee—my father's bookkeeper—remained on the payroll. Dad kept Rob engaged in helping to manage JHS's land and property holdings. Rob could speak and write in

French, an essential skill when dealing with the Quebec government and the towns where JHS's other properties were situated.

Dad involved Rob in the financial deals he was planning with the businesses in which he placed Steve, though no real deals seemed to be forthcoming with those companies. When my father and Rob had nothing to do, they played gin rummy for hours in the office. I was grateful that it was Rob and not me having to do that with Dad.

Rob and my father got close. Like a devoted third son, Rob arrived on time both to work and to Dad's birthday and holiday parties. On those occasions, the two of them hugged and kissed each other on the cheeks. They smoked and drank like comrades. Though their relationship seemed to get tighter over the years, I never felt threatened by Rob and his knowledge about my father's legitimate property holdings.

Dad had assured me that Simkovits blood was thicker than employee water. Rob was there for Dad when my father needed him, and Dad paid him well for his loyalty. Rob turned out to be a better companion to my father than Steve or I could ever be.

Because of his thick, handlebar moustache, Steve and I called our JHS bookkeeper "Roberto." He became a part of our extended Simkovits family, and I was glad that he was providing value for his remuneration, unlike some of us Simkovitses.

* * *

In early 1985, Dad purchased his Bahamian condo in Freeport. He made sure border officials stamped his passport every time he and Elaine made their island entries and exits.

Within a few years, Dad transferred the ownership of his Peru house from CANEX to JHS Holdings. He then told me he closed CANEX in Cayman, and that his money there was moved to Lux. He didn't even have to go down to Cayman to complete those transactions. They were carried out long-distance by phone, fax, and courier. My father's Cayman days were now officially over.

There was one thorn in my father's Canadian non-residency retirement plan. He had to give Elaine an extra three thousand dollars in after-tax cash each month so she could pay that money to JHS Holdings as rent for the Peru house. The company was then obliged to pay corporate taxes on those amounts. My father told me, "I hate having to pay taxes on the cash that comes to JHS through Elaine's house payments."

Nevertheless, he accepted the situation begrudgingly. It was a part of the price to acquire his Canadian non-residency. In time, he'd get the money back many times over. What he now needed was his Bahamian residency papers so he could leave Canada officially.

I wondered why Elaine went along with my father's money maneuvering. Could it have been blind love, or was it something else? I didn't dare ask her what she thought about my father's offshore plans. I didn't want to get between her and my father, and I didn't want to let her know what I did or didn't know about his offshore finances. I'd want her to go to Dad with anything I'd ask or tell her. That could get my father to roar at me. It was yet another Johnny Simkovits bind in which I felt entwined.

There was one consolation to the Peru house money snag. Dad siphoned the extra JHS income to my brother and me by way of our annual bonuses. Our personal tax rates were much lower than the company's rate or Dad's marginal tax rate, so Steve and I got a benefit from his Peru money maneuver.

Having a wife and a kid on the way, Steve used his bonuses to feed his growing family—he was obtaining only a modest salary from the small companies in which Dad had placed him. As usual, I turned JHS's bonus money into savings to make my future a little more secure.

I certainly didn't want to be left short if my father ever went crazy, unexpectedly giving his money away to reckless people or rash causes. I had read how some wealthy, divorced, and remarried men gave their wealth to their new, young wives, leaving their kids in the lurch.

If Dad was careless enough to play tax-avoiding games, he might become foolish enough to banish both Steve and me from his estate. He had told us that we came first in his mind and estate. But he had made similar promises to our mother, and I saw how she had fared.

I was glad my father had severed his ties with Cayman, distancing himself from the fair-weather island associates with whom he had affiliated. I didn't miss any of those people. I did wonder what new financial escapades The Bahamas would bring, and what would eventually happen with Dad's Peru house trickery. Would Revenue Canada catch on to his hidden money drift?

For now, I rode the churning waves of my father's black money seas. When my turn would come at the tiller of Dad's treasure ship, I prayed that I'd guide it into calmer waters that my stomach could manage. But no one knew what dangers or surprises lurked at the next Johnny Simkovits horizon.

* * *

It was the summer of 1985, a month or two after I had walked for my second graduate diploma. At the end of a workday at WISE, I came to visit my father in his office. He had been travelling back and forth between Freeport and Montreal almost every month during that winter and spring. Rob had left the office for the day, and Dad was alone.

Dad couldn't stop bragging. "You can't believe the tax-free income I'm making down there." I knew he was talking about Freeport. Maybe he was telling me because he had no one else to crow to. Perhaps he didn't want to risk putting that information on a drum for the wrong people to hear. But I soon found out he had another purpose in mind.

"Freeport's a gold mine! I can't wait for you to come and see for yourself, son." His eyes almost popped out of his head. He sounded like his gold-hauling Cayman real estate friend, Larry Younger. "I found a young fellow who can give me a 10% annual interest on my money, all in cash."

I sat in my old office chair across from Dad. "How is he able to do that?"

My father's voice was excited. "My guy has steady money suppliers and customers. He borrows cash at 10% and then lends it out at 15%." He raised his hand. "He works with well-to-do people. The money is tax-free, both in and out."

I wondered if Dad's Bahamian guy looked like a baseball player with a big bat to swing at the legs of any non-payers. I had seen enough Hollywood movies to know that there could be hardball endings to such money games.

My father got closer to his purpose. "Harvy, you received your company bonus recently."

I nodded and said, "Yes, Dad." Steve and I had recently obtained $50,000CAD each in JHS bonus money (about $38,000 net after government deductions and taxes). It was more money than my annual salary at WISE. But Dad's question made me feel apprehensive.

He spoke softly, "If you don't need that cash, I could take it 'down there' for you. I can get you the same tax-free interest that I'm getting." He smiled. "It's twice what you'd get from any bank CD here, and you don't have to declare the earnings on your tax returns."

Whoa! That's a new kettle of slimy Bahamian fish! Dad had never before asked me to join him in one of his offshore money ventures.

"Is it safe?" was the best objection I could produce. "Are you sure your guy would pay the money back?" I needed time to consider whether or not this Caribbean fish was to my taste.

"I trust the guy," Dad said. "He has many people he works with over there. He wouldn't screw them, or he'd be out of business fast."

Yah, if he didn't foot-scoff first with the money.

Dad added, "He's been doing this kind of business there for years."

"How will he specifically use my cash?"

My father seemed unfazed by my questions. "He has different people he lends to for various property and business projects. They get short-term money from him because they've committed their other assets elsewhere." He looked right at me. "The minimum term he offers is one year, but I'm in with him for three. He'll pay the interest every year and return the principal at the end."

That seemed like a long time. "How much did you give the guy?" I asked.

"$50,000 U.S. for now." Perhaps because of my hesitation, my father softened the risk. "Harvy, I'll personally take responsibility for your money. I'll pay you back no matter what happens."

My head whirled. *Was this a tax evader's test?* If I rebuked his offer, then he might wonder if I was worthy to inherit his larger stash. Or maybe this was his way to prevent me from spending my bonus money. Knowing that I was a saver, he might be giving me a gift of learning about an income-enhancing, tax-avoiding trick from him, the master.

I felt little recourse. "Okay, Dad, if you think it's okay."

Dad nodded. I felt a prick in my gut from swallowing Dad's offshore lure. I was now fully entrenched—hook, line, and stinker—into my father's tax-skirting sport.

I returned a few days later and gave my father a U.S. dollar cheque for a good part of my bonus money. I had made out the cheque in his name. That amount of money was small potatoes for my father but big bucks for me.

Dad took my cheque and placed it in his wallet. Later, he told he had deposited it into his Bahamian bank, turned it into cash, and then "lent" it to the money broker.

The next time Dad returned from Freeport, he handed me a short, handwritten IOU, signed by his money man.

I told myself that outside of this piece of paper, there was no indication of my illicit money deal. I had lent the money to my father, and he had made the loan to his Bahamas broker. He was the one with his hands in the tax-avoidance cookie jar.

For the next two years, Dad gave me the interest payments he received, in cash, every time he came back from his Bahamian winter vacations. Though I considered the money a gift, I couldn't wait until I'd get back the original amount and breathe easier about my potential tax-skirting sin.

* * * *

16

Sleight of Watch

Dad turned 65th on February 3 of 1985, six weeks after he closed JHS. He invited a hundred of his closest Eastern European, English, and French friends to his retirement party at the British Armed Services Club in Montreal.

One of Dad's best friends, a Czech-born man named Joe Bilek, had pulled strings to get my father into that exclusive club. Before WWII began, when Joe was nineteen years old, he escaped Czechoslovakia for England. He then enlisted in the British air force to fight against the Axis powers.

After the war, Joe immigrated to Canada, where he met my father. (I found it humorous how Joe spoke fluent Czech with his British-accented voice.) Getting my father into the Armed Services Club was Joe's birthday present to my father, though Dad paid for the event.

At the party, Dad stood at the front of the host's reception line. He greeted guests as they walked into the hall. Behind us, a small gypsy music troop played rapturous Eastern European melodies. Dad wore a new, slightly shiny, deep blue three-piece suit. He shook hands and gave big bear hugs to everyone, and he kissed the back of every woman's hand. The room reverberated with chatter as long-time friends and acquaintances from Dad's business days greeted and bantered with each other. Not a dull face was present—Johnny wouldn't have that at one of his parties!

Though the room was packed and loud with chatter, you could hear my father's voice rise in glee above the rest. He shouted, "Hey!" and "Hurrah!" as friends walked into the room. Elaine, dressed in a beige low-cut dress, was by Dad's side. Right after Elaine, my brother stood with his wife. I took my place at the end of the reception line along with my closest woman friend at the time. A videographer stood past me, shooting everyone arriving and through the whole event.

During supper, Dad nibbled at his shrimp cocktail appetizer and beef bourguignon meal. He found occasions to stand and walk to other tables across three rooms filled with guests. He had a toast with every man and a playful word with every woman.

As the many waiters served the main course, Jiri Varga stood, and then he clinked his glass with a spoon. Jiri, a Hungarian friend, had known Dad since he arrived in Montreal in the early-1950s. He raised his glass and spoke as he had done many times before. "What sets Johnny apart is that he's the best entertainer of his friends."

Many followed with a "Hear, hear!"

Dad didn't give a long speech to follow Jiri's toast. He stood, lifted his glass back to his compatriot, smiled broadly, and said to everybody, "Thank you for coming. Please enjoy yourself. Have a good time this evening, for you never know what tomorrow can bring."

He pointed his glass to everyone around the room. "Chin, chin," he offered and took a swig. Everyone lifted their glass back to him and took a sip of their drink. Many shouted, "Happy Birthday, Johnny!" Others jested, "Can't believe you're really retiring." Dad smiled and lifted his glass to the crowd once more.

My mother was not present this evening. No one dared disturb the air with her name. I tried not to think about her. Deep down, I knew how much she would have enjoyed this party and the milestone for her husband of over thirty years.

Tonight she probably was sitting alone at home rather than dancing here between the tables with her one true love. She would have bleached her hair in her kitchen sink instead of spending the day at a hairdresser. She might have worn a homemade dress rather than a store-bought one. I tried not to think about the unmendable tear in my heart on what should be a happy occasion for my father. It was undoubtedly a sad day for my mom.

Led by the hulky German, Hans, Dad's closest male friends presented him with a huge gift that they wheeled into the ballroom on a buggy. They had chipped in and bought him a wearable suit of black metal armour, shipped in from West Germany. The crowd stood, and everyone clapped and cheered when they saw the nearly two-meter-tall contraption, including long metal sword and matching face mask. Maybe they thought that the iron outfit well represented Dad's steely business character.

That menacing suit would stand at the base of the main stairs of Dad's Peru home for guests to see when they visited. It well represented my father's tough exterior as he went into business battle every day, rain or shine, healthy or sick, rarely backing down from a fight. Dad never tried to dress in that suit of armor. He didn't need to, for little could penetrate him the way he was.

At Elaine's suggestion, more than twenty friends and family members, including my brother and I, chipped in and bought Dad a build-it-yourself grandfather clock. Elaine had our names engraved on a bronze plaque attached to the clock's base. We figured my father needed a project during the first months of his retirement. Putting together that over two-meter-high, wood-encased device would keep him busy awhile.

The next time I went to his Peru home, I saw the clock's pieces and parts neatly strewn over the floor of the den. My father complained about the work and time it took to build that thing, especially assembling its moving clockwork, but he kept at it for many long weekends. With Dad's handiwork, that clock would tick true for decades.

As the retirement party came to a close, my father demonstrated his prowess by dancing with another one of his retirement presents. It was a voluptuous, exotic woman from the East who wore seven veils and lots of powdery makeup. She jiggled and gyrated to rapid Middle Eastern music, enticing Dad to follow her lead.

He took off his jacket but still wore his vest. Into his vest, the woman dancer inserted a couple of her veils, which flew around as Dad followed her moves. She bent her knees and lowered her body toward the floor and then stood back up on her toes, shaking her scantily-covered, robust breasts.

Surrounded by his friends, Dad wouldn't let her outdo him. He crouched down, clutched his arms together, and kicked his feet out as if he were a dancing Cossack. His face grew sweaty but remained joyful; his voice filled with laughter. Guests were gleeful as they watched both Dad and the dancer work to outdo each other. The crowd hooted, roared, and clapped with enthusiasm.

* * *

To self-commemorate his retirement, Dad replaced his thin St. Christopher necklace with a heftier gold choker. Around his wrist, he added a solid gold ID bracelet, which Elaine had bought him as a retirement gift. He also switched his long-time, sleek gold Omega watch for a much bulkier Rolex.

All this new gold went better with his new life partner's fancier shoes, dresses, hair, and makeup. I hated to consider it, but Elaine fit with Dad's gregarious style and late Troika nights, much more than my mother ever had.

During his later years in business, Dad's midriff had widened, his hands had thickened, and his arms and shoulders had gotten burlier. The Rolex timepiece and heavier gold chains suited his stockier physique much more than his slimmer Omega watch and St. Christopher pendant ever had.

Dad had told me, "I didn't spend much cash for the Rolex. I traded in my old Omega and a few 5-ounce gold bars I had sitting in my bank deposit box."

I was sad to see the Omega go. It was a fixture on my father since my youth. The pressures of business life now behind him, I hoped his heavier Rolex might slow Dad down in his older age.

I later heard from my father's good friend, Abe, that Dad wanted to dispose of his long-time Omega before obtaining the weighty Rolex. At a Slovak Scholarship Ball the previous fall, hosted by the Canadian Slovak Professional and Business Association, my father prestidigitated his signature gold Omega into the weightier replacement.

The Slovak Scholarship Ball was held every November at Montreal's Ritz-Carlton Hotel. The large oval ballroom felt like a royal court, with high ceilings and long beige and gold-laced draperies that covered the tall windows that reached nearly to the top of the walls.

More than 250 participants—local Slovak professionals and their Polish-, Ukrainian-, Czech-, Russian-, Hungarian-, English- and French-Canadian guests—were present that evening, dressed in their black tuxes and long gowns. They enjoyed *saumon fumé* appetizers followed by the Ritz's famed *rôti de bœuf* or *canard à l'orange*. A six-piece mixed Slavic band played lively European waltzes and soothing foxtrots.

Between the meal courses and short podium speeches, partygoers took swings with their spouses or mixed it up with the partner of a friend.

Every year, male and female Slovak debutantes, dressed in their coming-out best, were introduced to the community. These high school graduates were to receive a university scholarship from the association for their academic achievement. Dad's higher Jan Simkovits Prize went to the best overall student.

My father had invited many friends and colleagues to the event. Those ranks filled several tables. Throughout the evening, Dad spent more time walking around the other tables than he did in his seat. He chatted, laughed, and shared a drink with everyone he knew. Hellos, handshakes, and hugs flowed out of him as fast as the vodka flowed into his glass.

Later, in the middle of supper, the event's emcee rushed to the podium. Showing a concerned face, the man declared, "Attention, everyone! *Attention, s'il vous plaît! Pozornost', prosím!* Our esteemed member, Mr. Jan Simkovits, has lost his gold Omega watch somewhere in our ballroom." His tone was weighty. "Mr. Simkovits has been walking around to many of the tables this evening. Please be so kind as to look around your table to see if you might find the watch? If you do, please return it to him."

My father's stature in the association compelled many men (in their tuxes) and women (in their ball gowns) to curtailed their conversation and searched for the watch. Many bent down on hands and knees to crawl under white tablecloths to help find the Omega watch for their friend, Jani. In the end, no one recovered the timepiece.

An hour later, while everyone else continued to talk and dance in the ballroom, Dad stood alone by the bar in the ante-chamber outside. Seeing his friend, Abe, enter the room, Dad quietly motioned for him to come closer. The barman refilled my father's vodka glass while Dad puffed on a cigar.

As Abe came toward Johnny, he heard my father say, "Come here; I want to show you something." Abe noticed a boyish smirk on my father's face, which he initially attributed to the liquor Dad had been drinking. He then realized something else was going on.

My father put his index finger to his mouth and said, "Shh, don't say anything." Turning away from the barman, he reached into his tux pocket and pulled out his missing Omega.

My father knew that his long-time Ukrainian insurance agent, Yasko, was at the ball that evening. Dad had concocted a ploy to lose the Omega because he wanted to claim it for the insurance money.

My father often complained that he paid too much to the insurance companies that were covering his business assets and personal effects. He employed such ruses to recover some of his costs. The ball provided a golden opportunity to dispose of his long-time timepiece, his agent becoming a witness to the loss. Dad had had his eye on the Rolex, so he might as well obtain an insurance company down payment for it.

Years later, after Abe had told me that story, I smiled and said, "Yup, that's my dad!"

Though I cringed at my father's flagrant deceit, a part of me was in awe of his never-ending brazenness.

* * * *

See No Money Evil;

Say No Money Evil

It was 1986, six years into my parent's separation. They were nearing the seven-year separation-to-divorce timeline popularized by our Prime Minister Pierre Elliot Trudeau and his thirty-year younger wife, Margaret.

The official reason for that Canadian Camelot marriage failure was "incompatible differences." The word on the street suggested Mrs. Trudeau resented both being second fiddle to her husband's political career and having to raise their three children pretty much on her own. Pierre and Margaret's protracted 1977 break up, after only six years of marriage, regularly made for theatric news in both the Canadian and international press. Their divorce became final in 1984.

Having had six years of acrimony, my parents were pushing the Trudeau envelope. No marriage contract had existed between them. Mom's lawyer continued to claim that they had been living under the jurisdiction of Quebec common marital law, entitling Mom to half of Dad's assets. Dad's lawyer, Mack, claimed them to be separate-to-property (her having no claim on her husband's assets) as per 1949 Czechoslovakia civil law.

The only leverage Mom had was that her lawyer was able to freeze Dad's assets, which included his remaining apartment building and his JHS company stock. Dad couldn't sell or employ as collateral any of those assets without Mom's agreement and signature.

Dad countered that he had few assets other than the one building and his limited ownership in JHS. (That holding company, owned mostly by Steve and me through our common shares, held his factory building and other land properties.) I felt sleazy about keeping silent about my father's offshore assets in a Lux bank, but I was afraid to open my mouth about them.

I wondered what I could do for my mother. I had no access to the money locked in my and my brother's JHS shares—only Dad could unwind those holdings. I considered offering Mom a portion of my JHS bonus money to tide her over, but I imagined she would tell me, "Your father is responsible for me, not you."

Had I confronted Dad about his stinginess, or divulged what I knew of his hidden assets to Mom or her lawyer, it could have driven Dad even more underground with his offshore stash. I had no hard proof about his money over there—other than what he had told me—nor did I have access to those funds.

Dad said he'd take me to his Lux bank branch in Montreal, but he hadn't yet. Maybe he was waiting until his divorce was behind him. I had little in my hands, other than knowing about those Luxembourg bank business cards tucked away in his private office desk.

But that Lux banker could deny anything I alleged about my father's offshore money. Dad could switch his account or bank, and later tell the divorce court judge that I was mistaken about what I had heard from him. Even worse, if I broke his trust, I might lose my connection to him altogether and never see a penny of his offshore legacy. I felt that I had to play along with his dodging of not only the taxman but also my mother.

I felt my gut cramp in knowing about the raw deal that Mom was getting. But I saw no viable alternative without divulging what I knew and risking that Dad would then cut me off. Even decades later, I wondered what I could have done other than keeping my mouth shut about Dad's offshore finances. Thinking about my conundrum knotted my gut into a Johnny Simkovits bind.

Dad claimed to the divorce court judge that he owned little of JHS's assets, for he had transferred most of their value to my brother and me when we were kids. But Steve and I had no control over the company because Dad held the majority of its voting shares. He could do as he wanted with the company's money.

Though I saw what Dad had invested in his new home in Peru, JHS now owned the property. In that transaction, a chunk of JHS's cash had been transferred to CANEX in Cayman before Dad moved his offshore assets to the Lux bank. *What a finagler!*

With all this, Dad could legitimately claim asset poverty in addition to separate-to-property. I suspect that Mom, like I, knew none of it was true, but Dad's legal arguments were substantial enough to drag out divorce proceedings. Both Mom and Dad blamed each other for the lack of progress, and no divorce end was in sight.

Steve and I avoided discussing our parents' situation during visits with either of them. Even so, Mom found ways to speak about her plight. Over one home-cooked supper, she blurted out, "Your father is spending like crazy for Elaine in New York State, for suppers with his friends at the Troika, and for taking vacations all over." Her voice rose. "I don't even have enough money to pay for my lawyer."

I didn't know how Mom knew about Dad's whereabouts, but I guessed she had her sources. Though I didn't want to get involved, I was curious and sympathetic. "What about your lawyer, Mom? What is he doing to get a settlement for you?"

Her eyes glared at me. "My lawyer does nothing!" she said tersely. "The guy talks and talks, he promises and promises, but I see no results. I keep on getting his bills, but I told him I couldn't pay a penny until I have a settlement." She raised a fist. "There were supposed to be court hearings, but your father's schmuck lawyer, Mack, keeps on making excuses and delays."

She took a long breath. "Your father, the other schmuck, is giving me no more money than I had when we were together. I'm now paying all the house expenses myself." She shook her fist. "If I hadn't saved $5000 over the years before your father left me, I'd have nothing today." She pointed to herself. "I ate the cheapest food and didn't buy any new clothes."

I felt terrible for my mother. I knew Dad was stingy with her. I wondered what I could do.

I took a chance and asked Elaine out for lunch in the city without my father's knowledge. It was the first time she and I had ever met alone. After she and I ordered meals, I asked her, "I'm wondering if you could help me, Elaine." I could hardly look her in the eye.

She spoke calmly. "Sure, if I can."

I was shaking inside as I spoke. "Is there any way you could suggest to my father that he give my mother a larger separation allowance? She's hardly able to live on what he gives her."

Elaine looked away for a moment. Her eyes then turned back to me. "Okay, Harvy, I'm willing to help you out, but I have one condition."

I looked at her. "What's that?"

"I want you to talk to your father about this first. If you have no success with him, then I'd be willing to add my voice to yours and say something to him."

Although I felt afraid to confront my father about my mother, I realized Elaine was right. I had to face my father even if it raised his ire. I was the only one Dad might listen to, considering I rarely asked him for anything outside of his investing in my education. Our situation was a family matter, and it really shouldn't involve Elaine.

The next time I went out with my father for supper, Elaine stayed home saying she had something else to do. He and I went to Luigio's near their apartment.

As we walked up to the restaurant, a grossly obese man walked out. A moment later, when we sat down inside, Dad patted his stomach, smiled, pointed toward the entrance, and whispered to me, "I feel much better when I see a big guy like that."

I looked at him but said nothing about his coarse humour. I knew that any confrontational comment wouldn't make any difference with him.

We both had a couple of drinks. Dad devoured his fettuccini alfredo while I consumed my veal marsala. After we had talked about nothing special, I mustered my courage. I hardly looked at his face. "Dad, can I talk to you about something?"

"Sure son."

"I'm sorry to say this, but I don't think you're fair to Mom. She can't seem to support herself on the little money you give her each month."

Dad's hand made a fist on the table. He looked at me and spoke brusquely. "I want her to accept my divorce settlement." He banged the table. The water in our glasses shivered. "And I don't want her to feed the lawyers."

I was shaking inside, but I stayed as collected as I could. "Dad, it's not my business to get involved in that stuff between the two of you. What I can tell is that I don't see her able to live on the money she gets from you."

I took a breath. "And, Mom didn't ask me to say anything to you. It's just what I'm seeing, and it bothers me. She is my mother." My stomach churned to have to beg for her. My head ached from having to come up against my father.

Dad stared at me for a few seconds and then calmed his voice. "Okay, son, I'll think about it." He returned to eating his meal, and I switched subjects. What he had said was giving me hope.

Within a week, Dad raised Mom's "salary." I didn't know how much more he gave her, but she stopped complaining. I didn't tell her about the word I had put in with Dad on her behalf. I let her believe that her lawyer was the hero. Elaine and I didn't speak again about the issue.

It was hard to gauge if I had done more harm than good by my actions. Privately, I thought Dad wasn't generous in his divorce proposition. The $500,000 he had offered Mom, plus their house, seemed like small Hungarian dumplings for him, but I didn't know his total assets both onshore and offshore. From JHS financial statements, I did have a sense of what the company was worth. But those statements reflected only the cost of its myriad property assets, not their actual market value.

What I did know was that I didn't want to put myself any further into my parent's fight. Damned if I was going to risk more than I already had, in recently helping to increase Mom's separation allowance and in previously sneaking JHS statements to her lawyer via Moe.

Dad never gave any indication, but it seemed as if he were dragging things out with Mom so he wouldn't have to marry his current mistress. I didn't know if Elaine was seeking marriage. But from Dad's previous affairs, I wondered if he was hedging his bets with her. If life didn't work out with Elaine, might he head back to Mom's always open arms, as he had done before?

Though these thoughts unsettled my stomach, I wasn't going to confront my father about them. He might get angry at my questioning his motives. It irked me that he was lowballing my mother and possibly putting off his new partner simultaneously, but that was out of my hands. I felt I had done as much as I could and would do to help my mother with my father.

God knows if I were doing right or wrong for all of us.

* * *

What broke the divorce logjam between my parents was a personal tax matter for Dad.

A pending change in Canadian tax law was encouraging my father to transfer his last remaining apartment building to JHS. The legal and tax details were complicated, but that move would save him hundreds of thousands of dollars in income taxes if he consummated the transfer before the end of 1986.

Ideally, he should have sold his building to a third party before that year ended, but time was running out, and he had no prospective buyers. Considering his assets were frozen, Dad needed Mom's signature on the property transfer papers. The prospect of having to feed over 200,000 extra tax dollars to the government spurred my father into action.

While visiting Dad at JHS, he told me, "I want to settle with your mother this year. When that's complete, I can transfer my apartment building to JHS to save on taxes. This move will be to all of our benefits." He didn't specify who and how.

His voice turned stern. "Please don't say anything to your mother about this maneuver; I don't want her to know."

So why do you tell me such things if you want them to stay secret? I couldn't understand why he was putting me in another play-it-ignorant-with-Mom bind. Maybe he wanted me to nudge her to accept his divorce settlement offer, which hadn't changed from his original proposal six years earlier.

"Does Steve know about this?" I asked.

Dad spoke matter-of-factly. "He knows I want to transfer the building to JHS this year, but he knows nothing about the tax benefit."

I nodded my understanding. There would be hell to pay if I told Mom what I knew. Giving her such leverage in her divorce suit would yield a full-throated outburst from Dad. Though I was thirty-one years old, my father's yells, along with his banging or shaking fist, could still make my skin feel ripped from my body.

Halfway through my next supper at Mom's, she offered, "Your father's lawyer called mine earlier this week. He says your father wants to settle." She studied my face. "Why is he suddenly in a rush to divorce? Does he want to marry that other woman?"

I shrugged. "I don't know, Mom." I felt my stomach curdling from not being able to be open and straight with her.

Mom stared into my eyes. "What do you think I should do? If he's pushing for a settlement, should I ask for more money?"

I spoke in a naïve tone. "I don't know, Mom." I then saw an opportunity. My eyes looked up, but I kept my head down. "Why not ask for more? Unless you do that, you'll never find out what you could get." A shiver went through my side. "What's the worst that could happen? Dad would get mad, but what could he do?"

The prospect of sticking a spousal stiletto into her estranged husband's side seemed to intrigue Mom. After a reflective pause, she looked away and changed the subject.

The following week, when Steve and I were at Dad's office together, he raised his fist and screamed at us. "Now she wants $100,000 more from me! The lawyers will eat us alive!" He looked as if he were ready to punch someone. "Do you guys know anything about this?"

I both shuddered and smiled inside simultaneously. It seemed as if Mom had acted on my suggestion. I wondered how she picked an additional $100,000 as her ask, but that wasn't my business.

I was a fan of the *Colombo* television show. Its main character, Peter Faulk, was a frumpy, bumbling, yet smart detective. His motto was, *When you have no better idea of recourse, act dumb.* I showed a blank face to my father as I had done with my mother. "I don't know anything, Dad. I try to stay out of your and Mom's divorce business." Steve added the same.

I looked at my father's feet, though I wanted to look him in the eye. I desired to raise my voice and say, *Dad, why not give Mom the extra hundred grand. You'll get at least twice that back in saved taxes when you transfer your building to JHS.* I held back because I knew he was fully aware of that fact.

Although Dad's ire could reverberate through my bone marrow, Moe had taught me that my father's anger was his way of keeping everyone else off balance.

I worked to keep my body calm and face looking naïve until Dad was ready to change the subject. After again saying, "The lawyers will suck us dry," and shaking his fist in the air, he moved on.

After a few more weeks of grumbling, Dad met Mom's demand. It seemed he had no choice because Mom hadn't budged, and he needed her to settle.

At my next supper with Mom, she told me, "Before I tell my lawyer to accept your father's offer, I'm calling Moe."

I was amazed, for my mother hadn't seen Moe in five years. She continued. "I want his opinion on what I should do, whether I should sign the settlement with your father."

Through my surprise, I offered calmly, "Sure, Mom, if that's what you want."

A few days later, Moe unexpectedly walked into my office at WISE. He spoke quietly. "I talked to your mother on the phone the other day. I'm going to see her tomorrow about her divorce settlement. Do you have an opinion on how I should handle it with her?"

Moe had always told me to stay out of my parents' divorce, but now he was asking me to weigh in. Though I hadn't expected his question, and a part of me felt that he shouldn't have asked, I was glad he trusted me enough to inquire.

I thought for a moment. "It's whatever you and my mother think best, Moe." As with my father, I wasn't quite able to meet my mentor's eyes. "But after six years of animosity, she needs to end the stalemate with my father. He's never going back to her, and there is no point in maintaining the animosity. She has to find a way to settle with him and move on."

Though my voice stayed calm, I had loathed the years of fist-shaking and voice-elevating anger between my parents. I continued to talk as Moe listened. "It's not good for anyone to have their divorce linger any longer. Though my mother could hold out for more money, my father's settlement offer should support her the way she's accustomed to living."

I hoped I was right, and that Moe and I weren't ganging up on my mother. I had tried to do my best for her, but what did I know for sure? Part of me felt ashamed for not sharing with her (or Moe) what I had known of my father's furtive funds. Then again, even if I had spilled those offshore beans, would it have made any difference as to what she would have gotten in the end? Dad could have easily denied everything, and only he'd be better off.

Moe nodded, said no more, and left my office.

After Moe had returned from seeing my mother, he said nothing to me, and I didn't ask about his visit. A few days later, Mom agreed to the $600,000 settlement offer plus the house in which she was living. Dad was first to tell my brother and me that the lawyers were preparing the divorce documents for signing. I prayed for a better post-parental-divorce life for all of us.

The following week, over another home-cooked supper, Mom's voice was somber. She offered, "Moe came over for an hour last week." She looked down. "I could hardly stop crying for the whole time he was here." She took a long breath. "I asked him if I should settle with your father."

Her eyes looked away as if someone had touched a raw nerve. "Moe said that now, after six years, it looks like your father is never going to come back to me." Her eyes watered, and she rubbed tears away with the back of her hand. "He said that if I felt it was enough money to live on, then it would be good for everyone if I took the settlement."

She looked at me and said something I didn't expect. "Moe thinks that your father only came back to me the last time so that he could sell his buildings. He then turned those building profits into annuities for his retirement before he would leave me for good." Her voice was terse. "My divorce lawyer then wouldn't be able to freeze all his assets, except for his JHS shares and the one building he had left."

My eyes opened. *Could my father be that devious?* Or did my mother think that way and invoked Moe as the source of that notion? In my amazement, I just looked at her and said nothing.

Her face and fist tightened, and her voice elevated. "The next day, Moe sent me a bill for $300 for the hour he was here!"

She looked down at the table and calmed her voice. "A few days later, I called my lawyer and told him that I agree to the additional $100,000, as long as your father pays for the lawyers drawing up the divorce papers." She wiped the sweat off her brow and then said no more about her divorce settlement or Dad.

My father had his settlement stipulations too. He spoke to my brother and me the next time we were together in his office. "I want the three of you to have joint custody and joint signing authority for the money that I'm giving your mother." He raised a hand. "I don't want her to get remarried later and then have that guy steal the money. What I'm giving her is meant for you two boys to have eventually."

Dad had previously mentioned his remarriage concerns about Mom. I didn't take much heed of his warning because Mom had more than once told Steve and me, "I was devoted to your father for over thirty years. I wasted the last six years waiting for him to come back to me as he had done before. Who out there is going to want an old, separated woman like me?"

Steve and I nodded at our father's condition of joint ownership of Mom's divorce money. My brother and I could easily reassign the money to her if she wanted it that way.

Our mother didn't make a fuss about our father's terms. She agreed to joint custody and needing two of our three signatures on any bank cheque.

When both Mom and Dad announced that they signed their divorce documents, I took in a deep breath and exhaled with relief.

From the moment Dad had walked out on Mom in August of 1980, my parents hadn't laid eyes on each other. In September of 1986, they signed settlement papers at the offices of Mom's lawyer. Dad later told Steve and me that Mom's attorney shuttled back and forth between rooms where he and Mom waited separately. They wouldn't have to see each other in divorce court, for the lawyers would take care of everything. As on that paper signing day, my parents would never again be together in the same room.

One evening later that same week, over chicken paprika at Mom's, her eyes teared as she spoke to Steve and me. "The other day, your father and I finished signing papers." Dad had already told us that, but there was no sense stomping on Mom's news. She continued through her anguish. "I'm glad I didn't have to see your father's lawyer, Mack, *a nagy fasz!* [that big dick!] He's a *nagyobb fasz* [bigger dick] than your father. He left his previous wife, you know." She sighed. "Maybe your father would have stayed with me if it weren't for him."

I didn't know Mack's situation, but Mom's words about Dad's *schmack* lawyer rang with truth.

I kept my face expressionless while she continued. "After we finished signing the papers, I saw your father for a few seconds—through the conference door that my lawyer had left slightly open."

She looked away and then back at us. "I was glad your father didn't see me, but I saw him put on his coat in the reception area." She dropped her eyes. "He looked good—lost some weight, I think."

I looked at my mother and didn't utter a word.

* * *

Being a coupon clipper and penny saver, Mom could survive reasonably well on the interest from the money she received from Dad. She'd be able to take trips south to get out of our cold Canadian winters.

At our next supper with her, Steve and I said we'd put no restrictions on her spending. I added, "I'd be okay with transferring everything into just your name if that's what you want."

She replied, "It's okay. Leave it as it is. You boys will have it anyway when I die. I have no one else to give the money to."

Over the following weeks, I tried to get Mom interested in working with a money manager. "You could do a lot better than putting your money in bank CDs. A money manager can help you make good investments and earn more." She agreed to go to see a well-known private investment manager in the city.

Back home after our downtown meeting, she told both Steve and me, "I want my money to be safe and not have to rely on any strangers." Though I thought she was making a mistake, I acquiesced to her wishes. She had been through enough stress over the last years. She shouldn't have to worry about taking risks with her long-awaited settlement.

Without request or hesitation, Steve and I put one of our signatures on a bunch of blank bank cheques for our mother. She could add her signature later to obtain what she needed from the joint account. Steve and I agreed not to tell Dad what we had done for Mom. If asked, we'd say that everything was working out the way he had intended.

In addition to Dad and Mom's divorce papers, my father had Mack immediately prepare his apartment building transfer to JHS. With that, JHS was becoming a repository for just about all of Dad's legitimate personal holdings.

In my mind, I thanked Revenue Canada and their change in tax rules that encouraged Dad to settle his divorce with Mom. I hoped there now would be parental peace for our frayed family.

* * *

Some days after my parents' divorce papers were signed, my father asked my brother and me to meet him on a Saturday morning at JHS. He needed us to sign corporate documents.

In the mid-1970s, Dad had changed JHS's charter from provincial to federal—in light of his growing fear of the separatist movement in Quebec. At that time, Dad had made my brother the Secretary-Treasurer and me the Vice President of the company.

Each subsequent year, Steve and I were required to sign corporate minutes and papers for significant company transactions. Because Dad still held the company's voting power, such signing ceremonies were a legal formality. As the accountants in business and administrators in government say, "No one gets paid until the paperwork is complete."

After a round of hellos and hugs that Saturday, Dad said, "As directors of the company, I need your signatures to pay out your mother and, at the same time, to transfer my remaining apartment building from me to the corporation." He looked at us with intensity in his eyes as he motioned his finger in a circle to indicate the three of us. "These transactions will be to all of our benefits." He had said the same cryptic statement before, and he again didn't specify as to what that benefit was.

Dad motioned to two stacks of papers he had placed at desks on opposite sides of the room. "I need the two of you to sign this legal baloney. My property transfer to JHS will release enough funds for me to pay the divorce settlement to your mother."

This day's corporate proceedings were unusual in that many more papers had to be signed, in duplicate, and even triplicate. Wondering why there were so many documents, I took my time to glance through what I was signing—but not so slowly that my father would take notice.

Over the years, I had taught myself to read legal papers with their complicated "forthwith" and "notwithstanding" clauses. I had asked questions of our JHS lawyers and accountants until I understood the legalese. I figured my prudence as a son-of-a-business-owner would serve me well one day.

I scanned my pile of papers. After looking over and signing the customary annual shareholder declarations, I read, "Allocation of $1,000,000 of Class C Preferred Shares to John Simkovits in consideration of Dollard property." *That's what Dad's getting from JHS in exchange for transferring his last apartment building to the company.* I signed where my name appeared above the Vice President line and added the date. Steve and Dad's signatures would go on the other signatory lines on the page.

In the next document, I read, "Redemption of $600,000 Class B Preferred Shares."

Oh, what's that?

When Steve and I were kids, Dad had gifted money to us and then later bought us company shares with those funds. That cash—$475,000 to each Steve and me—was locked into those JHS Class B Shares. My brother and I together held $950,000 in tax-free assets in JHS, but Dad had locked that money into stocks that had no voting rights, paid no dividends, and could only be cashed with our father's signature. Like always, Dad had control.

My fingers squeezed my pen tightly as I looked more carefully at the document I was about to sign. It dawned on me what my father was doing with what he had referred to as "our company." In addition to transferring his personally owned building into JHS, he was redeeming $600,000 of my brother's and my combined shares to pay for his divorce settlement with Mom.

I felt my heart thump fast and the humidity rise under my shirt. *Dad is giving Mom both Steve's and MY money!* In effect, his divorce was costing him nothing personally.

My body started to tremble as I slowly signed my quivering signature on the multiple sets of papers in front of me. I tried not to attract my father's attention as I turned the document pages at a snail's pace. Out of the corner of my eye, I saw Dad behind his desk. He was lighting a cigarette. There was no telling expression on his face as to how he was screwing my brother and me. As my body shook in trepidation, I wondered what I should do.

What might Dad say and do if I refused to sign these papers? I could take a stand that I didn't want him to exploit Steve's and my ownership in JHS for his goddamn divorce settlement. But my refusal could affect my special place with him. Might I risk falling out of his greater graces if I didn't comply with his current wishes? *I can't frigging believe he's doing this to Steve and me!*

I glanced at my brother across the room. He was turning document pages quickly, and it looked as if he were signing blindly. Could I tell him what I saw was going on here and get him on my side? Would he raise a fuss along with me, or did he not care? My neck and armpits were getting wet with sweat.

I turned my head back to the papers in front of me. I wasn't sure if I wanted to create trouble. I needed more time to think. I looked over at my father. "Can I turn on the AC Dad? It's warm in here."

He nodded. I stood and sauntered to the wall AC unit. I turned it on and walked back to my seat.

What if I said nothing and went along with Dad's double-dealing? These funds were his money, made by his hands before he gifted the assets to my brother and me. If that cash remained in the company, then he'd still have full control over the funds. Steve and I held those shares only in name.

We had agreed that Dad's divorce settlement wouldn't go directly to Mom but sit in a joint bank account. In that way, Dad was giving us our money. That tidy sum would be out of JHS and work to support our mother for the rest of her life. Steve and I would have it eventually, after Mom passed away, and it would be out of Dad's control.

Why couldn't Dad *(the schmuck!)* fully explain what he was doing? Or maybe he thought he had. Might I be misinterpreting his words and seeing them in the worst light?

The seconds ticked away. My hand mechanically inked my signature onto the documents. *What should I do? What can I do? Should I say anything?*

I decided to do what my father had expected of me. Had I said anything, I'd be coming up against not only him but also his lawyer, Mack, who had drawn these papers. I didn't want a fight, and I didn't know if I could get my brother on my side. Only half the money going to Mom was coming from my JHS shares; the other half was from Steve. Why should I care about Steve's ownership if my brother didn't? I sucked in my gut and kept my sights on staying connected with Dad and the bigger pot of money he held offshore.

I let out heavy breaths as I finished placing my mark onto the legal pages. After Steve and I completed the paperwork, I could hardly look at my brother. If Steve had no inkling of what he was signing, then why should I enlighten him?

I quickly excused myself and left the premises, taking with me a sick-to-my-gut feeling. I wiped a tear from my eye that no one but I could sense.

I sat in my car for many long minutes before driving off. Why the hell had Dad held out for so long and with a lowball divorce settlement if he was going to give Mom Steve's and my money from JHS? There was still a chunk of money left in my brother's and my preferred shares. Our father could have given our mother more. *Should I feel sad, angry, betrayed, or what, by my father?* How could he do such a thing to his sons?!

On the other hand, maybe Dad did what he thought was his legal and ethical right. Then again, what about his moral responsibility to both Steve and me? More importantly, I had stood by his scheming, scamming, and skirting ways with few questions asked.

I now fully understood, deep down into my shallow pockets, how my mother felt in getting shortchanged by the man she loved. I wanted to slap my father in the face, scream at him like my mother sometimes did, but I couldn't raise my hand or utter a word. It would take me three decades to figure out that I did what I thought I needed to do to survive.

For my father, it was about winning the most or losing the least. From what I read in the documents I signed, Dad transferred $1,000,000 in property assets from his hands into JHS, much more than he had given Mom in their divorce settlement. He said that the transfer would be "to all our benefit."

Future corporate minutes would tell me that those specific shares were assigned only to my father. Steve and I would see money from those assets only if Dad played it in our favour—by leaving those shares to us in his will, or by permitting the profits from that building's eventual sale to remain in JHS. As always, Dad was in full control.

Our father had many times told us, "Boys, what's mine will someday be yours." Steve and I had little that was tangible to hold onto except for Dad's words. On this day, our father had compromised his promise, though he might have argued that he hadn't misled us.

I didn't know who was the bigger jerk, my father or me. I had played my negotiating games in helping Mom ameliorate both her separation allowance and her final divorce settlement. Dad was able to outmaneuver me by carving out JHS money assigned to Steve and me so he could fund that settlement. I thought I was his favoured son, and he would treat me differently than my brother. On this day, my belief proved not to be true.

But were Steve and I any worse off than before we signed those papers? Maybe I should have followed my brother in not closely examining what I was signing. My awareness only brought headaches and heartache that I preferred not to have. I wondered what other circuitous routes his money might take to find itself in my brother's and my hands, if we'd obtain any of it at all.

Thirty years later, I'm still not sure what I could have done differently without risking my brother's and my financial future with Dad. I felt as if I were in a Johnny Simkovits prisoner's dilemma. I was damned if I acted against my father and subsequently risked the loss of his favour. And I was damned if I stayed loyal and consequently risked my self-respect.

I told no one—not my new therapist or even Moe—about what had transpired on that day of signing corporate papers at JHS. I never asked my father why he structured the transaction the way he did. I had made my choice to sign, and I had to live with what I had done. As I once heard in a movie, "It's not so much the choices you make in life that matter. What counts more is how you live with the choices you made."

I consoled myself that Mom and Dad's tumultuous marriage and turbulent separation were finally behind us. The settlement was a lot of money for Mom, more than she, or the three of us, had controlled in our lives. It would give her a decent income for the rest of her life. She had no mortgage to pay and had Canadian Medicare to cover her health care.

Though the settlement sum was probably peanuts for Dad, and it didn't cost him anything out of his own pockets, Mom would do well on the money. Instead of that cash locked into JHS shares that Steve and I couldn't touch, it would be in a bank account assigned to Mom, Steve, and me.

Though I felt used by Dad, was my father's blatant transgression real or only in my mind? Were my brother and I better or worse off? I could hardly explain my father's deception to myself, let alone to anyone else.

If allowing Dad to win this money round would lead to peace in our family, then it was an acceptable arrangement. I sucked up my shock at my father's below-the-money-belt sucker punch and moved on. I vowed to be more watchful of his money maneuvers and better prepared the next time.

* * * *

18

WISE (or Unwise?)

Partnership Moves

One Saturday morning, sometime after my parents' divorce was finalized, Moe called me unexpectedly at my apartment. He asked if he, his partner, Irwin, and a guy named Jay could come over right away to my place. He wanted to determine if we could work out an investment deal in WISE.

Though Moe had once spoken about Jay, a former Montrealer who had moved to Boston, I hadn't met him. When the three arrived, I saw that Jay was about my age. Moe explained that Jay, too, had been a career counselling client of his.

Jay said more about himself. "I recently left my marketing and advertising position in Boston. I came to Montreal to obtain Moe's advice on my next career move." He smiled and gestured towards Moe. "That's when Moe told me about his and Irwin's management training centre idea." He looked at me. "And here I am now, talking with the three of you about making an investment deal." As it had been with me a year earlier, Jay's conversation with Moe had attracted him to WISE.

Moe and Irwin were still hunting for ten outside investors. At $50,000 each for a 2% stake in WISE, it made the firm worth $2,500,000 on paper in Moe and Irwin's view. Having younger guys like Jay and me as active investors, the firm would demonstrate a growing WISE team and offer a sustainable future for incoming passive investors.

As soon as I served tea and coffee, Jay came on strong with Moe and Irwin. "Using my marketing help to grow the business, and Harvy's technical assistance with our management training delivery, WISE could be worth the two-and-a-half million you guys are saying. But right now, you only have an idea and one WISE site with two employees."

He glanced my way again and then looked at Moe and Irwin. I kept my face blank as he continued. "At best, WISE is currently worth a third of what you guys are saying."

I was taken aback by Jay's aggressiveness, but he was also fighting for me. I had never been involved in a business start-up negotiation and had little idea what WISE was truly worth. Moe and Irwin then explained that three WISE training sites, with each producing $100,000 to $125,000 in annual after-tax profit, would extrapolate to a $2.5 million value for the firm, a number that was about seven times its total earnings.

Jay said, "Guys, that's two years down the line, but not today. You have only one site now, and it's not yet profitable."

I nodded my understanding. I let Jay do the talking for both of us; he seemed to be doing a good job.

Within the hour, Moe and Irwin accepted Jay's argument and investment numbers. I offered to invest $50,000CAD for a 6% stake in the firm, a third of the price that any passive investor would have to pay. Jay would put in $50,000USD for an 8% stake in the firm, his additional shares having to do with the higher value of the U.S. dollar. Jay also agreed to work without compensation on a WISE marketing plan and investment prospectus.

My investment would fund more salespeople for our Montreal operation. Jay's money would help to start up a WISE office in Boston, our second training site, to be managed by Jay. A third site would be opened in Toronto both after other investment money came in, and when Montreal and Boston became profitable.

We smiled and shook hands on our arrangement. Count on Moe for moving fast to seize an opportunity with Jay and me, and to close a deal quickly. Like my father, I wanted to make my business fortunes. Because Dad had limited my rise at JHS, and he had played games with my JHS ownership, I knew I couldn't depend entirely on him. I had to build or become part of something separate.

My head was spinning. In about a year, I had gone from a client to an employee to a business partner with Moe. Jay and I, a quarter-century younger than the WISE founders, saw the firm's future becoming ours. Though I didn't know much about Jay, and I had known Irwin only for a year, I trusted my mentor these last six years. If Moe felt our deal was right, then I was good with it too.

When I later told my father what I had committed to, he offered another warning. "Be careful with whom you get into bed." His eyes were intense. "I had minority partnerships when I started in business, and none of them worked out. I always got screwed one way or another."

He pointed a finger my way. "I may have once told you. After my company, Montreal Phono, was making money, I invested in another business. It was with a guy who produced spaghetti lighting."

I remember Dad bringing home one of those funny looking lamps when I was just a kid. It was the precursor to fiber-optic lighting. Thick strands of hot blown glass were twisted into different forms to channel light in different directions.

My father continued. "I invested a lot of money with that spaghetti-glass inventor guy. I stayed out of his day-to-day operations because I needed to focus my energy on Montreal Phono."

He huffed. "A year later, I caught the guy making cash sales on the side." Dad's eyes became intense. "I immediately threatened to sue him, even put him in jail, if he didn't return my investment money." Dad's face was stern, like a bulldog ready to bite. "The guy returned my funds, and then he later went bankrupt." He pointed his finger again. "You have to know who you are living with, or you'll get screwed."

I smiled inside of me, for I wasn't sure if my father was referring to his business or personal relationships.

I still felt the recent sting of Dad having used Steve's and my JHS money for Mom's divorce settlement. If I hadn't figured out anything else in my short business career, I knew my father liked to be the top dog in any business deal, the guy with the controlling interest.

In contrast to him, I was more cooperative and easygoing. As an involved investor and employee, I'd contribute to make my WISE partnership work and be successful for all its investors. I'd stay engaged in WISE's operations and finances so that I knew where my money was going. If WISE turned out to be a sour investment, which I hoped it wouldn't, then it would have been a worthwhile experience. I would learn much from Moe, a man I admired and trusted, even more than I could believe in my father.

Regardless of my dad's warning, I moved forward with my investment in WISE. The best part was that I wouldn't have my father looking over my shoulder.

* * * *

19

Dreaded Offshoring Day

As the mid-1980s continued, I wished that my father wouldn't become a resident of The Bahamas to save on Canadian income taxes. I didn't want to deal with my brother on JHS issues while our dad was baking on a Freeport beach or golf course by day, and hooting and hollering in the Princess Casino by night. I also didn't want to visit Dad at his so-called Grand Bahama Island paradise.

I had had enough of Dad's kind of fun during previous Princess Casino visits. There I had met gaming regulars. They stood or sat mindlessly for hours at a gambling table looking for a big hit or winning runs.

You knew them when they said, "I flew over from Miami for the weekend," or "It's not been my best year; last year was better." They chain-smoked cigarettes or slowly sipped on martinis as cards got dealt or dice got thrown. They told you about the big hauls they had pulled in on previous casino visits. They pointed to and talked about the high rollers who sat alone at $300 blackjack or poker tables. Those deep-pocket guys bet at all seven table spots at one time, putting $2100 at risk before the dealer dealt the first card.

I didn't visit Dad's Freeport condo even once during the three years he worked to establish his Bahamian residency, and neither did my brother.

Elaine said she found little to do there during the day, except to read books by the pool while Dad played golf with some Freeport chums—hopefully, better people than those he had met in Cayman. At night, they had supper at one of the few island restaurants. "Then your father threw his money away at the casino," she added.

Dad continued to come back from Freeport, full of stories about how he won thousands of dollars playing blackjack. Elaine told me privately that he could also lose the same any given night. She said, "Good thing that he's having fun and could afford the losses." She smiled. "He's lucky that his shirt is still on his back, and I'm still by his side."

Perhaps Dad surmised that his thirty-something sons no longer wanted to vacation with their father. As the years past, he told Steve and me, "Boys, you can go down to Freeport by yourselves. I'd be willing to give you the keys to the place so you can enjoy yourselves."

Neither my brother nor I ever acted on our father's "generous offer." After having married in '84, Steve had a daughter in'85 and a son on the way two years later. He told our patriarch, "My wife is pregnant, and my kids won't be old enough to travel awhile," and "I don't want to spend money on many airfares." He milked those excuses for years.

By his repeated offers, I sensed that my father was disappointed that I hadn't visited or made use of his place. I eventually told him, "Dad, I've been to Freeport many times. There's not much to do there." I didn't want to remind him of the horrible time he and I had had there years earlier.

I wouldn't want my mother to know about my vacationing with her ex or staying at his place.

By 1987, I was able to dodge Dad's offers with yet another excuse. "My girlfriend is not keen on Freeport. She prefers vacations where there's plenty to see and do, like at Club Med."

Three years earlier, Margie and I had met at a singles club dance in downtown Montreal. Eighteen months later, she and I became a couple. We then partook in the Turks and Caicos Club during one winter, and another Club in Corfu, Greece, the following summer. She enjoyed participating in *Le Club's* talent nights with the club's G.O.s *(Gentil Organisateurs)*. She reveled in singing along and mimicking the arm and hand motions to the Club Med theme song, "Hands Up."

Margie's exuberance for activity made it definite that flat, lifeless Grand Bahamas Island would not be in our vacationing future. Had Dad bought his condo in Nassau, I might have enticed her to take a trip to Club Meds' state-of-the-art tennis club on Paradise Island. But Dad's choice of Freeport offered no allure to her or me.

I continued to stop by Dad's office every couple of weeks to stay in touch. I joined him and Elaine for regular suppers at Hungarian, Italian, and Slavic Montreal restaurants. Margie and I ate the occasional Saturday supper and Sunday brunch at their Peru home—occasions that were hard for my mother to track.

I secretly hoped that Dad would recognize that he'd see less of his sons if and when he left Canada for his Bahamian tax-free oasis. I wanted him to see that light on his own, without having to flash a frigging flare in his bronzed face.

* * *

By the spring of 1988, Dad heard from his Freeport lawyer that the Bahamian government had awarded him residency status.

My worst fears were becoming realized. *Is Dad going through with this Canadian non-residency thing?* It seemed the gravitational pull of saving Canadian income taxes was bigger than seeing his sons stay in orbit around him. He wouldn't see us for many months, maybe even a year or more, in the pursuit of shortchanging his nemesis, Revenue Canada.

On one Monday afternoon, after Dad had received his residency papers, I made my regular pilgrimage to his office. I didn't get the chance to take my jacket off before he asked, "Harvy, can you come with me tomorrow afternoon to see Gregor Varga?"

"What's that about, Dad?"

"Gregor's father, Jiri, arranged it for us. As you know, Gregor is an international corporate lawyer who works with many wealthy people. He's going to tell us about Canada's current non-residency rules and procedures." Dad spoke as if he were conducting an ordinary business transaction.

A few years earlier, around the time he broke the news about his non-residency quest to Steve and me, my father had gotten advice from Roger Delliard's accounting firm. The accounting firm had provided a written report about the rules of claiming Canadian non-residency status. Dad showed me, and I glanced through the thick, bound document, which may have cost JHS a small fortune to have compiled. I remember reading in big, bold letters:

> Canadian non-residency rules and procedures are dynamic; they can change from year to year. Please keep our firm and your advisors abreast of your plans so that we can offer you the most up-to-date information and advice.

In 1985, after closing JHS, Dad ended the company's relationship with Roger's firm. My father now needed another professional to give him updated advice, or maybe he didn't want to pay for another full report. I suspected his friend, Jiri, wanted Dad to get his non-residency ducks in a row before he would fly offshore. When Jiri offered his son's legal advice for free, Dad couldn't refuse.

I agreed to visit Gregor with Dad. I wanted to know what the lawyer would say about my father's Canada departure plans. Might my dad try to shortchange or circumvent the legalities of his non-residency pursuit?

Though I had said yes to our seeing Gregor, I was apprehensive about our meeting. My father didn't have adoring affection for Jiri's son. Years earlier, it had been Gregor's firm that had helped JHS in our lawsuit against our Korean supplier, Jin Dae. Though JHS had won a million-dollar suit in Quebec court, Jin Dae had no presence in Canada, thus no assets to seize in our country.

To attempt to gain leverage over the Korean firm, Dad sent me to Seoul, Korea, for two days of bleary-eyed meetings with a Korean litigation lawyer. The lawyer said we would have a legitimate case to pursue on Korean shores. But my father balked when the attorney declared that it would require JHS put $50,000USD (more than twice what it cost to obtain the Quebec judgement) into escrow to cover Korean court costs. Plus, we'd have to pay a 30% contingency fee on any court judgment we'd win in that country.

The Korean attorney felt our Quebec ruling would hold up through the three years it would take to wind through the Korean court system. But Dad retorted, "I don't want to feed the bloody lawyers and wind up with nothing." After spending over a year and perhaps thirty thousand Canadian dollars on winning our Quebec court case, I couldn't understand why Dad dropped the case. Maybe he wanted something to hang over Gregor's head.

Even though Gregor's firm had adeptly won the Quebec litigation for JHS, Gregor might have led my father astray. Had he told Dad from the beginning that the Quebec judgment's money collection could cost more than the lawsuit, my father might have dropped the litigation before it started.

In seeing Gregor again, I hoped those old litigation wounds wouldn't get in the way of our having an informative meeting about Dad's Canadian non-residency pursuit. I certainly didn't want to deal with Dad's ingrained rubric of "These big-city lawyers have a licence to steal."

On Tuesday afternoon, I drove Dad into the city to meet Gregor at his firm. My father and I waited in a dark walnut-paneled conference room for an audience with this head honcho attorney.

Photographs of Gregor—in the presence of a long line of Canadian political and sports leaders—covered the conference room walls. In one, he was shaking hands with a prime minister. In others, he smiled with Quebec Premiers, provincial cabinet members, and Canadian sports heroes.

Standing around waiting, Dad said, "Those photos are only there to show us he's a big-shot attorney." His voice turned gruff. "And look at how he makes us wait. What kind of bullshit bigwig does he think he is?"

I looked at my watch. It was only twelve minutes past our appointment time. "Isn't Gregor giving you the courtesy of a free meeting, Dad? We can afford to wait."

"Yah, we'll see," my father retorted, his tone grouchy. "I knew Gregor when he was in diapers, and see how he treats me now."

I wondered if old ghosts of JHS lawsuits past were going to open today. My father batted his hand. "These professionals have a licence to take your money. When they solve one problem, they create others so that they can forever feed off you."

My father's words irked me, for I too was a consulting professional. I bit my tongue. At 68 years old, there was little chance of changing Johnny Simkovits's long-ingrained beliefs.

After another ten minutes of shifting around in our seats, Gregor walked in. He greeted us with a large, "Hello, Johnny," and "Hi, Harvy." He was a towering man, as tall as a professional basketball player. His face was well-sculpted, and he had a prominent jaw. He was thin and muscular, like his father, though I didn't know if he played more than golf as a sport.

My hands felt weak and puny as Gregor's firm grip swallowed them. His big hands crushed my fingers against my large MIT grad ring. "It's good to see you both after such a long time," he said. His voice was as deep as my father's, sans the Eastern European accent. "I'm sorry to keep you waiting, Johnny. I was on a call to the Far East that took a little longer than planned. I'm all yours now."

"Good to see you again, Gregor," I said. I didn't refer to when I had seen him previously. It was when my father had told him sharply to put our Quebec court judgment on hold. After our legal consultation had concluded,

Dad said to me, "We can wipe our asses with that piece-of-shit court ruling." I now wanted to keep that old lawsuit water under the JHS business bridge.

My father put on a better face with Gregor now in the room. "It's nice of you to spend a little time with us. I hope you and your lovely wife are well." A dozen years earlier, my father had been at Gregor's wedding.

Gregor offered another grin. "Yes, we are doing very well. We'll be off on a safari to Africa soon." He looked right into Dad's eyes, something I had trouble doing myself. "She sends her best to you, Johnny, and Elaine as well."

"Thank you, Gregor. And do send our regards back to her."

I sat quietly, waiting for the social talk to end so we could get down to business. Across the conference table, the tall, upright attorney stared with intense eyes at my stocky Dad who sat straight in his seat. I wondered which of these two stiff-spine big shots would have to bend more today.

Gregor took a long breath. "Johnny, my father tells me that you're seeking Canadian non-residency status. I'm happy to take you through the particulars, but first, can you share your plans with me?"

My father responded calmly, one hand on the table. "It's simple, Gregor."

Yah! Tell me another.

He continued. "I recently received my Bahamian residency. I want to retire there and take full advantage of not having to pay taxes in Canada, except for the usual retirement savings plan and company pension withholdings."

Between his pension funds, JHS preferred shares, and deferred-tax annuities, my father's potential savings were not small red potatoes but big bloody Idahos. If my estimates were correct, over his remaining lifetime, Dad could save more than a million Canadian dollars in taxes on his legitimate onshore assets.

Pulling up his Canadian roots and going non-resident could also legitimize Dad's hidden offshore assets. I didn't know how much cash he had stashed over there. I surmised he could save another million or more in taxes on those assets by not residing in Canada. If that many dollars weren't at stake, why would he go through the hassle of venturing offshore?

His right hand placed on his chin, Gregor eyed my father carefully. He waited a few seconds to see if Dad had more to say. He didn't, so Gregor jumped in. "We have dealt with many people who want to relinquish their Canadian residency to save income tax. It's not as straightforward as it might appear."

I hope he's not going to make his explanations too complicated. Dad hates when the professionals do that.

Gregor continued, "Johnny, the rules for Canadian non-residency status have been changing over the years. I want to make sure that you are fully informed and up to date."

He leaned forward. "The Canadian government is becoming more aware that people are moving offshore to skirt their tax obligations. Revenue Canada is making the rules more explicit and stringent as time goes on, and as more people try to get around them."

My father's face was blank as he sat calmly in his chair. I imagined him thinking, *Yah, such legal baloney!*

The lean and lanky Gregor raised his long arm and boney fingers as if he were conducting an orchestra. "To become a Canadian non-resident, you have to leave the country for at least a year, and more likely two years, unless you have a good reason to be back here."

The attorney's eyes stayed on my father. "You are permitted to come back anytime for special occasions, like birthdays, weddings, or special family gatherings, or important business meetings." His voice stayed firm. "But you would gravely risk losing your non-residency status if you were in Canada regularly within the first two years after your official departure."

It seemed as if Gregor had given this speech before. He stayed on his course. "After two years of being away are behind you, you could spend no more than six months in Canada each subsequent year." His voice remained steady. "You will have to make sure that immigration officials stamp your passport every time you enter or leave the country so that you can prove you were here no more than 180 days each year." He gestured my father's way. "The onus is on you to demonstrate where you are living, in case the government comes after you for tax avoidance."

Dad jumped into the conversation, his voice gruff. "What's with this 'one or two-year' business? I heard from my previous accountant that it was only one year I'd have to stay away."

Gregor pushed back. "It's been changing, Johnny. The government is not unwise to these things. They eventually catch on to what people are doing." He raised a hand. "The rule is now basically two years unless you have important business or political obligations here that require you to come back regularly, which I don't think you have." He raised a hand. "Your best non-personal reason to return to Canada would be for a JHS corporate shareholder meeting, but that would happen only once a year." Gregor paused to let his comments sink in.

I felt the temperature rising in the room. My father's face looked tense and flushed. I looked at Gregor and asked, "So how does one physically become a non-resident?"

I wanted to get the lay of our government's non-residency land so that I could help my father make honest footprints both on and off Canadian soil. He was hard to live with whenever the government was on his tail, as it had been when he had had federal tax-avoidance charges filed against Montreal Phono over a decade earlier.

Gregor turned to me. "To achieve non-residency, your father cannot have any permanent address in our country, no Canadian bank accounts, and no provincial driver's licence. He'll have to relinquish his home here and cancel any bills that come to him personally, like oil, electricity, telephone, and such. It has to look as if he were leaving the country for good."

Gregor glanced back at my father, possibly to make sure he was listening. "Johnny, you can hold onto your Canadian passport, and hold assets through your Canadian corporation, but that is it."

Then Gregor said something that I didn't anticipate. "And, you will have to relinquish your controlling interests in JHS to your sons or a third party." He paused for another second to let that comment sink in. "Otherwise, JHS would be taxed as a foreign-owned corporation, which carries a much higher tax rate." He took a breath. "By your staying a controlling shareholder of JHS, it could defeat your purpose of saving personal income taxes by leaving the country."

Wow! That's something I didn't know. I wondered if Dad would trust us with his company's ownership and its assets.

My father jumped in. "I can do that. Steve and Harvy are responsible enough that they could handle the company's assets." His voice indicated that what Gregor had said was no big deal. He continued. "Steve already signs cheques on my behalf when I'm away in The Bahamas."

He kept his eyes on Gregor as he batted his hand in the air. "Anyway, JHS doesn't make any profit these days; I give the income to the kids as annual bonuses."

I cringed at Dad's "kids" reference. Though Steve and I were in our early thirties, Dad still saw us as youngsters.

Gregor raised his hand. "It's not only operating income, Johnny. Your corporate income tax will be affected if JHS sells a property asset." He gestured toward my father. "You have to be careful with bonuses too. You would not be permitted to siphon big chunks of income to your shareholders without the government taking note."

His face and voice stayed stony serious. "Revenue Canada could overturn Harvy and Stephen's bonus income, reclassifying it as dividends, and force JHS to pay the requisite corporate taxes on those distributions. And, JHS would be liable for considerably higher tax rates if you stayed the controlling shareholder from offshore."

My father didn't flinch. "No big problem," he said. "I'll give controlling interest of JHS to Harvy and Stephen, and it will be no issue." He didn't look or even glance at me but kept his eyes on Gregor.

I was surprised by my father's statements. I didn't know he had given my brother cheque-signing authority at JHS. I guessed that Steve was more available to Dad because my brother didn't have a steady job as I did. I never expected my father would relinquish control of his company until the undertakers carried him out of his office in a cherry casket, his favourite type of wood.

Was Dad so determined to save on personal taxes that he would give my brother and me the authority to look after JHS's properties and cash? I imagined Dad calling us from Freeport every week to tell us how to feed and diaper his third child, or maybe it was his first.

Dad returned to Gregor's previous point. "It'll be easy for me to stay out of Canada. I'll spend a lot of time in The Bahamas or at our New York State home in Peru. The kids and our friends can come and visit Elaine and me there."

Gregor came back. "You have to be careful there too, Johnny, with spending time in New York State. You can spend no more than four months in the U.S. as a Canadian non-resident without the IRS declaring you a U.S. resident." He used his finger to make his point. "American authorities will then require you to pay taxes on your worldwide income."

His voice stayed lawyer firm. "Though U.S. federal taxes are less than what we pay here in Canada and Quebec, you'll also have New York State taxes to contend with, and they are not insignificant." He gestured with his hand. "Spending too much time in the U.S. will again defeat your purpose of benefiting from Canadian non-residency."

Dad now raised his hand along with his voice. "Then I'll travel the world and spend time in Europe. There are projects I could do in Czechoslovakia."

My father's tone turned a touch terse. "Anyway, how will the U.S. authorities even know I'm in Peru, NY? JHS owns our house there, and Elaine rents it." He pointed a finger too. "It's her name on the rental contract. When she drives us to Montreal from there, the Canadian border guards only ask to see her driver's licence, not mine." He kept his eyes firmly on Gregor as he swept his hand back and forth. "They never look at her passport, and they never ask for mine. There's no record of my comings and goings into and out of Canada."

Gregor's voice became as adamant as Dad's, but he didn't raise it. He tapped his index finger on the table. "That's maybe what happens today, Johnny. But computer systems are getting more sophisticated, and the Canadian and U.S. governments will be tracking these things better."

He leaned forward slightly. "One day, you'll need more than a licence to get across the border." His eyes stayed glued to his client. "You'll be taking a risk every time you cross a Canadian or U.S. frontier as to whether the authorities are keeping records on you."

Gregor leaned further forward in his chair and spoke calmly yet confidently. "What you are saying might work today, Johnny, but it may not work next month or next year." His voice was sure and steady. "If you are going to declare Canadian non-residency, you'll have to play by the rules. If they catch you skirting the law, the onus is on you to prove to Revenue Canada that you are not living here, or prove to the IRS that you are not acting as a U.S. resident."

My father was unfazed. "No problem, Gregor; I can do all that." He waved his hands as if he hadn't wanted another card from a blackjack dealer.

Gregor didn't fight or flinch. "Okay, Johnny. You now know what's needed if you want to declare Canadian non-residency, and what you can and cannot do afterward, and the potential consequences if the government catches you breaking the rules. The rest is clearly up to you."

I took calming breaths and then repeated Gregor's points. I wanted to make sure that I had gotten the facts right and that my father had heard them correctly. I didn't confront or contradict my father in front of the attorney. I kept myself collected throughout this repartee between a professional legal-advisor friend and my street-smart businessman father.

But my mind shouted, *Dad, what the hell are you thinking?!* Are you going to separate yourself from the country you have been living in for forty years, and the friends you have here, for pretty much the rest of your life? *Hell, if I'm going to visit you in goddamn Freeport!* I choked down my thoughts, leaving them to churn inside me.

Gregor allowed me to exhaust my questions. At this moment, there seemed to be little wiggle room between Dad's position of *I have my rights; it's my money; the government isn't getting into my pockets,* and Gregor's stance of, *You've got to play by the government's rules, or you'll risk the consequences.*

If I confronted or interrogated my father in front of Gregor, then he might dig his Hungarian-Slovak heels in deeper. I then might say goodbye not only to him but also to his offshore money. I prayed that he would see a father's light about his non-residency madness without my shining a son's flashlight directly into his eyes.

I was relieved that the jousting between Dad and Gregor had drawn no blood. Other than being impatient and a little loud, my bull of a father had remained civil.

During the car ride back to his office, Dad spoke animatedly. "These bigwig lawyers complicate things with their legal bullshit. What they want is to put their hands into your pockets so they can grab your money and your balls."

I nodded but said nothing until I could put more distance between Gregor and us.

Decades later, it would dawn on me that what my father had said about Gregor's "putting hands in client's pockets" was, in effect, my dad's modus operandi. My father was the kind of guy that could stuff his generosity, charm, and promises into your pants pockets until he had you by the short hairs. He had done that to everyone who let him, including me.

I wished to God that I had had my father better figured out back then. It could have saved lots of angst and anguish, or maybe not.

* * *

The next day, Wednesday, Dad telephoned my brother and me. "Elaine is inviting you both to our apartment for supper," he said curtly. "Can you please make it on Thursday evening?" His question didn't sound like a request.

It was rare that both Steve and I would be *chez* Dad and Elaine's for a family supper outside of a holiday gathering. As far as I could tell, my brother preferred not to be around those two. Maybe it was because Dad was never clear as to whether Elaine was his lady friend, mistress, live-in partner, prospective fiancé, or just the woman with whom he was living at the time.

Elaine was undoubtedly in the middle of Dad's non-residency pursuit. He may have told her that Steve and I were okay with his pending Canada departure. She probably wanted to hear our opinions directly rather than through our father.

I preferred not to come up against my father openly and directly. Though I thought it, I wouldn't want to say that he was wrong about chasing his Canadian non-residency craze. It was a long shot that he would keep faithful to the stringent government rules that Gregor had outlined. Dad was fooling himself about keeping his feet out of Canada for most of two years.

I had hoped Elaine could and would single-handedly stop my father from his folly. I gathered she needed a little help from Steve and me to get him to forgo his offshore wet dream. When I drove to their apartment on that chilly Thursday spring evening in 1988, I didn't look forward to our gathering of four Simkovits' psyches. I felt cold and wet under my tee-shirt, but I knew I had to be there. I had been the only other person present at the meeting with Gregor Varga.

I wondered what my brother thought about Dad residing in The Bahamas. I didn't know how much he knew about our father's growing offshore treasure. What I did know was that my brother and I never talked about Dad's plans.

Steve and I habitually stood on opposite sides of Dad, even in our family pictures. Though my brother prided himself in being an upright person, he could be as stubborn in his quest for transparency as Dad was in his desire for secrecy.

Though I usually leaned in my father's tax-skirting direction, I was beginning to feel weary in that perplexing position. I promised myself that I'd find a way to bring Dad's money into the light of day, but that possibility was still far away and not discussable today. Until that time, I had to find my way in my father's protracted money play.

The next day, the four of us sat for supper at Elaine's Chinese black lacquer dining room table. Asian artwork filled the adjacent living room. There was a large, black, intricately-carved lacquer room divider that separated the living area from the dining room. The apartment held colourful lacquer vases and glass flower-holders that sported high-quality fake flowers that looked incredibly real.

Placed here and there were assorted knickknacks: little wooden boxes and miniature statues, along with artwork and carvings that I had given Dad and Elaine for Christmas and birthdays. The room felt as if it were an Asian import store. Not a thing was out of place, not even Elaine's dark hair that was high and nicely shaped around her face.

Though Dad's non-residency loomed in the background, we had a pleasant meal. Elaine was a terrific cook, her cuisine less rich and more intricate than the Eastern European food with which Steve and I had grown up. She offered salmon baked in a teriyaki marinade. *Petit asperges* accompanied the fish, plus a side of tossed arugula and red leaf salad with sliced leeks, almonds, and tangerine wedges. For dessert, she served three flavours of sorbet, topped with fresh fruit. The only things missing were the printed menu cards.

I admired Elaine for her gregariousness. She could talk on and on about anything. Her topics this evening were where and how she found her Asian furnishings, her and Dad's trips to The Bahamas and Europe, and their Peru house improvements.

In the middle of her vacationing-with-Dad talk, she threw up her hand. "Having the apartment here, our house in New York State, and our condo in The Bahamas, it's hard to keep track of all our things. When last winter rolled around, your father was looking for his golf clubs to take them to Freeport. We couldn't remember where we left them, or when he last used them." She smiled. "We had to go to the trouble of buying a whole new set of clubs to keep year-round in Freeport."

She stopped to take in a long breath and then offered, "We had to buy ourselves three sets of clothes, one for each place." She looked at Dad, another smile on her face. "Neither of us can remember where we keep anything anymore." Her grin widened. "Looking on the bright side, we only need hand luggage whenever we go anywhere."

Elaine turned her attention to Steve and me. She wanted to know how my brother's young family was faring and how things were going with my fiancée. (Yes, we could hear wedding bells in the distance!)

Elaine got short answers from us. I didn't feel talkative with my brother around, and Steve was rarely revealing when Elaine asked questions. When she had partnered with our father, she hadn't realized how clammed up this Simkovits brood could be. Even her excellent food and hospitality couldn't loosen our tongues.

As the years wore on, even Dad had become quieter around Elaine. She seemed to consume the air and space around the three of us, and we seemed okay with that. As Elaine continued to chat, I thought of how women were so much better at sharing, communicating, and showing interest than men were, especially those with Simkovits genes.

Only one strain occurred during the meal. Dad said, "You boys can eat Elaine's rabbit food." He then turned to her. "Sweetheart, I'm not big on seafood, but the salmon is delicious."

Elaine smiled. I was glad that she let Dad's raw comments stay down.

Elaine wanted to know how things were going with Steve's church position and my work at WISE. When she turned to Steve and asked, "How's your work going at the church?" I cringed hearing about Steve's would-be job.

After Dad had decided not to invest money in the second company in which he had found Steve a position, the owner claimed poverty and let Steve go. Steve was then asked by his bishop to take charge of the church's family history centre. My brother performed projects for the centre, and he found ways to involve our father.

For one effort, Steve interviewed Dad to gather Simkovits family history. They then travelled together to interview our extended family in Montreal and Ottawa. My brother had told me, "Every Mormon conducts family history to 'seal' family members into the Mormon Church." He spoke with certainty. "Those sealed will reunite in the afterlife, and they will rise together in the second coming of Christ."

Dad was drawn into Steve's history quest and spent hours with him to review our family's past. My brother was doing what he thought right in his religion, but I saw his church work effort as nothing more than a reason to feed off our father.

Why couldn't my brother find a way to support himself like I was doing? I had worked hard in school, at JHS, and now at WISE. I wanted to make our father proud and to demonstrate that I was providing a return on his investments in my education.

But Steve was getting our father's support scot-free as if my brother had expected it that way. I had tried to talk to Dad about my brother's ways, repeating the adage, "Rather than give Steve more fish, isn't it better to give him a rod and reel so he could fish for himself? Why not send him to a job-hunting course?"

My father responded softly. "I know, son, but I feel responsible for your brother. He would starve without my support."

It irked me to see Steve continually at my father's fish market. Then again, wasn't I waiting for a future feeding frenzy from Dad's offshore school? Why did I feel so endangered?

Steve's tongue loosened a little with Elaine's question about his recent church activities. "With Dad's help, I found out that our Simkovits family goes back to a little village on a river in the hills north of Košice, a place called Veľká Lodina." His face was bright. "Dad says our family name, Simkovits, has been present in that town for many generations."

My brother's sweet talk tantalized our father. Dad offered, "My great-grandfather and his brothers lived there and were mostly farmers." He looked at me. "My father's father, Stefan, is who your brother is named after. I never knew Stefan because he died before I was born, but my father always spoke respectfully about him."

Steve added, "Stefan's son, Dad's father, Jan, was the first Simkovits to move into Košice, the biggest city in that region. Jan became a cabinet maker." My brother looked at our father. "Dad followed in his father's footsteps. He became the first to build console stereos in Canada by putting electronics into wood cabinets."

Steve looked sweet-faced at Dad. "Maybe we can visit Košice and Budapest and see how far back we can trace our roots."

Our dad didn't hesitate. "It would be my pleasure to do that with you, son."

I cringed again. My brother was shamelessly pandering to our father, and Dad was eating it up for supper. I felt a headache coming on. But wasn't I too pandering to our father for a distant offshore-money payoff? Was I being a favoured son pot calling an indulging brother's kettle black?

No! roared in my head, and I bit hard into a bone lodged in a forkful of my salmon. I'm trying to build my independence from Dad's money while Steve is breeding his dependency.

Elaine served her sorbet. She looked at me as we dug in. "So, Harvy; tell us what happened in your discussion with Gregor Varga earlier this week. Your father has said some things, but he tends to look at the bright side and to underreport the facts. I'd like to hear your and Gregor's take on your father's non-residency pursuit."

Dad looked at Elaine with a stern eye, but he said nothing. She continued to look at me. "I'm sure Steve would like to hear about it too."

Part of me had dreaded this moment, but I was ready for it. I took a long breath and shared what the attorney had told my father and me.

My voice was calm. "According to Gregor, Dad would have to effectively and honestly leave Canada for up to two years. He'd also have to give Steve and me controlling interest in JHS such that the company would still be considered a Canadian-held corporation."

Though I was feeling anxious, I powered through. "After that, Dad could come back to Canada for no more than six months each year." I raised a hand. "And he could be in the U.S. for only four months per year to prevent from being considered a U.S. and New York State resident and thus have to pay taxes there."

Steve turned to our father. "You'd give control of JHS to Harvy and me?"

Dad looked at him. "Yes, son, I would, so that government wouldn't tax JHS as a foreign-owned corporation."

Steve added nothing more. Maybe he, too, didn't want to reveal his thoughts about our working together in Dad's absence. I didn't address the point, for Steve and I could hash out our driving of Dad's company if and when he passed us the corporate keys. *God, help us!*

Elaine turned to our father. Her face looked a little stern. "Johnny, how are we going to carry this off? I don't want to be stuck in The Bahamas for two years." Her voice sounded a touch cold. "What about being able to see our Montreal friends? And what about my mother?! I can't leave her for all that time."

Elaine was exaggerating. She could come back to Canada as often as she wanted to. She might be giving Dad the message that he'd have to bachelor it in The Bahamas for the duration.

I twitched in my seat, but I don't think anyone noticed. I was very uncomfortable with Dad's self-serving, non-residency quest. Though his pursuit could offer Steve and me more control over JHS, and provide us a more abundant inheritance when he passed away, it meant we wouldn't see much of him for the next couple of years.

And if my brother and I went to The Bahamas to visit him, it would draw intense fire from our mother, even though she and Dad were now in the annals of Canadian divorce history. Neither Steve nor I had told her that we were here tonight, discussing family matters that no longer involved her.

Dad looked at Elaine and insisted. "Darling, we'd come to Canada often, for birthdays and holidays and any celebrations, even for JHS shareholder meetings. Our friends are welcome anytime to Freeport and Peru. I'll give Steve and Harvy joint signing authority at JHS, and I will transfer a portion of my voting shares to them so that I wouldn't have direct control over the company." His eyes projected assurance. "The boys and Jean can come to visit anytime, wherever we are."

While Dad and Elaine went back and forth for a moment, I wondered how Steve felt about Dad's plan. He hadn't divulged much of his thoughts. Steve's and my control over JHS seemed enticing, but I again imagined Dad calling us every week to give us marching orders for his company.

I felt a cold sweat forming down my back. There was irritation in my lungs from Dad and Elaine's cigarette smoke that hung around this apartment like a stinky Hungarian sausage in an Eastern European butcher shop.

Hell, if I wanted to get sidetracked from my consulting work and career at WISE. Damned if I desired to deal with Dad's holding company and its motley land and property assets. (As Dad sometimes said, "You can't ride two horses with one arse," and I wanted mine to stay in my WISE saddle.) Son-of-a-bitch if I was going to work with Steve concerning JHS. Fuck if I wanted to fly to frigging Freeport to visit Dad.

An opposing voice popped into my head. *Why not let him go as he wants to?* Wouldn't Steve and I be better off if he were a greater distance from our lives? On the other hand, might I miss his jovial smile, proverbial charm, fun parties, grandiose generosity, and being by his side? Was I as inextricably attached to him as my dependent mother had been? Did I fear that Elaine might fully take over my special place with him if they lived on an island two thousand kilometers away?

I don't know who said it first. As I glanced across the table at my brother, and then looked down at my sorbet, I felt a higher hand descend upon us. The words blurted out almost simultaneously from Steve's and my mouths: "Dad, I'm sorry; but I won't go to Freeport to visit you and Elaine."

The room froze for an instant. Dad and Elaine stopped talking, and they stared our way. My heart pounded hard in my chest. It was rare that Steve and I were of one mind against our father.

Gathering in my surprise at what had just been blurted out by Steve and me, I glanced at Dad. "I think Steve and I would still come down to your Peru home to see you and Elaine, and we'd enjoy seeing you in Montreal." I worked to keep my voice steady, though it stayed subdued. "But it looks like we both dislike the idea of having to travel to Freeport." I pointed to myself. "I know I'd never go there."

Steve nodded as his eyes looked down at the table, his voice as meek as mine. "That goes for me," he offered.

I hoped that our father understood that we were serious. During the three years that he owned his Freeport condo, we hadn't travelled there even once. Steve hardly went to Dad and Elaine's home in Peru, yet I figured we wouldn't punish our father by saying we'd avoid that place too.

Though I rarely, if ever, confronted my father in front of anyone, something compelled my speaking out this evening. I was relieved that my brother and I, and it seemed Elaine too, were on the same page regarding my father's senseless non-residency strategy no matter how much tax savings were involved.

Dad stared down at the table for a moment. Everyone else remained silent and motionless, including Elaine. He looked up and calmly said, "Okay, let me think about it."

Elaine jumped in. "Johnny, maybe we can talk more about this later." Her voice was upbeat, and her face hopeful. "Okay, anybody wants some more coffee, herbal tea, or sorbet?"

During the rest of our supper, we said not another word about Dad's Bahamas plan. We knew that he had finally heard us. I figured that Elaine now had the ammunition she needed to sail my father away from an island vagabond retirement.

Steve and I soon left for home. Elaine was grateful that we had come that evening, but she said nothing to divulge what she took away from our conversation.

On the elevator ride down, my brother and I had a brief chat as we both stared at the elevator doors. "That was an interesting supper," I said. "Did you mean what you said, Steve, about never going to Freeport?"

Steve's face was expressionless as he offered what I already knew. "I've never felt comfortable around Elaine. We hardly go to Peru, New York, to see them. Freeport would be even harder to do."

Elaine always worked to be considerate to my brother as she was to me. She carried the conversations, served great meals, and bought us thoughtful birthday and Christmas presents. But there seemed to be a snowbound void between my brother and Dad's life with Elaine. It was not her fault or doing; Steve would have been the same with any woman other than our mother by our father's side.

For myself, I worked not to shun Elaine or to see her as an awful person. Whether it was unconscious or intentional, I knew that the parent-targeted anger and disappointment I held was laid squarely on my father's shoulders. I didn't feel Elaine should be chastised or shunned for Dad's many transgressions with our mother or his misguided thinking about his money.

The elevator continued to descend. My brother turned his head toward me and added what I didn't know. "My wife doesn't like to fly, especially over water, so we'd never make it to Freeport."

I continued to stare at the elevator door. *Now there's a great excuse. I wish I had one like that.*

The elevator stopped at the ground floor. "I understand," I said to Steve. "For me, I've been to Freeport one too many times. I have no interest in going back there." And neither did my fiancée. There was nothing like Club Med on Grand Bahamas Island.

I turned to look at my brother's face, but I didn't quite meet his eyes. "I'm glad we feel the same way about Dad's non-residency pursuit." I didn't say it, but Elaine had orchestrated this evening well. She got what she needed from Steve and me.

Though my gut felt queasy, I kept my jaw tight about Dad's money hidden offshore. I wasn't going to tell Steve that our father's main non-residency motive was to legitimize that stash. Dad would have to find another way to deal with that buried treasure chest if he could.

"What do you think he will do?" Steve asked as we exited the elevator.

"I don't know for sure." I brought my hand to my chin. "I hope Elaine will convince him to keep his feet in Canada. It doesn't seem as if she wants to be away from Montreal for pretty much two whole years."

"I'll pray about it," my brother said.

You can do the praying, and I'll do the hoping.

Leaving the building, my brother and I shook hands, nodded to each other, and said goodnight. Then, as always, we went our separate ways.

* * *

On a late afternoon early the following week, I dropped in unannounced to my father's office. The events of Elaine's supper had bolstered my courage with my father. I wanted to say more to him, thinking I had a better chance with him if we talked in private. I sought to grab his attention by saying something provocative about what he was doing to what remained of our family. I felt he had to listen to me, his chosen son, more than anyone else.

We said a hearty hello, kissed each other on both cheeks, sat down in our familiar seats, and chatted for a bit. Then I gathered my courage and calmly proclaimed, "Dad, concerning your move to The Bahamas, you seem to care only about the money. . ."

I wanted to add, ". . . that you'd save by leaving Canada," but Dad immediately looked away and shouted, "No! Not at all!" He bolted from his chair and headed for the coffee machine in the little kitchen area in the office. He poured himself a cup as he kept his back to me.

I was taken aback by his forceful response. Though I was speaking my truth, I saw that I had hit a raw nerve in him. Perhaps I had said my piece with annoyance in my voice, not realizing how peeved I truly was concerning my father's non-residency goal. Maybe I hadn't thought through or presented my statement carefully enough or anticipated his potential thin-skinned reaction.

Though Dad was a money hoarder and money hider, he was generous to his friends, his church, and my brother and me. Though he saw himself as a magnanimous man, he could be notoriously stingy if one were on his wrong side, like my mother had been. What I had said and how I had said it may have been the last thing he ever expected from this son.

After a shiver of fear in my side, and a short, awkward silence, I changed the subject. Dad and I pretended as if I hadn't said my statement. Neither of us was good at approaching sensitive issues concerning each other.

I later figured there was little I could do to change Dad's view about building a money cushion that no taxman could touch. I still hoped that my off-handed barb might remain under his skin. I wanted him to come to his senses about what he was inflicting upon the rest of us regarding his non-residency pursuit. I wanted his acknowledgement, for once, that he was misguided about what he was chasing.

Decades later, I'd wondered if my statement, "You seem to care only about the money...," could have been as much about me as it was about my father. I was just as attracted to his stash, be it offshore or not. I admit that I may have, at that time, been no different or better than he.

Then again, I didn't want Dad to remove himself from my and Steve's life just so that he could accumulate more cash. I certainly would have missed him.

Some weeks after our supper chez Dad and Elaine, my father once more called Steve and me to his JHS office. After greetings, he looked at us and spoke casually. "I decided to let go of my Bahamian residency." He took a long breath. "I'm selling my Freeport condo. Elaine and I are going to buy a winter home in Florida, probably Boca Raton."

My jaw dropped into my pants, but I worked to keep it in my mouth. Steve, too, showed no reaction, though he did stare at Dad like a startled animal frozen in place. We both said, "Okay, Dad," and left the conversation there.

I suspected that neither Steve nor I wanted to rub any Canadian road salt into Dad's wound of forgoing his Bahamian tax-skirting desires. I would never say it out loud, but our father would have to find other pathways for his illegitimate stash. He did not indicate what that might be.

Though Dad's offshore Bahamian residency was now in our family's rearview mirror, I had no inkling of what was down the road regarding Dad's hidden money, and especially my part in it.

* * *

Twenty-five years later, I had an e-mail conversation with Elaine about her and Dad's Bahamian days. She wrote:

> Harvy:
> From as far back as I can remember, your father had these ongoing conversations with his accountant, Roger Delliard, about moving out of Canada. I couldn't understand why your father had to do this and what exactly he had to do. Then, one day, I was 'summoned' by your father to a meeting in downtown Montreal with Gregor Varga. I think your dad felt Gregor could make the case with me. Anyway, Gregor explained that we would have to be totally out of the country for a minimum of one year, and then only come back for short vacations. He said we needed to own absolutely nothing in Canada (sell the house, the cars, no phone numbers, no accounts, zip!)

It was intriguing how Elaine had gone through the same ritual with Gregor as I had. She continued.

> Johnny and I had our little apartment in Freeport at that time. Your father had applied for permanent residency in The Bahamas, and the papers were being processed in Nassau (he had already had one interview). I told Gregor and your father that I would not live on that little island year-round. Gregor said, 'Of course not, you can go to Switzerland for six months, then maybe a few months to Monte Carlo. The important thing is to stay out of Canada.'

I thought it interesting that Gregor seemed to have encouraged Elaine to join my father in his hunt for non-residency. But with me, Gregor had tried to warn my father about the challenges of that chase. Maybe Dad had hoped Gregor would have convinced me otherwise, but the attorney gave me the ammunition to take a stand against my father—with some discreet scene-setting by Elaine.

Elaine's e-mail went further.

> My first thought was, 'How much money is your Dad going to save if he spends money living and travelling around such places, plus having to pay guys like Gregor and Roger for ongoing advice, plus administrators for his money, etc. Why didn't he

stay in Canada and pay his taxes like everyone else?? Probably would have cost him less!!

It seemed Elaine knew little about my father's potential tax savings haul from his offshore cash. She went on.

> The biggest issue was that I had family in Canada (my mother in particular, and my brother too), and I couldn't see having to stay out of the country for such long periods. I remember telling your father, 'I'm not a gypsy. You can do what you want, but I'm not going to participate in that lifestyle. You can stay in The Bahamas, and I'll come and visit you once in a while.' Johnny's perceived tax problems were not my problems. Obviously, we never became non-residents, but it had been a battle!!

Some years later, Elaine divulged a little more about her part in extricating my father from his Freeport residency pursuit. Over dinner at a Boca Raton restaurant near to where she lived, she told me. "In the end, I had to put my foot down and tell your father, 'Johnny, I'm packing up my stuff in Freeport and not going back there.' After that, Johnny let go of his plans to move to Freeport."

I figured we all had played our part in getting my father to relinquish his offshore dreams. It was a good thing that the rest of us were pulling in a similar direction.

Forgoing his Bahamian residency, my father sold his Freeport condo within the year. He then bought and renovated a three-bedroom ranch home in Boca Raton. After his move was complete, he told me quietly in his office, "Our Boca home was purchased primarily with the money I have in Lux. I just made it look as if the house purchase had come from the proceeds of our condo sale in Freeport."

Once again, he said that only he and I knew differently.

* * * *

20

Wedding Alarm Bells

It was two years after my parents had signed divorce papers. Dad and Elaine's relationship and life seemed to be going well. Aside from Dad's foolhardy non-residency maneuvers, they had minor tussles about how much time Elaine could or would take off from her job to go to Florida or Europe with Dad.

I once heard from Elaine about the arguments they had regarding the remodeling of their new Florida home. During their first winter at their new Boca house, Elaine wanted to install expensive wallpaper that had to be special-ordered directly from the factory. Several times over that winter, she talked to my father about how that plush wallpaper would work in their kitchen and adjoining family room. She offered to put it up herself.

Dad acquiesced and handed her his credit card to place the order. She timed the delivery to come at the beginning of their second season in Florida.

When the wallpaper arrived, Elaine realized that the material was too heavy for her to install alone. I later overheard her tell the story to one of her friends. She knew I was listening as she spoke about it matter-of-factly. "I told Johnny I needed to hire a guy to help with that wallpaper." Her voice elevated. "He then started ranting and raving about not only how much that stuff cost but also how I now was going to spend another fortune to put it on the walls."

She raised her hand as if she were trying to stop his outburst. "I tried to explain to him that I couldn't put it up myself as I originally thought. But he kept on screaming as if I were spending his money like it was nothing." Her voice got edgy. "I finally got fed up and told him, 'Okay Johnny, forget it! I'm sending it all back. You go find something else with which to paper those walls.'"

She laughed. "That stopped Johnny dead in his tracks. He apologized and said I could keep the wallpaper." Her voice turned stern like a Mother Superior. "But by that time, I had had it with him. I shipped it all back. Hell, if I'm going to let him accuse me of spending his money like I didn't care what things cost."

The friend asked, "So what happened to your walls?"

Elaine batted her hand in the air. "We bought a cheaper paper at a local store." She smiled. "Johnny felt so guilty that he helped put it up."

I smiled too. I could imagine my father all day on a ladder, saying, "Yes, sweetheart." Like her dog Orphee, Dad's boisterous barks outdid any blood-letting bites.

Both Dad and Elaine were the types who rarely held grudges when conversations got heated. Elaine was especially good at giving Dad "the look" whenever she became frustrated at his stubbornness or persistence, as when he once again asked her to drive a station wagon load of materials from Montreal to their Peru house. She laughed it off, saying, "That Johnny! I can't believe what he made me do this time."

However, in 1988, after Dad and Elaine had been living together for eight years, their relationship changed. My plans to get married seemed to increase the friction between them.

* * *

Margie and I had met at a downtown singles party in the spring of '84. I was on the rebound after my American University depression, and it was some months before I started to work for Moe at WISE.

Margie had a tall, slender, size-six physique and flowing black hair that went halfway down her back. She was five years older than I, but she had young-looking round cheeks that made us look like peers. Margie enjoyed dressing well and eating at both fine restaurants and casual dining establishments. She worked out just about every second day and typically gravitated to salads for her meals. She wore stylish summer clothes and chic winter ski outfits, bought through routine end-of-season discounts from trendy Montreal stores. Before we started dating, I considered her a high-class friend.

Margie had quirks. She could completely deactivate the magnetically coded information on the back of any credit or bank card by just touching the black stripe. Whether it was the oil in her hand or her magnetic aura, any card became unusable as soon as Margie held it in her hand. She had to keep her ATM and credit cards wrapped in Kleenex and to handle them only from the edges.

Margie was extremely allergic to cats. She told me that she once owned a tabby. She added, "Because the doctor hadn't yet diagnosed my allergies, I sometimes got up in the middle of the night to pace the floors to regain my breath. The cat got up too and paced back and forth with me."

Her face was white as she remembered those moments. "When the doctor finally diagnosed me, he told me, 'I'm sorry, but you'll either have to get rid of your cat or die young from severe asthma.'" Her eyes turned sad. "I was mortified that I had to give away my sweet kitty."

After she and I had become a couple, we took a Lufthansa flight for a summer vacation in Europe. It was in the days when Lufthansa still used feather pillows. The feathers caused Margie to have an asthmatic attack. I held her hand for hours at the back of the plane as the flight attendants administered her oxygen.

It's no wonder Margie was so careful about how she handled things, what she ate, and even who she dated. It took eighteen months, and my resignation that we would never be more than friends, for us to become a couple.

One of Margie's prize possessions was a size 4, white, one-piece Bogner ski outfit, complete with a fur collar. Months before we met, she had worn that outfit while spending a week at the St. Moritz Club Med in Switzerland, followed by a week at the Val d'Isère Club Med in France. "It was during my ultra-slender phase," she told me while she showed me the one-piece in her apartment's front closet.

Her eyes saddened. "After those vacations, I went up a bit in size." That svelte Bogner would hang in her wardrobe for years, with Margie hoping she'd wear it again.

I believed Margie liked me because she saw aspects in me of her two most revered family members. I was an MIT engineering graduate, as was her brother, who worked in a big federal agency. Margie's sister-in-law, a woman who Margie also cherished, was a well-known organizational consultant, similar to what I was developing myself to become. I knew of Margie's sister-in-law through my professional training, and I revered her too.

Margie helped me to dress fashionably. I wanted to partake with her in the après ski crowd at St. Sauveur, Quebec, and the spring skiing diehards in Killington, Vermont. I wouldn't fit in on those slopes until I bought new banana-coloured Lange boots and both Bogner and Franz Klammer ski outfits. She said I needed two outfits with matching accessories if I were to make friends and find a girlfriend. (That was before she and I became a number.)

I prized my initial friendship with Margie, so we went on other shopping sprees to expunge the geek in me. I bought new dress suits and an opossum-lined trench coat, fashionable in Quebec at the time. After she and I had become a couple, I gifted her $1500 to buy herself a fur coat as both a Christmas and birthday present. She yelped with glee and then purchased a $3000 Tanuki (Japanese raccoon) coat that she wouldn't have bought on her own.

I saw Margie as a sophisticated and beautiful woman. Early one morning, after I had spent my first night at her apartment, she told me,

"Harvy, you are the first man in years to see me without makeup on my face." I felt honoured.

I particularly enjoyed Margie's outgoingness and intelligence. Unlike me, she made new friends effortlessly. She was a capable professional therapist and social worker. She masterfully handled challenging child foster placement cases in Montreal, saying, "I don't want *my* kids to get lost or forgotten in the system."

I didn't see Margie as "particular"—the term both my father and Elaine used to describe her. She'd push aside the wheat dumplings from Dad's Hungarian goulash, or she'd pick out the white-flour croutons from Elaine's salads. I saw Margie taking care of her physique and having discipline about what she wanted and who she was.

From the time I had met her, our acquaintanceship gradually turned into friendship, then courtship, then into living together, and then into wedding plans. She and I shared a wish to depart Montreal after we'd wed. We wanted to head to the U.S. under the auspices of Margie's big brother, who was an American citizen.

Margie and I were optimistic that we would rise together in whatever social circles we planted ourselves. We agreed to keep our intentions concealed from my parents until we felt the time would be ripe to divulge our plans. Because Margie's brother was helping us get to the USA, Margie's mother was more in the know.

* * *

In the spring of '88, after Margie and I had announced our wedding plans, Dad told me, "Elaine doesn't want the people at your wedding to see her as my mistress."

My eyes opened wide. "What's that about?"

Irritation was in his voice. "Now that you are getting hitched, son, Elaine wants to hook me."

I wasn't sure if he was irritated with me for getting married or with Elaine for wanting to marry him. He continued. "Now that I'm divorced from your mother, Elaine doesn't want her mother to see her as just living with me."

I wondered what Jean thought about Elaine being with a separated and divorced man these last eight years. I never had the gall to ask. Knowing Jean, I imagined her saying, "Elaine can live any way she wants to."

After many more months of stalling, Dad said he needed to comply with Elaine's wishes. That fall of 1988, before my wedding to Margie, Dad and Elaine wed in a private civil ceremony in Plattsburgh, NY.

Dad told Steve and me, "Elaine and I were able to get a marriage licence quickly in New York State." I figured he didn't want a record of his marriage in Canada. He didn't want Revenue Canada to find out that the renter of JHS's Peru house was the wife of a shareholder of the corporation that owned the property.

Dad asked both my brother and me to be his best men. Elaine's closest Montreal girlfriend came as Elaine's maid of honour. She, Steve, and I were witnesses. We wore dark suits or short dresses on that cool but sunny early-fall day. We participated in a quick service and signing ceremony with a Plattsburgh Justice of the Peace. Afterward, the five of us ate lunch at a local restaurant before driving back to Montreal.

In the men's room at the restaurant, Dad, Steve, and I washed up before lunch. The ink was dry on nuptial papers; gold bands were on ring fingers. As we stood by the sinks, my father raised his hand and voice as he looked into the mirror. "So now Elaine has me wrapped around her finger! She's trying to run my life. She cares only about herself and what her mother thinks."

I was taken aback by our father's unexpected and harsh declarations. He had shown a big, bright smile at the ceremony. I hardly knew what to say. "Dad, she's a nice lady. You get along, don't you?" I stammered, "Can't you just be happy with her?"

My brother nodded his acknowledgement of my statement, but he said nothing.

Dad huffed. "I don't know son. She's fun to be with, but I hate her controlling nature." He looked at us with piercing eyes. "She doesn't take care of me as well as your mother did."

Dad didn't realize how much he was talking about *his* controlling nature. And no other woman in the world would ever be at his call the way my mother had been.

Though I still felt awkward around Elaine, she was the best thing my father had going. But for him, everything had been fine as long as Elaine remained his mistress. A wedding band on his finger had set off an alarm bell in his head. "Can't you try to get along with her, Dad?" I repeated. It was the same message that Dad sometimes gave Steve and me when we didn't see eye to eye.

He looked down. "I don't know, son. I don't know."

It took me a long time to understand what my father wanted from women. He enjoyed being with an attractive lady, but not if it meant getting tied down. He appreciated having a worldly woman to display to his friends and around town, and he wanted someone who made hot soup and tea for him when he was sick and to sit by his side when he watched evening television. He wanted his women both ways, sans the ties. And, he wanted someone who expected little from him. What a guy!

Dad put on a smile for the rest of the day. That evening we had supper at the Beaver Club, the posh restaurant in Montreal's Queen Elizabeth Hotel. A dozen of Dad and Elaine's closest friends came for the celebration.

Placed in vases along the table were two dozen red roses that Dad had ordered. He raised his glass to his new wife, and everyone raised theirs to them. He was his charming self, and there was no further marriage balking.

I held my breath that it would remain that way.

* * *

After Margie and I had announced our wedding plans for late October of '88, my mother went on the offensive. At my next visit to her home, she looked at me with a pleading face. "I can't be present at your wedding with your father and Elaine there."

She wiped what seemed like crocodile tears from her eyes. "After what your father did to me, I can't be near him. Whether he is married to that woman or not, I won't be able to stay calm if I see him there with her." She raised a closed hand at me. "Harvy, please tell them not to come."

Three years earlier, in 1985, Steve had bent to the same demand from our mother. My brother had asked Dad not to come to his wedding and reception.

Dad grumbled about it for months. "After what I've done for your brother, he treats Elaine and me this way?!"

I urged him. "Dad, you should tell Steve how you feel." I, too, was peeved at my brother for slighting our father, but I didn't think it my place to say anything to Steve.

Dad could never confront his first son without anger, sarcasm, or judgement in his voice. Instead, he and Elaine suggested and catered an afternoon garden party for Steve and his new bride. The party was at Elaine's Pointe-Claire home, where she and Dad lived at the time. Afterward, Mom would attend the formal wedding reception held at the restaurant atop Place Ville Marie, Montreal's tallest skyscraper.

Steve invited our relatives and family friends to both parties. Guests could decide which event they wanted to attend, or they could participate in both celebrations if they wanted to. Most of Mom's relatives went only to the Place Ville Marie reception. Uncle Edo and his cousin Alex only came to the Pointe-Claire party. Though I felt awkward, I went to both. I brought a date, Diane—not Margie, because we weren't yet dating.

I was grateful for Diane's presence during my brother's wedding ceremony, held earlier that day at the Mormon chapel on Montreal's West Island. The following month, he and his wife would remarry at Toronto's Mormon temple, where only baptized Mormons could attend.

I made sure to time my and Diane's entry into the wedding chapel so that we were there just as the ceremony began. By then, Mom and her family were sitting in the front pews. I knew my father was going to sneak into the sanctuary late and without Elaine. He was going to sit in the back and then leave right after the service.

Diane and I walked quickly and quietly along one side of the chapel as the last attendees were getting to their seats. Halfway up the rows of pews, I saw an old high school chum of mine; John was sitting alone. He knew my brother from the summers we worked together at JHS. I grabbed Diane's hand and guided us stealthily to sit next to John.

I looked toward the front of the chapel. I saw my brother's best man, a Mormon friend. "Whew," I said to myself. "I'm glad Steve found someone."

Three weeks earlier, Steve had asked me if I wanted to be his best man. I had tried not to show my surprise at his request. I thought I was the last person he'd ask to be by his side on his wedding day. Maybe he had made that request because I was his closest family, or perhaps he had thought it was his brotherly duty.

I had told Steve I needed time to think about his best-man request. I wanted to say, "You and I are too estranged for me to be able to honour you." He had rarely deferred to me in our dealings, and I hardly respected my older brother.

I waited a week before I responded to him. "Sorry, Steve," I offered, "I appreciate your asking me to be your best man, but I don't feel right about it." I tried to come across both caring and candid. "There are lots of things our family does and says that's disingenuous, and I don't want to be that way with you. Please accept my bowing out, and I do hope you'll find someone more worthy than me to be there for you on your special day."

Steve's face stayed blank. "Okay, Harvy, if you feel that way," he said matter-of-factly.

From the church pew, sitting next to John, I looked at Steve standing at the dais. I hoped I hadn't let him down too much. I had been relieved he hadn't asked more about my decision. My answers might not have been kind.

After the wedding ceremony had ended, Dad slipped out the back unnoticed. My mother walked up to me. She smiled, said hello to Diane, and then looked at me with a stern eye, annoyance in her voice. "Harvy! Why didn't you come and sit with our family?"

I shrugged. "I saw my friend, John, sitting by himself. You remember him from our private school, BCS?" I looked directly at her and didn't let her answer. "I wanted to say hello and introduce Diane to him."

"You still should have come and sat with us in the first row," she retorted.

I kept my face as loving and naïve as I could. "I'm sorry you feel that way, Mom." But I wasn't sorry. I had sat where I should have.

After my mother moved on to spend more time with her family, I looked at Diane. "Hope you don't mind my mother."

Diane, too, had noticed my father enter late and leave early. She shook her head, and a half-smile came to her face. "You really have a screwy family, Harvy. I understand because I have one like that too."

I nodded. "I'm glad you're here to help me stay sane."

When it was time for my wedding to Margie, she and I nixed my mother's request to exclude Dad and Elaine. We decided to have one reception at the Ritz Carleton with both her and my family present.

I expected my mother's lobbying about keeping my father away. Over a home-cooked meal, I held my voice soft but firm. "I can't tell Dad and Elaine not to come to my wedding in the way Steve did for you."

Because Dad had buttered my life's bread, I couldn't mimic what my brother had done to him. Though I understood Mom's anguish about her ex, I couldn't let her rule Margie's and my wedding day.

Mom's voice got irritated. "So then, tell him to come by himself and to leave that American *büdös kurva* [smelly whore] at home."

"Sorry, Mom; I can't do that either." That would have been a slap in my father's face, especially since my father had said that Elaine wouldn't come to our wedding unless she and he were married.

I offered, "We'll keep you and your relatives separate from them. You'll sit at one end of our long head table while Dad and Elaine will sit at the other. You won't have to look at each other during supper, and we'll arrange a separate room where you and your family can gather." I felt that Margie and I had worked out a reasonable arrangement for her.

She looked sternly at me. Then you're a *kis fasz* [small dick], and your father's the *nagy fasz* [big dick]." Her eyes turned tearful; her face became long.

Her bitterness didn't move me; I couldn't let myself give in to her.

Irritated at her for trying to leverage my wedding day to get back at her ex, I gave Mom another blow as I ate the supper she had prepared. "Margie and I have decided to move to Massachusetts before the end of next year. Boston is booming right now. They're calling it the Massachusetts Miracle." I was trying to be upbeat. "Work and jobs are everywhere down there."

I looked at her. "Margie's brother lives in the U.S., and Margie has applied for U.S. immigration through him." I didn't tell her that those papers had already come through.

Mom glared at me and raised her voice. "What am I going to do here alone in Montreal?!" It was as if I had stabbed her in the heart. "Steve's married with a child, and he now has less time for me. You're getting married, and now you're going to leave Montreal." Her hands rubbed away tears. "I'll die without you here."

Considering that I perhaps had gone too far too quickly, I tried to console her. "Margie and I still have friends in Montreal, and her mother lives here too. We'll come back often to visit."

Though I felt concerned for my mother, my mind was firm about leaving Montreal. I didn't say it to her or my father, but I wanted a life far away from my family. I had had enough of my guilt-producing mother, my money-weaseling father, and my staunchly religious brother. I wanted to start anew with a better life a distance away. Hell, if I would permit my mother to ruin my new life with Margie.

Margie had hoped we'd move to California. But I felt the west coast was too far away, for I still wanted peace between my parents and me. Going to Boston, where I had spent nearly six years in college, was my compromise for their sake. Margie was kind enough to accept my wishes, with the hope that we would eventually make it to the west coast.

* * *

310

In late September, a month before my wedding, Mom came home from a day of shopping in the city. Because she didn't have a car, she had spent hours travelling on buses and subways. My mother had trudged up and down the aisles in several downtown department stores. She had been looking for a wedding reception dress. When she got home, Steve was waiting for her for his regular weekly visit.

An hour later, Steve called me at work. There was little emotion in his voice. "Mom was distressed when she arrived home. She said she had no luck finding a dress for your wedding. She wanted to look good if she was going to be seen by Dad and Elaine."

He spoke matter-of-factly. "After Mom changed out of her street clothes, she said her arms felt numb. I got her to sit down on the couch, and I loosened her clothing. I soon realized what was happening and called 911 to send an ambulance right away. She was having a heart attack."

He took a long breath. "The medics came within ten minutes. They put Mom on a gurney and are transporting her to the hospital as we speak; it's only ten minutes away. They just left the house a few minutes ago. I wanted to call you before I follow her there."

I was as shocked by my mother's sudden attack as I was surprised by my brother's coolness. I wondered if it was his religion that gave him such detachment. I was both envious and annoyed.

My pulse accelerated, and there was urgency in my voice as I offered, "Okay, Steve, I'm leaving right away. I'll meet you at the hospital."

He responded calmly, "Okay, I'll see you there."

During the ensuing hours, Mom had another attack on an emergency room gurney. Steve and I found out about it only a day or two later from an ICU nurse. Neither of us ever met Mom's admitting and attending physician. We got his name from the hospital and tried to call his office to learn more about Mom's condition, but the doctor never returned our call.

Damn the Quebec health care system!

During Mom's hospitalization, Steve and I alternated, each of us visiting her for hours each day in the hospital's ICU. She was under 24-hour care, tied to monitors, drips, and alarms. We couldn't locate her assigned doctor. We couldn't get complete information about Mom's condition and treatment, except for what little the nurses volunteered. We talked to our father about it. He offered, "Steve should have insisted the ambulance take her to one of the major hospitals in the city. Her local hospital is not as good."

It was too late for that hindsight. Steve and I had to do what we could for her where she was. We kept requesting to see her admitting doctor, or any ICU doctor, to find out more about her condition and prognosis. We got nowhere. It seemed as if she were locked in a hospital maze. Mom, still communicative, said she saw her doctor early every morning. But in her weakened and perhaps confused condition, she couldn't repeat what he had told her.

When it was my turn to visit her, I offered, "You'll get through this, Mom, just like the other difficulties you have had in your life."

She looked at me and said, "I hope so, son."

I massaged her back, sore from lying for days in her hospital bed. Her bed was tilted slightly backward so that her head was lower than her feet to ease the pressure on her heart. The nurses didn't allow her out of bed except to go to the bathroom, and only with assistance.

Though I was not a practicing Christian, I privately prayed for my mother's recovery. Neither Steve nor I expected the worst for her. We were optimistic those first few days. We didn't tell any of her local friends or far-off relatives that she was in the hospital.

Even if we had told them, they couldn't have visited her. She was in a small, cramped ICU where several critically ill patients lay. Only immediate family members were permitted to be there.

After four days of pursuing Mom's phantom doctor, another ICU doctor appeared. He was the night-shift physician, a 40-something guy. This time Steve and I were there together that evening with Mom. The doctor spoke calmly yet with concern. "Her blood pressure is considerably low. Her attacks seriously damaged her heart. It's beating irregularly and too fast."

He looked directly at us. "I'd like to consider installing a pacemaker into your mother's chest to stabilize her heartbeat." He explained how it would work. "The procedure should take place soon," he added. "Her heart could give out quickly if we can't get it slowed down and stabilized."

Steve and I looked at each other but said nothing. Our mother's situation was worse than we had considered.

Mom overheard our conversation with the doctor, but she didn't ask any questions or say anything until the physician left the room. She turned her head toward us and placed the back of her hand onto her forehead. "A pacemaker? I don't think I'll be able to live that way."

Steve said, "Please try for your grandchildren's sake, Mom." He and his wife had a second child on the way.

"Lots of people live with pacemakers," I said, though I wasn't sure how well they lived.

We received only a stare back from her.

During Mom's fifth night in the ICU, Steve and I each got a call at two o'clock in the morning from the ICU's night nurse. Our mother's condition had worsened. The night shift doctor wanted to pursue the pacemaker option. The hospital needed family members' signatures to proceed. The nurse wanted Steve and me to come to the hospital right away.

I became distraught that my mother could die. She had suffered and survived much: the bombings of Budapest in 1944, escaping Soviet communism in 1949, and the torment of a disgruntled brother. During her decades in Canada, she survived her husband's repeated infidelities, separation, and abandonment. But could she survive a failing heart?

What had given me solace was that Mom had come through other hospitalizations in the last number of years, including a psychiatric condition eight years earlier. By having survived all she had gone through in her life, I had hoped Mom could survive her heart attack.

After the ICU nurse had called me at home, I wondered if my mother might not survive this night.

On the way to the hospital this time, my eyes filled. I begged, "God, if you are up there listening, then please, please, please be gentle with her. She has lived a hard life and feels as if she had lost everything she had hoped and worked for." I wiped tears from my face. My handkerchief was getting soaked.

"Please show mercy on her. Please be gentle with her. Please don't make her suffer."

When Steve and I arrived at the hospital, the ICU doctor was waiting for us. He said, "Be prepared. Your mother could die from the implant procedure." His voice was matter-of-fact.

We signed papers. Steve and I saw her for a moment before they wheeled her into the operating room. Mom was groggy; she hardly understood what was happening to her. We held her hands and touched her arms, telling her we loved her and that we'd wait until she'd return. I wasn't sure if our mother understood what we were saying. She mumbled unintelligible words and gazed at the ceiling.

During her procedure, Steve and I called Mom's nephew, our cousin Ivan, who was a pediatrician in New York. He was the only doctor in our extended family. We explained what was happening to his aunt and asked what he thought we should do. After we had mentioned her high heart rate and low blood pressure, his tone rose, "Oh, oh. It doesn't sound good." He asked that we call him back after Mom was out of the OR.

An hour later, at four o'clock, Mom was back in the ICU. The doctor had successfully implanted the pacemaker in her chest. He said she was stable, but that anything could happen within the next hours or days.

Mom was barely lucid and needed rest. I felt helpless that there was nothing Steve nor I could do for her. We stayed for a few minutes, said goodnight to her, touched her arms and shoulders once more, and told her we would be back the first thing in the morning. She was in a daze and could barely speak.

As we headed out of the ICU, I looked at my brother and said, "I can't believe this is happening, Steve. She was fine less than five days ago."

"Yes," he responded, his face showing no signs of anything. "Mom could pass anytime."

I don't know why Steve and I didn't stay with her. There was hardly a place for us to sit in that small, crowded ICU full of severely sick patients. As Steve and I exited, I rubbed my burning eyes and glanced back toward our mother. I saw her raise one arm and hand toward the ceiling.

God, help her, please! I couldn't get those or any words out of my parched throat and dry mouth.

The sky was turning light when Steve and I got another call from the ICU nurse. Alone in her bed, Mom's broken and irreparable heart had given out for good. The nurse said she went quietly and peacefully. The nurse wanted us to return to the hospital right away to see our mother's body and to sign papers so they could release her to the morgue.

Mom was a month shy of her 68th birthday, and it was a week before my 34th. My throat ached; my esophagus felt as if it had closed; I could barely swallow. On the way to the hospital, as the light was brightening the sky, I sobbed uncontrollably. It felt as if a piece of my own heart had become broken too. I felt emptiness in my chest. My mother was gone!

Mom had been distraught by Dad and Elaine attending Margie's and my upcoming wedding. She had been disappointed by not finding a wedding dress that would make her feel first-rate in their presence. She had been distressed about my and Margie's plans to leave Montreal and head to Boston.

She must have felt as if she had lost me to Margie rather than her gaining a daughter-in-law. Might I have been the cause of her sudden attack and quick death? My throat and lungs felt like a desert.

When I arrived at the hospital, Steve was there, standing outside the ICU, talking to the doctor who had installed Mom's pacemaker. I hardly acknowledged them, walked past them, and went to see my mother.

I looked at her motionless body and blank, peaceful face. As I touched her arm and held her hand, I whispered, "I'm sorry, Mom. Goodbye Mom. I hope you'll be okay and happy where you are going." I talked through my tears. "Maybe I'll see you again in heaven—if I can get there myself." My eyes burned with tiredness. I wished I hadn't told her until after our wedding that Margie and I were moving to the States. That news, on top of everything else, had killed her.

Even worse, I felt sick to my stomach about having kept my father's secrets, being more loyal to him than open to her. Though I had helped her with her psychiatric illness years earlier and in her separation arrangement and divorce settlement with Dad, I still felt I had failed her. My head fell into my hands; my heart jumped out of my chest; my guts spewed over the floor.

I did my best to pull myself together and went back to where Steve and the doctor were talking. I quickly nodded at my brother then looked at the doctor. "What happened?"

The physician spoke softly yet matter-of-factly. "I'm sorry for your loss. The pacemaker helped for a short time, but her heart was too badly damaged." He switched gears. "With your and your brother's permission, I'd like to perform an autopsy."

"Why?" I asked, not knowing or caring if my blank-faced brother had already made that inquiry.

The doctor paused for a second as if he were looking for the right words. "For research purposes, to pinpoint the cause of her attack and the extent of her heart damage."

"When would you do that, and how long would it take?" Steve asked.

The physician replied calmly, "It's now Saturday morning; the procedure would have to wait until Monday. It would require a day to perform."

Steve and I turned to each other. We took a couple of steps away to confer for a moment while the doctor waited. Steve offered, "Mom wanted us to bury her as a Jew." He took a breath. "Jews need to be buried within three days of death. There won't be enough time for an autopsy."

I cut off my brother. "Don't you think it would be useful to know the true cause of her attacks?" I didn't say it, but I wondered if there might have been an improper diagnosis or insufficient care at the hospital or from her GP. That possibility may have precipitated or accelerated her death.

"There's not enough time," my brother insisted. "We need to get her in the ground before three days are up."

If it had been only my choice, I would have allowed the hospital to perform the autopsy. But I gave in to my brother's argument and what had been my mother's wish. Steve and I turned to the doctor and delivered our decision.

The doctor's face tightened. He looked disappointed but nodded his understanding. Unlike Mom's attending doctor, who I now saw as a dark angel of death, this doctor had had the courtesy to show and stay awhile.

I felt devastated. Mom had seemed as if she could recover from her heart attack. Now she was gone for good.

My brother's mood stayed businesslike, as if he had put his heart into his pocket. His voice stayed composed, and his eyes remained dry as he signed the hospital paperwork.

I again wondered if Steve's religion helped him to keep his feelings in check. He believed that he and Mom would reunite at the second coming. As for me, my hand shook, my heart burned, my sinuses filled, and my eyes ached not only from little sleep but also from rubbing away my start and stop tears.

Though it may seem trite, my only comfort was that my mother might now be in a better place. She had never acclimatized to her adopted country of Canada, the place where her one true love had brought her nearly forty years earlier.

Her best Montreal friends had been Jewish Hungarian women and men she had met here. Her well-being had come from writing to and receiving letters from her family in Hungary and Czechoslovakia. She also exchanged letters with extended homeland family and friends scattered in America, Germany, and Israel.

Mom's most cherished Canadian comfort had been her husband and children. She felt she had lost all of us—like melting Canadian permafrost turned to mud in the spring.

I wondered if I could ever get over the loss of her.

* * * *

Aftermath of a Loss

Steve and I agreed to meet the next day to share the arduous task of calling Mom's relatives and friends. Except for her nephew, the rest knew nothing about her attack and hospitalization. We'd make funeral arrangements to have her buried by the following Tuesday.

It felt a little fast to me, but my brother said, "It's customary in Jewish tradition to bury the deceased quickly. It shows respect for them and the mourners." Even though what he said made sense, I wondered why my brother always seemed to get his way.

Steve talked to Dad. We planned to meet at Margie's and my apartment to help with the calling and arranging—we had two landlines at our place plus a cell phone. Dad could inform his relatives and friends who had known Mom; Steve and I would inform hers.

Dad accepted our request without hesitation. Margie stayed with us and served food as we needed. She stayed mostly in the background or the bedroom as Dad, Steve, and I did our heavy-hearted work.

During the whole day with Steve and Dad, I felt as if I were dreaming with my eyes wide open—seeing my surroundings but sensing nothing being solid. I also felt as if I were at a remarkably amicable JHS board of directors meeting. Dad, Steve, and I were calm and cordial with each other. We kept focused on the tasks at hand, decided who would call whom, and who would do what regarding Mom's funeral arrangements.

Dad stayed quiet and somber. He offered a hand on a shoulder and a subdued, "You two should do what you think best," whenever Steve and I had to make an important decision. There was little tension between the three of us.

Since Steve had been closer to Mom than I had been, I let him continue to take the lead where and when he wanted to do so. For Mom's sake, none of us desired any arguments or angst on this day.

Our calls reached as far away as Czechoslovakia, Hungary, and Israel. I heard my mother's friends and family, one by one, gasp in disbelief then cry in pain for the loss of their beloved Nusi—Mom's Hungarian given name. They spoke of the strength and grace with which she had lived a hard life in Eastern Europe and Canada.

They grieved at the tragedy of losing her at such a young age. She was the youngest of her six adult siblings, only the third to die. Her family and friends mentioned how she had cared not only for her relatives but also for our family. They told me, "You and Stevie had been everything to her."

I could barely get out the words of how my mother was fine one week then gone the next. I cried with them. My heart sank each time I put down the phone receiver. Until those moments, I never realized how deeply I felt for my mother.

Though my head knew otherwise, my aching heart told me I had let her down. I felt partially responsible for her death.

* * *

Mom never practised Judaism in Canada. She never went to the synagogue on Saturdays nor celebrated Shabbat suppers at home on Friday nights. To reclaim her religion after Dad left her for good, she found occasions to try out her rediscovered Jewish cooking. She bought Jewish food at ethnic grocery stores in the city, carting her booty back to her suburban home via sidewalk, subway, and bus.

Even though her chicken soup was great, she could never quite get the little matzo balls right; they came out hard like rubber balls. Nevertheless, I found her ethnic dishes delicious, and the gefilte fish on matzo was tasty.

Over one supper prepared for my brother and me—some months after her divorce had been final—she sheepishly confessed, "I don't feel like I'm a good Jew." She looked down at her kitchen table. "On Yom Kippur, I can barely fast until noon."

We knew that Mom had been overweight for most of her life, and she was borderline diabetic as her sisters had been. Her sugar craving did her in on those days of fasting. "You're doing your best," Steve said. "That's what counts."

"God doesn't care," I added. "Trying is what's important."

"And being with your Jewish friends on those holidays is what counts," my brother professed. We knew that Mom celebrated the major Jewish holidays by getting together with her Hungarian Jewish friends in the city to play Gin Rummy or Kalooki.

Later in the meal, she added, "Boys, I need to tell you something." She looked at both of us and then at the table. "I might not be around too much longer."

I immediately retorted, "Mom, why are you talking that way? You have a lot of life left in you."

Steve jumped in. "You've always been a strong woman; you survived many hardships."

There was an uncertain look on her face. She took a deep breath and said, "Boys, when my time comes, I want to be buried as a Jew."

We stopped downing our supper and gazed at her. Almost simultaneously, we said, "Okay, Mom, whatever you want." Her wishes seemed both fitting and fair.

Our mother requested more of us. "Be sure to put my Tatransky name on my gravestone. My family's name will eventually disappear, so I want 'Tatransky' remembered where it could be."

Mom was right. Only one of her three Tatransky brothers had male children. Those sons, in turn, had only female heirs. Once my cousins passed away, it would be the end of the line for the unusual name Mom's family borrowed from Tatransky National Park in the Slovak Alps.

Steve and I nodded, and none of us said any more about it.

Steve found a Jewish funeral home and cemetery in Montreal that would accept Mom's body. If we had to, we'd have had Mom's many Montreal Jewish friends vouch for her Jewishness, but that wasn't necessary. The funeral home director knew of Anna Tatransky Simkovits and her small throng of Hungarian Jews in Montreal. It felt odd that I hardly knew any of those folks.

On the day before Mom's service and burial, Dad came with us to the Jewish funeral home. Traditionally, no one is permitted to view the dead body of loved ones. But the funeral home director knew that Steve, Dad, and I were Catholic. He wheeled the casket into a private room, shut the door, and opened the lid. Steve's wife was there for Steve, and Margie was there for me. Appropriately, Elaine was not present.

As the director revealed Mom in her casket, I could see that she was wearing her best greyish-black sequined dress that Steve had retrieved from her closet at home. Her hair and face were at its Sunday best. Her body was lifeless.

Upon seeing Mom resting motionless, my father brought his hand to his mouth and welled up in anguish. He turned away from Mom's body, barely able to look at his ex-wife lying dead. He had not seen her since he had left her eight years earlier. He could hardly look at Steve and me. His eyes filled with tears while his mouth tried to suck in air. His voice stuttered.

Dad put his hands on my and Steve's shoulders to steady himself. "She was a good mother to both of you," he said. He looked at the floor. "She took good care of me when we were together. She made sure I walked out of the house each morning with my clothes neat and clean. She made sure I came home to a good home-cooked meal."

I had seen my father cry only once before. It was after a big fight he and Mom had when I was a kid. Startled awake in the middle of the night by the opening of the garage door, I had heard Dad enter the house.

Having waited up for him, Mom laced into her loaded husband for coming home stinking of alcohol, cigarettes, and perfume. After many angry words between them, Dad broke down, moaned loudly, and then sobbed, "*Kérem, hagyja békén* [Please, leave me be.]" He repeated those words for what seemed like an eternity. Maybe my father had had a bad day at the office and wanted nothing more than to have sympathy from his wife and to get rest.

Hearing her husband's pleas, my mother stopped her offensive and went into the kitchen. She boiled water, made tea, put it down on the living room coffee table, and went back to bed without saying another word. For the whole time, I shook in my cold, sweaty bed. I couldn't return to slumber until I heard my father snoring on the couch.

My parents' marriage had been utterly turbulent and painful, and it was very much over. But today, at this funeral home, my father showed his deep feelings for his ex-wife. Had Mom been looking down from the heavens, I'm sure her bitterness would have subsided. She'd now know her one true love had acknowledged his sincere caring and appreciation for her.

The next day, before the synagogue services, Steve, our cousin Ivan, and I sat with the rabbi to discuss the service for Mom. Dad wasn't present because he felt Mom's friends and relatives might take issue with his being there.

After we had introduced ourselves, the rabbi looked at us, and he calmly asked, "How is everyone doing?" His voice was deep and somber.

Steve was the first to respond, his face smiling, "Fine, sir, just fine."

I jumped in, my eyes tearing. "Our mother's death was very unexpected. She had been a determined and giving woman. She survived many hardships, and she's now gone." My voice was frantic due to my mother's tragic life and sudden passing. "Her friends and extended family are devastated by her loss at such a young age."

Cousin Ivan spoke too. "She was my favorite aunt." His eyes filled, and his voice cracked. "We lived and hid together as Christians in Budapest during the war. She was like a second mother to me." Tears burst out of his eyes.

The rabbi turned to Steve and spoke softly. "It seems that not everything is fine."

Steve looked away, saying nothing.

The rabbi asked more questions about Mom's life. We told him about her family having survived WWII with false Christian papers. We mentioned her escape from communist Czechoslovakia with our father and their immigration to Canada with next to nothing. We shared how she relinquished her seamstress profession to become a housewife and mother, and how she became embittered and sad from three separations and eventual divorce from our father. We also said how caring and generous she was to her family and how they loved her for it.

An hour later, a contingent of Mom's friends filed into the synagogue. They entered one-by-one and two-by-two, in rumpled dark suits and out-of-date dresses. These were more elderly Jewish Hungarian Canadian men and women than I had ever seen together in one place.

During the service, the rabbi repeated for the whole audience what we had disclosed to him.

Steve, his wife, and their three-year-old daughter were sitting right behind me in the pews. As the rabbi spoke, the youngster babbled, her high-pitched voice competing with the rabbi's baritone. The rabbi stopped once in his tracks and looked the child's way. "Such youthful distraction," he said, and then continued the service. But the child didn't stop talking, even after a few soft "Shush!" from her mother.

I felt the heat rise inside me. I was trying to listen to the rabbi, but my niece was carrying on right behind me. Steve's wife wasn't taking care of it, and neither was he. I had given in to my brother many times in the last few days, but I couldn't let this one pass. I turned around, looked his wife in the eye, pointed to my niece, and whispered sternly, "Can you please, please take her out of here."

She looked at Steve. He didn't say a word, but his eyes told the story. She picked up her daughter and carried her out. The child blabbered through and out the back of the synagogue.

When my attention came back to the wise man, he was raising his arm and pointing to Mom's sealed casket. He looked at the crowd, raised his voice, and said, "Don't let what happened to Anna Tatransky happen to you!"

The synagogue was still as my mother's body while the rabbi's words of warning echoed through the hall. My torso shivered at his forthrightness.

Having been distracted by my niece, I hadn't heard what the wise man had said that led to his crescendo statement. I assumed he referred to my mother having become deeply embittered in her final years, and that she died with sadness and resentments.

Later, at the burial, I scooped shovels of soil three times, two times with the shovel blade upside down—a Jewish tradition—to symbolize the hard labour of life. I pitched the dirt onto my mother's casket as attendants lowered it into her grave.

Afterward, Steve and I held a reception at our childhood home. Mom's living room, kitchen, and hallways were wall-to-wall with people. No seat was left unfilled, and there was hardly a place left to stand. I don't know about my brother, but I was deeply touched and overwhelmed by the generous words everyone shared about my mother, and the heartache they felt about her death.

Although my mother said she had resigned her Jewish religion, my brother and I would never uncover any official documentation or certificates that showed that she had done that. We also didn't locate any documents indicating her claim to Christianity as her religion in Canada. We never found any papers with her middle name of Maria. Perhaps with Dad's encouragement, Mom might have informally bestowed Maria upon herself to seem more Christian.

Steve and I would continue to wonder how she might have officially relinquished her original religion or asserted a new one upon entering Canada in 1949. Maybe it was via a verbal declaration or by way of a simple mark she had put on an immigration form. It was another example of what she had given up to be with her husband.

While talking to guests at Mom's home, her longtime neighbours, Mr. and Mrs. Brisson, approached Steve and me. This elderly couple had known Mom as Anna for over 30 years—the whole time she and we had lived across the street from them. While Steve and I had been growing up in Dorval, Mom gave our house keys to Mrs. Brisson. The elderly lady watched over the house whenever our family went away on vacation.

The Brissons now divulged that they too emigrated from Eastern Europe soon after WWII, first spending a few years in France. Mrs. Brisson then offered, "Your mama was very lonely, *n'est-ce pas*? Whenever I saw her, I could tell."

"Yes, she had lived a hard life," I confessed.

I didn't say that, on lonely weekend days, Mom walked to the local multiplex movie theatre and spent the whole day watching movies for one entry fee. It was like she and Dad had done when they came to Canada, seeing the same movie twice, even three times in a row, to help them learn English. After Dad had left her, Mom became good at sneaking into a different movie after finishing an earlier film. At least my mother felt she was getting her money's worth.

Mr. Brisson looked at us with his eyes wide open. "We never knew your mother was Jewish."

My brother explained, "Mom hid her Jewish heritage from the community because of her harrowing experiences during WWII." He didn't mention that Dad had wanted her to keep her Jewish heritage hidden.

Mr. Brisson pointed to himself and his wife, and declared, "We are Jewish too! We, too, had hidden that from everyone when we came to Canada."

Steve's and my jaw opened wide. We had assumed these French Canadian neighbours, living a stone's throw away from our home, were as Catholic as the Pope. I now wondered—and I suspect my brother did too— what the Brissons and Mom might have shared had they known about each other's real history and heritage.

To my brother's and my surprise, Uncle Lali's wife, Martha, came to Mom's funeral. We hadn't seen or talked to her in over a dozen years, well before things turned unforgivably sour between our mother and her brother.

Martha's daughter, my cousin Janet, didn't come with her mother. Janet now lived in Toronto, and perhaps she held a grudge about my mother not having gone to her father's funeral a decade earlier.

After Mom's funeral, Aunt Martha came to our house to help with the reception. She put out and served trays of food, and she helped to clean up afterward. It was as if the years of strain between our two families had disappeared that day. She told us, "I know that things were difficult between Lali and Nusi, but you are still my family." She looked at us with caring eyes. "If it hadn't been for your mother and father, we wouldn't have known anyone in Canada when we immigrated here in 1950."

That statement was true for many Tatransky and Simkovits relations. Dad and Mom had paved the way for many of their family to follow them across an ocean.

Martha was certainly more gracious with us than my mother had been with her when Lali died. Mom had held onto her bitterness concerning her brother, who had put much angst into her marriage. We thanked Martha from our hearts for having come that day.

Sometime later, Martha moved to Toronto to live closer to her daughter. After Mom's funeral reception, I never saw my aunt again. After the start of the new millennium, my aunt passed away from a long-time illness. She was interred in Toronto.

Like Janet had done with my mother, I didn't go to my aunt's funeral. My brother didn't go either. I guessed the bad feelings that had lived between our parents got carried down to the next generation.

* * *

I had wondered why my mother named me Harvey. She gave me that name (with the "e") until I changed it to the shorter form while I was in college. To me, the extra vowel was superfluous, and "Harvy" looked unique and distinctive. For most of my life, I suspected my mother revered British male names, thus bestowing me with the English moniker.

Decades later, I met a Jewish man who had the same first name. He told me that it was common in Jewish heritage for one to take on the name of a relative, usually deceased. However, if the child was different in sex than that relative, only the first letter was carried forward. He explained that his name had come about that way, with the "H" taken from his grandmother's first name.

Steve had once said that my mother's name came from a great-aunt, Hannah Friedmann. Thus, to honor that relative and to generate a remembrance of herself, it seemed that Harvey became Mom's choice for me.

That one capital letter has undoubtedly had its effects.

* * *

One couple was missing at my mother's funeral and reception. It was the Meyers. Our family had been close to them when Dad and Mom had lived together. Years before Mom's death, Ned and Mimi had moved from Montreal to Toronto to be closer to their son and his family.

I was sad about our lost relationship with the Meyers. My brother and I had grown up with them as if they were as close as any Tatransky or Simkovits relation. We had spent time with the Meyers on many weekends, and we had driven in tandem to Florida for many Christmas vacations.

As we all had lounged poolside, Mimi and Dad downed endless gin and tonics. Ned and my mother were not drinkers and may have had only one libation. Though the four adults had laughed a lot during those times, there seemed to be tension in my mother's voice whenever Dad and Mimi whooped it up a bit too much.

After my father had passed away, a dozen years after my mother, I visited Mimi in Toronto. I was curious about our lost connection. Though she was in her early 90's, she made me a hearty Eastern European supper. I asked her, "What happened between you and my father after he left my mother for Elaine? Steve and I hardly saw you and Ned after that."

Mimi's voice got a touch edgy. "Ned saw Johnny from time to time, but it was never the same as before. Our two families never again did things together."

She drew a long breath. "I didn't like Elaine so much. She was not like your mother and me." Mimi's voice turned strong and expressed pride. "We are Eastern European *vimen*! We marry one man and stay by his side through thick and thin."

She shook her head. "Elaine was born and raised in North America, and it's not the same. Here, women are too independent. If a man doesn't suit her, she leaves him and moves on to the next—like that!" She snapped her fingers.

Her voice calmed. "Even Ned and I had our ups and downs, but we stuck together." She took a long breath. "When Johnny left your mother, it was never the same between our families." She glared at me. "Let's just say that Elaine wasn't my cup of tea."

Mimi took in a long and slow breath as if she hadn't many remaining and wanted to savour this one. She continued to look at me. "Your mother had a tongue on her too."

She raised a finger. "In 1960, Ned and I had planned to follow your family to Dorval, the suburb where you lived. When your mother found out about our intentions, she told me, 'Just because you are moving nearby, don't expect us to be good friends.'"

Mimi's eyes blinked a few times. "When I heard that, I told Ned we shouldn't move near your parents but stay closer to the city."

Ouch! It was hard to consider my mother not being welcoming of our close family friends.

Years after that conversation with Mimi, Elaine told me, "Your father once confided in me that he and Mimi had had an affair while he was still living with your mother. He said it didn't last long, and your mother didn't know."

Maybe Mom didn't know, but she may have smelled it on those two. She had a sensitive nose regarding her husband's infidelity.

Elaine's message explained a lot about the tension between my mother and Mimi, but a part of me wished I hadn't known.

* * *

Mom got small pleasures in her eight years of life after my father had left her that final time. She went on winter vacations with her Montreal Jewish friends to destinations in Miami, The Bahamas, and Rio de Janeiro.

Some of those friends had Nazi concentration camp serial numbers permanently etched into their forearms. Others had hidden in the woods of Poland during WWII, or they had concealed themselves with false papers as Mom's family had done in Budapest. My mother came back from those vacations with bronzed skin, her blond hair bleached almost white by the sun, and she sported a big grin.

For several weeks each summer, she travelled to communist Hungary. She stayed at spa resorts on Margaret Island, situated in the middle of the Danube River that split Budapest into its Buda and Pest sides. She invited her Košice sister and Prague brother to join her there, and she helped to pay for their stays.

Mom came to life around her siblings. Though she worried about going abroad—about what she should pack, about the long and tiring travel, whether she was going to have a good time—my mother always wore a smile upon her return.

Mom showed Steve and me the photos from her Margaret Island trips. She and her siblings stood by beautiful spa gardens that overlooked the Danube, possibly as they had done during less-horrific parts of WWII. I suspected that they found solace and support in each other's company. They probably reminisced about how they survived Hungarian fascism and German Nazism.

Mom learned about how her siblings lived under Soviet communism. She once told me that her brother had said, "Now that I'm retired, the CSSR government gives me three weeks a year to go to the spa for free. It's a part of my health care." Mom then admitted, "That's even better than our free health care in Canada!"

I was sad to think that Mom's brother and sister were among the last Jews remaining in Czechoslovakia. Even more surprising was how, after 39 years of living in Montreal—ten years more than she had lived in her homeland—Mom never fully adapted to our Canadian language or culture.

She stayed mostly in her small Jewish Hungarian and Slovak circle of family and friends.

Even her acquired English was not always comprehensible. When I had received letters from her during my time in summer camp, private school, and college, her spelling and grammar were things to chuckle about. But her generosity to her family was never something to laugh about.

Living alone after Dad left her had been excruciating. She once told my brother and me, "Some nights I can't sleep. I rise from bed in tears, and I walk sleepily down to the living room. I grab one of the window curtains and pray to my mother's mother, Matelaye."

Mom felt that her long-deceased relative, the wife of a Košice rabbi, had helped her and her family to survive the war. Mom hoped Matelaye would help her once more if she prayed hard enough. But her family's matriarch and savior never seemed to grace Mom again.

It took me years to understand Mom's bitterness and pain. She had sacrificed much for the man whom she stood by for over thirty years. For that husband, she had relinquished her seamstress career, had left her home country and city, had denied her religion, and had sacrificed her relationships with her siblings, especially her brother Lali. When her marriage became irreparably broken, a dark cloud enveloped her once energetic and resilient self.

She once reminisced by telling me, "I could tell your Dad stopped loving me after we were married for five years. But I never stopped loving him, and I still do." She took a long breath. "Though he hurt me badly with his other women, I would still take him back."

Sometime after Dad left Mom that final time, it was he who shared with me what my mother had meant about his "having loved her for only five years." As he and I sat together looking out the floor-to-ceiling windows at the Montreal airport, waiting for his flight to board for some southerly destination, he divulged, "You know, your mother had an abortion a year after you were born."

My eyebrows rose, and I turned my head toward him. He continued. "She didn't tell me about it beforehand, but she went to see an illegal doctor when she was pregnant with another boy." He took a deep breath. "I was furious at her for doing that. Afterward, she couldn't have more children. I couldn't completely forgive her for what she had done."

I responded un-profoundly. "Oh, I didn't know," and turned my head away. I felt a cold numbness come over me and wondered why my father needed to tell me such painful things. Was he trying to make my mother a terrible person in my eyes?

As a practicing Catholic, Dad's distress about losing a child that way was understandable. I gathered that Mom's choice to abort her third son was a pivotal point in their marriage.

Mom's taking of an unborn life felt unforgivable, but I could comprehend her decision. With Dad rarely home, she had pretty much been a single parent during Steve's and my upbringing. When I was a teen, I recalled her saying, "Your father left me home alone with two babies while he went away for weeks at a time on business trips and vacations with his friends." Raising a third child pretty much on her own would have been unfathomable to her.

During those years of my mother's life, it was hard for me to acknowledge her hardships with my father. Because of my fears of abandonment by my dad, it was easier for me to blame her for driving him away.

As Dad had made Mom disappear from his life, a part of me had wanted her to vanish too. That part of me thought that my life would be less stressful without her continually reminding me of her lost life and how she blamed Dad for that loss. Only after she had died did I realize how naïve that child part of me was; I just had wanted my parents' hostility to stop.

Though I know much better today, I can't tell her that I better understand her pain and suffering with her husband, nor can I ask for her forgiveness on my once limited view of her.

My closest Jewish friends tell me, "Your mother has forgiven you," but I still wonder if I can forgive myself for my foolishness concerning her.

* * *

A year after Mom's death, in the fall of '89, while visiting Montreal from Boston for my mother's tombstone unveiling, I was driving with my father to his apartment. I had recently participated in Werner Erhard's *The Forum*, where participants bared their souls about their lives and relationships.

That program compelled me to talk more to my father about my mother's death. I spoke as Dad drove. "I find that I still feel bad about Mom dying."

I looked out the car window. I felt agitated and weighted down inside as I continued to speak. "I wonder if she died because of my plans to marry Margie and move away from Montreal."

My dad took a long breath, reached over, and put his hand on my arm. He spoke softly. "Harvy, I know your mother well enough. If she were alive today and knew how you felt, she'd forgive you completely."

I didn't move a muscle as I stared out the car window. I instantly felt a heavy pressure come off my chest and shoulders. At that moment, Dad had offered words that only a father could say to a son to lighten a self-torment. It was the kindest thing he had ever said to me.

I realized that my mother would want me to carry on and not live with the tragedy of losing her. I kept my eyes looking away from my father so he couldn't see me wipe away a tear. "Thank you for saying that, Dad," I said. I looked at the sky and silently thanked my mother too.

According to Mom's will, Steve and I solely inherited her estate. Soon after her divorce was complete, she told us, "Boys, I don't know how much longer I have to live, but I want you to know that everything I own will go to the two of you." Now, after her death, I felt the weight of my mother's generosity like I never had before.

Mom might have had a grander purpose. She didn't want her two sons to be dependent on our father for money. She didn't wish Steve and me to fear his casting us aside as she had been. My mother wanted us to have children, to have money to support our families, and to remember her for the rest of our lives. She wished us a better life than her stay-at-home, keep-supper-warm, wait-for-her-man prison in which my father had kept her. I will never, ever forget that caring and generous side of her, and I continued to thank her from my mind and heart.

I wondered if Mom precipitated her death to remind Steve and me—maybe Dad, too—of her life of sacrifice and suffering. She may have wanted the rest of us to feel responsible, even guilty, for her lot in life. If she couldn't find happiness, did a part of her want us to be unhappy too?

Both of my parents had a knack for placing enormous defeats at the feet of my small victories—Dad in how he used Steve's and my JHS assets to pay for his divorce settlement, and Mom by dying as I was ready to begin a new stage of life with Margie.

Though Dad had lightened my guilt by his words on that autumn day after her monument unveiling, my gnawing feelings about my mother stayed with me for decades. I knew that I, too, had abandoned her by keeping my father's secrets.

For many years after Mom's passing, I had recurring dreams about being wrong about her death. I imagined that she had just been away (perhaps visiting family in Czechoslovakia or on a southerly vacation in Rio) and was waiting for me to visit her at her home. In my dream, I felt guilty that I hadn't gone to see her, and I felt an urgency to go to her home right away. Even when I startled myself awake, I had to ask myself if my mother was dead.

Those dreams stopped sometime after I had Yahrzeit plaques made for her and placed in Jewish temples in both Montreal and the town of Lexington, MA, where I lived. I wanted Mom's name to exist, beyond her gravestone and beyond my life, both in the cities she lived most of her life and where my family now resides.

I hope that my mother is at peace in whatever afterlife she has found. May I also find lasting peace and forgiveness before I join her.

* * *

Sometimes, I think about how my life has been affected by my Jewish heritage. Though my father raised me as a Christian, I find that I have my closest affinity with people of the Jewish faith. I have had many Jewish friends, clients, business partners, professional colleagues, Unitarian Universalist church friends, and associates in the many nonprofits I've served.

Perhaps I identify with Jews because of my mother and her family, or maybe I've been working subconsciously to compensate for the millenniums of Jewish persecution by other religions, or possibly both. After years of resisting my Jewish heritage, I finally gave into my observation that I seemed to be attracted to Jewish people.

Years after my father's death, I embraced my Jewish background. I helped to start and promote a Jewish Heritage Group in my UU church. Our group had many Shabbat suppers, annual Seders, and Chanukah gatherings. We saw movies and lectures to learn more about ancient Jewish culture, its fascinating history, and its best traditions.

My mentor Moe had once told me, "Because of all their human suffering over the millenniums, Jewish people can be very understanding." That certainly fits my observations.

Every year or so, when I visit friends or family in Montreal, I go to Mom's gravesite. I search for the largest stone I can find around her site and place it onto her tombstone. Both English and Hebrew engrave her headstone. The stone bears her full Canadian name, "Anna Tatransky Simkovits." Steve and I chose to keep Dad's last name attached to Mom's because she didn't stop using it after her divorce.

Every time I see her headstone, I stand for a moment and tell her, "Hi, Mom. I wish you well. I'm okay, but I miss you. I hope you are doing okay where you are. I'm sorry that I wasn't a better son; I hope you can forgive me."

I continue in my mind. *My biggest regret, Mom, was that I didn't see Dad as clearly as you did while you were still alive.* I look at her name again and say out loud, "You were right about him. He was an old fool with you and all of us."

I look down at her footstone. It reads, "Nusi – a determined and giving woman." I continue to speak to her in my mind. *Yes, you were that way in your life and with your family. You never cared for more than to see us be happy.*

I have never fully gotten over my mother's death, and maybe I never wanted to. I think about her almost every day, especially how she was shortchanged or let down by the ones she loved the most, including me.

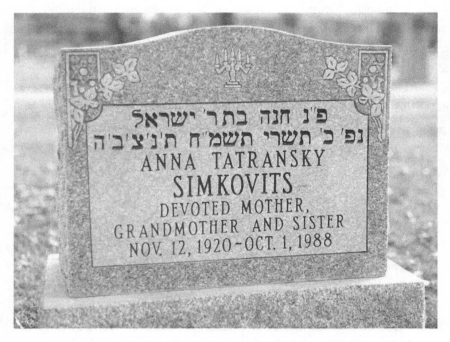

Mom's gravestone after its installation a year after her death, buried as she wanted to be. Oct 1, 1989.

* * *

After Dad had passed away, more than a decade after Mom, I came across their wedding rings in Dad's office safe. Steve placed Mom's jewellery in there after she had died. We had agreed to save Mom's other rings, charms, and chains for Steve's daughter, for when she would be old enough to wear and appreciate them. I'd get a portion of Dad's jewellery in return.

Among those precious things were Mom and Dad's simple, Canadian-made, 14kt wedding bands that were nested together in their original deep blue velvet jewellery box. I suspected, in my parents' haste to leave Czechoslovakia in 1949, they had little time to get rings for their civil wedding. Maybe they delayed the purchase because they didn't want to let on about their marriage before departing their communist homeland. If one of them got caught by the Soviets during their escape from Czechoslovakia or through the woods from Vienna to Salzburg, perhaps they didn't want to alert the authorities that he or she had a partner.

Today, those simple rings have remained within their box, sitting in a curio cabinet in my home. They symbolize my parents being together. The nested bands are a reminder of the handful of happy years they had with each other while we had been together as a family. That box has remained open behind the glass door, surrounded by other souvenirs from my trips—happier times—with my wife and kids.

I have never cleaned or buffed those aged, blemished bands, nor do I suspect I ever will.

* * *

Like my mother, my fiancée was Jewish but not a practicing Jew. Like my father, Margie had put her hand over her mouth when the funeral director opened my mother's casket for our private viewing.

Margie later told me, "I wanted to keep myself together and be there for you, Harvy." She put a hand on her chest. "When I saw your mother lying there, I was overtaken by her loss." A tear formed in her eye. "I know she was not a happy woman, but it's such a tragedy to see her gone."

After Mom's funeral was over, Margie looked at me and spoke softly. "In Jewish tradition, marriages are not postponed if a close loved one dies." She and I agreed that we should continue with our wedding plans.

We married four weeks later. Thanks to Elaine pulling strings, our wedding was at Montreal's posh Mount Stephen's Club, where my now stepmother was a member. To respect Margie's mother, we got married under a chuppah in this most English upper-crust establishment of raised wood-paneled rooms, flowing staircases, and ornate candelabras.

Our wedding ceremony was the first non-Christian ceremony the club had ever celebrated, complete with a glass that I stomped on at the end of the service while everyone yelled *mazel tov*. A Justice of the Peace led the proceedings, along with a cantor who chanted Hebrew prayers. I accepted these Jewish touches to our wedding because they were meaningful to Margie and her Mom—as long as neither of them expected me to convert or engage a mohel.

Before our wedding, Margie and I had gone to see a rabbi from a reform temple. We wanted to determine if I could legally claim, in the eyes of the Jewish faith, to be a Jew. But when that rabbi said I'd have to perform a Hebrew project or Torah study to reclaim my mother's religion within me, I told Margie, "That's not for me. I prefer to stay agnostic." She accepted my decision.

After the marriage ceremony, our wedding entourage walked the few blocks to the Ritz Carlton Hotel for the evening's reception. Between supper courses, I made a personal tribute to my mother. I said how much she would have enjoyed being at our wedding and reception this day. I called her by her various surnames: born Friedmann before WWII, changed to Gurcik during the war to hide from the fascists, and then changed to Tatransky after the war.

Because my father and Elaine were present, I didn't mention the Simkovits part of her life.

I called out my mother's given names: born Hannah, known by her Hungarian friends as Nusi, known by her Canadian acquaintances as Anna— all different derivations of the name Grace. For all that my mother had gone through, she had tried to live her life that way. And she did so on many days.

I didn't divulge the pain and bitterness that oozed through her veneer when it came to my father. I did say, "I hope she is looking down upon us this happy day. She'd know we love her and wish her well."

After my tribute to Mom, I made one to my father. "Thanks, Dad, for your support during my life, especially with my new career direction. You have been there for me if and when I needed your help." I saw the proud smile on his face as he raised his glass to mine.

I then made a tribute to another person in the room who I held in high esteem. Not mentioning the person's name, I spoke about my mentor turned partner turned friend. When I said Moe by name, Margie let out a gasp and nearly dropped her wine glass.

Later, during the supper, with a tinge of angst in her voice, Margie told me that she thought I had been talking about her. I explained to her that I wanted to honour Moe because we'd be leaving Montreal within a year and moving to Massachusetts. She glared at me but said nothing more.

Later that evening, Margie got on stage with our band and sang two songs. She dedicated "Evergreen" to me and "My Yiddishe Mama" to my mother. Afterward, some of my relatives approached her, with tears in their eyes, to thank her for her renditions.

When Margie and I later retired to our wedding suite in the hotel, we broke out a bottle of Brut. Glass in hand, her eyes narrowed. She spoke dryly. "Harvy, why were you not listening to the songs I was singing on stage?" She glared at me. "You continued talking to guests and paid no attention to me."

I was taken aback for a second time this day. "Honey—you were great! I listened as much as I could, but our friends kept on coming up to me to tell me how much they enjoyed our wedding." I shrugged. "What did you want me to say to them?" I considered, but did not say that perhaps some of our guests had not been stopped in their tracks by Margie's singing.

Alarm bells went off in my head as they had gone off after my father's wedding ceremony with Elaine. Had a spouse complaining switch suddenly turned on in Margie as it had happened in my father regarding his marriage to Elaine? Or had I been a schlep in not keeping my focus solely on Margie during her singing? I couldn't tell for sure.

Innumerable wedding gifts sat in the corner of our hotel suite. I pointed in that direction. "Honey, let's open some of our presents while we drink to our future."

She grinned, and I returned her smile. For the moment, we avoided more wondering about our wedding.

Claiming exhaustion, we went to bed early that night. We cuddled in our fluffy king bed before each of us fell asleep, she well before I.

* * *

Twenty-five years after my father's marriage to Elaine, Elaine e-mailed me after she had read these chapters.

> Harvy, it was your father who wanted us to get married before your wedding. After you and Margie had announced, your father came home one night and said that you didn't want him to be sitting with his girlfriend at your wedding ceremony and reception. So he insisted we wed before your marriage.

That was news to me; I was incredulous. Had my father played it one way with me and another way with Elaine? Or was Elaine misremembering or misrepresenting the situation? Dad had made it sound as if Elaine didn't want to come as his mistress to my wedding day.

As with all things Johnny Simkovits, one never knows such things for sure.

* * * *

Part III:

Ups and Downs of Moving On

22

Next Bumbling in Business

It peeved me to think my father was right. It took two years to figure out my partnership in WISE might not work the way I had expected. Like dominos wobbling and falling in a rising wind, things slowly toppled in my arrangement with Moe, Irwin, and Jay. It was mostly about money, and it had started with Irwin.

Soon after our WISE partnership formed in the summer of '85, we decided to engage Irwin as our full-time general manager. He had stepped aside from his computer consulting clients to run our computer-assisted-training operations, sales effort, and the firm's administration.

Irwin said he needed a monthly salary that was more than three times mine. He had a wife and kids entering college; he lived in an upscale Montreal community of mini-mansions with well-kept yards and gardens.

Moe, as company President and head of our training development, put half-time into WISE because he still maintained his psychology practice. Instead of taking a salary, an amount that was half of Irwin's, Moe took an IOU from the business. The business would pay off his debt after it had earned enough profits.

Jay, too, received a hefty annual salary, more than double mine, in line with what he had received in his previous marketing and advertising position.

344

He agreed to forgo a part of his remuneration for the first year, until we established the Boston office, and it achieved profitability.

Though I didn't like to be the low man on the WISE salary totem pole, I was fresh out of grad school. I couldn't ask for more than what Moe considered my fair market value.

Irwin spent most of his time selling our management training software products and finding new clients for WISE's training centre. Moe encouraged his small company clients to sign onto WISE to develop their growing supervisory teams. Moe and I worked to establish and document our WISE training approaches so that we could install them in large corporations and duplicate them as we opened new WISE locations.

After eighteen months of effort, our Montreal office was performing at barely breaking even. Over that time, Irwin's salary was steadily draining the $50,000 investment that I had put into the firm, and our debt to Moe was building. And, during the second year of the partnership, WISE had to hold back Jay's and my salaries, amounting to $25,000 each. We agreed to do that to keep our Montreal and Boston offices afloat.

Irwin couldn't cut back on his salary, saying he needed the money. Fairly, he added, "If WISE can't afford me, then I'll go back to my computer consulting work. That would mean I could work only one day a week for WISE."

We knew that WISE's Montreal sales efforts would be at risk without Irwin. Moe still had his private psychological practice, and I wasn't about to become a salesperson for our Montreal branch. Though I was developing into a good "farmer" of our existing clients, learning how to keep them well served and to grow their involvement in WISE, I wasn't a good "hunter" for new business. I had an aversion for rejection.

At Moe's recommendation, we consented to Irwin's salary needs. As my father might say, "I wonder how that guy could live so hand to mouth."

* * *

Late into the second year of our partnership, and nearly three years from WISE's founding, Moe sensed the growing tensions among us about the firm's finances. Though Jay had effectively redrafted our WISE business plan, Moe and Irwin hadn't found any passive investors. Our cash was running low.

Moe called a special Saturday morning partnership meeting in a restaurant at our office building. Irwin was his predictably perky self, smiling and chatting as if he had few cares in the world. I could see Jay's face was a little tight; mine probably was too. I shifted back and forth in my seat as we started on breakfast.

Irwin reported on how WISE stood financially. "We had a $3500 cash loss last month across the whole firm." I noticed he avoided the word "another" before stating the loss number. He smiled. "We still have $20,000 left in our bank line and $15,000 in client receivables due." He said nothing about our partner and bank liabilities that WISE had amassed. He continued, "Our Montreal training centre is generating income, but we haven't sold any training packages or services to any big corporation."

We all knew it was Moe's clients who were keeping WISE afloat in Montreal. We were riding the edge of running out of cash. We were working hard, but the business could run out of money before the year ended.

Jay and I had mentioned to Moe our concern about WISE's "Irwin overhead." It was more than what our fledgling firm could afford. Moe knew he needed to act. Otherwise, Jay might walk from the partnership and find another position in Boston. Jay was our Boston centre, and his site was now paying for itself because it didn't have to support Irwin's salary—my cash investment had been doing that subsidizing.

Moe's face was blank and business-like as he looked at Jay and me. "To get the pressure off our short-term liabilities, what if we turn your deferred salaries into preferred shares in WISE?"

Jay, Irwin, and I glared at Moe as he continued. "And, with us reaching our second anniversary in business together, it would be fair to say that the company is worth more today—with two training centres in operation—than it was when our partnership started." His voice was even-keeled. "If all of you agree, we can revalue our shares at 50% more than the original value. That would make Jay and Harvy's preferred shares (in exchange for their deferred salary) worth that much more, and everyone's common shares would reflect the higher share value as well."

Irwin, Jay, and I glanced at each other and then back at Moe. I felt relief about reduced debt in our business. Jay and I would hold additional company shares that had long-term and growing value. Though Jay's face looked a bit more relaxed after Moe had aired his idea, Irwin sat blank-faced. I couldn't tell if he knew beforehand about Moe's shareholder hocus pocus.

We quickly accepted Moe's proposal. Jay and I would share equally in $75,000 of WISE preferred shares to pay us back for our $50,000 in deferred wages. It sounded good, but only if WISE could generate the profit to pay out those shares.

Moe came forward with another corporate trick. He turned to Irwin. "What if I relinquish the firm's debt to me for my unpaid time for these last two years? I'd be willing to do that if you, Irwin, are willing to transfer three percentage points from your WISE shares to me."

Moe raised a hand. "Three percent of our shares are now worth that same amount on paper, based on our new higher evaluation." He took a big breath and gestured towards all of us. "We can then call it even between me and WISE." He put his hand back on the table. "That adjustment would take a lot of pressure off the liability WISE owes to me."

Irwin looked at Moe. Jay and I looked at Irwin. Irwin was nodding. His eyebrows rose as if he had been surprised by Moe's proposal, but he didn't hesitate. "Okay, that works for me."

Jay and I looked at Moe, our heads now nodding too. I don't know about Jay, but I was impressed by Moe's shareholder magic and surprised by Irwin's quick acceptance.

Moe's transaction meant that Moe now had the largest voting bloc in the firm, 46% of our voting shares. Moe addressed that point. "No matter how big our percentage ownership is in the firm, I still want our major decisions to be consensual. We are working as a team of equal voices to see WISE succeed."

So why is my salary so much lower than everyone else's? But this wasn't the time or place for that conversation—or maybe I didn't have the nerve to confront my partners about it.

I focused on the good news: in the last few minutes, my $50,000 initial investment and $25,000 in deferred salary were now together worth $112,500 on paper.

Moe and Irwin's verbal commitments were enough for the edginess to dissipate from all of our voices. We unanimously voted for Moe's proposals. Moe had saved the day with his wise money manipulations that fit the moment. Our focus turned back to growing the business so that all of us could come out ahead.

* * *

Another WISE domino wobbled and tumbled in the wind.

Moe and Irwin had taken WISE's business plan and share-offering memorandum to the wealthy business people they knew, including WISE's biggest and most committed clients. Moe and Irwin hoped to raise half a million dollars to open more training centres across Canada. Even my father was sticking to his offer of throwing in fifty grand for a 2% stake if Moe and Irwin could find other investors for the additional 18% stake in WISE.

Over supper with my father sometime after our second WISE-partnership anniversary, I told him something he could have easily said to me. "Dad, it looks as if Moe and Irwin had gotten some nibbles, but no new investors are on the hook."

I didn't want to give my father a chance to say, "I told you so," so I kept on talking. "Moe and Irwin also decided to stop selling our management training software to bigger corporations with training departments. No large company has wanted to buy our software and hire us to educate their trainers." I raised a hand. "Instead, we are focusing on selling management education memberships—like a gym membership—to our Montreal and Boston centres. Managers will come to us for training rather than us becoming management training consultants."

My father looked at his drink. "Your company still doesn't have its act together and can't seem to attract money. I guess I'm not going to invest either." He put his intense blue eyes on me. "How deep are you in with them?"

I hesitated and then responded, "I'm in for my original $50,000, plus some deferred salary that the firm converted into shares at a good price." I thought my father would be proud of my having followed his earlier advice about working for free and getting company shares as remuneration.

His voice was terse. "Don't put any more money into it, son. And don't let those guys take your salary away!" Dad perhaps didn't realize his inconsistency. I nodded and said nothing.

I later surmised I was learning an old marriage adage the hard way: "Never share with a parent too much about your spousal problems." That's because, even after you and your partner work out the difficulties, you risk that your parent holds onto the negative impressions you had initially given them. I shouldn't have been talking to my father about my business partnership issues.

At our next WISE management meeting, Moe proclaimed, "It's not a problem that we have no outside investors. We'll continue to open training centres across Canada; Toronto will be our next site."

He was upbeat. "Instead of raising investment seed money, we'll sell franchises across the country to trainers and consultants who have the cash to invest." He motioned to Jay. "Look! Jay was able to get our Boston office running with only $50,000 in seed money and some months of taking no salary. He's running a decent profit there now."

Yah, he doesn't have to feed Irwin. Jay might have been thinking the same.

Moe raised his hand. "Montreal will remain our flagship site. We'll do our research and development here, and experiment with new training methods. We'll train our trainers and franchise owners here too." He pointed to Jay. "Boston will be our franchise model going forward with every city in the country."

He drew a slowly rising line in the air. "Our growth may slow, but it won't stop. Once we have new sites open, and a couple of years of positive cash flow record behind us, investors will flock to us. And our price for them to play won't be as low."

I handed it to Moe. He had crooked teeth and a balding head, yet no one could fault him for his big grin and eternal optimism.

Having over $110,000 at stake in WISE, I was staying put.

* * *

During another supper with Dad, I explained how my work was going with WISE. I was optimistic. "Moe and I are developing many tools and an inventory system for our training software and our growing array of materials. Recently, we created an assessment process to help WISE trainers develop a personalized training program for each manager we work with."

I glance at my father's face. Though he looked pensive, I continued. "When our clients can't break away from work to come to our centres, we bring a portable computer—weighing just thirty pounds—to their company office to do training sessions there." I felt proud of our efforts and technology.

I continued. "For higher-up executives, we don't even use the training software but mentor them face-to-face." Moe and I had determined that the more senior folks received more benefit from interacting with the trainer than they did from our software programs.

My voice elevated with enthusiasm, as my father's tone could be when he had a new project or deal. "We call it 'one-on-one management training.'" (This was years before the terms "management coaching" and "executive coaching" were coined in the training or consulting vernacular.)

Dad's JHS never had a human resource department, let alone performed any supervisory training. My father had been the guy to hire people straight from Quebec Manpower, set salaries (typically minimum wage to start), agree to any promotions and wage increases, and have his secretary keep employee records. When he fired people, he did it with a scream in their ear or a virtual shoeprint on their backsides as he showed them the factory door.

The only employee development at JHS was my father's "seagull approach" to performance improvement. It was his practice to swoop into the factory, flap his arms and make a lot of noise about something, anything, not going right, and then crap on a line worker or the foreman. He then swooped back into his office, leaving behind gawking faces, downed heads, and rattled nerves. He never wanted anyone to forget who the boss was.

Dad's nose stayed pointed at his meal as I continued to talk about WISE. "In addition to working with clients, I'm our head training instructor. I work with Moe to teach our software and training methodology to WISE's other trainers." My voice stayed buoyant. "Sometimes, I have a whole employee team in front of the computer, and we go through a program together. Their supervisor or I lead a discussion on what they are learning on the screen."

My father lifted his head. "I always thought you'd be a good teacher, son."

I appreciated his remark. It was rare for my father to say anything nice about my capabilities. But he asked no questions and soon changed the subject.

I didn't know if my father couldn't or didn't want to understand my efforts to make company managers more effective. Perhaps he didn't believe in that kind of profession, or he still had a hard time with Moe replacing him as my boss, mentor, and now business partner.

As the months elongated into years, I spoke less and less to my father about my work at WISE.

* * *

More time passed, but my "wobbling domino" worries about WISE didn't. I felt I could no longer confide in my father about my partnership misgivings. I thus shared more with Margie about my growing frustrations.

Over one supper at our apartment, after downing a second glass of wine, my concerns came pouring out of me. "Irwin's monthly salary nut is still hard to crack. Our Montreal centre is losing money in most months so that we can meet his money needs."

Margie looked at me as she sipped her Chardonnay. Her long black hair flowed halfway down her back, making her look youthful and non-threatening. "That's crazy, Harvy. Have you talked to Moe about it?"

I took a long breath. "Moe is working to find ways for Irwin to pay for himself. As you know, years ago, Irwin's family was a client of Moe's. Out of that, he and Irwin became friends." Frustration grew in my voice. "I don't think Moe would ask Irwin to leave WISE and go back to his former computer consulting career."

An unexpected edge entered my wife's voice. "It seems very incestuous, Harvy." She pointed my way. "In one way or another, Irwin, Jay, and you were connected to Moe as therapy clients before he formed WISE. Doesn't that sound unhealthy to you?"

My psychoanalytic wife knew how to stick a supper fork into my side. "I know! I know!" I said. It wasn't the first time she had such things, but her voice was a little more piquant this time.

I opened my arms and hands. "Moe has been good to me. He's a brilliant man, and a good mentor and consultant. I'm learning a lot from him. I trust him more than my father, and he's never steered me wrong." I responded as if she had asked me to cut off my right arm.

"Sounds like the man's perfect," she said with sarcasm. "Is that what you're saying?"

I was irritated. "No, of course not!" I felt I had to defend my relationship with Moe not only to my father but also to Margie. "Moe has his shortcomings," I offered. "He doesn't win over every client or every prospective trainer we try to bring into the firm, but he does get their attention and make them think about things."

I looked down at the table. "If I fault Moe for anything, he sometimes tries to make too big of a splash."

"What do you mean?" Her face looked puzzled.

I laid down my fork and looked at her. "Not long ago, we saw one of our long-standing retail clients that we hadn't worked with for months. Moe and I met with the president and his top manager to review our past projects and to determine what else WISE could do for them."

I raised a hand. "During the meeting, Moe suggested many endeavours we could initiate in their business. One was starting regular top-team conferences. Another was developing in-store sales training modules on top of our one-on-one manager training." Margie's eyes were on me. "In front of his key manager, the president agreed. He even said, 'By George, Moe, you've done it again!' It looked as if our client had come back on board with us."

My eyes turned down. "Though I supported Moe in front of that President, I privately thought that he was going a little overboard with his plans." I pointed to myself. "I like to walk my clients more gradually into deeper water, adding projects one at a time, building on previous efforts and successes, etc., etc." I looked again at her. "Moe likes going after all the fish in the barrel that he can see and catch at once."

Margie leaned forward in her chair. "So what happened, Harvy?"

"Everything seems great after we all met. But a few days later, the company president had buyer's remorse and decided not to move forward with any new efforts." I picked up my fork again. "I even tried to reach out to the manager who had been at the meeting. I knew the fellow from having mentored him previously." I sighed. "But he just put me off. I guess that the president didn't want to have Moe and WISE too deeply entrenched in his business."

Margie stared at me as if flashing lights were going off in her head. She poked the table with her index finger. "That's my point, Harvy! Moe tries to get himself entwined too deeply with his clients as he has done with his business partners. Whether that president realizes it or not, he was fighting his feelings of dependency on Moe."

I couldn't look at Margie but glared at my supper. A part of me knew that what she had said made sense.

It was dawning on me that I had effectively replaced my father with Moe. From the moment I had joined WISE, I worked to impress my mentor with my smarts and capability, as I had tried to do with my father at JHS. I wondered if I was becoming as dependent on Moe professionally as I was reliant on my father for his promised legacy.

Had Margie told Moe what she had just said to me, my professional mentor and business partner might have retorted, "Harvy and I have a healthy 'interdependency,' one to learn from and build on. Harvy is important to WISE, and he's growing professionally from being here with our team and me." Margie never fully understood that perspective. Or if she did, she never acknowledged it.

I looked sternly at my wife. "Please stop making Moe the bad guy!" Margie had a knack for focusing on the deficiencies in men, including me. The only man in her life who could do no wrong was her tall, handsome, smart, MIT Ph.D. brother. He seemed akin to the Mickey Mouse Club theme-song that some MIT students mockingly sang. The lyrics went:

"M-I-T…..P-h-D….. M-O-N-E-Y."

My voice elevated. "So what if Moe's not perfect! We've done great work for many companies. Moe and I have effectively served many executives and managers for years, and they've gotten a lot from us." I took a breath and tried to calm myself. "For me, the more serious problem is Irwin, not Moe."

I changed the subject and focused on my supper. Margie, too, went back to her meal and, for the moment, added nothing more about Moe.

A few days later, over another supper, Margie soothed her tone and changed her approach. There was a curiosity in her voice. "Okay, Harvy, what's Moe doing to get Irwin to better pay for himself?"

I placed a piece of bread roll into my mouth to gnaw on my rising angst. I huffed. "A lot of stupid stuff has gone on." I looked away and then back at her. "After Moe and Irwin realized that our software sales would never take off, Irwin focused his efforts on selling WISE's training services."

I raised my hand. "Yet the guy has no knack for selling such services. When he worked to get WISE in the door with some companies, he told their president, 'Give us your most problematic managers. We'll fix them for you.'"

My voice rose to join my hand. "We then wasted months trying to fix the unrepairable. In one case, we tried to train a mid-level sales manager who was angry at his boss and not very committed to the company." I squeezed my knife and fork harder. "One can't expect unmotivated people to develop."

I sighed. "It affects WISE's credibility and track record to work with managers who can't or don't want to improve." I pointed to myself. "And I'm the schmuck that has to come in behind Irwin and perform the miracles he promises our new clients. I then look bad when a manager doesn't improve."

"That's ridiculous, Harvy. Is Irwin still doing that?" I was relieved that Margie was now seeing things my way.

I huffed, "Fortunately, he's now more aware of what he's doing." My voice calmed. "Once Moe and the rest of us figured out what Irwin was promising, we changed his approach. He's now working to sell WISE's assessment package to the whole management team of every prospective company he meets. He's not just targeting one or two problematic individuals, causing us not to know what we're up against."

I loosened my hard grip on my fork and knife. "Our assessments will then tell us which managers are best to develop." I took a deep breath. "Irwin says he's now setting better expectations, but who knows. I'm not at his client sales meetings."

Margie threw the bottom line at my feet. "It sounds like Irwin might be a liability. Do you think he's learning?"

I answered sheepishly. "I'm not sure. Moe has been trying to morph Irwin into a management consultant to help the guy earn his keep. Though Irwin seems to be an expert computer consultant, he doesn't provide the best solutions to management problems."

I took another long breath. "One time, Irwin told a company president, one we had been working with for years, 'All your managers seem to be bored with their jobs.' He was serious when he added, 'Let's get them to switch positions to rejuvenate their careers at your company.'"

"Wow! That seems radical. Did Moe know?"

"I think Moe knew in general but not the specifics. He trusts Irwin, like he trusts the rest of us, to do the right thing, but Irwin certainly needs supervision. Moving people around in a company isn't like installing new computer workstations."

I looked at Margie. "I didn't quite feel right about Irwin's idea, but I thought he had a transition plan in mind." I moaned. "But, like switching on a computer, the guy expected that people would start doing each other's jobs starting on a particular day—like the inside sales manager switching places with the marketing manager, and vice versa."

I raised a hand. "Most of these company managers had worked with each other for years. So perhaps Irwin thought it would be simple for them to move into each other's positions and take on each other's array of inside and outside relationships." I looked away. "Half a dozen managers were affected by those moves."

Margie's eyes stayed on me. "So, what happened, Harvy?"

"The worst!" I bellowed. "The company president went along with Irwin's idea!"

I worked to keep my speech steady. "The president and Irwin set a date to make the changes. Every manager came to work on that Monday morning and moved into their peer's office."

I shook my head. "Not having had time for people to learn each other's jobs, the place became chaotic." I raised my hands again. "Everyone was so focused on his or her new position that no one helped their counterpart get grounded in his or her old job. They all ran to the president for guidance."

Her voice rose again. "Oh, no! What happened then?" The drama drew Margie as if she were an exuberant child jumping into a swimming hole in the summertime. She liked to feel the murky bottom.

My voice rose again. "Within two weeks of the changes, the President called an emergency meeting with Irwin and me." I pointed to myself. "I was there because I had been working with the company's operations manager and a couple of the other managers."

I looked again at Margie. "The President was perplexed. He told us, 'Every person who reports to me is now paralyzed and doesn't know what to do in their new jobs. I have to spoon-feed each of them.' He looked at Irwin, raised his voice, and half-seriously said, 'When can I switch my job like everybody else?'"

"Wow!" Margie's proclaimed. Her childlike eyes were wide open. "So, what did you and he do?"

"Except for one important job move the company sorely needed, Irwin and the President agreed that every other manager should go back to his or her original position." I shook my head again. "Irwin came out smiling from that conversation as if he had done something terrific for that president and his company. But I knew we were now nothing but toast there—Irwin couldn't see the scrambled eggs on our faces."

I wanted sympathy from Margie for what I had to deal with regarding Irwin. Instead, she asked a poignant question. "How did you let that situation happen, Harvy?"

In her social services job, Margie dealt with complex, even crazy foster-family situations that involved lawyers, psychiatrists, problematic birth parents, and troubled children. She was talented at diving into the deepest, darkest family waters and swimming through them to save a child's future. My wife could be very sharp, in both the best and worst sense of that word. "Didn't you realize that Irwin's plan wouldn't work?" she asked.

It irritated me how Margie was spot-on. From the time we got serious as a couple, she was good at pointing out my shortcomings. Perhaps my sweetheart wanted me to be a better man, someone admirable, like her big brother. It sometimes felt as if she were sticking barbs onto my behind. Though I felt the pricks, I let them stay right where she put them.

I looked down at our supper table and responded. "I wish I would have said something sooner to Irwin, but I figured he knew what he was doing."

My voice shook as I avoided her eyes. "Irwin's a senior partner in our firm! At the time, I thought he'd know how to work with the company's president to manage employee moves, or that he had consulted with Moe." I raised my eyes. "I was working with only a couple of the managers, and I've never been involved in such comprehensive management moves."

I took another long breath. "After we met with that president, I told Irwin that he could have arranged the changes one or two people at a time, over several months, giving the managers a chance to get stable in their new positions before making more moves."

Margie nodded. "That makes more sense. What did Irwin say to that?"

I shrugged. "Not much. It was as if Irwin couldn't admit he'd done anything ineffective or out of the ordinary. Anyway, it was way too late for my Monday morning quarterbacking."

I shook my head. "Other than the operations manager who I still work with, and who wasn't affected by the crazy job moves, the other managers no longer want to sit down with Irwin or me." I sighed. "My operations guy tells me that everybody had been looking forward to their new positions. They were very disappointed about our failure to make those job moves stick."

Margie's voice calmed but remained concerned. "Harvy, maybe you should talk to Jay about this. Could the two of you speak to Moe, to get him to do something about Irwin?"

Margie did have good ideas. What she offered was what I might have suggested to a client who was having issues with a partner. The adage was right: *If trees surround you, then it's hard to see the whole forest.* I couldn't find my way out of our Irwin dilemma.

She fired off more questions. "Can you trust Jay to hear you out? Will he keep your concerns in confidence? Will he go with you to talk to Moe?"

Though Margie's queries seemed fitting, her rapid-fire approach gnawed at me. It felt as if she were like my mother, who interrogated me incessantly about my father and wanted me to betray his trust. It now felt as if Margie were pushing me to do the same regarding Moe, by my aligning with Jay. My armpits started to sweat.

I looked at Margie and kept my voice steady. "I'm not sure, honey. Outside of our monthly partner group meetings, I don't work much with Jay. I don't know how he truly feels about Irwin." My gut tightened. "Jay does know that Irwin's salary is a big drag on the firm. But, like me, Jay may not want to confront Moe on this issue."

Margie was adamant. "Listen, Harvy! You should talk to Jay. Maybe he feels the same way as you do."

Finally, there were no more questions from Margie, just a "listen" and "should," as my father might say. I nodded, yet my gut stayed tense. "Okay, I'll see. I'll keep my eyes and ears open for a good time to talk to him."

I said nothing to Margie about my irritation with her. I hid my angst the best I could.

* * *

It turned out that Jay came to me first, some months after Moe's successful sleight-of-hand with our WISE shareholdings, and some days or weeks after my talk with Margie. On the Friday before one of our monthly Saturday morning partner meetings, Jay walked into my office and closed the door behind him. "Harvy, can I get your thoughts on something?"

"Okay, Jay," I said hesitantly.

His penetrating blue eyes were on me for a moment. Perhaps seeing my discomfort, he changed his gaze to the shelves of professional books behind me. He raised a hand. "What's your assessment of Irwin and his efforts at WISE?"

I noticed that Jay was asking for an opinion before he stated his reason for the question. I responded cautiously. "Irwin's heart seems to be in the right place. I think we know that he has his challenges in setting the right expectations and making the right things happen with clients."

Jay stayed quiet as I searched for words. "Irwin may be a good 'expert consultant,' as he was in his computer consulting practice, but he's not versed in being a 'collaborative consultant' who can do our kind of management development work."

Jay jumped in and was direct. "Don't you think that Irwin's both a financial drain and client liability to our firm?"

I responded slowly. "That could be true, but..."

I wanted to be as compassionate as I could be in my comments about Irwin. But Jay pointed a finger in my direction and didn't let me finish. "If you agree, Harvy, would you be willing to meet privately with Moe and me this Sunday for breakfast?" His voice didn't waver. "It may be best for WISE if Moe encourages Irwin to go back to his other consulting career."

My cohort drew a long breath. "Irwin can certainly remain a passive partner in our firm, but the guy's not adding enough value to the partnership to justify his salary. We need the right guy to sell our WISE training services, and Irwin isn't the right guy."

Though I worried that Moe might see Jay and me circling our wagons against Irwin, part of me was relieved that Jay, too, had his concerns about Irwin. I nodded my accord and added nothing more for now. We needed a solution to our Irwin situation; otherwise, WISE would run out of cash, and our firm's future and all our investment money would disappear.

Jay arranged the meeting with Moe. I just had to be there and let Jay do most of the talking. Privately, I supported my junior partner. He had more courage than I did to come up against Moe, but I hoped he wouldn't be too harsh with our WISE leader and my mentor.

The three of us met over breakfast. Jay repeated his views as I looked on. I felt uncomfortable being in this anti-Irwin offensive. I nodded at Jay's words and added, "I agree that we need to do something." I took a breath. "Moe, it's no different than with our clients that are family businesses or peer partnerships. Things have to change when owners or partners aren't contributing effectively in their roles."

Moe raised his open palm. He spoke calmly but firmly. "We always try to work with and improve the weaker partners."

He glanced at me as he took a breath. "Irwin relinquished his career in computers to join this venture. He was also the guy that originated our computer-assisted management training idea. He has sacrificed too much; I can't ask him to step back or away."

Moe's voice didn't falter. "Irwin's computer consulting skills have gotten stale because of the over two-and-a-half years he has spent with WISE." He pointed our way. "And he believes in what we are doing." Moe eyed both Jay and me as he put his open hands firmly on the table. "I do agree that we need to find better ways to get him to pay for himself."

Though I didn't say it, I admired Moe for his unwavering loyalty to his founding partner. The three of us agreed to see what Irwin could do in the next few months with more help from the rest of us. Jay said, "I reserve the right to surface this topic again if Irwin's not cutting it."

Moe looked at him. "If deep down, you want Irwin to fail, then he will fail. If you focus on him succeeding, as I am working to do, then he will succeed."

I hoped Moe would be right, but I also wondered how we would measure Irwin's success or failure.

That evening, I told Margie what happened. "Jay and I got the Irwin issue aired with Moe, but not much will change for now. Moe wants to work to increase Irwin's value to the firm." I let out a breath. "We'll see what happens."

Margie responded, "I don't know, Harvy. WISE seems to be perpetuating an intolerable situation." She put her hand on mine. "You should seriously think about what you want to do." She repeated, "Don't you think it's unhealthy for you to work as business partners with your ex-therapist and other former clients of his?"

Though Margie may have been right, I felt as if she were placing another barb on my backside.

* * * *

Next Phase in Partnership

I considered what my father might do if he were in my shoes at WISE. For sure, he would have never gotten himself into a minority position in a company unless he needed an investor's money. During his early years in manufacturing (before he raised enough cash to start a company on his own), a former boss had chiseled him out of bonus money. In a subsequent business partnership, he caught the major shareholder trying to start a factory fire for the insurance proceeds.

Dad, too, had done his share of partner chiseling. In the year I was born, Dad had partnered with his friend Ned Meyer to birth Montreal Phono's cabinet making business. Ned and Dad became 50/50 partners in a company they called Dor-Steve, named after both of their first sons, Doran and Steve. Both Dad and Ned invested equally in the new company. It was incorporated separately to Montreal Phono, to take advantage of small business tax incentives.

Ned's wife, Mimi, related the story when I visited her in Toronto. "My Ned invested $5000 in Dor-Steve to help get it started." Her voice rose. "With $5000, you could buy a house in the suburbs back then!"

Her face looked tense, but she spoke matter-of-factly. "Your father controlled the pricing of Dor-Steve's completed record-player cabinets built for Montreal Phono." Her tone heightened. "The way Johnny set those prices, Montreal Phono made money, but Dor-Steve didn't."

Her face tightened. "My poor Ned got frustrated. After a year or two, he went to Johnny and said he wanted to get out of the partnership. Johnny accepted, but he also said he couldn't give Ned back his investment money."

She looked away and then back at me, her voice raised once more. "I had to go myself to plead with Johnny about giving Ned back his money." She calmed down. "Johnny eventually agreed to give us $500 a year." She shook her head. "At some point, he stopped paying, and I don't remember if we ever got all our money back—it was so long ago."

Her face relaxed. "That Johnny could be one tough son-of-a-gun, but Ned and I still loved and admired him. We stayed friends and did things together until your father left your mother twenty years later." She sighed. "After that, we drifted apart." There seemed to be a frown on her face for a past that was now long gone.

Mimi then waved a finger and repeated something my mother had once said about my father. "Ned and I learned the hard way that if you have Johnny Simkovits as a friend, then you don't need an enemy."

* * *

I shunned my asking Dad for his advice. I didn't want to operate his way, applying threats or coarse language in dealing with partners. I didn't turn to Margie because I knew her broken record mantra: "It's not healthy to be partners with your ex-therapist and his former clients."

I certainly didn't want to see my WISE investment completely consumed to support Irwin's needs. As Ned Meyer had done with my father, could I ask Moe to let me out of our WISE partnership? Moe wouldn't maneuver me out of my investment the way my father did Ned, or might he?

I kept my WISE thoughts and feelings to myself. I tossed and turned in bed for days and weeks of sleepless nights.

After three years of worrying about WISE's ability to stay afloat, and seeing little prospects for profit, I called Moe for a private conversation.

Though I was developing into a capable management coach, I was perhaps too cautious (not aggressive enough) as a businessman. Most of my work and business experience had been in the area of internal operations at both P&G and my father's company. I had grown up as a saver of resources, emulating that aspect of my father's MO.

In contrast, Jay and Irwin were marketing and sales guys who were more concerned with how much money we had available to spend. It bothered me that our firm had a mounting line of bank credit and significant debts to both Jay and me. Perhaps I wasn't as entrepreneurial as they were; they seemed able to live on the edge of running out of cash.

From the way Jay looked at me out of the corner of his eye during our partner meetings, I felt he might put me into the same "not adding enough value" box as he had put Irwin. Perhaps Jay wanted to be the one-and-only heir to Moe and WISE. Maybe he wished to usher me from the partnership with a smile and "Thanks so much for your service." Had Irwin given up his General Manager position at WISE, and gone back to computer consulting, I might have become Jay's next target. Or was it I who had a hard time dealing with another junior partner, as I had had when working with my brother at JHS?

I believe Moe had recognized our firm's cash flow challenges and Jay and Irwin's looser spending. Perhaps he thought I would feel more secure, and the firm's finances better managed, if WISE gave me some say over the firm's accounting. At one of our monthly Saturday partner meetings, he raised the topic of my becoming WISE's Comptroller, taking WISE's money administration job away from Irwin.

After a few seconds of dead silence, Jay said, "That's not necessary, Moe." Irwin added, "Between Jay and me, we've got the money issues covered." They didn't even look my way.

There go those sales and marketing guys! Those two don't want anybody watching over their shoulder while they spend what little war chest we have.

Being a pleaser type, I hadn't found my confident voice in our partnership. Maybe I should have called for a shareholder vote then and there, which Moe and I could have won. Then again, Moe always sought consensus, so such a move may have yielded little change. I offered no thoughts as Moe acquiesced to Irwin and Jay's assertions.

I was limited by having worked only *in* a business and never *on* one. What I knew for sure was that our Montreal center was hardly breaking even, and WISE's accumulating debt to Moe was continuing to mount. I couldn't fathom working hard to support Moe and Irwin. I felt as if I were at the bottom of this partnership totem pole, though maybe that thinking was only in my mind.

Moe and I met for breakfast in the café near our WISE offices. After ordering, I told him, "I'm sorry, Moe, but I'm worrying too much about WISE's money situation. It's affecting me."

"What are you saying, Harvy?" He spoke with sincere curiosity.

"Our partnership is not working for me. I'm feeling on edge about our firm's finances." I stammered my words. "WISE always seems to be on the verge of running out of money. I can't sleep well at night because of it."

He eyed me carefully. "Does this mean you want out of our partnership?"

I nodded shyly, hoping not to disappoint my long-time mentor. "I'd like to get out if I can."

Moe paused for a moment; his eyes moved back and forth. He focused on me again. "Okay, Harvy, I understand."

His eyes softened as he put his hands flat on the table. Perhaps he had figured this day was coming. His voice was adamant. "Harvy, I commit that you'll get your money out of WISE, the full amount we owe you."

He paused to think for a second, and then continued. "It may take a year or two to give you what WISE owes you, including the increased value of your shares, but I promise you every dollar."

I was stunned by Moe's unfailing fairness. He was a stand-up guy—one reason why I would honour the man at my wedding reception. Moe had stood up for Irwin against Jay and me. Now was standing up for my wanting to get out of our partnership.

Moe and I worked out that I would remain on contract as a WISE trainer. I'd obtain a fair 45% of my client revenues as remuneration. I had grown a steady stream of repeat training and mentoring business with companies that Moe and Irwin had brought to the firm. I'd be able to make good money as long as I maintained those relationships and my client billings.

The other 55% of my billings would work to repurchase my WISE shares over the next couple of years. In effect, I'd be working for myself under the auspices of WISE. There would be no more stressful Saturday morning partner meetings for me.

I appreciated Moe for looking for a win-win solution.

I figured my father would be pleased to see me get out of WISE. When I broke the news to him, he said, "It's one thing to have a promise. It's another thing to see the money in your pocket."

I responded, "Dad, I trust Moe. If WISE doesn't pay me, then I can withhold my client billings. WISE will then show less income to its bank, and the bank then would reduce the firm's credit line. Moe and Irwin wouldn't jeopardize WISE's bank line."

My father looked at me with skeptical eyes. "I hope you're right, son. In my experience, anything can happen in business."

* * *

A few days after Jay had heard from Moe and Irwin about my departure from our partnership, the Montreal Gazette published a feature business article entitled *The Three WISE Men in Management Training*. It included a photo of Moe, Irwin, and Jay on the front page of the paper's business section.

Jay had planned that article—and title—for months. He had been waiting for a shoe to drop with either Irwin or me. *What a guy!* He and I had joined forces for a bit, as my brother and I had done at JHS. But it now became clear as to who Jay had been working for.

As Moe had promised, I did get my money out of WISE over the next two years. Though there were delays because WISE needed my monthly billings to stay afloat, I did get my every penny due. Whether WISE had to cut back on its partner salaries to pay me out, or to dig deeper into its bank line, I didn't know, and I now had little reason to care.

Because of a quirk in the Quebec tax law that gave tax breaks to investors in startup companies, I hardly paid any taxes on my WISE investment gains. Though my take wasn't big bucks, the mostly tax-free benefit was more than a year's salary, and it represented a lot to me.

I felt good to come out of my first business venture with a significant profit. My father told me, "Son, I'm glad you are out of that WISE mishigas."

Years later, Jay and I met for lunch in Boston. By then, he too was no longer associated with Moe and Irwin. He confided in me. "Harvy, you were the only original investor who made any money on your WISE investment and shares. We had a couple of other partners and franchise owners come and go, but they never walked away with anything to speak of."

He took a swig of his drink and looked at me with his intense eyes. "I had my own falling out with Moe and Irwin a couple of years after you left the firm." He didn't elaborate on the details. He did add, "I got angry at those two for spending money without telling me."

He took in a long breath. "We separated our branches of the business. What I got for my original investment was spinning off the Boston office that I had built with my own time and money, and I was able to take ownership of the WISE name here in the U.S."

I hated to admit it, but my father had been right about those WISE guys. Though Dad was pleased about my departure from that partnership, he was kind enough not to say, "I told you so." During a subsequent restaurant supper, he moved his index finger in a circle on the table and said, "Son, I'm glad you got off that horse that was running around in circles, and you didn't lose your shirt along the way."

I hoped I was learning about making it in business, by surviving and leaving an unhealthy partnership, and in executing that move a little better than my father might have done it.

* * * *

24

Next Chapter in Career

There's an expression in my organization development field: "Protégés eventually expel their mentors."

Margie continued to urge me to distance myself from the man who had saved my life from my family and helped me find a worthwhile career. On a trip to the west coast to visit Margie's brother and sister-in-law, her big brother confronted me about my relationship with Moe.

Two minutes after he and his wife picked us up at the airport, he started to pepper me with questions. It became quickly evident who he was speaking for, and who had been filling him in on her doubts and concerns about my relationship with Moe.

Margie stayed silent next to me as her brother fired query after query. He was so bothersome that his wife got peeved at him, telling him to stop pestering me. When he persisted, I told him—without looking at Margie— "You're beginning to sound like your sister."

He got the message and stopped his grilling.

Eventually, I acquiesced to the static I was getting about Moe from Margie and my father, for there was some truth to their concerns.

Looking back at my evolving relationship with my mentor, I knew the man had boundary issues. Before Margie and I became a couple, Moe twice suggested that I ask one of my female clients out on a date. I felt awkward about doing it and didn't act on his suggestion, though I had considered it with one woman manager with whom I felt some chemistry.

Whether I was fully aware of my reluctance or not, I sensed that once one crosses a professional boundary, it changes everything. Perhaps guys like Moe and my father were good at handling ambiguous relationships, but I preferred my connections clean and single-purposed.

It concerned me that I had gotten too entrenched with Moe. My irritation grew regarding his having chosen business partners, including me, who had been therapy clients of his. Also, none of us were on par with his professional credentials and capability. Was he somehow unaware of the problematic dependencies he had been breeding? I guess he saw it as a healthy interdependency, and so had I, but my view was evolving.

At one client review meeting with him and Irwin, my irritation oozed out. "Moe, my client wants practical solutions that they can apply today. If I present your complicated analytic model to them, they'll kick me out of their company." Moe stopped talking and soon stepped out of the meeting; I continued the conversation only with Irwin.

Moe now joined Irwin as an impetus for me to leave WISE Montreal and head to the U.S. with Margie. My father had won the father-figure competition between himself and Moe. But Dad didn't realize that he too would lose me to Boston, the city where I had spent most of my college years.

* * *

When Margie and I became serious about leaving Montreal, I figured I had good reason to repatriate the cash I had invested with a money broker in The Bahamas. I needed it to support my new life with Margie. I also found it interesting how much a spouse could change a frugal person's spending habits, but I viewed it as a part of my desire to be with her.

Concerning that money invested offshore, I worried about not disclosing the income to the IRS when I'd have my feet on U.S. soil. I had heard from JHS's accountants that the IRS was more stringent with tax evaders than Revenue Canada was. I didn't want to be shackled by U.S. authorities, accused of tax evasion, and then sent back to Canada on a freezing winter day on top of a frigging dog sled.

As the three-year term of my offshore loan was ending, I asked my father if he could repatriate my cash from Freeport. By now, he knew I was moving to the USA with Margie. I added, "I could use my money from over there to help fund our move to the States."

Over the subsequent months, Dad returned from each of his Freeport vacations with small packets of new U.S. hundred-dollar bills. He said, "I'm giving you your money piecemeal so that I don't have to carry so much cash at one time." He then had me count the bills in front of him.

After he returned all my cash, I wiped the hot-money sweat off my forehead for being out of my father's tax-free interest game. Maybe he was cut out for these black-money pastimes, but I was finding out that such pursuits were not to my money-making liking.

* * *

The time had come.

In August of '89, ten months after our wedding, Margie and I said goodbye to Montreal. We tucked our new U.S. immigration cards into our wallets and struck out for Boston. I liked Boston because it was as walkable as Montreal, and it was more manageable in the winter than the city of my birth. (In Boston, daytime temperatures rarely got below 20⁰F, while temps below 0⁰F were typical in a Montreal winter.)

I may have felt a tad like my father did in 1949 when my parents immigrated to Canada from Czechoslovakia. Different from him, I never had to go through the oppressive regime changes that he had survived—unless one calls Quebec's separatist movement a brewing regime change. Perhaps like my father, I left Canada with the anticipation of abundant work and a vibrant Boston lifestyle for Margie and me.

Boston was more professionally active than Montreal in my training and consulting field, with a plethora of business associations and networking groups. I wouldn't have to communicate in French, a language I didn't practise enough to be able to work as a bilingual professional in my home province. When I tried to consult or train in French in Montreal, my clients politely said, "Harvy, it's okay if you speak English. We'll translate among ourselves." I had had a hard time with languages in school, even in English, and it showed in my adulthood.

Boston was a hotbed for high tech. My clients there would be more sophisticated than those I had had in Montreal.

As an example of the difference, one of my Montreal garment industry clients had formed an executive team on Moe's and my advice. The President then decided to conduct his weekly top-team meetings in the backroom of a tavern situated on the ground floor of the building in which he was a tenant.

That location was okay, except for the continuous hardcore pornography that was showing on a TV placed high up one wall. I had been at one or two of those meetings, and it was hard to keep my eyes from glancing at the monitor.

Months later, I convinced the President to add the first female employee to his management team. I also told him, "With your leadership team getting larger, maybe it would be better to have your weekly meetings in your company's conference room." I hoped he'd get my indirect notion of finding a more suitable venue for his top team gatherings.

A few weeks later, I asked the woman how being a part of the company's management team was going for her. Pointing upward, she said, "It's good except that we have our meetings at that place—you know the tavern downstairs with the TV on the wall."

I asked her how she managed that. She responded, "I'm the first one there, and I sit with my back to the video." I gritted my teeth and gave her a painful grin. Being still young in my field, I hadn't the gumption to ask that passionate President directly to change his manager meeting location.

I knew my work would be more challenging in Boston. Montreal had become consulting heaven for me. I had had enough steady clients doing ongoing work that I didn't have to prospect for new customers. If I needed work, I employed a clever technique that Moe had taught me.

On a slow day, I dropped in on a number of my clients without forewarning. I said to their receptionist or secretary, "I was in the area seeing other people." I wasn't lying. "I figured I'd stop by and say hi."

About half the time, my client came out to greet me. We'd then have a conversation, which often led to another project in their company. Other times, my unplanned visit led to a follow-up appointment. For every three doors I knocked on, I landed a new project. Sometimes, I even got a free lunch, though the client did receive a taste of my expertise over those meals.

My impromptu practice had worked well with the people in Montreal who knew my work. I'd be starting from scratch in Boston. Because the Massachusetts economy was growing gangbusters in '87 and '88, I said to myself, "How hard could it be?"

In 1949, my parents had courageously dodged Communist authorities and walked cross-country under the moonlight to escape Soviet-occupied lands. They then crossed an ocean by steamship to reach Canada.

In sharp contrast, Margie and I casually drove over the U.S. border to our new city, with our van of apartment furniture arriving a day behind us. On our U.S. immigration day, I was 34 years old, five years older than my parents had been when they immigrated to Canada. I wanted to prove to my father that I could do what he had done. And I was glad to be further away from his shadow and reach.

Though Margie had initially wanted us to go to the west coast where her brother lived, I pushed us toward Boston to stay closer to my father. I said to Margie, "We are two bright, well-educated people. We ought to do well in Boston, and you won't be too far away from your mother." I touched her hand. "We can visit Montreal often to visit our families."

She acknowledged my reasoning, as long as we would keep our longer-term sites on a city like San Francisco. I accepted her wish, but I wasn't sure if I wanted to be that far away from my father.

* * *

In the spring before Margie and I packed our bags, I had asked my father, "Want to go see a Montreal Canadiens playoff hockey game?" He and I hadn't gone to a professional sporting event since I was in my twenties. I felt it would be nice if he and I did a couple of father-son things before I left the country.

Dad didn't hesitate. On the evening of the event, we drove to the Montreal Forum and bought scalped tickets for $100 a pair. Montreal was playing the Calgary Flames in the Stanley Cup final series.

Inside the Forum, we cheered from the high rafters. We devoured mustard-laced hot dogs and cold beer. I don't remember which team won; I do remember that Dad and I jumped up and screamed, "Hurrah!" every time *les Canadiens* scored. We slapped each other on the back, and our seat-neighbours' backs too, no matter if they were English, French, or any other ethnicity.

Before Margie and I departed Canada, we went one Sunday to visit Dad and Elaine at their Peru home. Elaine whipped up a delicious brunch of multiple quiches with a side of tossed salad. Of course, Margie didn't touch the quiche's crust, and she picked out the croutons from among the lettuce.

We talked about the new apartment that Margie and I had rented in Boston's stylish Back Bay. I offered, "Our new place looks out at the Sheraton Hotel and Prudential Center." I spoke with excitement. "Dad, do you remember we once stayed at that Sheraton when I went to MIT? You and Elaine can come and visit us anytime."

Dad wiped a stray tear from his eye and turned to us. "I'm going to miss both of you. I hope you will come to stay with us here in Peru or back in Montreal."

"Yes, of course," Margie and I emphatically echoed.

In contrast, there had been little emotion when I had said goodbye to my brother at my father's office. As we shook hands, Steve said, "So long, brother. Enjoy the more tropical weather down there in Boston." He smiled. "And I hope you don't root for those pesky Bruins."

I returned a small grin. "I'll keep my faith with *les Canadiens*."

Steve and I never got into mushy stuff. I wasn't going to miss him, and I doubt he was going to miss me.

During our Sunday brunch, I turned to my father. "Dad, I'll be back every two or three weeks to see my Montreal clients." Though I was leaving Montreal, a couple of my WISE clients still wanted to work with me rather than a different WISE trainer. Having those clients would give me some steady work until I could establish myself in Boston.

I looked with caring at my father. "I'll come and see you every time I'm in town. It'll be as if I had never left." I hoped the greater physical distance would make us closer in some ways.

"I know, son, but you'll be a *Baauustoner* now." He offered a small smile.

Elaine jumped in. "Will the two of you two become American citizens?"

I looked at her. "No plans for now. I feel too connected to Canada to want to change my citizenship."

Margie nodded but said nothing. I wasn't sure if she wanted to stay Canadian or become a U.S. citizen like her brother. Whichever she wanted, I'd support her choice.

Canada was the country of my birth and the adopted land of my parents. As a Canadian, I appreciated the warm smiles and friendly greetings I received from people I met in Europe and other parts of the world where I had travelled.

We Canadians are a friendly lot. We have a much less violent history (perhaps more boring too) than our southern neighbour, and less contentious politics. I didn't want to let go of my more congenial Canadian heritage.

My mind was settled. I'd remain a Canadian, *eh*.

* * *

In 1987, when Margie and I first considered moving to the U.S., the Massachusetts high-tech economy was roaring past the rest of the country's economy. Massachusetts Governor Michael Dukakis was running for President based on his "Massachusetts Miracle" record.

I hadn't wanted to work for Jay at WISE. After Jay had shown his partnership colours, I sought other organization development and management training jobs in Boston. In '88, one well-known Boston HRD placement agency with whom I interviewed, told me, "Call me a couple of months before you get down here. I'll arrange interviews for you. Jobs in your field are everywhere."

By mid-'89, the Massachusetts Miracle no longer looked miraculous. The state and the whole country were heading for a recession. That same recruiter told me, "HRD professionals like you are being laid off all over the Northeast." He then asked, "How about a job in the Midwest? I can find you openings there."

I declined. I didn't think that Margie, a stylish woman who went for croissants and *café au lait* in outdoor cafés, would care to go to Kansas or Missouri.

I continued to report to Moe and Irwin regarding my Montreal clients. My ex-partners were pretty much hands-off with me, as long as I kept them abreast of my projects, and I billed for my work every month. With my WISE's share repayment now complete, my only tie to them was my Montreal client work. I liked it that way.

Soon after Margie's and my move to Boston, with no other job prospects in view for the moment, I found myself reluctantly walking through the doors of WISE Boston to work for Jay.

Jay was more hands-on with me. Irrespective of our previous partnership, he spoke as if he were my big brother who knew better. "The first client I'm giving you, Harvy, will be a $5000-$6000 per month user of our services."

My eyebrow rose, for I didn't know how he got that number.

He continued. "You'll be part of a team of three WISE trainers working in different parts of the firm. You'll lead the inside work with the client's new Director of Operations."

His intense eyes were on me. "I want you to work with the ops guy to generate billable projects. Because he's young and new to his position, he'll need a lot of one-on-one mentoring." Jay pointed his finger at me. "I want you to bill at least $3000 a month."

His forceful comments took me aback. "Jay, shouldn't we figure out the projects and efforts first and then create a budget based on that?"

My new boss didn't waste a breath. "Harvy, I did that already! I'll be doing outside work with the sales team at $1000 per month. One of our other WISE trainers will be mentoring the business owner's nephew for another $1000 per month. I want you to generate $3000-$4000 per month of work with the Director of Operations and his supervisory team."

Jay's eyes were penetrating. "The company owner wants his new ops director to take control of things inside the company and not let the old-time production supervisors walk all over him. He needs to build confidence and capability in managing those well-established employees. Moe and I had recommended that the owner hire this new ops guy, so we want him to be a leader and successful."

He pointed my way again. "You need to assert yourself into what's going on in the company and sustain your work. I could see you there for a year or two." I didn't know whether Jay was presenting a carrot or a stick.

"Okay, Jay, I get it." Though Jay was a native Canadian, originally from Montreal, I could see he had adopted a more aggressive Made in America approach. Having limited alternatives, I said nothing more until I got the lay of the territory with WISE Boston and my new client.

Jay added, "Harvy, here in Boston, you'll make 35% of everything you bill, plus expenses."

I was still making 45% of my revenue with my Montreal clients, as per my informal agreement with Moe. WISE had subsequently moved to a 35% formula firm-wide, similar to big accounting firms. Moe and Irwin allowed my remaining at a higher percentage in Montreal because I needed minimal supervision. There, I had helped to develop other WISE trainers, and I had billed acceptable annual revenue.

I don't think Jay appreciated my special status in Montreal. He wanted me lumped in with his other Boston trainers. "I know, Jay," I said. "I'm the new kid on WISE Boston's block. I know I have to fit into your formula."

I worked to return his intense look. "But for that percentage, please don't expect me to train or mentor any staff here as I did in Montreal." Until I found other prospects, I'd have to live by Jay's rules.

"Okay, Harvy. That's acceptable."

He turned to his desk, retrieved a couple of documents, and handed them to me. "I need you to sign these papers before leaving today."

"What's this?" I asked.

"Our standard employee agreements," he responded matter-of-factly.

I glanced at the papers in my hand. I saw that there was a non-compete among the documents. I looked at Jay. "I never had to sign anything like this in Montreal. Moe, Irwin, and I have worked together on trust."

Jay's voice rose. "This is not Montreal, Harvy!" He pointed to the documents. "Everyone else here has signed these papers, so why can't you?"

His tone was edgy, and he didn't wait for a reply. "If you want to move forward with your new client tomorrow, I need this signed before you leave today." He got up from his chair, walked past me, and exited the room.

I spent a few moments looking over the papers. Along with the non-compete, there was a comprehensive employment agreement that covered my client work firm-wide, across all WISE branch locations.

Had I been a little smarter that day, I might have told Jay, "I need a day or two to have my lawyer look this over." Had I had that time, I might have countered, "Jay, your contract should only relate to my Boston clients. My informal arrangement with Moe and Irwin will be my covenant in Montreal."

I was not so smart that day. I needed the work. WISE was my only game in town for now, and Jay made it sound as if I wouldn't get any clients unless I signed.

I put my signature on the agreement, put it on Jay's desk, and walked out of the office. Though I had felt strong-armed, I hoped I wouldn't regret my quick acquiescence to my ex-partner, turned boss, turned big brother.

* * *

The following week, I was back in Montreal to see my clients there. I had lunch with a WISE training colleague, Raymond, with whom I was close.

Half-way through lunch, he looked at me. "One late-afternoon last week, I overheard Jay speaking to Irwin over the speakerphone. It seems that Jay was calling to boast about how he got you to sign WISE's employment agreement while Irwin couldn't."

"What day was that?" I asked.

Raymond searched his memory. "It was Monday, Harvy. Irwin didn't realize that I was still in the office when Jay called."

My muscles tensed. *What a schmuck that Jay could be.* My signature hadn't even dried on his employment agreement and non-compete. He couldn't wait to brag about how he got one over on me, and how he even one-upped Irwin in getting me to sign those documents.

I looked away and said, "Yah, Jay made me do it to get a Boston client. I felt I had little choice." I looked back at Raymond. "What did Irwin say?"

He obliged. "Irwin sounded impressed; he congratulated Jay."

My friend lowered his voice. "You've got to watch those two, Harvy. They don't have the trainer's best interests in mind." He tapped his finger on the table. "I don't think I'm going to stay here much longer. This place is a revolving door for guys like us."

"I understand." My heart pumped hard, and the heat rose under my collar. Over the years, many professional trainers had come and gone from WISE. I found that the most promising ones didn't stay long.

I fumed inside. The strikes with Jay were building, and I had lost count with Irwin. I didn't want to give my new boss a chance for another slap in the face. I decided not to go to Moe with my sour grapes—he'd point me back to Jay and Irwin as the General Managers of their branches.

I felt that my WISE brothers had treated me poorly, but I didn't think there was much I could do. But the writing was now on our conference room whiteboard concerning my pending departure from WISE.

Four months later, in early 1990, I left Jay and WISE for good. I struck out on my own as an independent consultant and trainer. I seamlessly returned my Montreal and Boston clients to WISE, except for one big Montreal client.

That client had made it clear to Moe and Irwin that they only wanted to work with me. Because I had signed Jay's non-compete, I had to negotiate with Irwin to purchase consulting rights to the client.

I mentioned my WISE negotiation to my father. He raised his voice. "Don't give those WISE guys any money upfront! You don't know what will happen to your client. Don't give WISE any cash until some money is in your pocket." I felt my father had a reasonable thought, though I knew my client was expanding and wouldn't go out of business anytime soon.

To push Irwin to forge an acceptable buyout figure, I delayed my WISE client billings that month. Because WISE was still living on the edge with its finances, and it needed every penny of its portion of my client revenues, it wasn't long before Irwin accepted my offer. We agreed I would pay WISE a fixed monthly sum for one year for my gaining unilateral ownership of that one client.

Over the ensuing years, my client expanded my work with his company. My work there carried on for another decade, until the client sold his business.

After Irwin and I completed our deal, my father said, "I'm glad you are out from WISE, Harvy. You'll do much better working for yourself."

I wasn't sure, but I appreciated his thought.

There was one snag in my WISE exit plan. The early 1990s recession was in full swing. Unemployment in Massachusetts would continue to rise for two more years, to levels higher than in the rest of the country. Even so, I felt I'd be better off seeking business on my own rather than work with Jay, especially since he had offered me only one client in Boston. I felt protected by having safeguarded a security blanket client in Montreal.

Dad continued to give me—as well as my brother—end-of-year bonuses from JHS. I hadn't needed that money before, but the cash came in handy for an underemployed guy like me in a more expensive city like Boston. I did appreciate my father showing his love through his assets. It brought me a little more financial freedom, though it may not have loosened the money knot between us.

* * *

After I had departed WISE's Boston branch, I hardly stayed in touch with Moe. Months later, he asked Jay to engage me as a subcontracting consultant for a Boston high-tech company, but I played hard to get. We couldn't reach a fee arrangement. *Twice Jay burned, thrice Jay shy.*

I believed that Jay reached out only because of Moe, for my WISE brethren quickly dropped our negotiations once I balked at his fee-sharing offer. By then, I didn't want to take more WISE flak from Margie or my father.

Part of me felt a loss in my not having more chemistry with Jay, though we did complement each other's capabilities. He would continue, with the WISE trainers who stuck with him, to do bigger and better consultations in Boston. He was probably more successful, perhaps also more ambitious than I was in the field of executive mentoring and business consultation. He was a more accomplished marketer, and he had had Moe as a management consulting mentor longer than I did.

Over the decades, it even seemed to me that Jay became a better person. Once or twice, he tried to flip a client opportunity my way with no strings attached, though I never fully grabbed onto his gifts. Maybe Jay was working to mend our relationship, but I kept a distance from his advances and prospective clients. I was never sure of his "no strings attached," but maybe it was just my inherent sibling skepticism at play.

To my detriment, I had had difficulty with big-brother figures. I continued to wonder if my reactions to Jay might foreshadow my future interactions with my brother regarding his and my partnership in JHS. But as long as our dad was alive, Steve and I had limited strings to pull in our father's business and his other holdings. Time would reveal as to what Steve's and my interactions might be like after my father's passing.

Years after I left WISE, I heard from Jay that Moe had experienced something like a mini-stroke. The next time I was in Montreal, I went to see my former mentor.

Moe was cheerful and pleased to see me. I sat on his couch, where I had sat during my years of counseling. As always, he sat in his high-back chair, his stocking feet placed on the floor under him. It felt a little odd to be back in his office as a non-client, but I tried not to think about it.

Moe offered, "The doctors don't quite know what's ailing me." He was optimistic. "I'll be fine after some rest at home."

He looked at me with his wide but crooked-tooth smile. "I'd like you to see this new product we've recently created at WISE. It's an organizational assessment. We're going to market it through established consulting professionals like you." His grin widened. "I'd enjoy getting your opinion on it."

There was the part of Moe that was a pure salesman, as my father had been in his career. At training expos, Moe was the kind of guy who'd go right into the aisle and pull people into the booth to view his business offerings.

His salesmanship had reeled me in before, but now I wasn't taking the bait. I raised an open hand, "Moe, please don't sell me on anything. I only came to see how you're doing."

He raised an open hand too. "Okay, sure, Harvy. I just thought you might be interested. We built our new product for capable consultants like you."

"Yah, Moe, I know." I then changed the subject.

Half-an-hour later, as I stood to leave, Moe came back. "Do keep us in mind if you're looking for a good tool with which to augment your consulting services."

I looked at him. "Is Irwin involved in this new product?"

"Yes, sure," he said without losing a beat. "He's now selling it across Canada and the U.S."

One could never fault Moe for his loyalty, and to try to make something more out of Irwin. I looked at him. "You know I have a hard time with that guy."

Moe nodded his understanding and took my hand in his. "Then, I hope you stay in touch."

I nodded, but I didn't stay in touch. It was time to move on.

That was the last time I saw Moe. Some years later, whatever had stimulated Moe's health event had gotten him for good. I didn't even hear about his passing until over a year after his funeral. Neither Jay nor Irwin told me that Moe had died; I heard it from a former WISE trainer.

Moe had done a lot for me. He helped to move me along in my life, well past JHS factory life and my father's overbearing hand. I had felt a tremendous loss when Dad cast Moe aside from our family business.

Before my mother passed away, she had told me, "After your father left me for the last time, Moe saved my life. I started to go out and do things again rather than sit at home and cry for your father." But even she curtailed her relationship with her lifesaver.

Moe had assisted me in finding a new and exciting career. He gave me my first job in my new field and brought me into a business partnership. I had been his first WISE protégé, and I learned much from that creative, optimistic, and inspiring man.

He and I had been a great team. For every new brilliant method Moe brought to WISE, I found ways to improve upon it. There are consulting and coaching practices I continued to employ and evolve in my work that originated from my discussions with my mentor at WISE.

Though my father won out in the Moe versus Dad competition, Moe had won my spirit. I sometimes wondered how my career and life might have turned out had he not enticed me into WISE and away from moving to Vancouver. Though my mentor had had his shortcomings, he was one to emulate. Sometimes, when I get stuck with a complicated client situation, I ask myself, "What might Moe do?" I rarely consider, "What might Johnny Simkovits do?"

I never thanked Moe directly for his efforts with me, but I hope he somehow knew how I felt about him.

* * *

Years after Moe's death, I got in touch with his wife, Dee. Over a restaurant supper in Montreal, I apologized for not having been at Moe's funeral. She offered, "His death happened so fast and unexpectedly. Even until the last day, Moe was optimistic about his prognosis and recovery."

I smiled. Unlike me, and perhaps even more than my father, that man had had an optimism gene.

"Tell me, Dee. How did Moe get the idea to start WISE?" I wanted to hear her perspective.

Searching her memory, she said, "Harvy, he came home one day after having lunch with Irwin and said he was starting a company. And that was it!" Her response reminded me of my parents' good friends, George and Mimi Meyer. In some ways, maybe Moe and Dee had also been alternate parents to me.

I figured that Moe had helped many small business owners to build their company and success, so why shouldn't he create his own? He just needed a loyal partner like Irwin and a management training product like Edware with which to get started.

I looked closely at Dee and took a deep breath. "I feel that Moe did a lot for me. I want to do something in return for him. Might there be a cause or project he wanted to support, but couldn't because his life was cut short? I want to provide some funds for whatever it is. I'd do it in his name."

Her eyes opened wide. "That's very nice and generous of you, Harvy."

I looked at her, my eyes not quite meeting hers. "Dee, I feel as if I owe Moe for how he had helped me."

"Okay, Harvy. I'll put my thinking cap on and come back to you with options."

"Thanks, Dee. I appreciate it."

Weeks later, she e-mailed me. "Thank you again for supper. I'm still thinking about your offer. I appreciate your considering Moe in that way."

I e-mailed her back. "Once my memoir is complete and published, you'll better understand why I feel that way about Moe."

I'm still waiting to hear back from her.

* * * *

25

Next Bother with Brother

There is a Canadian expression that goes, "When the U.S. sneezes, Canada catches a cold."

When the 1990 recession hit North America, the Canadian economy was even more affected. Unemployment rates in my homeland were four percentage points higher than in the USA.

For the second time since JHS closed in '84, Steve found himself out of work. (He had been the purchasing agent for a second company in which our father had helped to place him.) Not wanting his first son's family to be without, Dad brought Steve into a new business.

After the Iron Curtain had fallen in late '89, the Quebec government and Czechoslovakia embassy approached my father. Dad later told me proudly, "Representatives from both those places knew I had been in manufacturing. They asked me to get involved in a venture to distribute Canadian building technologies to Slovakia."

Dad was introduced both to an Ottawa builder who held a patent on structural panel technology and to potential Slovak partners in Bratislava. The Quebec government offered a grant to cover half the cost of marketing the panel technology overseas—to build inexpensive homes and simple office buildings. Dad liked the ideas of free money and of helping his home country, so he grabbed onto the new venture. He called it Canexco.

My father later told me, "I lost a lot of assets in Czechoslovakia when the Soviets took over my country in '48. The communists appropriated my business bank accounts and inventories." He huffed. "I had nothing but a modest salary in what had originally been my own business." He raised his hand. "This Canexco project will now give me a chance to get something back."

Count on my father for being able to make capitalist lemonade from communist lemons, forty-three years after the Soviets took over his country and nationalized his business.

Because Steve was out of work, Dad took him under his Canexco wing.

Weeks afterward, when I was in Montreal, Dad and I had supper at Luigio's. He ordered his customary fettuccini alfredo. I asked for my usual veal marsala.

After Dad had downed his first vodka on the rocks, I asked him, "So why is Steve back working for you, Dad?" I spoke calmly. "When Steve was at JHS, you complained about his work ethic, so what's changed now?"

Dad's voice was sarcastic. "Now that your dear Mormon brother is out of a job, he wants to gather more family history in Slovakia. He wants to go there with me when I travel on Canexco business."

His face tightened. "Steve asked me to take him around to meet our living relatives. He wants to ask them questions about our dead relatives and still-alive family so that he could make a record of it for his church."

Dad twirled the ice in his vodka glass while his tone turned edgy. "Your brother also wants to visit the cemeteries where our ancestors are buried. He wants to dig up church and city records over there to trace my and your mother's roots." His tone stayed a touch terse. "He doesn't speak Slovak or Hungarian well enough, so he needs me to translate."

I couldn't believe my brother's nerve. "So how do you feel about that, Dad?"

My father's voice elevated a bit. "If Steve wants me to do that for him, then he should do something useful and get involved in Canexco. The new company will eventually need purchasing help, and Steve could easily do that job."

My stomach started to feel queasy. "Are you sure you want Steve involved with you again? You know how he can be unreliable." I pointed at my father. "You've complained about him before. What makes you believe it'll be any different this time?"

I was perhaps channeling my mother, interrogating my father as she might have questioned me about his whereabouts during their separations. Or she might have done the same to him when they were still living together.

Dad gathered himself and responded calmly. "Maybe Steve has grown up since he last worked for JHS."

I kept on pressing. "Didn't you say some months ago that Steve's boss had complained that Steve's Mormon activities got in the way of his job?"

My voice became a touch elevated, but I tried to keep it in control. "Didn't the guy grumble that Steve often came late to work, or he departed work early because he had things going on at his church?" I raised a finger in my father's direction. "If you want Steve to grow up, he has to find his own way and his own job." *Just as I have done these last six years!*

My father continued to look down into his nearly empty glass. I took a long breath. "Don't you want Steve to become more self-sufficient?"

My father deflected my comments and questions. "A job with Canexco would give your brother the flexibility to do his church projects as well as work for me." He raised a finger back at me. "Canexco isn't nine-to-five like his previous jobs were. Your brother's work for Canexco would be flexible, with occasional meetings at our office."

Following his finger with his hand, he stayed on his track. "We have a construction show coming up in Bratislava; there'll be a lot of preparation for that. And Steve's time and travel to Czechoslovakia will be a part of Canexco's expenses, which the Quebec government will pay half, up to $75,000 in reimbursements." My father seemed confident. "It should work out."

I wasn't so sure who was deluding whom. Was Steve going to put in the time at Canexco that Dad expected? Was Dad leveraging the Quebec government grant only to help his first son travel to Czechoslovakia to gather family history? It seemed as if my brother's family research had become his excuse for not finding a job. What would Dad do if his arrangement with Steve didn't work out? Would he have to dissolve Canexco, like he did JHS, to cut the cord once more with his first son?

"Dad!" I said, perhaps a bit loudly. "Don't you think your plan with Steve is unhealthy for both of you?" Now I was beginning to sound like Margie. "I would say the same thing to any family business client of mine."

I pointed my finger again, perhaps encouraged by my ability to support myself, though I was still receiving annual bonus money from my father's company. "You're actively working to breed Steve's greater dependency on you. I've seen the same thing happen in other family businesses with which I've worked. It rarely comes to a happy ending."

Some of those overly sympathetic, family business monarchs kept their incapable and otherwise unemployable kin engaged in their business, giving them a deductible salary. These hanger-on relatives should have never entered those family businesses. It was hard to extricate them once they were entrenched. Another employer would never match the inflated salaries and elevated positions they received from their company patriarch.

Here was my father doing the same damn thing with my brother. Dad was demonstrating the definition of insanity: repeating the same move with Steve, once again, yet expecting a different result from his son. Why couldn't my brother support himself like I was working to do? I couldn't envision him having much to offer Canexco. It boiled my sibling blood. Then again, could I have been overly judgemental?

My father looked at me and raised his tone to match mine. "You're off in Boston, and your brother is here in Montreal." He took a breath. "I'm no spring chicken." Dad had recently turned seventy years old.

His eyes stayed fixed on me, but his tone quieted. "I need something to keep me busy for now. And who else can I give this Canexco project to when I want to back away from it, or when I'm gone to St. Peter?" He glanced at the ceiling as he pointed upward.

He continued. "And Canexco is a 50/50 partnership between me and my long-time Slovak friend, Jan Dubinsky. Jan knows the construction business better than I do. When I'm gone, Steve will have someone around who has the experience to help him if they want to continue the project together."

My backbone bent; I slumped in my seat; my voice surrendered. "Okay, Dad, whatever you want." There was this son's signature line. I knew that it wasn't right that Steve worked for our father again, but I realized I had no leverage in the matter. Maybe I should keep my mouth shut and bear with their craziness.

In part, Dad was right. I was in Boston developing my career while Steve was here and available to him. There was probably nothing I could say to either of them that would sway them away from their father-son lot. They had developed a marriage of convenience. It was perhaps a misguided union that would end when Dad was in his grave, or if my brother ever moved to the Great State of Utah to be among his Mormon kind. Then again, why would Steve ever move if he had our father's favours here in Montreal to fall back on?

I calmed my voice and cut back on the intensity in my eyes and face. "I hope it'll work out for you and Steve." There was no point blowing against my father's brisk but deluded wind.

Decades later, after our father's death, it came to me that something else could have been going on for him with my brother. Though Dad had closed his CANEX Corp in Cayman, he had created that offshore company to syphon and stash money offshore. My father then moved his illicit assets to Luxembourg. He had promised them to me after his passing.

Maybe Canexco was our father's way of being equitable with Steve, giving my brother a shot at a legit onshore business. The similarity in the names of both those ventures gave me pause. Maybe Dad was attempting to spread his financial legacy equitably to his sons in the ways he thought we each could digest them.

* * *

A half-year after Dad had gotten Steve involved in Canexco, I was at another supper with him chez Luigio. I was curious to know how his grand Canexco plan with my brother was coming along. They had taken one extended trip to Slovakia together, and other outings were in the works.

Before we ordered our meals, Dad huffed. "Canexco is feeding Steve and his family. Your brother then turns around and gives that money away to the church." Steve had once said that it was typical for Mormons to tithe 10% to 20% of their income to support their church.

Dad fumed. "Steve wants to be a Mormon big shot. He's giving away 20% of the salary Canexco is giving him." His eyes glared at me, and his voice was terse. "And he has us going all over Slovakia and Hungary to find our dead relatives." He made a fist. "It's as if I had nothing better to do than to help him with his fucking family history." Dad rarely held back on his coarse language when he was upset.

I wasn't surprised, but I stayed collected. "So if it's bothering you, Dad, then stop doing what you're doing. You're the one enabling all this."

I pointed my finger, but not directly at Dad. "If Steve would make his own money, rather than living off your salary, he can give away as much as he wants, and you wouldn't care. He could then pay for his trips to carry out what family history he wants."

My father squinted; his eyes seemed in pain. "I can't leave him on the goddamned street to fend for himself." He then added something I didn't expect. "I know it's partially my fault that Steve turned out the way he did, with his religious conversion and running off to Timbuktu as he pleases."

He calmed his voice, but his closed fist remained on the table. "Maybe I should have been tougher from the beginning. I've been too lenient in letting him get away with his baloney."

I nodded my understanding, though I felt it wasn't belligerent toughness but compassionate straightforwardness that Steve needed from our father. If Dad could have talked honestly with Steve without screaming at the guy, it might have helped.

I didn't repeat that message now because I had said it before. It felt way too late for such advice, or to be punitive with an "I told you so." Both

Dad and my brother had become locked in their ways, and it had been that way for a very long time.

Dad turned his head away. "Your brother wouldn't have two sticks to rub together if it weren't for me."

I tried another angle. "Dad, Steve would say that Mormons work in this life to build chits with God to reach heaven in the afterlife. It makes no difference if you pay him or not. He'll have his church and spiritual teachings to fall back on whether he has more money or less money." I kept my voice as caring as I could. "By paying him for what little work he is doing, you are letting him do what you are complaining about—not stand on his own feet."

My father looked down at the table. "I can't abandon him," he repeated. "It would be like cutting off my arm."

"So, what's going to happen when you're gone?" I declared. "How will Steve support himself?"

He looked down at his drink and then back at me. "There will be enough money and assets in JHS to keep paying something to both of you every year. It should be enough to support him and help you, too, for a good while."

I was peeved, not only at my brother in using our father to bankroll his religious life but also at my father for enabling Steve to get away with it. Though I stayed collected, my upset caused me to prey on my father's fear. "Are you ready to see Steve give twenty percent of his half of your assets to the church as soon as he gets his hands on them?"

I knew that Mormon tithing rules applied to annual income and not inherited assets. But after our mother's death, Steve said he had given the church a percentage of his inheritance from her estate.

Dad's forehead cringed, but he ignored my comment and kept on his line. "If your brother needs more, I trust that you, son, will help him out from the money I have put over there for you." Dad pointed east, toward Europe and Luxembourg, where his offshore bank's head office was situated.

Dad never had any trouble abandoning women, but he could not cut off his first son, even for my brother's benefit. I wondered why I was trying to be the good and responsible one in Dad's brood. I could have similarly gotten my father's handouts with minimal effort, the only consequence being that he'd complain about me. On the other hand, I wanted my father's respect, and I couldn't tolerate myself if I didn't earn my keep.

I did hand something to Steve. He had found a way to leverage our father's favours and fortunes to support his spiritual enlightenment. Though his ways irked me, there was little I could do about it without sounding exceedingly self-serving. It was yet another Simkovits double bind in which I found myself.

I slowly nodded agreement to my father's point about my helping out Steve with Dad's offshore assets after his death. A negative response would have caused more pain for my father, or it might have jeopardized my coveted position with him.

Though I had implied I'd help Steve if he needed it, I loathed the idea of becoming my brother's keeper. For now, I said nothing about my resentment. I accepted my father's wishes because I didn't want his thinking lesser of me. But I considered that it might take Mormon hell to freeze over before Steve got a penny when I'd finally have ownership of our father's offshore legacy.

* * * *

26

Next Fiasco with Family

Four months after Margie and I moved to Boston, Dad insisted that Steve and I come to his Peru, NY home for the last Christmas Eve of the 1980s. Our wives didn't join us for supper that evening. They had gone off to their Montreal families instead. They'd join us the next day for a Christmas brunch and to open holiday presents.

We sat for supper at his dressed-up dining room table that night. Little did I know that my father would reveal a secret he had held for my whole life. Ironically, the breaking news didn't even come from Dad.

We were nearing the end of Elaine's delicious turkey and stuffing supper, cooked to perfection. Dad had filled the house with strings of decorative lights. Other bulbs and ornaments dressed a nearly three-meter-tall fir tree in the living room. The mood was festive, and Elaine, as always, did most of the talking.

When she gathered the finished main course dishes to take them to the kitchen, she blurted, "Harvy and Stephen, did you know about your having a sister in Slovakia?"

Dad looked at her sternly and raised his voice. "Why are you opening your mouth? I wanted to tell them myself."

"So tell them, Johnny," she said. Plates in hand, she stood and headed for the kitchen. "You've had all supper to speak, and you haven't. I wanted to get the ball rolling."

I glanced at Steve. He looked as confused as I felt. He chimed in first. "What's this about, Dad? Is that true?"

Our father looked down for a moment as if he were searching for words. In that void, Elaine spoke again as she stood by the swinging door to the kitchen. "Your father was married before your mother. They had a child who survived."

"Elaine, let me talk!" my father barked. His eyes looked like a hungry fox ready to pounce on a squawking turkey.

"Go ahead, Johnny. The floor's yours." Elaine pushed through the door and disappeared into the kitchen. The only sound left in the room was the door swinging back and forth.

So Mom was right! Years after he had left our mother for the final time, she had told my brother and me about our father's previous marriage. "That's why we only had a civil marriage in Košice," she had said to us. "Your father couldn't be married a second time as a Catholic because he had had a previous wife."

Mom had alluded to a baby from that union, but she said he had died as an infant. I didn't want to believe her when she added, "There was a second child, a girl."

Steve and I had stared at our mother, but we said nothing. We were worn out by her continuing dramas as if she had seen too many TV soaps. We shrugged off her comments as a left woman's bitter tale. *Dad would have told us about a sibling, wouldn't he?*

I didn't want to know about any other family tied to my father. I already had contentious parents and a brother who I steered clear of. Hell, if I wanted to know about a half anything that would compete for my father's attention. I looked at Dad and repeated my brother's words. "Is that true?"

In '68, during our family's summer vacation to Eastern Europe, Steve and I had driven with Dad from Košice back to Lausanne, Switzerland. My brother and I were to go to an international teen camp. Mom had remained in Kosice with her relatives. On our way, Dad stopped our car in a rural village outside of his hometown. He told Steve and me to stay in the vehicle while he "visited someone he knew."

Over an hour later, he returned, and we continued on our way. He told us, "Please don't tell your mother about us having stopped."

Both Steve and I had nodded our acceptance, and we asked no questions.

That was twenty-one years ago. I now wondered if Dad had gone to visit his first wife and their kid. Dad had never said a word about having a daughter in Slovakia. Was he now getting such things off his chest because Mom had died?

Across the dining room table, our father glared at my brother and me. He spoke slowly and calmly. "Yes, boys, it's true." He looked like a remorseful child; his jaw stayed slack, and his eyes looked down. "I had a short marriage in Košice right after the war was over in Slovakia, at the very end of '44, just as the war was ending in Slovakia."

His eyes shifted back and forth. "I had gotten the woman pregnant, and both my father and grandfather said I should do the right thing and marry her." He took a long breath. "I didn't want to, but they insisted that it was the honorable thing." He sighed. "I respected my father and loved my grandfather, so I agreed to marry the woman."

He took a sip of his mimosa. "However, before the boy was one year old, he got sick with pneumonia and died. I didn't love the woman, so I applied for a civil divorce." He looked past Steve and me, seemingly into a distance. "Before our divorce was final, she got pregnant again, with a girl, Emilia."

What! Couldn't my father avoid impregnating his soon-to-be-divorced wife? *What the hell is wrong with you?!* Or could it be that Dad's first wife hoped he'd stay with her if she had another child with him? With my father, who knows what was real.

I was numb and didn't utter a word. My brother asked, "How did you get reconnected with her?"

Dad spoke calmly. "Sometime last year, Emilia found Edo in Košice."

In '88, after nearly twenty years in Canada, Dad's brother returned to his homeland after retiring at 57 years old. In Kosice, Edo could live inexpensively off his Canadian and Quebec pensions and not have to work.

Dad continued. "Edo wrote to me. He said that Emilia wanted to meet me." His voice rose. "Last month, when Elaine and I were in Košice, we went to see them."

I was grabbing at short straws. "Are you sure Emilia's your daughter? Is she a Simkovits?"

Elaine returned into the dining room. She carried her home-made, hot blueberry pie. It was my favourite, but this time I expected it to taste like corrugated cardboard in my dry mouth. "Yah, she's his daughter all right!" she blurted. "Emilia's the spitting image of Johnny, just twenty-seven years younger."

"Elaine, let me talk!" burst from our father's mouth. His eyes were intense, as if he were ready to jump out of his chair and claw his—*Oh my!*—third wife.

"Okay, Johnny; I just thought you needed a little help." She gave him a look.

Dad turned to Steve and me. "Emilia is not a Simkovits. She took her stepfather's last name. Her mother remarried after I left the country with your mother in '49."

Steve looked at Dad. "So, what's her situation? Are her mother and stepfather still alive? Is she married? Does she have children?"

Dad looked at him. "Emilia's stepfather died years ago, and so did her second husband.

Emilia has had two husbands! She's not just emulating Dad's looks.

"She's living with her son," Dad offered. "His name is Igor, and he's a young teen." He looked at us. "Emilia's mother is still alive, but she didn't want to see me. We've had no contact since we divorced."

Elaine couldn't help herself. "Igor is Emilia's son from her second marriage. She has two daughters from her first husband, but he divorced her years ago, well before he too passed away."

She took a big breath, and Dad let her talk this time. "When we were in Košice last month, we met the whole kit and caboodle—Emilia, her son, her two daughters, and their two kids." She smiled, or was it a smirk? "It was one big Slavic Simkovits reunion."

Dad's hometown clan was growing by the minute. I could barely breathe. There were now more mouths open to my father's favours, and possibly hands grabbing for his fortunes. One of my hands held onto the edge of the table to keep myself steady. My other hand was crumpling the tablecloth that hung over the side of the table.

"So, Dad; what's Emilia like?" Steve asked. Though he seemed curious about his new relatives, I wondered how my brother was taking in our now bigger Simkovits brood. Outside of his inquisitiveness, he showed no reactions.

Our father replied, "She's a nice person, and Igor's a good kid. They were happy to see me."

Elaine exclaimed, "And you should see how Emilia hangs onto your father's arm! She nuzzles against him like a long-lost orphan. I felt invisible around her."

"Elaine, please!" my father pleaded.

"I want them to get the whole picture, Johnny. You only give them the highlights that suit you."

Dad took a breath, and his face softened. "Boys, I don't want you to be concerned. You two are first in my heart. I wanted to meet Emilia before I got too old. I feel morally responsible for her." His voice was calm. "But please don't worry. You are first as my beneficiaries. I don't owe Emilia anything financially, just morally."

I did quick calculations in my head. My half-sister must be about 43 years old, seven or eight years older than me, and a couple of years younger than Elaine. No wonder there might be tension between those two.

Though my father said that he didn't feel financially beholden to Emilia, I wondered if my half-sister had an eye out for Dad's money. Her nuzzling up to her birth father indicated she wanted to be in Dad's good graces. Maybe she wanted something for her three children.

My mind kept on getting away from me. I wondered what Dad meant by "owe his daughter morally," but I didn't ask. I held down my angst. "How does she support herself?" I asked.

He responded, "She's not working anymore. She has pensions from her deceased husband and from an office job she had for many years in Košice."

"So are we going to meet her?" my brother asked.

I screamed at Steve in my head. *Why the hell do you want to meet her? Let her stay in Slovakia!* The less we know her, the less we have to deal with her. Let her remain Dad's stashed-away daughter in his faraway homeland.

Elaine offered, "She and Igor are coming to visit us here in Montreal and Peru next summer. Your father invited them for six months."

Uh-oh and oh no! Dad couldn't have them here just for a few weeks or a month. He has to play big shot father and grandfather by taking care of them for half a year.

Elaine continued. "Your Dad is arranging everything. He promised to take Igor to Disney World in Florida." I again couldn't tell whether Elaine was smiling or smirking. "Your Uncle Edo and Aunt Eboya [Edo's newlywed] are coming too."

"That's great!" came exuberantly from my brother. I now definitely knew where he stood.

My brain bellowed, *Oh my frigging God! More Simkovits relatives in our hair with their hands out!* I started to feel sweat ooze from my sides.

My father couldn't have left enough alone with his faraway kin. He had to make our North American lives more complicated. I had enough with one brother with whom I don't get along. Now I had a half-sister and her brood with which to contend.

And there would be more people on Dad's dole—a situation he had created with pretty much every Simkovits relation in the world. Even Elaine had knuckled under to Dad's retirement desires. She had quit her real estate job to be more attached to Dad's hip, travelling with him to Europe and Florida whenever he wanted.

But I didn't fret about Elaine's enjoyment of Dad's largesse. She was providing value, not only socially but also as a good business head. It was the rest of my father's relations that troubled me.

It was admirable that my brother wanted to know more about our half-sibling. Perhaps I was petty, but my half-sister's presence seemed an incursion into our North American Simkovits realm. Would Emilia turn out to be dependent on Dad as much as my brother was? I took slow, deep breaths to prevent my heart from jumping out of my chest. I needed time to process all these Simkovits revelations and relations.

My father had surprised me with his hidden Slovak family. For the moment, I told myself that I was better than the whole lot. Being perhaps the only working Johnny Simkovits relative on this planet, I was glad I lived in Boston. It was a distance away from this family craziness, and I had my career to console me.

There was nothing more I could do but ride this sibling spring tide that Dad had created. For as long as he remained the giant star around which our family constellation revolved, I hoped that he wouldn't Super Nova and consume the rest of us.

* * *

That spring through fall of 1990, Dad had his Košice clan live at his Peru lakeside home. There, I met Emilia, Igor, and Eboya for the first time. Except for my Uncle Edo, none of them could rub more than a few English words together, and my uncle was no linguist.

I didn't speak their shared Slovak, Igor's first language. Igor didn't converse in Hungarian because Slovak public schools no longer taught the language. (Hungarian language learning had been replaced by Russian after WWII, and now German after the Iron Curtain's fall the previous year.) Edo, Eboya, and Emilia spoke Hungarian, but Steve's and my Hungarian was rusty. Elaine, too, spoke no Eastern European languages. So Dad acted as translator for us North American Simkovitses.

At this first gathering, Emilia was cordial but reserved with me. She offered her hand, a hearty *Hallo,* a subdued smile, and a peck on the cheek. I returned the favour, but I didn't feel much warmth from or for this woman.

I noticed that she resembled my father, including aging facial lines and liver spots on her face and arms. She dressed fashionably, and her greying hair was pinned up nicely on her head. She showed no signs of poverty or malnutrition. Maybe her premature grey was from having lived a harder life in a former communist country, where fresh food and advanced medicines were hard to obtain. I wondered whether Dad had been helping her along the way.

Eboya, like many Slavic women, was stocky and round-faced. She was friendlier than my half-sister. She presented a wide grin and was excited to meet Steve and me. She gave a big hug and a kiss, and I returned both to her.

Perhaps I wasn't as warm with my step-sister because I didn't trust her intentions with my father. I tried to keep a smile on my face, and openness in my mind and heart for a hidden sibling I hadn't known for, *ouch*, 35 years.

That first evening with Dad's Slovak brood, I noticed what Elaine had said about my half-sister. At dinner, Emilia sat right next to Dad. She held his arm for a time as if she were entitled it. The word "papa" came out of her in every second or third sentence that she spoke in Slovak or Hungarian.

I glanced at Elaine and sensed her discomfort in Emilia's hogging Dad's attention and appendage. Though Elaine said nothing about Emilia's behavior, she sat with her lips pursed and cheeks tight.

Weeks later, during one of our regular Sunday night calls, Dad's voice was enthusiastic. "I put everybody to work in Peru," he said. "They're doing spring gardening, weeding, and house chores for their keep. Edo is good with outdoor work, and Eboya is helping Elaine in the kitchen."

Dad's family guests still had a lot of spare time on their hands. I didn't know what they did between the weeding, gardening, and cooking. I never considered their Peru stay would be a fun way to vacation for six months. Dad's outboard motorboat and 200-channel TV satellite dish wouldn't keep my interest for that long. "What do Emilia and Igor do for you?" I asked.

"They help out here and there," he said.

"So, are you with them in Peru the whole time?"

"No, son. We leave them there from Monday afternoon through Friday morning while Elaine and I go do my business in Montreal."

Dad was working on his Canexco project and had been elected President of his Canadian Slovak Business Association. Elaine was his part-time secretary. I imagined it was good that Dad and Elaine took a break from his family—especially for Elaine's sake.

Though I came once or twice from Boston to visit my kin in Peru, I mostly stayed away. I used the excuse of needing to seek more consulting work after having departed WISE earlier that year.

That June, Dad rented a minivan. He and Elaine drove everyone to Florida for a month, staying mostly at their home in Boca Raton. When he called on the weekends, he told me everyone was having a good time. I wondered how any of them wouldn't like Disney World, SeaWorld, and Florida's beaches and open-air restaurants, especially when Dad was paying.

I consoled myself that if Dad's entourage made him happy, then why should I say anything that would stand in the way of his enjoying them? I was glad he had stable annuity income and private pension funds to feed his houseguests well. Maybe, in time, he'd have enough of their company.

* * *

To stay abreast of our family happenings, I visited Dad in his JHS office whenever I was in Montreal for business. On one visit, in mid-September of 1990—four months after his Slovak clan had descended upon our Canadian shores—I asked him, "How's it going with your relatives?"

Dad threw up one hand. "They're getting on my nerves. I want the whole bunch of them to go home."

My ears became excited, but I stayed collected. "What happened? Didn't you have a nice time in Florida?"

"Yes, but I had enough of them." He flicked his hand in the air. "I now want them to *foot-scoff* back home."

I was curious but didn't want to show meanness. "So, what's going on that makes you want your family to leave?" There was no need to motor this tipsy family raft down a rough Canadian river when it seemed to be floating swiftly by itself.

Dad threw his hand in the air again. "It's stupid! Eboya and Emilia are not getting along."

"What do you mean?"

His voice elevated. "They sometimes get mad at each other and then don't talk to each other for days. Even Elaine is complaining that Emilia walks around like a prima donna, hardly picking up a thing or helping with anything."

Elaine would later tell me, "'Princess Emilia' always arrives for breakfast with her face entirely made-up, and wearing a nightgown and earrings. She then sits down and waits for me to serve her breakfast!" After a long breath, she added, "The only thing I ever asked her to do was to keep clean the rooms she and Igor sleep in." Her voice turned terse. "But one day, when I stripped the bedcovers, I was amazed to find dried peach pits, soda cans, among other things, under the beds. Neither she nor her son ever thought of throwing that trash into the garbage can I keep in the adjoining bathroom.

My father took a long breath as he looked at me from across the office. "Eboya occasionally cooks for us, making good Slovak *haluśky* [Slavic stuffed cabbage] and Hungarian chicken paprika." He smiled, trying to be positive. "Eboya is an excellent cook."

I smiled too. Such cooking reminded me of my youth; my mother had made those dishes.

Dad's smile morphed into a frown. "Eboya says that Emilia hardly lifts a finger to help her."

I wanted a complete picture. "What about Edo and Igor? How's it going with them?"

His tone started even-keeled. "Edo helps here and there with house repairs." His voice became agitated. "But he sometimes needs to do things three times before he gets it right."

Dad liked to leverage his family resources to save money where he could, though he often got what he paid for. I knew from my JHS days that Edo didn't always like his big brother telling him what to do. Though my uncle complied with Dad's requests, he might down a beer or more when he had had enough of his older sibling.

"Is Edo drinking?" I asked.

"No," Dad said emphatically. "Eboya watches him like a hawk. She doesn't let him go near any alcohol." He pointed downward. "And I hide the house liquor in the basement so he can't find it."

I was relieved. Edo could get pretty happy and uncontrollable after a couple of drinks. He'd swagger around, click his tongue, point to himself, and say, "Now, who's the big boss?"

"And Igor?" I repeated.

My father looked at me. "Igor's a good kid. He pitches in and does whatever I ask. He cuts the grass and waters the gardens every week. It keeps him busy for a day or two."

I wondered what my nephew did the rest of the time. Elaine would later enlighten me. "Emilia has her teen son so spoiled that she even cuts the meat on his plate. Other than taking care of the lawn and gardens, he does nothing for himself or others."

I tried to stay on the bright side. "So what's the big problem, Dad? So what if Emilia and Eboya aren't best of friends. They can spend time in different parts of the house."

Dad's voice rose. "I'm getting tired of feeding and entertaining them; you should see the food bills I'm paying!"

He was edgy. "I also want peace from Elaine. She's jealous of Emilia. She complains more and more about how she has no time with me when my daughter's around." He looked down at his cup of coffee. "I want no more arguments with her. I want to send all of them back home."

"Then tell them to go back to Košice," I stated emphatically. "Can't you change their plane tickets to leave sooner, later this month rather than when you planned in November?"

Dad's mouth twitched as he shifted in his seat. "I can change the tickets, but I can't insult them. I don't want them to feel unwanted. I don't want to throw them out." But that was what he wanted to do.

My father couldn't find his way out of the patriarchal quagmire he had created. I put on my Moe Gross consultant hat and pondered for a moment.

I looked at my father. "What if you tell them you have an important business trip happening in October, and that Elaine has to come with you? You don't have to mention the details." I smiled. "Just say that you and Elaine won't be around for a few weeks, and it would be better if they go back to Košice earlier than planned."

His eyes shifted back and forth. "That's a good idea, son." His face looked more relaxed. He pointed to his forehead. "I like the way you think."

After Dad and I worked out the details, he gently put his hand on mine. "Son, I've meant to talk to you more about the money I have over there. I want you to come with me soon to my Lux bank." He smiled. "A new manager is coming, and I'd like to introduce you to the guy after he has gotten here from overseas."

I nodded and kept my voice subdued. "Sure, Dad, whenever you think best."

Dad had said the same thing before. This time, it seemed as if he hadn't been just trying to impress me. There was something different in his voice.

That day, my father had explicitly recognized my ideas, my counsel, and my worth. It was a touch of a father's hand to a son's shoulder for the right thing said, or a nod of a head for a job well done, or a kind word of appreciation that only a father could provide. I yearned and even ached for that acknowledgement.

I never heard Dad bestow such reverence on my brother. I suspected that his lack of recognition of Steve caused my brother to defy our dad. My older sibling now sought anointment from higher fathers.

I·took in my dad's pronouncement with rapture. Breath came out of me that released my remaining fears concerning my Czechoslovak half-sister and kin. My shoulders, having felt burdened from the deluge of relatives that had descended onto my continent, now relaxed. The knot in my gut found relief. Once again, all became right in my corner of our Simkovits world.

It didn't matter if my father had only $1000 in his offshore accounts, though a million or more would be nice. I realized that it was his genuine appreciation that I deeply desired. Though Dad could be a jerk in how he tried to run other people's lives with his "Just *lassen* to me!" pronouncements, I desperately wanted his respect and positive regard.

Thinking back to those days, I wondered whether Dad and I had stooped to the lowest common denominator to gauge our love for each other—the dollar signs he had stashed in Luxembourg. Though I steadfastly hoped his offshore money would come to me, being acknowledged and loved by him was what I truly longed for.

And the cash would be sweet too, like the Maraschino cherry on a double fudge ice cream sundae, as long as that richness didn't cause me to throw up.

* * *

Our Slovak relatives soon returned to their homeland. The next time I was at Dad's Peru home, Elaine told me how my father had broken the news to his brood. "Your father and I had talked in the car vis-à-vis telling everyone calmly and quietly over supper about our needing to leave the country on Canexco business."

Her eyebrows narrowed. "But your father couldn't help himself. We weren't in the house five minutes before he blurted out, 'I need to go to Europe on business, and everyone needs to go home!'" She raised and waved her hand in the air as my father had done to get everyone's attention.

She laughed. "The way Johnny had expected it, everyone would have shot themselves for having to leave early, or they would shoot him for kicking them out. After everyone had said, 'That's too bad,' in three languages, they said they liked the idea. They went to their rooms and started to pack. Your father then called to change the plane tickets."

She took a long breath. "Before the week was out, they were gone back to where they had come from." She let out a big sigh. "We finally had peace in Peru."

Though I had anticipated family hell in having this family crew chez Dad for six months, I never said anything about my trepidations to my father. I now knew unequivocally that my Czechoslovak kin was no threat to my favoured position with him.

No matter how much attention and money Dad doled out to his kin, I figured he had plenty to spare. My half-sister may have hung onto my father's arm, but I had his ear. Destiny made me my father's first relation.

I made prudence and patience this offspring's virtue.

Well into the 1990s, my father continued to support his boatload of family: Elaine, Edo and Eboya, Steve and his wife and two kids, Emilia and Igor, and maybe Emilia's other daughters. Some had their hands out more and some less, but they all depended on Dad one way or another.

I didn't know how much cash was involved, and I didn't want to know—it would have aggravated me. I surmised that Dad was doling out only small potatoes from his money sources. I hoped I wasn't wrong.

After coming back from fall trips to Slovakia, Elaine said that my father enjoyed his Košice clan as they surrounded and paid homage to him. He bestowed gifts on everyone to show his love and generosity. Who was I to stand in the way of his happiness? But I wondered if that kind of attention truly made him happy. Little did he realize—or maybe he did—that he was a co-creator and enabler of those family dependencies.

Though I too was attracted to my father's largesse, I told myself that our relationship was different, both special and real. I felt I was a better person than those Simkovits panhandlers, my brother included. I hoped I wasn't deluding myself.

I continued to protect my future by focusing on my consulting practice. I swore to myself to be never again dependent on my father's money. My work to support myself bolstered my self-worth. My career was my insurance policy if my father didn't come through on his offshore promise to me.

Over the ensuing years, Dad complained about the money he was spending on his relatives. "She now wants this from me," or "He now needs that from me," came out of him at almost every private supper he and I had.

But my father never stopped his money tap, even after Emilia extracted a couple of grand from him to buy a casket, gravesite, and church service for her mother's funeral in Slovakia. I winced every time Dad or Elaine mentioned another family foreign-aid story, but I said nothing. It was Dad's money and not mine, at least not until his passing.

I never pried into my father's financial aid to my brother. I trusted that there was an "offspring balance sheet" inside my father's head, and I'd get my fair share of benefits at the right time. I also didn't want to come across as jealous or selfish. I kept my sights on Dad's potentially bigger fish that lay offshore, and I hedged my bets by investing in my consulting career.

I continued to receive my father's recognition, and he continued to confide in me about his money and relations. But I still wondered if I ever could be 100% sure of my position with him. Might he be telling me things that he thought I wanted to hear?

* * *

Years after Dad's death, I asked Elaine how she first learned about Dad's first wife and their daughter. She e-mailed me.

> Harvy:
> I was with your father for eight years before I found out he had married before your mother, and that he had a daughter in Košice. I learned of her when we were at a party at the home of Edo's cousin in Ottawa. Cousin Alex mentioned Emilia's name and her relationship to your father, but he then realized I knew nothing about her. He swore me to secrecy. You can imagine how I felt, but I never let your father know I was aware of his daughter or who had divulged that info to me. For a couple of years, I pretended not to know.
>
> For fun, from time to time, I said to your father, 'Aren't you sorry you never had a girl, only boys?' He always responded, 'Yes; it would have been nice to have had a little girl!' He never let on regarding the truth hidden in his home country.
>
> One evening, we were out for supper with Hans and his wife, Kathy. I remember the evening vividly. We were waiting for our reservation at The Beaver Club in Montreal's Queen Elizabeth Hotel. We were having drinks at the bar outside the restaurant. The subject of a friend's daughter came up. Out of the blue, your father said, "Once, I was accused of having a daughter back in Czechoslovakia. But I took a paternity test, per court order, which provided proof that she wasn't mine."

My father had his excuses. He was never the bad guy, rarely took responsibility for his mishigas, and never admitted to any problem or situation he had created.

Elaine's note continued.

> I had previously told Kathy about Johnny having a daughter. I said to her that Cousin Alex had mentioned that Johnny had been in contact with her on several occasions, without anyone else knowing. The first time was when she had gotten married, and your dad gave her a dowry. So, that evening at

The Beaver Club, Kathy kept asking Johnny questions, and his answers were bizarre.

I imagined a poor little girl that had been abandoned in a communist country, struggling to survive. I figured that her successful, North American father should do the right thing. I said to him, 'You know, John, if you have a daughter you left there, she has a right to know her father after all these years. You should attempt to contact her!'

Oh boy, was that a mistake!

The way Emilia competed with Elaine for my father's attention was palpable. At gatherings of family and friends in both Montreal and Košice, Emilia pushed herself to be front and center around Dad. In photographs I had seen, Elaine faded into the background behind Dad's shoulder, her face flat or expressionless.

Other photographs, taken during meals, showed my father sitting with each woman on either side of him. Elaine sat straight, her smile restrained. Emilia, her face bright, leaned into Dad, allowing no arm space between her and her father.

Maybe my father was working to compensate for being an absentee dad, and he basked in his only daughter's attention. I suspected the situation would lead to a wife versus daughter struggle, but I said nothing to my father about my concern. It wasn't my place to get into the middle of his women.

Elaine went on in her e-mail.

One day, in the fall of 1989, your father came home from the office. He was very excited. He said, 'Edo called to say he made contact with Emilia. He's going to arrange a meeting when we are next time in Slovakia,' which was happening soon. Little did I know then that it was Edo—as per your father's instructions—who had reached out to Emilia and not vice versa.

Within a day of arriving in Košice, we grabbed Edo and took a cab to Emilia's apartment. She embraced your father at the front door as if he weren't a stranger. I didn't understand Slovak but certainly understood her gestures and the big hug for your father. At one point, in the living room—I will never forget this!—she reached toward a bundle of envelopes sitting on a wall unit. She held them to her chest as if she were embracing them, saying 'Papa...yak, yak, yak' in Slovak. I thought, 'What?!'

You'll recall that your father's Montreal Phono and JHS letterhead had red and black logos. The bundle of envelopes she held was from both companies, which meant your father had been writing her FOR YEARS!! And, of course, Edo knew—he just went along with your father's desire to make this a grand family reunion.

Emilia and her tribe (Igor, and her other kids and grandkids from her previous marriage) were in our lives from then on. I could tell you so many stories, but one tires....

May God bless and keep the lot of them, my dear ol' Dad included.

* * * *

27

Next Plays (and Ploys) for Pelé

Speaking about Edo, my uncle had been a very long story with Dad. Those two were even more different than my brother and me.

My father had supported Edo throughout his nearly twenty years in Canada. Not only had Dad offered his half-brother a low-rent apartment, but he had also provided Edo a steady job. He later gave him a company station wagon to drive.

Dad had also put many a stiff drink into his brother's hand. After Edo had had one too many auto fender benders, and once having put a person in the hospital while driving drunk, Dad didn't give Edo another car to drive.

Not able to afford a vehicle on his own, Edo boarded buses or obtained lifts from friends during the rest of his remaining days of working for his big brother. My father still took Edo, in addition to Edo's cousin Alex, on vacations with him and Elaine.

After JHS closed in '84, Edo became laid off like every other employee. He picked up occasional, short-lived labourer jobs, eventually going on unemployment for nearly a year. I suspected that not too many other bosses were tolerant of Edo tying on the occasional bender.

Dad had promised his stepmother that he'd take care of her son in Canada. But in 1987, Dad urged Edo to go back home to Czechoslovakia. He offered that suggestion with as much zeal as he had enticed Edo to come to Canada in 1968.

"Edo won't have to be on my payroll anymore," my father proclaimed during a Luigio's supper. He mentioned Edo's most recent vacation episode. "On our first night in Rio de Janeiro with Elaine, Alex, and me, Edo got tipsy and fell off the dancing stage. He hurt his knee, had to keep ice on it the whole week, and could hardly walk. We had to get a wheelchair at the airport to get him on the flight home." My father shook his head, batted his hand, and raised his voice. "I'm fed up with the guy."

I later heard from Edo that he went to the ER after they had returned to Canada from Brazil. The hospital diagnosed him with water on the knee. Edo needed treatments for months, with a big syringe inserted into his knee to remove excess fluids. He had to use crutches and then a cane for over a year.

Even after months of physical therapy, Edo sported an ongoing hobble. When anyone pointed out his limp, Edo adamantly declared, "My leg is fine!" But the accident ended his days of bouncing a soccer ball on his head and feet like his favourite soccer player, the Brazilian Pelé.

At the end of 1987, nearing the age of 57, and with no additional prospects in Montreal, Edo acquiesced to his brother's urging and returned to his hometown of Košice, Czechoslovakia. He and I had a deli lunch together before he left the country. Smiling like the big kid he was, he said in his limited English, "Better I be a rich man in a poor country than a poor man in a rich country."

A week later, Dad drove Edo to the airport to head back from where he had come, including his mother's arms. I wondered whether my uncle's departure was partially swayed by his having had enough of his big brother's advice about everything.

It seemed best that Edo would return to his homeland. Dad told me, "Back home, he could take care of his ailing mother. He can cook and clean for her and put drops of medication in her eyes—she's nearly blind, you know."

My father looked away and then back at his drink. "When his mother eventually dies, he'll inherit what she has there and get her apartment too. I want and expect nothing from her."

Edo could reside cheaply in communist Czechoslovakia. In addition to his mother's small estate, he'd obtain a modest income from the money he had put into his Canadian retirement savings plan. He'd also receive his Quebec and Canadian pensions after he turned 60 and 65, respectively. He'd never again be wanting from his big brother.

A year or two after he returned to Czechoslovakia, Edo's mother died. He subsequently met a woman, Eboya, and they married in early 1990, the year after the communist walls had tumbled down in Eastern Europe.

After returning from his next autumn trip to Slovakia, Dad smiled when he told me, "Hallelujah! Eboya got Edo off the bottle." His grin widened. "Maybe it's because of her good Hungarian cooking. She makes wonderful beef goulash and chicken paprikash, both of them with a smooth sauce and just the right spice."

After meeting Eboya in Dad's Peru home during the summer of 1990, I often heard her tell her new husband, *"Vedd fel a lábad, kedves Edo* [Pick up your feet, dear Edo.]" She said that whenever Edo dragged his shoes or summer sandals. She sometimes said those words lovingly and sometimes with a motherly edge in her tone.

* * *

All had gone well with Dad's plan to have Edo return to Košice. At the end of 1990, months after Dad's whole Slovak family had returned to Košice post their long summer visit, something unexpected happened.

In one of my Sunday evening phone conversations with Dad, he said, "Edo called from Slovakia. The guy was panicky." My father was breathing quickly. "You know he's turning 60 next year, in May. He told me that he applied for his Quebec and Canadian pensions, but those governments won't allow him to obtain his pension payments in Slovakia while he's living overseas."

Dad spoke frantically. "Edo asked me to look into it for him. He said he couldn't survive in Košice without his pensions."

Not another Edo headache! "What are you going to do?" I asked.

He calmed his voice and said matter-of-factly. "Rob will look into the matter with the government when we get to the office on Monday. They only speak French in Quebec City. Rob could speak to those provincial bureaucrats in their language."

On my next trip to Montreal, I had supper again with Dad and Elaine at our Luigio's haunt. After we had ordered our drinks, my father revealed more concerning Edo.

"Edo was right about his pensions," he groaned. "He lived and worked in Canada officially for only nineteen years. He needed to have lived here a full twenty years before the Quebec and Canadian government would send his pensions overseas."

I don't know how my money-maneuvering father had missed that fact before he pressed Edo to go back to Košice. I said nothing; there was no point stirring the muddy water under the Edo bridge. Instead, I asked, "How much money are we talking about?"

"It would amount to $1500 or more per month for Edo."

That amount was a pittance in Canada—and for my father too—but was big bucks for Edo in Slovakia. During the communist era, a loaf of bread or a bottle of beer in Czechoslovakia was tenth the price than it was in Canada.

Dad continued. "Now that the Soviets are no longer in control of the country, prices are rising, even doubling or tripling from what they had been under communism. That pension money will be important for Edo to live on, on top of his retirement savings."

My father turned to look at Elaine. He repeated, "Edo can't get his pensions paid to him outside of Canada unless he can prove he has lived here for twenty years."

Elaine's face looked glum. "So, what's he going to do?"

Dad blurted, "Edo and Eboya will have to come again to Montreal and live here for a year. With that, he can officially show that he has spent the requisite time in Canada."

Oh no! I kept my mouth shut; I figured Dad wanted me here for my moral support with Elaine. I glanced at her. She raised her voice. "Johnny, where is the 'here' that Edo and Eboya will live?"

My father didn't hesitate, and his face stayed serious. "With us, of course, in our Montreal apartment. We have a spare bedroom."

As eager as Dad had been in shipping Edo back to Czechoslovakia some years earlier, he seemed as keen to see his brother and sister-in-law come back to Canada.

Elaine's jaw opened, and her eyes rolled back. "So now I have to entertain your relatives for another year? Didn't we have enough of them when they were here last summer, Emilia and Igor to boot?"

My eyes went back and forth between those two as if I were watching a tennis match. Perhaps seeing Elaine's skeptical and annoyed eyes, Dad continued to sputter, "Like we did last time, we can leave them down in Peru during the summer to work at the house—there's lots of gardening, grass cutting, and cleaning they can do." He pointed south. "They can watch over things there while we're here in Montreal."

He swirled the ice in his empty vodka glass. "In the winter, we'll take them to Boca. Eboya's a great cook and can help us there." Dad was playing like a pro working to slam aces at his opponent. "Both Eboya and Edo would be happy to be with us, and it will be much simpler without Emilia and Igor."

Two more mouths to feed again. And I figured Elaine was thinking: *and to house, watch over, and clean up after.*

Dad hadn't finished. "If they don't live with us, then I have to get them an apartment. Edo doesn't have the money, and I'm not going to give him anything more if I can help it." His voice was edgy but in control.

Elaine's eyes and head pointed down at our supper table. She didn't look convinced.

I jumped in. "So how is this going to work, Dad? How will this prove to the Canadian government that Edo has been in Canada for twenty years?"

My father looked my way and spoke calmly. "When Edo went back to Czechoslovakia, I told him to take his Canadian citizenship card in addition to his passport."

He spoke matter-of-factly. "When Edo entered Czechoslovakia, the communist immigration officials right away took his Canadian passport. They told him, 'Since you are coming back to Czechoslovakia to live, you don't need your Canadian papers anymore.'"

Dad smiled. "But, as I had told him to do, Edo hid his Canadian citizenship card in the bottom of his shoe so the Czechoslovak immigration officers wouldn't find it." Dad's grin widened at his little cross-continent residency trick.

He raised a hand. "Now that the communist government is out of power, Edo will use his citizenship card to apply for a new Canadian passport. He'll tell the Canadian consulate in Bratislava that he lost his old passport and now needs a new one." Dad picked up steam. "With his new passport, he can buy plane tickets to come back to Canada with Eboya."

His hands were animated. "It'll be as if he had departed Canada for a long vacation—to take care of his dying mother, to get married, and to have a long honeymoon with his new wife." Dad smiled again through his false teeth, yellowed by years of cigarette smoking. "The Canadian government, especially the pension office, won't know otherwise."

My father continued to serve verbal balls at us, adding a wink to his smile as he looked at me. "Right after Edo returns to Canada, he'll apply to receive his Quebec and Canadian pensions here. After spending a year living here, he will have a record in his passport to show he was in Canada for a full twenty years." He kept on serving. "He'll then reapply to both governments to send his pensions directly to him in Slovakia."

Elaine's mouth was wide open, her jaw almost on the table. I put my hand to my pounding head. "Would that work?" I asked.

"It's all legit," Dad responded. "Edo will open a new bank account in Montreal for the pension cheques that will come to him here. After he goes back home, Steve or Rob could make those deposits for him, and wires the money afterward, until the government starts sending his cheques to Slovakia. Rob can even file Edo's Canadian income taxes for him, and I'm sure he'll get refunds every year because he has no other income."

"But what about Edo's drinking?" Elaine cried. She was thinking the same as I was, but she had been the first to say it. "If he's left alone, he can go through a few beers in no time. You know, it doesn't take much to get him intoxicated. You remember what happened on our vacation in Rio?"

Dad huffed. "You already know that Eboya got him to stop drinking before they got married. He hasn't touched a drop in more than a year. She keeps her eyes on him like a hawk. He won't be any trouble."

Yah!? Spending another year being told what to do by his big brother could get that guy going again. Eboya was going to need hawk eyes on both sides of her head. Elaine might be thinking the same.

My father's eyes were wide with his Edo ideas. I turned to Elaine. "Elaine, it's your and Dad's home, so it's your call." Hell, if I was going to put a stop sign directly in front of my father.

"How are they going to get around town, Johnny?" she responded. "You also can't trust Edo's driving."

After Edo's many fender benders, Dad's company station wagon swayed on the road as much as Edo wobbled on his feet after having a few. "We'll have to drive them around," she added. Maybe she figured that she'd have to do most of that driving.

Dad was calm. "Sweetheart, I'll take responsibility for getting Edo and Eboya from place to place. Your mother, too, can help drive them here and there if we need her."

Elaine's voice turned terse. "Don't bring my mother into this, Johnny! She has better things to do than babysit Edo and Eboya."

Dad's voice softened. "I'm just saying, darling, that your dear mother can help once in a while, if we need someone when we are away." Dad could be as sweet as sugar when he wanted something. "Otherwise, I'll be happy to take them around," he added. "Anyway, they can easily take the bus to the city from our apartment."

Elaine's voice stayed stern as she pointed a finger in her husband's direction. "Okay, Johnny, but if they're any trouble, then they, and you too, will go sleep in a hotel."

She looked at me and added a quick wink. "And be sure to tell Eboya to bring her Hungarian and Slovak recipes. I want to add to my collection of your country's cuisine."

My father raised his head and smiled. "Okay, sweetheart." His eyes were thankful. "Edo already put in his application for his new passport. He will book his and Eboya's flight ticket to Montreal for May of next year after we come back from Boca."

Dad was serving aces. "Rob is going to make Edo's application for his pension sometime this winter, having his cheques sent to our home in Montreal." He hardly took a breath. "I already told Edo to buy their tickets from over there—it's cheaper than if I buy them here—and for them to keep the return flight open."

My head was spinning. Dad had wanted me here so that Elaine wouldn't scream at him for his crazy ideas. It seemed as if Dad had already blueprinted Edo's Canadian reentry. I wondered what Eboya had to say about this.

I imagined Elaine agreeing to Dad's plan because she figured Edo would be a good companion for Dad, now that my father was seventy.

Edo liked to stay fit. He could get exercise by golf caddying for his big brother in Peru or Boca Raton. Eboya, who was retired too, could be useful in the kitchen and help Elaine tidy their homes. Eboya was more helpful than Emilia. Elaine could also get some freedom from having to be around Dad 24/7.

Whether it was his age or a fear of dying, Dad never liked being left alone for too long. Unlike my mother, who sat by her man during supper and while he watched evening TV, Elaine wanted time for herself.

Elaine looked at my father, her voice a bit edgy. "Johnny, what about Emilia and Igor? I hope you don't want to add them into the mix any time this year. The last thing I need again is a house full of your Slovak relatives."

She pointed a stern finger toward him. "If you're going to continue to do that to me, having your relatives in and out like Hungarian nomads, then you'll have to buy a bigger home here in Montreal. Our small apartment won't do."

"Don't worry, sweetheart," Dad said right behind her. "I learned my lesson last summer."

But did he? Elaine needed to apply every ounce of leverage she could marshal to curb my father's dogged finagling with his family.

* * *

Edo and Eboya arrived in Montreal in the following May of '91, just as Edo turned 60. Rob then helped Edo apply for his provincial pension.

After they had spent six months living with my father and Elaine, Dad told me, "Instead of coming with us to Florida for the winter, Eboya wants to go back to Košice." His voice sounded concerned and disappointed. "She's homesick and misses her family. She spends most of the time in her room crying and writing letters to her closest relatives, her brother and his two kids."

It sounded like a repeat of when Dad's kin had visited North America a year earlier. They had been happy to head back home after four months *chez* Johnny and Elaine. Maybe living with Johnny Simkovits was like being in a cushy prison, having all the free time and comfort in the world but no place to go. I didn't ask more about why Eboya wanted to go home, and Dad and Elaine said nothing more about it.

After Eboya had departed, I heard from Dad that Edo occasionally snuck out from their apartment to buy a few brews. I was relieved that I never heard about any incidents or accidents.

In the spring of '92, with Canadian and Quebec pension requirements complete, Edo flew back to Slovakia. At a second "goodbye Canada" family supper in his honour, a dry Edo boasted, "My first job was with Johnny in Košice in '48, and my last job was with him in Canada in '84." He smiled. "I even worked for him now in my retirement." He was talking about the work he did at Dad's Peru and Boca homes.

I smiled at my uncle's statement, but I wasn't sure if his brag was something to be proud of.

* * *

Dad could complain vehemently about his problematic sibling, but he felt responsible for Edo's survival as if his own life had depended on it. I don't know where his instinct came from—his parents or culture—but it was an admirable quality. Be it with my mother's relatives or his own, or even Elaine's family, Dad offered open arms and helping hands to his blood relations where he could, even to a fault.

Part of me wished my father's helping ways would have rubbed off on my brother. If Steve had looked out a little more for me, I might have felt a bit more indebted to him. Then again, no matter what my brother might have done for me, I may have fought fang and tail not to feel beholden to him.

I didn't want to rely on my sibling, as my uncle had depended on his brother. That dependency could send me, like Edo, to a bar for liquid relief, or maybe back into a debilitating depression.

What lurked at the horizon of my mind was that I was better than all my problematic Simkovits relations put together. But I hoped my feeling of superiority wasn't showing. And I prayed that I wasn't deluding myself, or wouldn't drive myself stir crazy, concerning Dad's offshore treasure that I could sense but still couldn't touch.

* * * *

28

Next Muddle in Marriage

It would be no surprise to say that I was prone to mysterious ailments throughout my younger life. Stomach upsets had plagued me—sometimes for months—during my years at MIT. Insomnia was my nemesis at Harvard. During my partnership days at WISE, I occasionally left work early with headaches, nausea, or feeling overly fatigued.

Once, I felt so out of sorts at work that I left early and went to a hospital emergency room. After I had told the doctor what was going on, he drew blood for testing. While I was waiting for results, he approached me. "Your symptoms seem to be hepatitis-related. You don't use any needles, do you?"

I was taken aback and responded immediately, "No, not at all. I don't even smoke."

He stared at me. "I didn't think so. You don't look the type…"

So what type do I look like? I wondered.

The doctor continued, "…but I had to ask. We'll wait to see what your test results say."

Finding nothing concerning in my blood, the doctor sent me home. I felt much better the next day; I chalked up my odd illness to work-related stress.

In preparation for our Montreal wedding, Margie and I took six months of Arthur Murray dance lessons. Margie wanted us to do a five-dance, twelve-and-a-half-minute performance for the nearly 150 family and friends coming to our wedding reception. The reception was my father's wedding gift to us.

At our very first dance lesson, Margie looked at me, her face serious. "Harvy, sweetie, I've ballroom danced before, so I know what to do. You just need to learn how to lead me."

So it's all up to me?

Unfortunately, I did some stepping on toes. Thankfully, we had a very patient dance instructor. Monsieur Charbonneau knew how to handle Margie when she once stated impatiently, "Harvy, you've got to stop leading me astray. You'll whittle down my little feet to nothing by the time we're done."

Le petit et très gai Monsieur Charbonneau knew that Margie wouldn't listen to my observations or suggestions. He immediately took her hand and put her through the paces. The professional led her as if he were towering above her, though he was considerably shorter. The instructor then gave equal time to me, with his stepping through the woman's part.

Margie and I then danced together. We beamed with smiles as we glided across the floor without sliding out of step or stepping where we shouldn't.

Weeks before our wedding, Margie and I performed in front of an Arthur Murray dance assessor to get our Level 1 Diploma. Margie dressed in her white reception gown, and I wore my tux. We went through our chosen five dances: rumba, cha-cha, tango, swing, and triple swing. I found that if I counted out the beat in my head, I could relax and focus on how I lead Margie. Monsieur Charbonneau watched from the sideline, both urging us on and seeing the result of his five months of twice-a-week lessons.

At the end of our twelve-and-a-half minute performance, the Arthur Murray assessor stood, clapped softly, and then took our hands in his. His Parisian accent came through. *"C'était merveilleux,"* he offered. "You are a tribute to your instructor."

Margie was beaming, and so too was Monsieur Charbonneau. I was relieved that I hadn't messed up any moves.

After our wedding, I started to have second thoughts about our dancing. Margie continued to put the onus on me to lead her properly. It was like in the old dance adage, "The man's job is not just to lead the woman but also to make her look good." In Margie's case, the man makes damn sure the woman looks good; otherwise, there might be a frustrated face or terse tongue with which to contend.

One Friday morning, before our last dance class in a series, I woke with a throbbing ache in my left heel. I couldn't walk or put much weight on my foot. Every step sent a sharp pain shooting up my ankle and into my calf. I told Margie that if my condition continued during the day, I wouldn't be able to go to our lesson that evening.

I hobbled to my car that day and got myself to WISE. Luckily, I didn't have to commute anywhere else. Only a few clients were coming to see me at the office. I was able to sit without pain to conduct my mentoring sessions.

That afternoon, I continued to hobble around. I decided to leave work early and drop in at a sports clinic on the way home. A doctor examined me. He asked, "Have you fallen on this foot or had significant trauma to your leg recently?"

"No, I just woke up this morning with this awful pain in my heel. The pain doesn't go away unless I put no weight on my foot."

He looked at me. "It looks like a pulled Achilles tendon. Go home and ice and rest this foot. Keep it raised on a chair or ottoman over the weekend."

"But I have a dance lesson tonight! And my wife and I have plans for the weekend."

The doctor's face looked serious. "I'm sorry, but you won't be able to walk on this foot for at least a couple of days. If it's not better by Monday, you'll have to come back to see me."

I called Margie at work and left her a voice message. "I'm sorry, honey, but I can't go to our dance class tonight." I explained my situation and doctor's visit and then added, "If you want to go without me, I'm okay with that."

Margie, too, decided to skip our lesson that evening. She later said, "Tonight was our last lesson of this series. Do you want to sign up for another?"

"I'm not sure, honey. Let's see after my heel feels okay."

When I rose the next morning, my heel was miraculously healed—no pain, nothing. I took that as a sign that I didn't want any more dance lessons for now.

After Margie had asked again about another series, I said, "We're immigrating to the U.S. in a few months. Maybe now's a good time to curtail our lessons here. We can sign up again in Boston after we relocate there."

Margie looked down as she nodded her acceptance. She later broke the news to Mr. Charbonneau. She told me afterward that he was disappointed but understood.

* * *

Unexpectedly and unabashedly, the 1989-1990 recession pulled a tendon in Margie's and my relationship.

From the time we arrived in Boston in August of '89, and until Margie could develop her private practice, each month, I paid out at twice the rate than it had cost to live in Montreal. I even gave Margie a stipend so she could take a counselling psychology program to build her network in the city.

Before our first year in Boston had passed, I had spent the proceeds from my WISE share redemption, not just the gains but also the original investment. I was also out of the funds that my father had repatriated for me from his Bahamas broker. I told myself it was the cost of making a new life with my love, though it irked me to see that much money flow out of my bank account so quickly.

After departing WISE Boston, I joined and attended every professional consulting and business networking organization I could find. I called and sent my resume to headhunters and every sizable high tech company I could locate. Margie's sister-in-law, well established in the HR and OD fields, offered a connection to a high-tech HR professional she knew in Boston. I sent the woman'my resume and called her a week later to follow-up.

Over the phone, she ripped into my qualifications, saying, "There's nothing memorable about your credentials and experience. Organization development professionals are now a dime a dozen in this city." She offered no useful advice to beef up my credentials to make me more marketable or my resume more appealing.

I felt mortified that a friend of my generous sister-in-law was so harsh. I dissolved into a funk. I had once told Margie, "Two smart people like us should be able to do well in Boston." Now I wasn't sure.

* * *

Margie had subtle ways of being disapproving of me. Perhaps she wanted the perfect romantic man, and I fell short through my more count-out-the-steps analytical mind. Nearly every time before or after we made love, she offered suggestions. "Can you kiss me this way . . . touch me more there . . . lead rather than wait for me to guide you."

One night, I made a yeoman's attempt to do everything she had previously pointed out. I kissed her on the lips the way she said she liked; I held her firmly the way she had asked me to; I moved my body in sync with hers; I let her become satisfied well before me. We laid together afterward, arm in arm, sweetly exhausted by the moment. In less than a minute, the very first thing she said was, "That was nice, Harvy. And next time, if you could..."

My body stiffened, my heart raced, my chest burned, my hands clenched, my mind shut down. I couldn't hear another word of Margie smothering what manhood I had mustered. Couldn't she tell I had been working hard to please her? Maybe I could never be the man she desired. Or was she just playing out a timeless human habit of wanting to make one's spouse perfect?

I said nothing and stewed inside for weeks, perhaps even months. As Margie did to her bank cards, she deactivated any magnetism I had by having touched me the wrong way. From that moment, our romantic life curtailed.

I was angry at her for her continual criticisms, be they unintended or not. But in my habitual way, I couldn't say a word to my spouse about my festering resentment—just like I couldn't confront my father about what he had done to our family. I was afraid of what my dismay would mean for our still young union.

* * *

By the summer of 1990, I told Margie I wanted to separate. She acted surprised and didn't understand. I told her I could no longer be myself with her. I said I needed space to regain my professional footing in our adopted country. I couldn't go as far as to tell her that I might no longer love her.

Margie then did something that peeved me more. She called every friend and some family members I was close to, entreating, "Something is wrong with Harvy. He says he wants to separate from me. I don't know what to do to hold our marriage together. Can you talk to him and tell him to stay with me?"

When my friends called to tell me about her outreach, they said they were embarrassed by Margie's advances. I told each one, "I recently discovered that she might not be the right woman for me. Her calling you is certainly not the way to get me back." Her behaviour reminded me of what my mother might have done to keep my father from leaving her.

To my relief, every friend agreed with my position. Not one tried to sway me from my departure path. I became even more resolved to leave my former love.

I started looking for another apartment in the area. Margie asked if I'd be willing to do couples counselling with her—as we had once done in Montreal. But who was going to pay for our therapist in Boston? Me, of course! Though we did see someone for a couple of meetings, I sensed the sessions were mostly about my shortcomings. After I abruptly (Margie might say "rudely") exited our second session, I told her I wasn't interested in continuing.

As recommended by a close Boston friend, Margie and I did agree to participate in Werner Erhard's *The Forum* for back-to-back weekends. After that, we'd make some decisions about what we might do next.

On the second weekend of the workshop, in front of everyone, the group leader picked on me. "Harvy, you always play the nice guy, even when you are angry and disappointed. Do you ever tell people what you think and feel deep down?"

I turned red. The trainer had summed me up perfectly. I realized I had much work to do in stating my emotional needs and divulging my deepest disappointments. I worked too hard to accommodate others, not only Margie but also my father.

The leader similarly took no mercy on Margie. (She and I had sat separately in the audience so people wouldn't know we were together.) He looked at her intensely and offered, "Margie, you have a real racket going. I bet you have shattered some fellows with your innocent charm followed by your sharp intellect."

That was all I needed to hear. I cursed myself for having married a woman with a controlling nature, as both my parents had been. Though Margie's methods were much more subtle and subdued—more like wielding a barrage of paper cuts rather than brandishing a single stiletto—her ways took their toll.

I had appreciated that Margie saw me as a smart, compassionate, and easy-going guy. Early in our relationship, I had held her hand one Friday evening in a quiet restaurant. I listened for hours as she told me about her boss, who had put her through a hell that week. Months later, she shared, "From that evening, Harvy, I started to see you as more than a good friend. I started to fall for you."

When we once entertained Margie's family at a Montreal restaurant, one of us accidentally knocked a glass of water, which spilled all over the table. Shattered glass went in every direction, and several of us got wet. Margie's brother immediately jumped up and away from the table, and he presented a peeved look.

Unlike him, I laughed off the spill. Employing table napkins, I corralled as much water and broken glass as I could, and I hardly lost a beat in the conversation. Margie and her sister-in-law smiled and later commented on "Harvy's coolness under that water pressure."

I thought I loved Margie. She attracted me from the moment I met her at that singles club gathering in Montreal. She was a handsome woman who worked hard to maintain both her slim, shapely figure and long, flowing black hair. She dressed fashionably and used makeup well to accentuate but not exaggerate her facial features. She had a kid's way of putting her hand in front of her mouth or over her heart when she laughed, as if she were slightly embarrassed or very much touched by what a person had said or done.

Margie made friends quickly, and she kept them for a long time. She could spend thirty minutes on the phone with her best woman friend, going back and forth to figure out a workable date and time to meet for coffee. She strived to get back into that Bogner ski outfit that had hung in her closet for years—though she felt I had led her astray by my love of *les croissants amandes et café au lait*.

I imagined Margie the classy, gregarious catch I sought, and with whom I wanted to be seen out in the world. Margie desired to look her best, to say her piece in any conversation, and to enjoy the finer things in life. But Margie also focused on her needs, to the point of being unyielding, or "particular," as my father and Elaine might say. I worked to please her until a switch in me suddenly flipped, and I could accommodate no more. Indeed, my inability to push up against her well-crafted "racquet," and effectively state my concerns and needs, contributed to our marriage downfall.

There had been only one other time when Margie had deeply upset me during our courtship. I had taken her to the Esalen Institute in Big Sur, California, where we participated in a weekend of massage training for couples. We had fun exploring the crooks and curves of our bodies.

Over that long weekend, I couldn't understand why Margie kept on running off to talk to a fellow we had met there. She later said that he had told her about his rough childhood.

But she's here with me! I had paid for the weekend, but she kept on disappearing to talk to that other guy.

I said nothing about it at first, thinking that she was trying to help out the fellow with an abusive childhood. After the third or fourth time she ran off, I got a splitting migraine—another one of my mysterious ailments. I wondered why she continued to excuse herself to go to him, though it was never behind a closed door.

I saw her taken in by his stories of childhood neglect. She wanted to rescue the fellow like she did the foster kids she served. I suspected that the guy, attracted to Margie's dark eyes and child-like charm, was working to reel her in and away from me.

I finally said something to her when we drove away from the retreat center after our stay. I offered sheepishly, "I'm a little disappointed about you running off during the weekend."

She offered, "I'm sorry for not having been with you more, Harvy. I was trying to help out a guy who had a horrible upbringing."

But what about me?! Haven't I had a rough childhood too?

I was angry inside, but the considerate part of me kept my mouth closed. I wanted to scold Margie, to say that her insensitive actions deeply hurt, but I held back. I didn't want to berate her as my father had done to my mother.

I, too, had been far from the perfect partner. I felt my biggest failure was in how I handled Margie wanting to have a child.

One night over supper, some months before our wedding day, she surprised me, saying, "I'd love to have a child together. My doctor tells me I can get pregnant anytime."

At that moment, I felt as if I had put my finger into a light socket. I looked at Margie. "Honey, we are about to get married and then move to the States. Wouldn't it be better to wait?"

Her eyes wetted. "Aren't you happy that we can have kids if we wanted? I don't have many years left in which I could. Sooner might be better than later."

I back peddled. "Yes, of course; I understand, sweetheart." I looked down at the floor and then up at her. "I'm just saying that now may not be the best time."

I didn't tell her that the idea of our having a kid scared me senseless at the time. We were getting ready to move to the USA. I didn't want the added complication of a child to take care of—in addition to supporting Margie—either just before or soon after we crossed the border.

"Can we at least think and talk about it more?" she added, her voice calm but begging.

My breathing became a little choked at the prospect of being a father soon after our wedding. But she was right; we had time to think and talk before we made such a decision. I hugged her and offered, "Okay, honey, but let's not tell anyone about this, for now, especially not my parents or your mother."

"Okay, that makes sense," she nodded. "We don't want to get their hopes up and then let them down."

I didn't feel that now was the right time to share my doubts about being a parent with her. My gut told me she might be an overindulgent mother, dressing our child as a doll and hovering like a helicopter over the kid. I wanted to be better prepared for such prospects. I needed to have a secure job in Boston before we crossed such a demanding bridge.

A week or two afterward, Margie and I talked again. I looked at her. "Honey, I am happy we can have kids, but I don't think I'm ready to be a father right now. It will complicate our plans to move to the U.S. We can certainly address it again after we resettle in Boston."

Her eyes oozed wetness, but she nodded her agreement.

Some days later, as I arrived home late one afternoon, I could tell from Margie's red eyes that she had been crying. I asked her what was wrong. She said, "There's never a perfect time to have a kid," she blurted. "I'd love to have a child with you."

I repeatedly apologized for any insensitivity I may have shown to her wish. I took her hand and spoke softly. "We can try after we have resettled in Boston, and when we both have good prospects."

For the following weeks, I could feel Margie's disappointment with me in her quietness over supper and at bedtime. A month later, I tried to rekindle her spirits by taking us for an impromptu spring vacation to Club Med in Florida. I hoped that a little spring sunshine, and Margie singing at their nightly talent show, could help refill the emptiness she felt.

At *Le Club,* we unexpectedly met a close friend of mine, Kathy, who lived in Toronto. She was on vacation from studying to become a counselling psychologist.

Over several days, Margie and I spent much time with Kathy, together and separately, working through our wishes and desires about having children.

I held back on sharing my concerns, perhaps even fear, about being a parent with Margie. I focused on the timing. After we'd become settled in our new city, I might be better ready for fatherhood.

By the end of our vacation, the cloud had lifted from Margie's mood. On the plane ride home, she offered, "We'll talk about having children again after we resettle in Boston."

I took her hand, "Yes, of course." But I wondered if I was being like my father had been to my mother, making promises that I couldn't or wouldn't fulfill.

Though I was glad at that time that everything seemed to be back on track between Margie and me, I still held doubts that I feared giving voice to.

Now in Boston, less than a year after our move, and twenty months after our wedding, I felt the stress of being the sole breadwinner and of seeing money fly out our front door every month.

I found that Margie's continual cutting criticisms about my clothes, my eating habits, and my role as a sexual partner, was her way both to undress and redress me as her "ideal" husband. Though she may have felt that she was doing me a service, it made me feel as if I weren't good enough and would never be. I could no longer offer myself to her. She also came out of our *The Forum* weekends, saying, "I don't know what that leader was getting at with me. I didn't get much out of those sessions."

By now, I unequivocally knew that I could no longer commit to our union. Our marriage had perhaps been a mistake. The economic recession had taken its toll on us. Margie was blind to what she had been doing to me, and I no longer saw a future with her. I was unable to speak to my concerns and disappointments to her. Maybe I just lacked the courage to confront myself and her, and I might have taken the easier way out.

A week after our Forum sessions concluded, I moved down the street, leaving Margie for good. It was a calm yet somber moment between us. She offered quietly, "I'll stay in the bedroom while the movers are here." I figured both of us were full of feelings, but we could hardly look at each other or say a word.

I directed the movers to pack what little furniture I was taking, mostly from our second bedroom, and to walk it down the street. Margie came out from hiding only to close the front door behind me. Her eyes were red, and her face was looking down and seemed incredulous.

Though my shoulders felt a touch lighter as I walked out of the building, my throat was parched and chest heavy with disheartenment. I couldn't speak to the anger and disillusionment I held, not necessarily toward Margie but toward myself for having gotten myself into this daunting situation. I wondered how I (and we) could have misled myself (and ourselves) about our being right for each other.

Years later, during a therapeutic men's retreat, I came to realize that my repressed anger—even rage—was mostly about having been taken in by my father's charms and elusive promises. I had heaped resentment onto myself for trying to please him in exchange for his fatherly attention, respect, and—I had never quite forgiven myself—offshore money. I had been wedded to him more than Margie, and it pained me to think as to how much.

Right before I left Margie, I spoke to a divorce attorney. She urged me to get out fast and not pay Margie anything until we had a signed divorce settlement. I couldn't do that to Margie, so I pressed her to allow us to work with a divorce mediator rather than confrontational lawyers. She accepted.

With the mediator's help, I gave Margie enough money to live on, without having to work, for the following two years—longer than the time we had been married. I offered her the settlement payments monthly during our separation, and then the rest in a lump sum upon our divorce. She wouldn't have to pay any taxes on those amounts. I footed the bills for professional and court fees. Our divorce ended up costing me over half the money my mother had left me in her estate. I was willing to compensate Margie adequately for my failures.

I had paid for our move to the U.S., and I left Marge most everything we owned together, except for the furniture in our second bedroom. My only regret was that she kept my engagement ring—with a one-and-a-half carat diamond. The stone had come from a brooch my father had had from his late mother.

A jeweller friend of ours had designed her engagement ring around that large diamond. I then spent more money to nest four smaller diamonds around the big stone. After we had divorced, I said to Margie, "You can keep my engagement ring, but I would like to have back my grandmother's stone."

Though that stone might fetch $5,000 from a diamond dealer, she replied coldly. "I'll give it back to you for its full insured replacement value of $10,000."

I felt a pain in my face. "Forget it. You keep it," I said.

My father was kind enough to have never said anything about missing his mother's diamond.

As a part of our divorce agreement, Margie requested, "I'd like you to put another sum for me in your will in case you die before I do."

I stared at her but accepted her request. She knew that I had insurance policies on my life, and my estate could afford to give her some cash after my death, especially if I unexpectedly died well before her.

As to friends, I backed away from every relationship we had developed in Boston, allowing her to maintain those connections if she chose to. I didn't desire to keep any friend who might try to play it both ways, potentially reporting back to Margie about my life without her.

I wanted to be unlike my father, who walked away from my mother and gave her as little as he could in their separation arrangement and divorce settlement. If it hadn't been for the work of Margie's brother, she and I couldn't have immigrated to the U.S. That effort was worth my generosity.

I figured I would be better off starting anew than spend the rest of my life working on my relationship with a woman I felt I could never satisfy. Whatever money I had given to her, I figured I'd save it in couples therapy and my sanity.

When I left the mediator's office after Margie's and my settlement agreement had been finalized, the professional followed me into the hallway. He raised his hand and looked at me. "Margie seems devastated in seeing your marriage over." He patted then placed his hand on a hallway railing as if he were steadying himself. "When I met with her privately, she cried inconsolably at times."

I looked down at the floor and then up at him. A took a deep breath to firm myself. "I'm truly sorry about what happened between us, but I can't see us able to mend what has become so broken. I wish Margie well, but I can no longer be a part of her life."

He nodded. I then turned and walked out the front door.

Nearly a year later, I appeared with Margie in Massachusetts court to officially dissolve our marriage. Our voices stayed subdued. We spoke politely with each other and matter-of-factly with the judge. After the hearing, she and I just nodded to each other and said goodbye.

Like with my parents after their divorce, Margie and I were never again in the same room together.

Ten years after our divorce, Margie called me unexpectedly. I was living in the Boston suburbs with my second wife, and we had just had our first child. After short salutations, Margie hesitated. She then said, "Harvy, I need to ask you something." Her voice was meek. "Can you tell me why you left me? I need to hear it again."

Though her question came by surprise, I spoke calmly and caringly. I figured she still needed healing, so I was as kind as I could be while keeping any critical thoughts in check. "Margie, I guess I hadn't been mature enough to tell you what hadn't been working for me in our marriage. At that time, I found it easier to leave you than work to build on any good we did have together." I kept the critical part of my mouth shut, perhaps because I was fearful of her potential criticism and caustic manner toward me.

I didn't tell her that she had been too picky and prickly, critical and controlling of me. I didn't tell her that, just after our separation, both my father and Elaine had told me, "Margie was too demanding and particular . . . She wasn't for you, Harvy . . . We all make mistakes; don't worry too much about it".

I was relieved that Dad and Elaine had taken my separation and divorce well, but I wondered why my father hadn't told me his actual impressions about Margie before I married her. Then again, would I have listened to him if he had been straight with me? Might I have acted counter to his wishes for me as my brother always did?

Either way, I'm sure I would have taken my father's warnings to heart and mind had he offered them. I didn't berate Dad for not having shared his candid views on Margie before my marriage. I did tell him, "Thanks, Dad, for your support."

Feeling depressed after our separation, I went to see the couples' therapist that Margie and I had seen a few times in Montreal. After I had told him what had happened between Margie and me, he offered, "Harvy, I can understand why your relationship didn't work. Margie could be hard on guys like you who try to please."

Though I felt absolved of my separation and divorce guilt, I sensed his statement was as much about me as it was about Margie.

On that phone call with Margie, ten years after our divorce, I was thankful that she accepted my answer and relieved that she didn't press further. She thanked me, said goodbye, and hung up. She asked nothing regarding me, my second wife, or my young child, which was understandable.

Except for sending occasional e-mails for birthdays and holidays, Margie and I didn't see or talk to each other again. Years later, I learned she remarried. After that, I never initiated any further contact with her. I hoped, deep down, that she had found a more suitable partner than I could have ever been for her.

Margie and I did experience love for a time. And there had been other benefits to our relationship.

Two months after our Montreal wedding in '88, Margie and I honeymooned in Asia. We visited six countries in three weeks. When we got to Hong Kong, our most extended layover, she said, "A well-travelled friend of mine told me about a custom tailor here. Let's go and buy some hand-tailored clothes."

I didn't realize at the time that she was perhaps still working to extricate the geek in me. Over the next few days, I had summer and winter suits and a dozen dress shirts made, half of them from silk. They were a third of the price of similar fashionwear in Canada.

She too bought a business suit and a dazzling dress. She told me, "Now we can go to that Montreal Hungarian Ball that your father keeps on inviting us to." My Hong Kong suits stayed in style and lasted many years, well past my marriage with Margie.

Years after the divorce, a dress-for-success consultant I knew from one of my professional networks told me, "Harvy, you dress perfectly for your colour and personality. You have earthy shades in your suits, warm-coloured shirts, and complex, bright ties. It suits you well."

I smiled. "You can thank my ex-wife for that."

She glared at me with a puzzled look.

I explained. "I used to be a very geeky guy. I owe my ex as to how I dress professionally. That was a positive thing that came from our marriage."

And what about that opossum-lined trench coat I bought to be better dressed during the time Margie and I had lived in Montreal? It took twenty years for me to muster the courage to wear that fur in more politically-correct Massachusetts. If anybody subsequently asked me about its styling and materials, I told them, "It's amazing what Montreal designers can do with fake fur."

* * *

A year after I left Margie, my father showed his colours as a remarried man.

Elaine told him that she no longer felt the fresh water from Lake Champlain was sanitary enough to use within their Peru home. Though the house's access pipe drew water from the lake's floor a hundred meters away from the shoreline, more boats were using the nearby launch site. In late summer, algae grew along the lake's edge. After Elaine had raised the issue several times, Dad agreed to drill for fresh water on the property.

My father asked around and located a diviner to come and find the best place to drill. With a stick in hand, the guy ambled around the backyard. A few meters from the sunroom, the rod pointed downward. The man marked the spot. He told my father that this was the place to find fresh water.

Dad hired a drilling crew. He recounted caustically, "Construction work is much more expensive in New York State. The goddamn drilling company is charging $15 U.S. per drilled foot."

"So, what are you going to do?" I asked.

"I'm limiting them to 250 feet before they call for further approval." His face became peeved. "I can't believe I'm doing this baloney, but Elaine wants better water for the house."

I nodded my understanding. I hoped Dad would find well water without spending a fortune.

After several days of drilling, the contractor called my father in Montreal. He said he had reached the 250-foot limit. He hadn't located water and asked if he should continue.

"How much more pipe do you have situated on-site?" Dad asked.

"About 75 feet," the guy replied. "We can drill that in another day or so."

"Okay, use that up," my father told him. "But stop everything if you don't hit any water by the time you reach 325 feet."

Dad's Catholicism kicked in. He voiced to Helen and Rob, "I said a prayer to St. Christopher [Dad's favourite saint]. I asked him to have the driller strike water before he reaches 325 feet (about 100 meters)."

Dad then called the priest at his Montreal Slovak church. "Father, can you say a prayer tonight for my driller to strike water before he runs out of piping? I'll put $100 into the plate this Sunday if God comes through for me, and I'll give you another $100 personally."

The priest accepted Dad's terms.

The next morning, Helen came to the office saying she too had said an extra prayer the previous night for the Peru driller to reach water at Dad's N.Y. home. My father called me later that day. "We are sitting on pins and needles here waiting for my Plattsburgh contractor to call."

I responded, "I wish you luck, Dad. May God be with you."

That afternoon, the driller called with good news. The contractor's crew had struck water at a depth of 315 feet.

Helen and Rob cheered, congratulating Dad on his achievement, good fortune, and powerful ways with the Almighty. Ecstatic, Dad called the Slovak priest. Together they howled for joy. Their belief in the power of prayer was confirmed. As promised, Dad handed out two Canadian hundred dollar bills at church the following Sunday.

Ten days later, the water tests came back from the state laboratory. The report said that the water was at or above the limit in iron and sulfate content. The high iron would make the water undrinkable. The sulfates would build in the house's water lines, eventually clogging them.

After hearing Dad's complaint about his bad luck, I called a Boston fellow who was an expert in the water filtration business. He said to fax over the water test results so that he could recommend what my father should do.

A couple of days later, my guy confirmed, "The iron and sulfate levels are at the upper limit of being filtered well enough to be safe for both pipes and people. I could give your father a fancy and expensive filtration system for that kind of water, but the filtering media would have to be flushed weekly and changed often. It's probably not worth the trouble and expense."

I called my father and smiled through the phone. "I'm sorry, Dad, but God works in mysterious ways." Tongue in cheek, I added. "You should have asked your priest to pray for better quality water."

Dad and Elaine checked out the water for themselves. They left a glass of it on their kitchen counter for over a week. When the liquid evaporated, the inside of the glass became coated with white sulfate dust and red iron streaks. The water was not drinkable.

For the next six months, Dad let the water run out of the ground in the hope that its mineral concentration would diminish. After several retests and more calls to the Slovak Catholic priest in Montreal for his prayers, the water's iron and sulfate content didn't decrease appreciably. Dad and Elaine let go of their wish for well water. They upgraded their lake water filtration system and lived with that.

Dad complained about the over $5000USD that Elaine had cost him on a fruitless freshwater search. Then he got an idea.

The next spring, my father installed a concrete fountain on top of the well site. He located the fountain in full view from the kitchen and sunroom. That fountain would remind Elaine of her wish for freshwater—though she later told me that it had been a mutual desire from both of them. No pump was needed for that fountain, for the water surged out of the ground on its own volition.

Dad showed his new home feature to every visitor. He called it, "My most expensive gift to Elaine."

As the years passed, that fountain got gradually redder from the iron in the water. Even though Elaine and Dad kidded about it, I sensed that my father's feelings about his marriage to Elaine were growing darker as gradually as that fountain.

* * * *

29

My Tunnel's End, Revisited Again

November 1999.

No mishaps occurred during my supper with Dad and Suzie. It was the evening after I came to their apartment following my meeting with my latest lawyer, Bernard, from Elliot Trudell. Though I was nervous about what I was plotting in a quest to legitimize my father's offshore holdings, I was able to keep my mind off my angst during supper. *Was I becoming as conniving as my father?* Dad smelled nothing fishy in the air but Suzie's cooking.

Suzie served a low-fat meal of braised chicken cutlets, slightly buttered red potatoes, roasted Brussels sprouts, and a side salad. It wasn't my mom's rich Hungarian fare, but it was still delicious. Since my mother's death, I always appreciated anyone who cooked for me, and I made sure Suzie received my accolades.

Suzie eyed my father as she said to me, "It's always nice to cook for you, Harvy."

Though Dad had commented favourably about her cooking, he had hardly touched the salad or Brussels sprouts. *A meat and potatoes man stays a meat and potatoes man.*

This time, Suzie didn't nag him about not eating his vegetables. If she did, Dad might retort his signature line, "I don't like rabbit food."

After supper, I said I was tired. I excused myself and went to bed in the guest bedroom. Dad and Suzie stayed up and watched TV.

I lay in bed awhile, with my eyes alternating from staring at the ceiling to closing them to try to fall asleep. I thought about all the murky water that had flowed under our Simkovits family bridge these last two-and-a-half-decades.

There had been Dad's belligerent bullying: his continual yelling and screaming at JHS while I tried to grow and expand my wings working there; my feeling attached to his hip during an exhausting trip to the Far East and while he smoked, drank and gambled at a salacious Bahamas casino; his unceremonious firing of our counselor Moe Gross when I thought we had been making progress in our business and as a family; and holding on tightly to his business as he went down as the captain of his sinking JHS ship.

There were also my father's sexual escapades and money finagling: the temptations he put in front of his chums at places like the Moulin Rouge in Paris; his cavorting with dubious Cayman Island money bedfellows; his screwing his insurance company as a down payment for a new gold watch; his utilizing his children's assets to pay off his divorce settlement to Mom.

Then there were my dad's perpetual tax avoidance schemes: his multi-year attempt to gain Canadian non-residency status to cheat the government of their rightful taxes; his flitting from one offshore tax haven to the next (from Switzerland to Cayman to the Bahamas to Luxembourg); his getting me involved in his illicit tax-free money games with a money broker in Freeport, and his luring me into a bogus annuity scheme with an international university.

More so, there was his appalling treatment of my mother: his constant cheating on her; his abrupt and brutal third leave of her; his perpetual financial and emotional stinginess that prevented her from living a secure and happy life; and his years of putting off marriage to another in case he ever wanted to go back to her.

And there were his secrets: his hiding of my Slovak half-sister for most of my life; his keeping knowledge of his offshore money schemes away from my brother; his drafting me to keep my mouth shut about his hidden money.

And what about the dependencies and counter-dependencies he had propagated? Dad enabled my brother's continual defiance, his half-brother's ongoing drinking, and his daughter's endless doting. He allowed his first son to wield his religion as a sign of his superiority while, at the same time, letting Steve hold him up for money handouts.

It was a lifetime of Johnny Simkovits' immoral deeds, deceptions, dependencies, and deceits that he had placed at my feet, with the promise of "Everything I have will someday be yours, son." The transgressions were becoming innumerable; I could hardly list them on just one page of writing paper.

But had I been any better?

I had played along with my monarch's money manipulations, and I had held private his money secrets for twenty-seven years. Like him, I had had both a failed marriage and a disastrous business partnership.

Maybe my divorce from Margie had happened because I chose to see more of my father and mother's controlling nature in her rather than what I hoped that she and I could have become as a couple.

Maybe my extrication from WISE had been partially propelled by seeing more of my brother's behaviour in my partners rather than seeing the good in them as professionals. Perhaps my separation from my mentor was because I could no longer digest the father-figure competition between him and my dad.

I wondered how much free-will I had consciously wielded in my former marriage, my previous partnership, my change of career, and my overall life. Was I perhaps following a path that was fated for me and totally out of my control?

But was I now being a bad son? I was plotting against my father to divulge his hidden money haven, just as he had plotted against the government to build it. It was hard to close my eyes to my complicity and parallel life to my dad's, even though I never wanted such an existence. It was hard to close my eyes and get some rest on this day of wrestling with my father and reckoning with my conscience.

Uncensored thoughts continued to fill my mind. I had tried to be a decent son to my parents and a collaborating sibling to my brother. I had come home from Harvard to make inroads with the lot. I had secretly helped my mother in her divorce fight with Dad. I had worked to make my father proud of me in his business. I had reached out to build a friendship with Steve. My brother's lack of support then caused the demise of our relationship.

When my efforts at JHS didn't work out, I attempted to make my dad proud of me for finding a self-sufficient career and building my independence from his money. I hope he appreciated my efforts to become like the parts of him that I held in esteem.

But why did I still feel unfulfilled as a Simkovits son? This plotting against Dad for the sanitization of his secret stash didn't feel good one bit, but I saw no realistic alternative. Dad wasn't going to restrain his offshore shenanigans by my just requesting him to stop.

I hoped I wasn't heading for another breakdown or depression. I looked up at the ceiling again, hoping for a sign, perhaps from my deceased mother. I saw no guiding light in the darkness, except maybe a flickering light that was housed and growing in me.

For now, I had to stop thinking about my failings!

For now, I had to keep my eyes focused on my father!

For the foreseeable future, I had to clean up my dad's finagling as best as I could, either before or after his death.

It was my duty to my mother, to my brother, and most importantly, to me.

* * * *

Excerpt –

Just Lassen to Me!

Book Four: Survivor Surviving

Next Juncture for My Dad and Me

In February of 1993, my girlfriend, Gloria, and I visited Dad and Elaine at his renovated Boca Raton winter home. We were celebrating his 73rd birthday with a gang of his Montreal friends. Gloria was the only American-born person at the party. Besides her and Canadian-born Elaine, everyone else was a Canadian-immigrant snowbird who could converse in at least three languages: English, French, and at least one Eastern European dialect.

My father had hired a Polish fiddler and accordion player who were also winter vacationers from Montreal. The two men dressed in red and green vests typical for Slavic folk singers, dancers, and musicians. They serenaded guests with both lively and soothing melodies from the old country. Most everyone knew and sang the refrains in Hungarian, Slovak, Polish, Ukrainian, and Russian, all languages in which my father could converse.

Dad sang along, mixing words, changing syllables to spice up the lyrics. One Russian song lyric went something like, "I'm looking at your beauty with my sad eyes." Dad turned the last phrase into the Ukrainian, "…with my excited eggs." Howls of laughter emanated from the Slavic men, and blushing smiles came from their wives.

Gloria later told me, "I'm here on American soil, and I feel like a foreigner in my country." She looked at me. "By the way, what are those men howling about?"

Knowing my father's word plays, I told her.

She blushed too.

Gloria and I had met six months after I had left Margie. Unlike Margie, she had a more easygoing personality. My closest Boston friend called Gloria "an adorable person," and she was. Gloria had an engaging smile and a wide-mouth laugh that could fill a room. She wore her brownish-red hair in a curly perm that dropped onto her shoulders.

Gloria and I had met at a Christmas party at our Boston racquet club. There, she and I had danced, talked, and laughed with ease. She enjoyed hiking, tennis, and skiing as much as I did. I felt light around her.

After my father first met Gloria at one of his Peru house garden parties, he jested with me privately, "Margie was too thin." He gritted his teeth and closed his fist. "I like Gloria because she has a little more to grab onto."

I cringed and smiled at the same time. I told myself that I wasn't going to match my father's three marriages and other women on the side. I hoped he was staying faithful to Elaine.

The three-bedroom ranch house Dad bought in Boca was in the Royal Palm gated community between the intercoastal waterway and Federal Highway 1. It was a two-mile drive to the boardwalk at Hillsboro Beach. There Dad and I went for early morning walks with Muffie, Elaine's Tibetan terrier. As it had been with Orphee, Dad was enamoured with Muffie and continually played fetch with her. To Elaine's chagrin, he fed the dog scraps off his plate as he had done with her former pet.

The Boca house had a mesh-screen enclosed swimming pool, complete with a rooftop solar heater to warm the water to near bathtub temperatures. Every day I stayed chez Dad, he watched as I swam across that small, kidney-shaped pool, timing me for twenty minutes. I'd be across its length in five good breaststrokes, and then I'd turn around to do it again, and again, and again. He never tired of our having such moments together.

What I particularly enjoyed doing at my father's Boca property were the fruit trees: one orange and one grapefruit. They filled the small backyard adjacent to the pool. My father rose early every morning to pick the fruit right off the branches before breakfast. He squeezed fresh juice for guests who stayed over, Gloria and I included.

As he had done with his Peru, NY property, Dad had gone on a construction spree to spruce up his and Elaine's new southern home. He turned a small library into a big family room, and he opened and renovated the kitchen. Engaging his electro-technician skills, my father single-handedly rewired the whole house for stereo, both inside and out by the pool.

Elaine later complained, "Your dear father just had to pull speaker and power wires through the attic by himself, as he did in my Pointe-Claire house years ago." She pointed upward. "But it's loose fiberglass up there! He itched and scratched for days until that stuff worked its way out of his skin."

Elaine, too, kept busy by furnishing their new digs with wall mirrors and black-and-white furniture everywhere. Colour came from large paintings that filled the walls. Some of the pictures were mural-size, purchased from Slovak- and Hungarian-Canadian snowbird friends who were amateur painters.

As in Peru, NY, Dad and Elaine didn't permit any guests, including Steve and me, to come and visit until the renovations were complete. When I saw it finished, I went ooh, ah, and wow until my mouth was sore.

Today, at Dad's celebration, we mingled outside by the pool, complete with an open bar area that connected to the kitchen. The Slavic men chain-smoked strong cigarettes they had brought with them from Quebec. While Beth and I sipped on piña colada and rum punch, Dad and his male friends stuck to Russian vodka, straight or on the rocks.

My father approached Gloria and me. He smiled and said, "Those sweet drinks are for the ladies."

I pointed to my mouth and retorted, "I know, Dad, but I don't need that straight stuff to grow any more hair on my tongue."

He chuckled and continued to walk around and talk with every guest. He made sure their hands were full with drinks and canapés, and that they were having a good time. Every so often, he'd grab a bosom buddy, and they sang along with the music. They laughed, clinked glasses, and downed healthy swigs.

I watched my father work his pool party. Like a sun worshiper, he soaked in the heat of his comrades' attention.

I thought of the many years our family used to come to Florida. For almost every winter while my brother and I were growing up, Dad drove us from Montreal to Miami, Hollywood, or Fort Lauderdale for the Christmas and New Year holidays. Our winter trips to Florida surely beat the blustering blizzards in Montreal.

My biggest regret was that my mother, in her later years, never had a chance to take these long southerly sojourns that my father now took with Elaine. Though I didn't hold a grudge against Elaine for anything to do with my mother, I still felt a loss for what Mom's life could have been like with Dad during his retirement.

Dad's Boca birthday was not a time to dwell on such skeletons. I was glad that my brother bowed out of Dad's birthday party here in Boca; it offered me more of my father's attention. I think Dad, too, felt freer with Steve not present. I worked to stay focused on Gloria and to give her a sense of the food, music, people, and culture of my forebearers.

Ensuring that Gloria had a good time with me at my father's party was what mattered most.

* * *

Six weeks after Dad's Boca birthday, Elaine called my home office in Boston. It was a Monday morning.

She was matter-of-fact. "Harvy, I'm sorry to tell you, but your father had a serious stroke yesterday. He's in the hospital on blood thinners." She spoke as if she were taking no breaths between her sentences. "Right now, his left side is paralyzed, but the doctor says that movement could come back in time. The good thing is that he's out of danger."

I had anticipated such a phone call from Elaine one day, be it my father having a heart attack, a stroke, or another severe health emergency. But her call still came as a surprise. "How did it happen?" I quickly asked, forcing the breath out of me.

Though her voice expressed concern, she was business-like. "The stroke was progressive, happening gradually over several hours. It started yesterday morning. Your father could hardly get out of bed."

She continued to speak rapidly. "I put Johnny into a hot bath and immediately called his doctor in Montreal. When I reached the doctor, he told me to get your father to the hospital right away. I called the ambulance, and they were here in ten minutes."

She stopped for a millisecond to catch her breath. "Your father couldn't get himself out of the tub, and I couldn't lift him by myself. When the EMTs got here, they had to pick him up buck naked and carry him out on a stretcher."

She paused for a long breath and then continued to speak rapid-fire. "When they got Johnny to the Emergency Room, the doctor found out he had a blockage in the artery in his neck. By then, his whole left side was paralyzed."

The words were pouring out of her like a fully opened faucet. "The emergency room team immediately put Johnny on anti-stroke meds and blood thinners. It's too early to say how much motion he'll recover. He'll need lots of physical therapy."

There was another pause. Elaine shifted gears, now speaking slower. "Your father's asking for you to come down here. How quickly can you be here? Can you stay for the week? You'd be a big help to him and me."

"Oh my," I said. I was fifteen hundred miles away in Boston, but I felt my father's gravitational force field through Elaine's voice. I didn't hesitate. "Okay, I'll check flights and cancel my appointments. Can I get back to you later this morning?"

"Sure, Harvy; reach me at home." She was speaking more normally. "I'm going to spend this afternoon and evening in the hospital with your father. I really can use your help to be with him."

Her voice accelerated again. "I need to get our house down here closed so we can get back to Montreal as soon as Johnny is physically able. We had planned to drive back in two weeks, but the stroke has put a hold on that." The words were again flowing out of her like smoke out of a drag-racing car on a high-speed track. "I'm trying to get him into rehab as soon as possible so he can start physical therapy. He can get a good start on it here and then continue in Montreal."

I interrupted. "Okay, Elaine. I'll come as soon as I can get myself organized."

"Thank you, Harvy." She took a long breath. "I know he had a choice of asking you or Steve to come down here, and he wants you. Maybe he figures your brother's too busy with his wife and two small kids."

Yah, Steve is always busy with something. If it weren't with his family, then it was with his church work. And if not with his church, then it was in helping his Mormon friends and the church's missionaries.

But now wasn't the time to get into that. "Sure, Elaine," I said. "I'll try to be there tomorrow, or the next day at the latest. Let me catch my breath."

She said, "Okay, Harvy. Thank you." She then hung up.

I put down the phone and sat stunned for a moment. I knew that Dad's careless live-for-today self-neglect would catch up with him eventually. I wondered if this could be the beginning of his end.

If he survived the stroke, which Elaine said he would, how long might he last with a partially paralyzed body? Would he play golf again, be able to lift his grandchildren, stand and walk, drive a car, or even grab both of my shoulders to offer kisses on both of my cheeks?

My hand closed into a fist. *What a schmuck he is for letting this happen to him!* My father continually entertained customers and colleagues in smoke-clogged restaurants, and he filled ashtrays with umpteen cigarette butts. He ate fatty meats with the passion of a Hungarian butcher. He drank hard liquor with everyone, clinking glasses and offering *chin-chins* as if there would be no tomorrow. Now there may be many fewer tomorrows for him, for he had played Russian roulette with his Slavic *yaytsa*.

Though Steve and I had urged him to stop smoking, he paid no mind. "Smoking relaxes me," he told us. "And I'd rather do that than put sweet cakes in my mouth and then blow up like a balloon."

I took in deep breaths as I further digested Elaine's news. My father's smoking like a Canadian chimney and drinking like a Russian fish may have now caused a grizzly bear hit to his health. I wondered how I might have to pay for his vices besides now having to drop everything in Boston to attend to him in a Boca rehab hospital.

I stared at a blank wall for a few seconds. I considered what my father's sudden illness might mean for him and me regarding his offshore money. Will changes come there too?

I rose from my chair and went to my office door. "Gloria!" I yelled down the stairs. She had spent the night at my condo and was making coffee in the kitchen.

"What's going on?" came her reply.

"My Dad's in trouble. He had a stroke yesterday and is now lying half-paralyzed in a Boca hospital. I've got to get down there right away."

* * *

Acknowledgement

Outside of the usual suspects who have helped over the years to perfect my writing and this book series, I want to thank my closest *Just Lassen to Me!* readers. I appreciate their ongoing support and encouragement of my work, both in my writing and for my maturation.

Special thanks to my wife and kids for putting up with my sometimes focusing on *Just Lassen to Me!* as a Johnny Simkovits mistress. I can console you by saying that the end of my diversion is near.

Thank you to my wife for your invaluable help with my manuscript.
Thank you, Susan, for your careful proofreading.
Thank you to my ex-wife for your input and feedback on our years together.
Thank you, Moe, for your ongoing encouragement and guidance.
Thank you, Mom, for your never-ending love and caring.
And thank you, Dad, for your unwavering investments in my life and future.

About the Author

For too long, Harvy Simkovits followed in the path of his crafty and conniving patriarch. Harvy's WWII surviving, Soviet-communism escaping, Canada immigrating, Montreal business building, government tax skirting, and blatant womanizing father told him, "Harvy, I want you to finish engineering school, business school, and then law school." The family's flamboyant forbearer longed for his second son to become somebody. He then wanted Harvy to come into the family business where he'd brashly say, "*Lassen* to me, son, for I have more experience than you!"

A loyal and impressionable youth, Harvy heeded his predecessor's wily wisdom for a while. After completing his bachelor's and master's degrees in engineering at MIT, and a stint at Harvard Business School, Harvy realized that he was following his father's designs and not creating his own dreams.

Harvy dropped out of Harvard and discovered his passion in the fledgling field of organization development. After completing another master's degree in that discipline, Harvy enjoyed a twenty-five-year career in management consulting and executive coaching. He helped many owner-managed companies and family businesses not to make the same mistakes that his father and family had made in their business of over thirty years.

Then, in 2005, years after the death of his dad, Harvy felt he had to make peace with his past. He started to write not only about how his charming, hard-driving, and finagling father built his success in Canada, but also about how those qualities had had an insidious impact on their family, the family business, and (of course) Harvy. The second son of Johnny had to reconcile, repudiate, and rectify the moral and ethical dilemmas he faced with his furtive father and the rest of his thorny family so that he could successfully survive his survivor patriarch.

Harvy Simkovits has been writing and publishing stories about his Canadian immigrant family and their family's business since 2005. *Just Lassen to Me!* is Harvy's full-length memoir turned book series. He resides in Lexington, MA, with his wife, two kids, and two cats.

Visit Harvy at his website:
www.HarvySimkovits.com
to read the latest news regarding his memoir series.

Just Lassen to Me!

Book Four: Survivor Surviving

Available in 2020 in e-book and paperback formats
through all online outlets.

Volume Four of *Just Lassen to Me!* brings with it the culmination of the Johnny Simkovits and sons saga. We learn how Harvy survives his father's furtive finances and his brother's bold-faced brashness.

More twists and turns, ups and downs, and ins and outs will emerge regarding Johnny's legacy, both onshore and offshore. See what happens as the family monarch slowly loses his faculties after surviving a severe hit to his health. Watch as Johnny undergoes a falling out with his third wife, and how he mismanages his money over the waning years of his life. Can his offspring reign in, mitigate, and overcome their father's flagrant falls and foolish failures?

Meet more characters in Johnny Simkovits's money-hiding world. They will entice Harvy to keep up his father's hidden empire, but will Johnny's second son succumb to their advances?

After his dad's passing, Harvy will endeavor to make amends with his brother. But will the confreres be able to work together to dispose of their father's empire fairly and to treat each other as equals? Watch as the departed Johnny continues to show up between them no matter what they attempt to do to survive their survivor patriarch.

Both soft landings and hard endings will culminate with Harvy's stepmother, half-sister, uncle, and brother. Experience the conclusion of Dad's unashamed straying with sordid people, and the disposition of his legitimate holdings and clandestine empire. Most importantly, will Harvy be able to put his Dad's distasteful dealings behind him, transcend his father's legacy and family history, and come into his rightful own as a son of Johnny?

© 2020 Wise Press

Just *Lassen* to Me!

Book Four: Survivor Surviving

Harvy Simkovits